S0-EWT-566

The Master and the Devil– A Study of Mikhail Bulgakov

THE MASTER AND THE DEVIL—
A STUDY OF MIKHAIL BULGAKOV

Andrzej Drawicz

Translated from the Polish by
Kevin Windle

Studies in Slavic Languages and Literature
Volume 18

The Edwin Mellen Press
Lewiston•Queenston•Lampeter

Library of Congress Cataloging-in-Publication Data

Drawicz, Andrzej.
   [Mistrz i diabel. English]
   The Master and the Devil : a study of Mikhail Bulgakov / Andrzej Drawicz ; translated by Kevin Windle.
      p. cm. -- (Studies in Slavic languages and literature ; v. 18)
   Includes bibliographical references and index.
   ISBN 0-7734-7500-1
   1. Bulgakov, Mikhail Afanas§'vich, 1891-1940. 2. Authors, Russian--20th century--Biography. I. Title: Master and the Devil. II. Title. III. Studies in Slavic languages and literature ; v. 18.

PG3476.B78 Z6513 2001
891.78'4209--dc21
[B]
                                                                                            00-048709

```
This is volume 18 in the continuing series
Studies in Slavic Languages and Literature
Volume 18  ISBN 0-7734-7500-1
SSLL Series ISBN 0-88946-290-9
```

A CIP catalog record for this book is available from the British Library.

This project has been assisted by the Commonwealth Government through the Australia Council, its arts funding and advisory body.

Copyright © 2001 The Edwin Mellen Press

All rights reserved. For information contact

        The Edwin Mellen Press   The Edwin Mellen Press
                 Box 450   Box 67
        Lewiston, New York   Queenston, Ontario
        USA 14092-0450   CANADA L0S 1L0

                The Edwin Mellen Press, Ltd.
                Lampeter, Ceredigion, Wales
                UNITED KINGDOM SA48 8LT

            Printed in the United States of America

**FLORIDA GULF COAST
UNIVERSITY LIBRARY**

Table of Contents

Foreword by Lesley Milne vii
Acknowledgements xiii
About the Author xv
About the Translation xix
From the Author xxiii
The Master and the Lesser Devil 1
Chaper One: The City, the House, and the Years of Wandering 5
Chapter Two: The Years of Study and Apprenticeship 31
Chapter Three: An Essay in Satire 69
Chapter Four: An Essay in Honest Reporting 97
Chapter Five: An Essay in Recovered Dignity 129
Chapter Six: An Essay in Comedy and Compromise 161
Chapter Seven: Breakdown and Attempts to Leave 187
Chapter Eight: An Essay in Normality 219
Chapter Nine: Essays in Almost Everything 263
Chapter Ten: Victory 287
The Master 325
The Devil 331
Glossary 335
Select Bibliography 341
Index of Names 345

Foreword

I first met Andrzej Drawicz in 1975, in Cologne, in the international community of Russian scholars that Wolfgang Kasack attracted to the University there. This tall Polish gentleman had, I learned, written a book about Bulgakov, a book that had been well received in manuscript, but the publication of which had been suddenly abandoned without explanation. This pattern was drearily familiar in that era of Soviet domination in Eastern Europe. It was of course also the pattern to which Bulgakov had had to accustom himself. I speak no Polish, and the manuscript, like the copies of the articles on Bulgakov that Andrzej had been able to publish, was thus a 'closed book' to me. I looked at the Polish text with the sad realization that all I could recognize with any confidence was the titles of Bulgakov's works. At that moment I was keenly aware of what I was missing, and indeed what we were all missing, because publication of this book seemed infinitely deferred. It took *glasnost'* and *perestroika* in the Soviet Union and liberation from Soviet control throughout Eastern Europe before the book could enter public discourse, first presented as a doctoral dissertation in 1987 in an abridged form, then in 1990 as its full self. This is the book we have before us here, in an English translation that opens it up to those of us who do not have sufficient command of Polish to appreciate Andrzej Drawicz's achievement in its original language. The translation is a *tour de force*, conveying all the excitement, passion and laconic authority of Drawicz's scholarship along with what Drawicz himself, when speaking of Bulgakov, calls 'the extra-literary warmth of the author's touch' (p. 318).

This is a book that was written more than twenty years ago. The dates of items in its bibliography betray this fact. But what it also reveals is how much could already be intuited from the information about Bulgakov that had, by the end of the 1970s, been discovered by scholars working in archives, Andrzej Drawicz among them. Most of this archive material has now entered the public domain, along with revelations such as Bulgakov's first published piece of work: a newspaper article entitled 'Future Prospects', written in November 1919 when he was a doctor in the White Army, and full of inflammatory rhetoric directed against 'the social revolution'.[1] Simultaneously with the appearance of Andrzej Drawicz's book, the *doyenne* of Russian Bulgakov scholars, Marietta Chudakova, was also able to publish her exhaustive biographical study *Zhizneopisanie Mikhaila Bulgakova*.[2] Bulgakov's drama and his association with the Moscow Art Theatre were illumined in that same period of *glasnost'* by Anatolii Smeliansky (Al'tshuler) in his book *Mikhail Bulgakov v Khudozhestvennom teatre*.[3] All these scholars were working in parallel and all were able at the end of the 1980s finally to make public the material that they had gathered over the preceding decades. However, the cautious hope expressed by Andrzej Drawicz in his first chapter has been justified. None of this new material has yet upset 'the hypotheses which the present book poses on the basis of circumstantial deduction' (p. 19). Such additional details as have emerged under *glasnost'* have served only to corroborate, not contradict.

There has undoubtedly been progress, in that much of the scattered source material cited in the notes and bibliography to this present volume has now been collected and republished in more accessible form. Compilations of Bulgakov's letters have appeared, along with a five-volume 'collected works'[4] and two

---

[1] 'Griadushchie perspektivy', text discovered by Grigorii Faiman and first published by Marietta Chudakova in her *Zhizneopisanie Mikhaila Bulgakova, Moskva,* No. 11, 1988, pp. 72-75.

[2] The full text appeared in the journal *Moskva,* nos 6, 7 and 8 (1987) and nos 11 and 12 (1988). An abridged version appeared as a separate volume (Moscow: Kniga, 1988), 496pp. In the same year the complete journal text appeared in book form (Moscow: Kniga, 1988), 672pp.

[3] The first edition (Moscow: Iskusstvo, 1986) had been passed by the censor pre-*glasnost'*. The second edition (Moscow: Iskusstvo, 1989) contained much new material and indeed a whole new chapter, 'Ukhod' ('Departure', pp. 316-385). This book has been translated into English by Arch Tait under the title of *Is Comrade Bulgakov Dead? Mikhail Bulgakov at the Moscow Art Theatre* (London: Methuen, 1993).

[4] Mikhail Bulgakov, *Sobranie sochinenii v 5 tomakh* (Moscow: Khudozhestvennaia literatura, 1989-1990).

scholarly editions of his plays.[5] Various publishing houses have issued 'selected works' that have made Bulgakov texts widely available to the Russian reading public. No longer does an enthusiasm for Bulgakov mean locating rare periodicals of the 1920s in major Russian libraries and somehow persuading the guardians of ideological purity in the photocopying department to make a duplicate of this material, which shrieked 'ideologically dubious' from every line. In those days access to photocopying facilities was under total state control, and a decision by the functionary behind the little window to accept material for copying meant that he or she was answerable should any ideological 'error' subsequently be detected. The shade of this period in Bulgakov studies is evoked in Drawicz's brief afterword, entitled 'The Devil'. He recalls this strange half-life of Bulgakov's novels, stories and plays in the Soviet Union from the 1960s through to the mid-1980s, when only some of these works were published, and then only in small print-runs. Many of these volumes never found their way into the hands of readers in Russia because of a practice of using books to earn foreign currency, either by sending them abroad or selling them to foreigners for dollars in the special foreign currency shops. The result was a spectacular black market in Bulgakov that only disappeared with *perestroika,* when commercial principles took over and publishing houses orientated themselves to demand from readers rather than command from above. Commercial decisions based on entirely on the principle of 'what will sell' bring another set of problems for Russian culture, of course, but that is another story. Suffice it to say here that, as far as ready availability of works by Bulgakov is concerned, huge progress has been made since Andrzej Drawicz wrote his afterword to the present volume. It does no harm, however, for today's students of Russian literature to have a historical sense of the barriers erected by ideological bureaucracy between so many books and so many of their readers in the Soviet Union and Eastern Europe in the years of what we now call 'stagnation'. It was always a struggle to overcome these barriers, and that struggle is written into this book also. Indeed it is one of the things that give it its special insights.

Andrzej Drawicz was another man of letters who knew from personal experience the stratagems for maintaining existence and retaining integrity in a

---

[5] M.A. Bulgakov, *P'esy 1920-kh godov*, ed. A.A. Ninov (Leningrad: Iskusstvo, 1989); M.A. Bulgakov, *P'esy 30-kh godov,* ed. A.A. Ninov (Sankt-Peterburg: Iskusstvo SPB, 1994).

situation where there are powerful pressures to compromise and conform. When he says that for Bulgakov '*real* literature' was 'an element of secure order' amid surrounding chaos (p. 25), one suspects that this was no less true for Drawicz himself. After all, why else would he have chosen such a deliberately independent path? In a Poland always fiercely resistant to foreign domination and at that time smarting under Soviet rule, he chose to devote himself to Russian authors, which alienated him from one category of patriotic resistance. On the other hand, the authors he chose lay outside the official Soviet canon, and so he alienated himself from the official literary world that took its cue from Moscow. This independence of path showed itself to the end, as can be deduced from Kevin Windle's introductory remarks 'About the Author'. And yet there is nothing austere about it, as is revealed in this study of Bulgakov and his times. The book is a brilliant display of knowledge, energy, discipline, perception and a sheer stylish élan that one is tempted to call 'very Polish'.

This Polish outsider with his burden of personal experience also retains his independence of judgement when it comes to critical analysis of Bulgakov's works. He is not of the opinion that all are equally strong from an artistic point of view. But whether his judgements are positive or negative, the analysis itself is always judicious, illuminating and sharply to the point, a wonderful stimulus to develop an argument either of agreement and amplification, or disagreement and refutation. With a measure of fellow-feeling and instinctive sympathy, but without a trace of arrogance or condescension, Drawicz approaches Bulgakov as an equal, and this gives him a right to his independent view, which even when negative is tactful and never unjust. Bulgakov, who set great store by intellectual honesty and social courtesy, would have appreciated the integrity, acuity and scholarly decorum of these critical encounters.

Bulgakov would also have appreciated Drawicz's swift pen-portraits of periods in Soviet history, such as the aphoristic delineation of the immediate post-revolutionary era, the setting for Bulgakov's *Notes on Shirt-Cuffs* and 'Diaboliad'. Drawicz summarizes it as a time when 'people who barely acknowledged the new regime were compelled to go to it for employment and they pretended to work, and the regime had to tolerate this while being incapable for the time being of assuring these half-working workers even a subsistence wage' (p. 44). The atmosphere of the 1920s during the New Economic Policy is captured with the same authoritative laconicism. Drawicz also evokes such specifically Soviet phenomena as the 'communal flat', a mysterious historical detail for today's Western reader, but an experience that left its mark upon the literature of the time, including Bulgakov's own. Drawicz describes how 'one's own room ceased to offer protection, and the kitchen, bathroom or corridor became cause for great distress' (p. 36). This awareness then leads him to note that it is very convenient to have one's own devil, who can make a communal flat 'non-dimensional and inaccessible to all earthly powers'. This literary devil, which Drawicz calls the *diabolus minor,* thus becomes a mediator in the relationship between Bulgakov and his environment, and later between him and his awesome patron, Stalin, whose regime is the major devil, the *diabolus major.* As Drawicz puts it in another of his succinct formulations: Bulgakov 'had the measure of the tyranny, but enjoyed the protection of the tyrant' (p. 292).

The book is full of such *aperçus,* sometimes tumbling out like crystals in a dazzling cascade, as when Drawicz examines *The Master and Margarita.* Here, for example, he notes that 'we see airy frolics of the pen beside the firm tread of prose dealing with the things that matter most' (p. 320). Not the least enjoyable aspect of this book is its literary style, which Kevin Windle renders into English with correspondingly inspired flair. Written in the 1970s and published in the early 1990s, Andrzej Drawicz's book comes to us now in translation with a delay of yet another decade. The time lag is appropriate to a book about Bulgakov, the majority of whose works were published posthumously and at least a full quarter of a century after they were written. Like *The Master and Margarita,* this book reaches us removed from its own chronological context, but with a corresponding gain in historical perspective. And, like Bulgakov's novel itself, it is still as fresh as on the day it was written.

Lesley Milne
University of Nottingham

Acknowledgements

I am grateful to the Australia Council for financial support provided to me in completing this translation into English.

My thanks are due to *Australian Slavonic and East European Studies* for permission to reprint some biographical material about Drawicz, used in a different form in an obituary published in Vol. 11, Nos. 1/2.

It is a pleasure to record my gratitude for unstinting help with a difficult translation to a number of friends and colleagues, in particular Vera Drawicz, Anna Wierzbicka, Mary Besemeres and Jerzy Włodarczyk. Andrew Barratt, James Grieve, Rosh Ireland, Lesley Milne and Margaret Travers read a complete draft with great care and suggested many improvements, in the process helping me to pinpoint and rectify serious flaws in the translation.

I am conscious of the fact that, while presuming to correct occasional slips in Drawicz's text, I may have committed more serious mistranslations and factual errors which have remained undetected. For these and any infelicities that remain, full responsibility must, unfortunately, rest with me.

KW
Canberra
October 1999

About the Author

Andrzej Drawicz was born in 1932. The family was evacuated from Warsaw to the Eastern territories as the Germans invaded in September 1939. The death of his father at the hands of the NKVD produced an understandable fear of all things Soviet, as he recounted in an interview in 1996, but these feelings were overcome a few years later when he witnessed the liberation of Częstochowa by Soviet tanks.[1]

As a young man, Drawicz was one of those whose idealism led them to support the new communist order imposed upon their country in 1945. His enthusiasm for the cause quickly waned, however, with his deepening understanding of Russia and its literature and his personal experience of Stalinist rule in his own country. His love of Russian literature remained with him throughout his life.

Drawicz's early studies were in Polish literature. One of his early books dealt with the poetry of Konstanty Ildefons Gałczyński. In his student days he demonstrated an uncommon theatrical gift and was an enthusiastic performer in the well-known Student Satirical Theatre (Studencki Teatr Satyryków), as he fondly recalls in his light-hearted autobiography *Holiday under the Gun-muzzle*.[2] Literary study and his interest in Russia gained the upper hand, however. From his first visit to Russia in the late '50s he developed a wide circle of friends in the literary world. Books on Russian literature, in which he managed to indicate the achievements of a number of writers who lay outside the Soviet canon, soon followed.

---

[1] Andzhei Dravich, 'Ia prosto liubliu literaturu' (Interview with Tat'iana Bek), *Voprosy literatury*, No. 2, 1997, p. 219

[2] Andrzej Drawicz, *Wczasy pod lufą*, Warsaw, 1997.

In the mid-'70s Drawicz was invited to sign an open letter protesting against a clause in Poland's new draft constitution which stipulated 'compulsory' friendship with the Soviet Union. Fully aware of the dangers, he signed. The inevitable consequences soon followed. Being barred from entering the USSR was by no means the worst of these. Drawicz became a prominent member of the political opposition in Poland. He was active in the Workers' Defence Committee (Komitet obrony robotniczych, KOR) and the 'flying universities' of the period, helped to establish the influential opposition journal *Zapis,* and soon after this participated energetically in the open breach with communism which began in the Gdansk shipyards. He was interned under martial law in December 1981, with other leading intellectuals, including his friend, Wiktor Woroszylski, another specialist in Russian literature, whose death preceded his own by some eight months. He later spoke good-humouredly of this period and the intellectual companionship which he clearly enjoyed.[3] During the latter years of communist rule his difficulties continued. He remained unable to publish his work legally.

In the first post-communist government he was appointed by Tadeusz Mazowiecki, the Prime Minister, to chair the important Radio and Television Broadcasting Committee, in place of the long-familiar Jerzy Urban. In this position he later came into conflict with the anti-communist president, Lech Wałęsa, and in the 1995 election he switched his allegiance to Aleksander Kwaśniewski's ex-communist camp, thus alienating many of his earlier admirers. In his last years he was an adviser to the government on eastern matters.

His book on Bulgakov was written over many years in the face of seemingly insurmountable political obstacles. Though finally accepted as his Habilitacja (higher doctoral thesis) at the Jagiellonian University in Cracow, it did not see publication until after the fall of the communist system.

Even when active in politics he remained deeply involved in Russian literature, and made television appearances to speak of Bulgakov's novels or interview Joseph Brodsky. He had long since established a reputation as one of Poland's leading experts in Russian literature and affairs. Possessed of great erudition, he was also known as one of the most accomplished translators of modern Russian prose and poetry, having produced outstanding Polish versions of

---

[3] Dravich, 'Ia prosto liubliu literaturu', p. 227.

works by Brodsky, Akhmatova, Platonov, Vladimov, Nadezhda Mandelstam and, of course, Bulgakov.

He died suddenly of a heart attack in Warsaw on 15th May 1997, a few days before his 65th birthday.

KW

About the Translation

This translation is based on the Polish text published by Znak of Cracow in 1990.

Where the author quotes Bulgakov's works in Polish translation, the English version given here is made from the original Russian. In the rare cases where the Russian and the Polish diverge significantly, it is the Russian which is followed rather than Drawicz's Polish. The same applies to the correspondence and the critical commentaries and reviews cited in the text, except in a small number of cases — mostly newspapers of the 1920s — where the Russian source was inaccessible to the translator.

In preparing this English version, I have been guided by the assumption that the reader will have no knowledge of Polish, but, being interested in Bulgakov, may well have some knowledge of Russian and possibly of German. For this reason, when Drawicz quotes Russian poetry in the original, I have preserved the original Russian but added an English prose translation in the notes. Similarly, when Drawicz cites a Polish translation of Thomas Mann, the passages have been traced and cited in the original German, with an English translation and full references supplied.

Occasionally, where the Polish text shows an obvious slip of Drawicz's pen, I have made the necessary correction, as when an account of a film version of *The Government Inspector* names the hero as 'Chichikov' instead of Khlestakov (Chapter Eight).

Drawicz undertook his research into the life and works of Bulgakov in the 1970s. Exercising great patience and determination, he succeeded in gaining access to much material which was not widely available, and to editions of the writer's work from the 1920s which had long been collectors' items. Thanks to his connections with Western scholars and an extended stay at the Australian National University, he was able to study Western editions of Bulgakov's writings, which were not easily available in Poland or the Soviet Union.

Since Drawicz wrote this book, new editions have appeared of many of the works by and about Bulgakov to which he refers. Several important texts which were difficult to obtain in the 1970s and early '80s were published in the late '80s as *glasnost'* took hold. Others have become available since then. In some cases therefore, Drawicz's references have been adjusted to take account of this and refer the reader to sources which are easier to trace. Often a new reference, introduced by the words 'also in', has been added to Drawicz's original reference. This has not, however, been done in systematic fashion, as my own range of available sources has been far from comprehensive. No doubt there are many more notes where I could have added references to newer editions.

At other points where I have felt a need to add notes of my own, these are marked *Trans.* to distinguish them from the author's. On occasion, for example in Chapter Eight, where Drawicz confuses similar quotations from two of Bulgakov's letters on the same theme, these have been corrected and the new references stand alone. In places where Drawicz's references are incomplete or unclear, I have done my best to amplify them, but this has not always been possible.

I have reproduced Drawicz's Select Bibliography with minimal change, resisting a temptation to include sources which the author could not have consulted. The version of his Bibliography presented here is the shorter for the omission of a list of Polish-language editions of Bulgakov's works.

Russian place-names and the titles of Soviet institutions, as used at the time Drawicz was writing, have not been modernized in the translation. Where the author speaks of 'Petrograd' and 'Leningrad', I have preserved these forms. Where he refers to the Lenin Library, this title will be found in the translation.

A note is called for on a very few items of Drawicz's terminology. In describing Bulgakov's method of shaping and delineating his characters Drawicz makes frequent use of the terms 'kontaminacja' [contamination] and 'konfabulować' [to confabulate] (and the related noun 'konfabulacja' [confabulation]). For the former I have in most cases preferred 'cross-fertilization' to the more literal translation. For the latter, however, I have often retained the literal version. Although it may be unfamiliar to students of literature, it is a term used in psychiatry (by English as well as Polish specialists), with a very specific meaning: 'to replace the gaps left by a disorder of the memory with imaginary remembered experiences consistently believed to be true' (*Collins English Dictionary*, London, 1979). This is close to the sense in which Drawicz intends the word to be understood. Bulgakov's characters, he tells us, are often based on individuals whom he knew, but usually display added features which are the product of his imagination.

'Woluntaryzm' has in most contexts been translated as 'free will', rather than the more literal 'voluntarism', since Drawicz does not usually intend a philosophical sense.

Transliteration

In the transliteration of Russian names I have applied the Library of Congress system with the following exceptions in the main text and the Index of Names:
- the names of emperors (e.g. Nicholas I, Nicholas II, Alexander II);
- names judged to be familiar in other English guises: Babel, Joseph Brodsky, Gogol, Gorky, Ehrenburg, Mandelstam, Meyerhold, Joseph Stalin, Tchaikovsky, Bolshoi when this refers to the theatre (otherwise 'bol'shoi, bol'shaia' etc.), and Bolshevik. This category includes some familiar first names: Natalia, Olga, Tatiana and Leopold rather than Natal'ia, Ol'ga, Tat'iana and Leopol'd;
- names in which the LC system produces curious or comical effects: Semion and Manya rather than Semen and Mania;
- in place of -skii and -yi, masculine surnames and adjectives are given the endings -sky and -y;
- most non-Russian surnames of Russified or partly Russified individuals are given in their original form rather than a transliterated form. Thus d'Anthès, Williams and Herzen rather than 'Dantes', 'Vil'iams' and 'Gertsen'.

In the references and the Select Bibliography, however, for the benefit of specialist readers who may wish to investigate Drawicz's sources, I have tried to apply the LC system with greater consistency. This does, unfortunately, mean that that some names occur in two different forms.

In *The Master and Margarita*, established practice dictates the use of 'Yeshua' rather than 'Jesus' and Yershalaim rather than Jerusalem. For other non-Russian names of characters in this novel I have followed the usage adopted in Michael Glenny's translation and avoided transliterated forms: thus Woland, Azazello, Frieda and Baron Maigel. The same applies to Eve – rather than 'Eva' – in *Adam and Eve*.

From the Author

This book has had a lengthy prehistory, which I shall briefly relate. The first draft was written in 1972-73 for the 'Profile' series, on commission for the 'Wiedza Powszechna' publishing house. Though initially accepted, it was later hastily rejected, though the reasons were not specified. For those relatively conflict-free times (this was 1974) the latter decision was evidence of exceptional foresight and vigilance. I took the opportunity to rework the text thoroughly, having dismissed my internal censor; in its revised form the text found its way to one or two publishers, but to no effect. However, in 1987 a version of *The Master and the Devil*, abridged to about three quarters of its length, was published by the Jagiellonian University as a higher doctoral dissertation, in a print-run of fifty copies. In the end, thanks to the patience and determination of Znak, the matter was brought to its proper conclusion. This seems to me the best and most logical outcome: that this publisher should provide a home for such a Bulgakovian creative venture.

I also feel that, while living for so many years in Bulgakov's world, I have done my best to understand him. In doing so, I have become to some extent a pupil – if an unpromising one – of the great Master. If this means that the product even distantly approaches Bulgakov and grasps something of him, it should not have an easy life, because an easy life would be essentially un-Bulgakovian.

I still reflect with a certain melancholy that the chance to be first to publish the source materials – a chance dear to the philologist's heart – passed me by. When I was rummaging in private and public archives nearly twenty years ago, many of these were completely unknown. Since then, however, other researchers – quicker-thinking and more fortunate than I – have published almost everything, and it is right that this should be so. I remain hopeful that all interpretative avenues have not been exhausted, and that I shall still be able to contribute something of my own.

I remember with gratitude those who helped me; the list is long and still cannot be published in full, life being what it is. As for those who tried to raise obstacles, by hastily writing all that was demanded of them, standing guard over ideological purity and thundering from various rostrums or holding up printing – I have already forgotten them, for they deserve nothing better. In the end the fate of a book such as this, although it represents a substantial portion of my life, is merely a tiny fragment of the endlessly great order of things, whose purpose emerges most clearly to me in Bulgakov's sentence, adopted here as a motto: that everything will be as it should. I deeply believe this to be so.

This book owes most of all to my wife Vera, to whom I dedicate it.

AD
Cracow
May 1988

The Master and the Lesser Devil

We must admit that it is convenient to own one's own devil.

We must admit this without going into detail on the satanic condition or into semantic distinctions between 'devil', 'demon' and 'Satan'. We can leave aside the genealogical considerations stored away in myth, legend, creed, religion and literature. It does not concern us whether the Devil is an expression of a Manichaean belief in the eternal duality of the world or a traitor punished by God; the spokesman and implement of reprisal for men's sins or a secret emissary from Heaven putting human virtue to the test, and therefore a kind of superior *agent provocateur*; a basically harmless jester, tolerated by the Creator as a Faustian 'spirit of negation' and the leaven of human progress, or as a magician and master of ceremonies, revealing human secrets by a wave of his fiendish wand.

We may move on to the fundamental dual perception of devils in tradition, folk belief and art: on the one hand as tragic rebels with the aura of former angels and shattered power, and on the other as grotesque fixers, seducers and inept fishers of men, dangerous but comical, at once deceiving and deceived, widely known in folklore and having their origins in pagan times.

All of this may be very important, but not relevant to the subject or the man we shall be dealing with. Here the broadest outlines will suffice for the moment. We may take refuge behind a quotation from Thomas Mann's *Doctor Faustus*, in which the Devil says to Leverkühn, 'Lohnt es zu fragen, ob ich wirklich bin? Ist wirklich nicht, was wirkt, und Wahrheit nicht Erlebnis und Gefühl?'[1]

---

[1] [What serves it to ask whether I really am? Is not 'really' what works, is not truth experience and feeling?] Thomas Mann, *Gesammelte Werke*, Vol. 6, *Doktor Faustus*, Frankfurt am Main, 1960, p. 243. The English translation is from Thomas Mann, *Doctor Faustus*, translated by H. T. Lowe-Porter, Harmondsworth, 1960, p. 235.

The effect on us is a need to invoke the name of the Devil. Here he appears as a scapegoat, ready to accept responsibility for all our failures, everything that goes wrong or frustrates our hopes, and which we dismiss casually with the words 'The Devil only knows!', 'The Devil take it!' or 'To the Devil with it!' We send him ahead of us into dark, treacherous or dangerous places, using him as our defence against our fear of ourselves or the outside world, our own weakness or our shame. He is the master-key to doors which we prefer to push gingerly ajar rather than open wide. He is our alibi and partner, having unlimited responsibility, of which he relieves us. Baron d'Anthès, in his dotage, irritated after years of being asked about his fatal duel with Pushkin, apparently retorted angrily, 'Le diable s'en est mêlé !' – and who could have put it better?

The Devil may also be to us the possessor of enviable powers not yet explained by science, and a relative of magicians, wizards and famous spiritualist media, seeming to be one of them, but with substantially enhanced capabilities. This is the *diabolus ex machina* who pushes back space and time, jumbles fixed parameters, punishes villains and rewards the virtuous (or vice versa), makes fools of presumptuous know-alls, confounds determined rationalists with illogical absurdities – and vanishes as suddenly as he appeared, to reappear when next invoked, or not invoked.

For anyone who is not such a devil as this, I repeat: it is convenient to have one of one's own and to have the ability to 'go to the Devil'.

Russian literature has 'gone to the Devil' many times. Among the best exemplars are Gogol's phantasmagorical tales, seemingly harmless at first, when set in the Ukrainian countryside, but later assuming more sinister forms in the hallucinatory landscapes of St Petersburg. Gogol himself summarized his own strivings in terms of calling forth the devil, grappling with him and finally succumbing to him. One of Pushkin's last draft outlines is a plan for an epic poem about the Devil and Satan's ball. The Russian Hoffmannists – Aleksandr Vel'tman, Vladimir Odoevsky, Osip Senkovsky and Aleksandr Bestuzhev-Marlinsky – treated the Devil without ceremony, in the spirit of the time. The Devil peers through the sinister transmogrifications of Sukhovo-Kobylin. The Devil appeared to Ivan Karamazov, the two of them being one and the same individual; this signalled the start of a new era in the Devil's modern existence. He was present in Remizov's dreams and became a perverted monster in Sologub's novel, then passed across easily to the other shore of time, to Zoshchenko, whose early hero Sinebriukhov suddenly noticed beside him 'something small, black, impish and shaggy, a small child, urchin-like in appearance', re-emerging in the gloomy fantasies of Vsevolod Ivanov. Towards the end of his life Gorky urged others to write plays in which the moving spirit would be the Devil. In his view, this would be a particularly suitable project for Nikolai Erdman, the author of *The Mandate* and *The Suicide*. A little earlier he had reproached Mikhail Slonimsky with the words, 'While you have a good sense of the irrational concealed in reality, in facts, you do not go far enough to expose fully the unreal element, the semi-fantastic, the devilishly Russian element. Zoshchenko is bolder and this is what makes him so good.'[2]

Mikhail Bulgakov 'went to the Devil' by following above all in the footsteps of his master, Gogol. In his hands too – seemingly at the merest wink of an eye – reality was easily transmuted into fantasy, just as Gogol's Foma Grigor'evich in *Evenings on a Farm Near Dikan'ka* was able 'from a distance to take his own coat at the head of his bed for a devil rolled into a ball'. From childhood he had been a prankster, a fantasist and an often irritating joker; as a friend would later write, 'his imagination twined itself in fiendish fashion round reality.' The Devil as a traditional symbol of the mysterious nature of the world made manifest and the Devil as the focal point of forces unknown must have seemed to him a person for whom there was a natural need in the bizarre order of things around him. He felt himself to be on easy terms with him, constantly used his name and invoked him as witness, and could use his presence to explain simple matters. In *The Life of Monsieur de Molière* for example, he asks, 'What connection can there be between an old man and a boy?' and answers without hesitation, 'It must have been the Devil himself. Yes, I'm sure it was the Devil.' He constantly compares things with him: 'The little bells shrilled [...] as if Satan had climbed the belfry [...] and was amusing himself by raising bedlam.' He sees around him signs of the Devil's presence: 'The figure of a policeman materialized out of thin air – there really was something Hoffmannesque about it.' That something was a devil, a tame devil, an errand boy or printer's devil with horns. Thanks to a family joke he assumes a new form. A drawing has been preserved in the Bulgakov archive, showing a little demon named 'Horns' giving the writer's second wife a splendid diamond ring. Such a gift was the stuff of dreams, far beyond Bulgakov's actual resources. But

---

[2] *Literaturnoe nasledstvo. Tom semidesiatyi. Gor'kii i sovetskie pisateli. Neizdannaia perepiska*, Moscow, 1963, p. 387.

why should an agent of Hell be presenting it? The sixteenth-century Milanese physician Hieronymus Cardanus maintained that he kept a small demon, a *spiritus familiaris*, for help around the house; a twentieth-century Kiev ex-doctor could equally well call on him.

Let us call this devil or demon, modelled on traditional folk magic and pagan black arts and made into a stock figure of the contemporary imagination, Bulgakov's Lesser Devil. It is convenient to own one's own devil. Bulgakov has this one and uses him repeatedly. Sometimes this will be comical, sometimes dangerous, sometimes even fatal. After all, in the work named after him, 'Diaboliad', it will drive a modest clerk insane, having first stripped him of any sense of his own identity. To some he will appear in dreams, others will see him in their daily lives, and to yet others he will be a cause of confusion and frustration while making the cause look accidental. He will be everywhere: in speech, where the word 'devil' can be heard every moment; and in the imagination.

As a jester and prankster, a seducer and tempter, an agent of destruction and chaos, balancing precariously on the frontier between dream and reality, *diabolus minor* will accompany his master and maker.

But along the way something will happen to him and around him. Traditional devilry will be put to the test of supernatural power. And it will then transpire that his powers are limited.

But we should not run ahead of the facts of the story. This is only the beginning.

Chapter One

The City, the House and the Years of Wandering

I. The Street, the House; parents and family. School and medical studies. First marriage.
II. War. Apparent front-line service. Work in Nikol'skoe and Viaz'ma. End of the Old World. Demobilization and return to Kiev.
III. Kiev under the Hetman. Power changes hands. Presumed links between Bulgakov's experiences and later literary works.
IV. Leaving Kiev. Further autobiographical connections.
V. The decision to change career. The Caucasus. First steps in literature, and educational work. Departure – via Kiev to Moscow.

I

The street is called Andreevsky Hill. It runs down from the escarpment above the Dnieper, from the Church of Saint Andrew, one of Rastrelli's masterpieces, to the district known as Podol. The steep slope is negotiated by flowing bends – to right, left and right again – and its time-worn cobbles resemble the bed of an invisible river. There are probably few streets like it, especially in the evening when the old street lamps are lit. The houses seem to squat on the slope. There are one or two solid stone-built houses with peeling façades that tell of past prosperity; one of them is even adorned with pretentious neo-Gothic turrets. But most of the trees are taller than the houses; gateways, behind which lie steeply sloping courtyards, conceal the usual jumble of sheds and lean-tos. Little seems to have changed; reconstruction has hardly touched the buildings and the war left relatively few marks. There is little traffic. The bustle of the city is behind you over the escarpment and that of Podol does not reach here. When you look towards it you can see the greenish bulk of the Kiev Academy, known to readers of Gogol, for this is where poor Khoma Brut received his education after being frightened to death by the monsters of Vij.

Number 13 stands on the very elbow of a bend and to those going downhill is seen first from the side. It is a single-storey house. Because of the way it clings to the slope it possesses an appealing lack of symmetry. Its front wall facing the slope is lower, and its back wall, looking towards Podol, is higher. From the back its ground floor is the first floor and the basement is the ground floor, as faithfully described in *The White Guard*.

It was not here that Mikhail Afanas'evich Bulgakov was born on 3rd May 1891, and not here that he spent his childhood.[1] The Bulgakov family moved to Andreevsky Hill in 1907. This was their fifth Kiev address at least.[2] As things turned out, however, this was the house which gained particular importance first for the writer, and then for his readers. In it Mikhail Bulgakov spent his adolescent years, matured, took on the role of head of the family, married, and later spent the years of the cataclysm and collapse of that order for which the house, or rather, the House, stood as sign and symbol. Previous homes may have left certain traces and combined with the image of the House in a synthetic whole. 'Cross-fertilization' was Bulgakov's favourite descriptive method; he hardly ever reflected anything directly, but took features of people and various situations, shaping them into something new, attached more or less tenuously to reality, sometimes deceptively similar, yet not identical. Perhaps this was what happened with the House; there are good grounds for supposing that its authentic furnishings were less lavish than in the well-known descriptions of old upholstery, Turkish couches, silverware, portières and precious trinkets. However, this has no importance since Bulgakov chose precisely this house to be the House and situated it very carefully, peopled it with characters who have clear links with real people from his family and circle of friends, and lent it significance in his works – as a fragile, threatened, yet enduring safe haven. Today's Number 13, like the houses nearby, is run down and showing its age. There is no visible sign of the presence of Bulgakov, no memorial plaque on the wall, and only thanks to a kindly quirk of fate is it still possible to find a living witness to those years in the Bulgakov home, now completely changed.[3]

---

[1] All dates from the pre-revolutionary period are given according to the Julian calendar then in use.

[2] See A. S. Burmistrov, 'K biografii M. A. Bulgakova (1891-1916)', *Kontekst 1978*, Moscow, 1978, p. 252. This study publishes for the first time genuine biographical facts based on the official Kiev municipal archives.

But all the same we know that this is the House. All that it has lost is more than made up for by Bulgakov's imagination, which becomes more real than reality, as is the way with literature. This is the House which people come to Kiev to see, and this House is the beginning of the story.

Mikhail Bulgakov's parents came from the province of Orel, from the middle-ranking clergy. They had moved to Kiev after their marriage. His father, Afanasii Ivanovich Bulgakov (1859-1907), was on the staff of the Kiev Theological Academy, a respected historian of religion and the author of many scholarly works, towards the end of his life a professor at the Academy. His mother, Varvara Mikhailovna, née Pokrovskaia (1869-1922), bravely kept house and brought up her numerous children after the premature death of her husband. Mikhail was the eldest; then came Vera (1892-1973), Nadezhda (1893-1971), Varvara (1898-1957), Nikolai (1898-1966), Ivan (1900-69) and Elena (1902-54). During their studies in Kiev two nephews of Afanasii Ivanovich also stayed in the house, as did other close and distant relatives and children taken in as lodgers. In this way Varvara Mikhailovna supplemented her widow's pension and the modest salary she received as a kindergarten teacher in the so-called Fröbel Society.

The father must have been an outstanding scholar, but he was probably something of an introvert, immersed in his scholarly writing; or perhaps his departure from this life (he died of nephritis; his eldest son was to fall victim to the same disease at the same age) simply came too early for him to exert much visible influence. However, without launching into the mysterious chemistry of heredity, there is good reason for thinking that he did in fact exert an influence. The father's interests, his circle of friends and the reading matter absorbed in that circle could have told on the design of *The Master and Margarita*, and there is no doubt at all that they influenced the implementation of that design. Some time later Bulgakov *fils* would state, and leave a permanent record saying, 'If my mother provided the impetus for *The White Guard*, in my view the image of my father should serve as the point of departure for another work I have planned.'[4] A little earlier in the same

---

[3] At the time of writing such a witness was Inna Konchakovskaia, the daughter of the engineer Vasilii Listovnichii, the owner of Number 13 from 1911 and a friend of the younger members of the Bulgakov family.

[4] *Zametki avtobiograficheskogo kharaktera*, a record based on Bulgakov's own account of himself, set down by his close friend Pavel Popov in 1926. It is faithful in terms of content while

text we read, 'The image of the lamp with the green shade has special meaning for me. It is a very important image that reaches back to my childhood, from my memory of the figure of my father writing at his desk.'[5] Every reader of Bulgakov knows full well that the image of the lamp whose shade must not be removed really is important; it is the tangible symbol of the strength and permanence of hearth and home. Perhaps Bulgakov *père*, who died during the period of stability before the assassination in Sarajevo – with his expression of tense concentration, his high balding dome and spreading beard – was imprinted in his son's memory as a symbol of order, a psychological constant which gained added importance when the fire was extinguished and scattered.

The standing of his mother in the family emerges rather more clearly. She had great individuality and was an energetic person who struggled bravely against the vagaries of fate. Although she had tyrannical characteristics she knew the art of diplomacy and turning a blind eye; she also possessed much maternal warmth. She had enormous authority but she managed gradually to share her family responsibilities with her elder children. She did not give up hope of a private life for herself and in 1918, recognizing perhaps that her children were already sufficiently independent, she married Ivan Pavlovich Voskresensky, a surgeon. They set up house nearby, further up the hill, near the church (38, Andreevsky Hill). Her open, expressive face, with lively flashing eyes and characteristically prominent nose with deeply carved nostrils, has much in common with the features of her first-born son. Her mother, Anfisa Ivanovna, bore the maiden name of Turbina.

This last shared Bulgakov home, the most important, was lively, at times even uproarious, held together by strong family bonds, subject though these were to rights of seniority. There was plenty of social life as the atmosphere attracted friends, and their individual features would later be immortalized by the elder brother. There was a tradition of music-making, much singing, and plays based on family events were staged by the joint efforts of all. All of them enjoyed drama and opera. Mikhail Afanas'evich shared these interests with the rest of his family and even dreamed of a theatrical career. During their holidays the family usually

---

showing little respect for Bulgakov's style. *Zametki avtobiograficheskogo kharaktera*, Manuscript Department of the Lenin Library, Fond 218.

[5] Ibid.

repaired to nearby Bucha, a summer resort where they had their own little house. Their life thus was fairly typical of the milieu of the educated Russian intelligentsia of the period – and the permanence of that life must have been taken for granted.

'Those days belong to legend,' Bulgakov would later write. 'Days when a carefree young generation lived in the gardens of the most beautiful city in our country. That was the time when the certainty grew in the hearts of that generation that all of life would sail by quietly, calmly, amidst bright colours; dawn, sunset, the Dnieper, the Kreshchatik, sunlit streets in summer, and in winter big flakes of friendly snow, not cold, not penetrating...

And everything turned out quite differently.'[6]

Until this happened, however, our hero proceeded up the steps of life's ordinary initiation ceremonies. In August 1900 he entered the first year of the First Kiev Grammar School in Bibikovsky Boulevard. Later the school was renamed in honour of Alexander the First. It had a good reputation and many of its pupils made their mark in the world. One of its pupils, a year younger than Bulgakov, was Konstantin Paustovsky, who gives a lively account of his youth in the first volume of his autobiographical cycle. This is valuable evidence, although the information in it should always be taken with a grain of salt. Paustovsky was an inveterate embroiderer, convinced of the memoirist's right to refashion reality so as to make it richer and more colourful than it actually is. Furthermore his knowledge of Bulgakov's later life could have unconsciously shaped the resurrected images of a schoolfriend. But even when treated with the greatest caution the following passage does not sound exaggerated: 'Bulgakov was a great one for pranks, invention and mystification. It was all carried off with ease and grace, on any occasion, and demonstrated his generosity of spirit, the power of his imagination and his gift for improvisation. But there was nothing in this that removed Bulgakov from real life. On the contrary, as you listened to Bulgakov it became clear that his brilliant imagination and free interpretation of reality were purely

---

[6] 'Kiev-gorod', *Nakanune*, No. 377, 6.7.1923. This and other sketches by Bulgakov published in *Nakanune* have been collected in M. Bulgakov, *Ranniaia neizdannaia proza*, ed. by V. Levin, Munich, 1976. Also in M. A. Bulgakov, *Povesti. Rasskazy. Fel'etony*, Moscow, 1988.

symptoms of that same life force and that reality. The world existed, and Bulgakov's youthful creative imagination was one of its components.'[7]

Paustovsky was right in saying that a brilliant imagination is part of reality; in this sense the things about Bulgakov which were embroidered or simply invented in recollections of him are also part of the truth about him. From the accounts of various japes and escapades on the Dnieper, of secret outings to the theatre, there emerges a picture of a clever and witty schoolboy whose imagination was laced with a large admixture of naughtiness. It also seems that his younger siblings were rather fearful of their elder brother's sharp tongue. From Bulgakov himself we learn immediately of his early enchantment with Gogol ('I first read *Dead Souls* when I was nine; at first I thought it was an adventure story'); of his first attempts at writing ('I wrote my first story, "The Adventures of Svetlana", when I was seven... After that I wrote nothing until the fifth form of grammar school. After a pause I started writing humorous pieces'); and of his own awareness of his situation as a pupil ('I wrote my school essays well, but on the whole it was poor, second-rate scribbling on hackneyed themes. The teacher of Russian was a nonentity... Grammar school left me with very vivid impressions; university with very much paler ones').[8]

It must be agreed that there is nothing extraordinary about this; no early signs of future distinction. As usual in such cases, certain details become significant only by the will of later biographers who consider them with closer attention after the event. Young Misha is a normal child and adolescent with a taste for literature; he writes scripts for family theatricals and entertains his peers with jolly improvisations. He leaves school in the usual way in 1909; a comical photograph has survived in which he can be seen smoking his first officially permitted post-matriculation cigarette – head thrown proudly back, a defiant look in his bright blue eyes, an assumed seriousness, yet with a touch of self-mockery... For his university studies he chooses medicine. When asked later what prompted this choice he seemed to shrug off the question with a joking reply: he was drawn to a 'meteoric career' and 'couldn't resist microscopes';[9] from this we may

---

[7] Konstantin Paustovskii, 'Bulgakov i teatr', *Mosty*, 1965, No. 11, p. 380; also in *Vospominaniia o Mikhaile Bulgakove*, Moscow, 1988, p. 96.

[8] *Zametki avtobiograficheskogo kharaktera*.

[9] Ibid.

conclude that, like many bright boys, he had not fixed on a definite sphere of interest. In the meantime there was already a medical presence in the family; Varvara Mikhailovna's two brothers were doctors, as was her husband-to-be, who was much loved by all the Bulgakov family. Whatever the case, Mikhail Afanas'evich began his studies in the Faculty of Medicine at St Vladimir's University. Here he spent the years 1909-1916. The first half of this period was overshadowed by political unrest which had a marked effect on university life. Typically, however, there is not the slightest indication that Bulgakov was aware of it. Politics seemed to play no part in his life, or at least there is no evidence that they did. All the indications are that the family had a strongly conservative leaning, without any extremist tendencies. This was a fairly typical, middle-of-the-road position in this period and this social milieu. Bulgakov apparently needed nothing more.

Should this surprise us? In recalling the 'carefree young generation' he may generalize excessively but he clearly has his own background in mind. Besides learning, he is interested in literature, art and the theatre. He is surrounded by 'the most beautiful city in our country', which he will later remember with the words, 'Spring turned the gardens white with blossom; the Royal Gardens were covered in green and the sun caught all the windows and lit fires in each one. And the Dnieper! And the sunsets! And the Vydubetsky Monastery on the escarpment. A sea of green with arms running down to the gentle, variegated Dnieper. The dense blue-black nights over the water, and the electric cross of St Vladimir suspended in the air... In short a beautiful city, a happy city. The mother of Russian cities.'[10]

He also married young. He met Tatiana Nikolaevna Lappa, a year younger than himself and the daughter of the director of the Department of Revenue in Saratov, at the home of her aunt, a friend of the Bulgakov family. The marriage took place on 26th April 1913 in the church of St Michael in Podol, a short distance from his home. The service was performed by Father Aleksei Glagolev, a friend of the family; their student friends and a cousin, Kostia Bulgakov, were the ushers. It was all honourable, cosy, friendly and familial in that last year of the *belle époque*, when there still remained the certainty that 'all of life would sail by quietly, calmly, amidst bright colours', and nobody could imagine what *The White Guard* would later relate:

---

[10] 'Kiev-gorod'.

'The walls would crumble, the startled falcon would fly from the white gauntlet, the flame would gutter in the bronze lamp, and "The Captain's Daughter" would be burnt in the stove. Their mother would tell her children that they must go on living.

But suffering and death awaited them.'[11]

II

We are still dealing with the pre-literary prehistory of a literary career. It is important – like everything else from which outstanding people appear – as the raw material for future achievements and the foundation which made them possible. But it is not in any direct fashion recorded in those achievements.

That, however, would follow a little later. Literature would enter into life, and life – his own and that of those close to him – would become the stuff of literature. History would see to that.

But first, war would break out, filling Kiev with wounded soldiers, refugees, staff officers, auxiliary personnel, a mass of uniforms of paramilitary organizations whose functionaries cut a dash while carefully avoiding front-line service. The university was partly evacuated but the Faculty of Medicine continued to function. In April 1916 Bulgakov passed his qualifying examinations with honours and became a doctor. Immediately after this he was apparently conscripted into the medical corps. His officially published biographies are silent on this point; there exists, however, a plausible version which tells of a member of a second-line militia detachment volunteering for the south-western front in 1916 and working in field hospitals in Kamenets-Podol'sk and Chernovtsy.[12] Tatiana Nikolaevna is supposed to have accompanied him as a nurse. But in the autumn of that year Bulgakov was called to Moscow and then assigned to the Smolensk region, where, like other graduates from his year, he was to take the place of an older country doctor who had been sent to the front. In September he reached the village hospital in Nikol'skoe, with the wife who was his inseparable companion and assistant.

---

[11] M. Bulgakov, 'Belaia gvardiia', in *Izbrannaia proza*, Moscow, 1966, p. 113.

[12] This version has been officially confirmed. See T. Kisel'gof, 'Gody molodosti', *Literaturnaia gazeta*, No. 20, 13.5.1981.

For a city-dweller born and bred, and a novice doctor at that, this was undoubtedly a stern test. A little later Bulgakov would embark on a description of it in his *Notes of a Young Doctor*. There is no doubt about the autobiographical nature of that description.[13] Only occasionally does Bulgakov apply certain screening devices to try to weaken the impression that the author and the narrator are the same person. For this he had definite and specific motives. While exercising caution, we may therefore take the scenes showing the young doctor confronting serious medical emergencies, his own inexperience, physical fatigue and rural ignorance as facts of Bulgakov's biography. He received patients from morning till evening, taking charge in his own hospital in the intervals and being called out at night to accidents and women in childbirth. There were dangerous adventures too: marauding wolves and the experience of being lost in blizzards. Doctor Bulgakov had his successes, which contributed to his fame in the district, and his failures, which he felt bitterly for long afterwards. He made up at first for a lack of skill by self-confidence and sidelong glances at his textbooks. Later he would write of himself unsentimentally, soberly and with self-deprecating humour, but also with honest satisfaction at having come unbroken through the school of hard knocks and professional practice.

In fact it is fair to suppose that there was a moment when he did break down, but that he overcame his weakness. It is not the role of the biographer to retail gossip, but this instance, seen as shameful in the circle close to Bulgakov, was made known in the recollections of Tatiana Nikolaevna, as reported by an anonymous acquaintance.[14] From these we learn that to counteract the pain caused by an anti-diphtheria inoculation Bulgakov injected himself with morphine and that his organism became so conditioned to it that he developed an addiction. This state of affairs is said to have endured for a year; the drama of it suffuses the cruelly accurate short story 'Morphine', which was included in *Notes of a Young Doctor* (though here Bulgakov masked the autobiographical nature of the story). Tatiana Nikolaevna takes the credit for rescuing her husband from his addiction and there is

---

[13] For a description of Nikol'skoe today compared with archival data see A. Burmistrov, 'Poezdka v proshloe', *Zvezda*, No. 5, 1981, p. 19.

[14] See 'Beseda s T. N. Lappa', in *Neizdannyi Bulgakov. Teksty i materialy*, ed. by E. Proffer, Ann Arbor, Michigan, 1977, p. 18.

no reason to disbelieve her. But the patient-doctor's will power probably also played its part.

During this period of rural practice we begin to see Bulgakov as a personality. The earlier image of Mikhail Bulgakov – as far as it has been recorded – is made up of his outward appearance and a certain attitude. We see an elongated triangular face with a prominent nose and 'Shaliapin' nostrils, as somebody later described them; a fair forelock constantly falling on his brow and being tossed back; very light blue eyes with a hint of wickedness dancing in them, witty to some, caustic to others; jerky, angular movements; much personal charm, natural, but consciously deployed. These features are now filled out by character. A trait which was to become important is now visible: his calm acceptance of the inevitable, and determined action in the face of adversity, driven by an inner imperative, to do all that can be done and all that must be done, and do it as well as possible, to help others, unsparing of oneself.

When Bulgakov left Nikol'skoe in September 1917, a year after he had arrived there, the district authorities testified in the then-accepted style that he had 'shown himself an energetic and tireless employee in the field', and the details read like a detailed confirmation of the contents of *Notes of a Young Doctor*:

'He has performed the following operations: amputation of leg at hip – 1; amputation of toes – 3; termination of pregnancy – 18; circumcisions – 4; delivery with correction of breech presentation – 3; manual removal of placenta – 1; removal of lipomas – 2; tracheotomy – 1. He has also performed suturing of wounds, lancing of abscesses and carbuncles, treated perforated ulcers (2), and reset dislocated limbs. On one occasion he removed fragments of ribs shattered by a bullet, using anaesthetic.'[15] Being immersed in his work, Doctor Bulgakov may well not have heard the ever-growing rumblings of 1917, particularly as Nikol'skoe was a remote backwater. The October coup found him in Viaz'ma, working in the local hospital. The feelings with which he greeted the change in the cycle of history are easy to imagine, as they could not differ from those which predominated in his milieu. There is clear evidence of his state of mind in a letter to his sister Nadezhda written on New Year's Eve 1917:

---

[15] Institut russkoi literatury (IRLI; Pushkinskii dom), Leningrad, Fond 369; reprinted in *Neizdannyi Bulgakov*, p. 13.

'From the train to Moscow and Saratov I recently saw it all with my own eyes, and I never want to see it again. I saw grey crowds smashing the windows of trains and people being beaten up, shouting and cursing vilely. In Moscow I saw houses that had been sacked and burned. [...] I saw hungry queues outside shops, harried and pitiful officers, and newspapers all devoted in essentials to one thing: the blood that is being shed in the south, the west and the east.'[16]

Politics was the last thing likely to interest Bulgakov at that period. He felt not the slightest urge to change the world. By nature he was a supporter of enlightened order; a spasm of horror at the brutality with which scores were settled, and of fear in the face of the chaos which had been unleashed, was powerful and irresistible. Later this reaction would constantly return, although he would succeed in muting it by reflection. There is nothing surprising in this: the Russian *demos* had heard the catch-cry 'grab' nagrablennoe' [seize back what's been stolen], with which the Bolsheviks set in motion the chain of mutual acts of violence and ever-crueller vengeance by the 'Whites' and 'Reds'. What followed must have come as a shock to all dispassionate and intelligent observers, even those who had successfully anaesthetized themselves by becoming persuaded in advance of the justice of historical revenge in all its manifestations. A dose of determinism eased the pain, but Bulgakov did not apply this method.

What could he do with his honours degree and his references when his world had crumbled about him? He took his discharge from the army, left his position, returned to Kiev and set up in private practice as a venerologist.

The winter of 1918 was just giving way to spring.

III

He found his home town fundamentally changed; its agreeable stability had vanished forever and its finer features no doubt seemed blurred amidst the nervous agitation of people who had no time for calm contemplation. Kiev had already stepped onto the roller-coaster of changing governments: the Ukrainian Rada was followed by the Bolsheviks, then the Germans, who installed Hetman Skoropadsky

---

[16] Quoted in A. Al'tshuler, *'Dni Turbinykh' i 'Beg' M. Bulgakova v istorii sovetskogo teatra 20-kh godov*. A dissertation presented for the degree of Candidate of Art History, Moscow, 1972, p. 80. Also in Mikhail Bulgakov, *Dnevnik. Pis'ma. 1914-1940*, Moscow, 1997, p. 10.

as their puppet ruler. The illusory nature of his authority was plain to see; the surrounding countryside seethed with peasant unrest, only just held in check by German punitive expeditions; the city teemed with agents and conspiracies of every possible orientation and trend. Relatively speaking, to those newly arrived from Bolshevik Russia, this seething vortex seemed an oasis of order and prosperity. They brought with them a passionate desire for stability and an awareness of its fragility, premonitions of new upheavals and a readiness to flee yet again, a fatalistic sense of powerlessness and concern to preserve the appearance of normality in a life of make-believe. The upholding of these forms did little good, and reality, which was to surpass even the most catastrophic presentiments, made itself felt again and again. As the year 1918 waned it moved increasingly towards new shocks, and it is no surprise that in the opening sentences of *The White Guard* this year is presented in tones of pathos and menace like those of a biblical or mythical prophecy.

This was only the beginning. 'According to the calculations of some citizens of Kiev,' Bulgakov would write later, 'power changed hands eighteen times. Some refugee-memoirists have counted twelve such changes. For myself, I can state quite precisely that there were fourteen. Moreover I personally experienced ten of them.'[17]

His experience of the change of government in December, the second in the series but probably the first to find him actively involved, assumed particular importance. The fall of Skoropadsky, the German withdrawal and the entry of the Ukrainian Rada forces led by Semion Petliura, must have been felt as the very end of the old world. In the fastness of Smolensk province the doctor had not witnessed any of this; fate therefore arranged a repetition of the scene, drawing him into closer involvement.

What sort of involvement? A diary entry tells us laconically: 'On 14th December I was in the streets of Kiev. I found myself in situations resembling those in the novel.'[18]

'The novel' is clearly *The White Guard*. The word 'resembling' permits the cautious supposition that in essence the experiences of Aleksei Turbin and Mikhail Bulgakov could have been similar, though the situations may not necessarily have

---

[17] 'Kiev-gorod.'

[18] *Zametki ...*

coincided fully. In the novel the experiences of various members of the family could also overlap and intersect.

The regular appearance of certain motifs linked to the events in Kiev and recurring in various guises in Bulgakov's prose is noteworthy. One such is the flight before Petliura's forces on the day they enter the city, in one case filled with danger and drama (*The White Guard*), in another quasi-grotesque ('The Unusual Adventures of a Doctor'). Another is the dragooning of the doctor-narrator into Petliura's army and his escape during its night-time retreat (a story entitled 'The Murderer' in the cycle *Notes of a Young Doctor*; a fragment in 'The Night of the Second', probably taken from an earlier version of *The White Guard* which has not survived in full; and again 'Unusual Adventures...'). And finally the scenes in which Petliura's men interrogate and torture their defenceless victims, (*The White Guard*, 'The Night of the Second', the story 'The Raid', the sketch 'To a Secret Friend', 'The Murderer', *A Theatrical Novel*, and the first two versions of *The Days of the Turbins*). The vision of the interrogation, torture and murder of innocents, in particular, varying in the detail but recurrent in its central features and in the spasm of rage which it elicits, becomes a true obsession, a nightmare which haunts the memory. We may see this as a mark of authenticity. Just as striking is the exceptional clarity and almost tangible precision of the record of the experience of Doctor Bakaleinikov, who is thrown from a bridge by Petliura's men ('The Night of the Second'). Stylistic analysis alone would probably suffice to prove that such complete identity of description and subject, such total immersion in the hero's emotional life, is achieved when Bulgakov is writing about himself.

From this we may conclude: that he was probably mobilized by Petliura, probably witnessed his brutality (he was capable of fair assessments, in spite of his own feelings, but his deeply-felt shock at Petliura stayed with him, although he certainly witnessed things as bad later), and probably sooner or later escaped. Perhaps Aleksei Turbin's desperate escape in *The White Guard*, also featuring a seismographic recording of his feelings, is Doctor Bakaleinikov's bid for freedom, displaced in time, and both are literary versions of some escape by Doctor Bulgakov, which must have occurred.[19] In all the works mentioned except the

---

[19] It is also possible that there were two escapes, at the beginning and the end of Petliura's occupation. This is suggested by the overlap between the episodes in *The White Guard* and 'The Unusual Adventures of a Doctor'.

story 'The Raid', there are numerous traces of real individuals from among Bulgakov's family and friends, though in most cases subjected to a degree of 'cross-fertilization'; we shall return to this topic later. All of this is substantial corroboration of the notion of 'similar situations'; to this extent, but no further, a *literary* work which is not a diarist's record and not amenable to such treatment may be treated as one.

This is about as much as we may surmise about Bulgakov's life during this period which was so important to him – before he turned it into literature.

IV

In the meantime the vicissitudes of the city of Kiev were gaining pace. In February 1919 the Bolsheviks drove out Petliura. On 1st September they withdrew before the Whites and Petliura but in October two Red regiments gained control of the city for two days.

In autumn of that year, probably in September, Bulgakov left the family home for the last time.[20]

The circumstances of this departure are passed over in silence in all autobiographical sources. This very silence appears to be evidence of something. It is possible that some of the same motivation operated here as in his silence about the period he spent at the front in 1916. There may be more weighty motives too: the greater part of a generation of writers served in the Tsarist army and this was rarely concealed. With the White Army things were different. There is no doubt that Bulgakov left while the Whites were in Kiev. Why? And in what capacity?

To this day there is much archival material about Bulgakov to which researchers have no access; here we see in operation the ubiquitous hypocrisy which dictates that uncomfortable facts did not exist and will not exist as long as no one mentions them, as well as the ambiguous attitude of the writer himself. When the archives are fully opened it will immediately be possible to verify the

---

20 'I lived in Kiev without a break from February 1918 to September 1919,' (*Zametki* ...). A sentence in a letter to his cousin Konstantin dated 19.2.21 is therefore surprising: 'You and I parted about a year ago.' Perhaps Bulgakov did not after all leave Kiev immediately and for good. At the moment further evidence is lacking on this point.

hypotheses which the present book poses on the basis of circumstantial deduction, in full consciousness of the risks involved in this procedure.

In 1922 Bulgakov published the story 'The Unusual Adventures of a Doctor'.[21] It is the spasmodic record of the experiences of a doctor specializing in bacteriology who is mobilized by 'the fifth government in succession', torn from the peace of hearth and home and dispatched to the Caucasus front. Here too the seismographic nature of the record is perceptible; its style clearly matches that of the *Notes on Shirt-Cuffs*, written at the same time. But while the *Notes* are openly presented as autobiographical, the 'Unusual Adventures...' are placed in the conventional quotation marks: they are supposed to be the diary of a friend who has fled the country, made available to the author by his sister. This would not be the last time Bulgakov would resort to this gesture of symbolically distancing himself from a text – said 'authentically' to be the work of another hand. No doubt he had various motives for doing this, but who can say? Perhaps on this first occasion he was driven by simple necessity.

Bulgakov's doctor evades the 'fifth government', Skoropadsky's; then, as we know, there is his grotesque flight before the sixth, Petliura's; later he is mobilized by the Bolsheviks, and then, after an interval – a row of dots – he turns up in the Caucasus as a doctor with the White Army. The nature of the diary allows us to suppose that Doctor Bulgakov himself was recruited into this army and left Kiev in its ranks. This was, after all, quite natural. His two younger brothers had also joined this army and were evacuated abroad from Odessa.

The story 'The Red Crown' presents significant material for circumstantial deduction.[22] The narrator, a patient in a mental hospital, is tormented by the memory of a brother who was killed in the war. The narrator had promised his mother that he would bring him safely home, but the brother, a young cavalryman, had refused to go, saying he could not leave his squadron and charging into an attack in which he was mortally wounded. This motif – the wounding and death of a younger brother – would also recur several times in different guises. As early as the surviving fragments of the story 'A Tribute of Admiration', regarded by

---

[21] *Rupor*, No. 2, 1922. Reprinted in Mikhail Bulgakov, *Ranniaia nesobrannaia proza*, ed. by V. Levin and L. Svetin, Munich, 1978, p. 171; also in M. A. Bulgakov, *Povesti...*, pp. 153-163.

[22] 'Krasnaia korona', *Nakanune*, 22.10.1922; reprinted in *Ranniaia neizdannaia proza*, also in M. A. Bulgakov, *Povesti...*, pp. 183-188.

Marietta Chudakova, the most serious and best-informed Russian Bulgakov expert, as his probable début in print, we find a characteristic story told by a mother of how her younger son shielded her with his own body during an exchange of fire. Her listener is her elder son, who is also the narrator.[23] Elena Zemskaia, the writer's niece, who has published some important Bulgakov material which was preserved by the family, has written in her introduction, 'The stories of that period, "The Red Crown" and "A Tribute of Admiration" are profoundly autobiographical. They record Mikhail Bulgakov's anxiety about his mother and his younger brothers.'[24] From other family accounts it is clear that Nikolai and Ivan Bulgakov were cadets and that they really did try several times to leave home and go off to the war, but their mother demanded that the elder son restrain them.

It is easy to imagine the depth of the elder brother's anxiety; he had a great sense of responsibility for the family, but at the critical juncture was he powerless to prevent its being broken up, or was he unwilling to act? Perhaps he had a sense of the hopelessness of the anti-Bolshevik resistance; it is likely that by nature he had little of the man-at-arms about him. *The White Guard*, for which the works mentioned are his preparation, the tuning of his instruments, grapples with the injunction to be true to one's oath and one's honour come what may, – an injunction which must be rejected as it imposes suicide. Does this mean that the injunction ceases to exist? In *The White Guard* the elder brother is a grotesque 'outsider'; he oversleeps and is late for parade; he stands outside the struggle; he is exposed to danger purely by chance, whereas his younger brother faces live bullets. Is this not also a reflection, in the carefully planned construction of the novel, of actual events?

---

[23] See Marietta Chudakova, 'K tvorcheskoi biografii M. Bulgakova 1916-1923', *Voprosy literatury*, No. 7, 1973, p. 237. Chudakova suggests that this might be the story alluded to by the writer in his autobiography (see Note 24) and that it should be regarded as Bulgakov's literary début.

[24] M. A. Bulgakov, 'Pis'ma k rodnym (1921-1922)', published by E. A. Zemskaia, *Izvestiia AN SSSR. Seriia literatury i iazyka*, Vol. 35, No. 5, 1976, p. 452. See also a fragment of a letter from Bulgakov to his sister Vera dealing with the sending of some fragments of the story 'A Tribute of Admiration' at the same time: 'These are merely scraps, but I somehow feel they will interest you.' Ibid. p. 458; also in Mikhail Bulgakov, *Dnevnik....*, p. 18.

For over two years Bulgakov heard nothing of his younger brothers; only in January 1922 did word come from Nikolai, and a little later from Ivan. Family solidarity had carried over into exile, where the elder of the two had assumed the role of guardian of the younger. Nikolai studied medicine in Zagreb, then moved to Paris, became an expert in bacteriology, lectured in Mexico, and during the Second World War distinguished himself in the French Resistance. Ivan, apparently made of less stern stuff, turned his musical gift to advantage by playing in balalaika ensembles *à la russe*. Both remained in touch with the family at home and the middle brother was often involved in the literary affairs of the eldest.

To return to the eldest: he burdens the narrator of his 'Red Crown' with the torment of shared responsibility. Not only for his brother, but also for the idea to which his brother was sacrificed and which turns out to be brutal in its manifestations – people are hanged in its name. This is a separate thread running through this immensely important story and intersecting with the main one; the shock experienced by a witness to physical violence – of which we already know – is expressed in an accusation levelled at himself and the White general who gives the order to hang a Bolshevik agitator:

'General, I agree I was just as much to blame as you, that I bear a terrible responsibility for that man with the soot smudge on his cheek, but my brother had nothing to do with it. He's only nineteen.'

And further on:

'For all I know that man swinging from the lamp-post in Berdiansk, the one with the soot on his cheek, might come calling on you. If he does, it's right that we should suffer. I sent Kolia to help you hang him, but you're the one who did it.'[25]

This is the background to the narrator's insanity, which is depicted in the story, but is that all there is to it?

The vision of the fallen brother constantly returns, insistently repeating his last sentence: 'I can't leave the squadron.' This is the categorical imperative of loyalty. For the narrator, does the emphasis here not rest on the word 'I', with the unspoken question 'What about you?'? Are he and his creator not haunted by the thought that they have deserted their squadrons? And are they not trying by this story, apart from everything else, to find justification for that decision?

---

[25] 'Krasnaia korona'.

Knowing Bulgakov's later career, we have no right to suspect him of faint-heartedness. It is certain that he was not seeking a convenient alibi. On the contrary: in what he wrote about the period of the Civil War and the way he sought to judge it, he was also seeking a fair appraisal of himself. And in studying recent history he traced in it the basis for decisions he had made or failed to make. His conclusions regarding himself may well have left a bitter taste. There is a point in *The White Guard* where the authorial voice calls Aleksei Turbin a 'milksop'. Recalling the brutality of Petliura's men, Doctor Bakaleinikov weeps and cries out: 'Bandits!... But I... I'm an intellectual louse!' At this point the narrator adds that he said this '... again for no apparent reason', but this is a literary device, an assumed naïveté.[26] While there is 'no apparent reason' in the strict sense, we nevertheless sense that this constant recourse to the position of the 'outsider' and the re-examination of it from all angles reveal an urge to scratch a sore spot. To what extent is this literature, and to what extent life? There are no accurate gauges by which to measure this. To what extent is Bulgakov fair towards himself, to what extent too hard on himself? Again we do not know. In filling in the biographical lacunae, we must emphasize that we are dealing not with facts but with the next best thing – conjecture.

One way or another Bulgakov makes his way to the Caucasus; if he had earlier been with the White Army, here he parts company with it. Along the way, as he would write in his autobiography, his 'first little story' came into being – 'in a rattling train, by the light of a candle stuck in a paraffin bottle.' It was published in a Vladikavkaz newspaper. 'After this,' the author goes on, 'several of my feuilletons were published. In early 1920 I set aside my degree with honours and began to write.'[27]

V

Thus the decision to change careers came about. In addition to reasons of an unverifiable nature covered by the word 'vocation', it is possible that he was

---

[26] The scene described here is from the story 'V noch' na 3-e chislo' [The Night of the Second], *Sobranie sochinenii v 5 tomakh*, Moscow, 1989-1990, Vol. 1, p. 523. (Also in *Povesti...*, p. 201). *Trans.*

[27] *Sovetskie pisateli. Avtobiografii*, Moscow, 1966, p. 85.

tired of being repeatedly mobilized, anxious that this should not happen again, and that this played some role. Literature was still a guarantee of independence; the time when writers too would be mobilized still lay in the future.

The motivation for this decision had been taking shape for some time. It lay in the early literary efforts – no longer childish efforts – which he had left in his study in Kiev. 'The archive material,' writes Marietta Chudakova in her pioneering account of the Bulgakov collection in the Lenin Library, 'testifies that by autumn 1919 "Sketches of a Country Doctor" already existed, as did the sketch "Ill Health" [Nedug] (which may be related to the future *White Guard*) and "The First Colour" (about whose content nothing is known), as well as "The Green Dragon".'[28] In spring 1921 Bulgakov asked his sister Nadezhda to collect all these, as well as certain pieces he had written while in the Caucasus, and throw them into the stove. He repeated this request more than once and with some insistence. His wish was carried out. It is a great pity that his authority as elder brother carried such weight, but Bulgakov had set himself high standards right from the start and had evidently decided to erase the traces of his first steps.

He was tormented by a sense of having wasted time. '...I was four years late in starting what I should have started long ago – writing,' he confided to his cousin Konstantin in February 1921

'[...] At night I sometimes look over the stories I have published (in newspapers, newspapers!) and think to myself: where's the collection? Where's the name? Where are the wasted years?'[29]

Now he wanted to make up for all the lost time, but conditions were against him. He was a particle in the human mass which was being shaken and tilted this way and that across the former empire. The nomadic existence became the norm. Hardly had Bulgakov halted in Vladikavkaz than he wanted to move on. All the indications are that he then intended to emigrate; there are perfectly transparent hints

---

[28] M. Chudakova, 'Arkhiv M. A. Bulgakova. Materialy dlia tvorcheskoi biografii pisatelia', in *Zapiski Otdela rukopisei Gos. Bibl. SSSR im. Lenina*, Moscow, 1976, p. 35. (The first title given here, in Russian *Nabroski zemskogo vracha*, appears to belong to an early version of *Zapiski iunogo vracha* [Notes of a Young Doctor]. Bulgakov mentions this title in a letter to his brother Konstantin. *Dnevnik. Pis'ma 1914-1940*, 1997, p. 14 – *Trans.*)

[29] M. A. Bulgakova, 'Pis'ma k rodnym', pp. 454-55; also in Mikhail Bulgakov, *Dnevnik. Pis'ma..*, p. 13.

at this in several texts. But he was stricken with typhus, and when he recovered Vladikavkaz was in Bolshevik hands (they entered the town on 31st March 1920).[30] Later he confided, 'on 15th February 1920 I experienced a spiritual crisis.'[31] Thus he encoded an accumulation of circumstances which undoubtedly determined his fate.

For the next year and a half this fate kept him in exceptionally beautiful surroundings, at the foot of the majestic Mount Stolovaia, among avenues of lindens above the River Terek, and the creaking carts and the hubbub of eastern bazaars. The exotic surroundings, appealing in normal circumstances, could only irritate the new arrivals from the north, exacerbating their sense of loss and instability. Swept here from different corners of Russia, they carried with them a sense of the ambiguity of the nomadic life, as they tried to sit out the time of uncertainty, doing any work they could find.

Bulgakov did the same. He started work in the local organ of the newly-established educational and cultural administration, a body with a suitably long name. His friend from those days, Iurii Slezkin, already an established writer of the drawing-room modernist school and therefore no doubt an authority to the novice writer, left a credible sketch of Bulgakov in his novel *The Girl from the Mountains* [Devushka s gor]. In it he appears as Aleksei Vasil'evich, and his appearance and attitudes match Bulgakov's no less than what he says about himself:

'I'm just a private individual, a journalist who knows a little about books and literature, no more. I'm not a doctor. I'd like you to bear that in mind in the name of our long friendship... That's right, no fixed profession. A member of the union of cultural workers and head of the literature section of the District Committee's sub-committee on art.'[32]

And from other viewpoints: 'What does he do anyway? He's a failed journalist dreaming about writing a novel; a doctor doing his best to forget all about

---

[30] According to some versions he went to Batum and fell ill there.

[31] *Zametki* ... In mid-February the disastrous situation of the White Army in the Stavropol' region and the Kuban' became obvious. It is possible that this had some connection with the date Bulgakov chose to give.

[32] Iurii Slezkin, *Devushka s gor*, Moscow, 1925, p. 72. The discovery of this coincidence is the work of a researcher into Bulgakov's Caucasus period, V. Chebotareva. 'Mikhail Bulgakov na Kavkaze', *Ural'skii sledopyt*, No. 11, 1972, pp. 74-77.

his profession. A man with a gift for observation who manages to observe one or two things. But from the moment he was evicted from his flat, given a number and told to report to a certain place, then shunted from one war front to another, having to say that the side who'd claimed him was "his side" – from that moment he ceased to exist, he died.'[33]

Bulgakov was soon to give an autobiographical record of his experiences and activities during this period in *Notes on Shirt-Cuffs*. If we set this record beside Slezkin's novel, the basic features, factual and psychological, overlap. The two describe similar episodes showing someone's daring escape before the fall of the city, scenes from literary life, local tribal troubles, the harsh and clumsy moves of the new authorities. Above all they show the painful reality of the unreal situation of Aleksei Vasil'evich and Mikhail Afanas'evich, who are equally dazed and react equally impulsively, conscious of living a life of make-believe.

However, this is not the whole truth, for Bulgakov is already advancing with determination into the world of literature, and in the surrounding chaos this is what becomes for him an element of secure order. *Real* literature. Slezkin also noted, 'The only thing he would like to write is a novel. And write one he will, you may be sure. His novel will be written... All those jottings, feuilletons and reviews are only to earn his keep. The same goes for such fruitful activity as running LITO (the literature section – A.D.) and giving lectures in various courses. All this is very important of course – but that novel will be written no matter what.'[34]

Before the dream of real literature came true, he would produce writing of a more utilitarian nature, to earn his daily bread, which was very hard to find. It consisted of attempts at drama, which the author would later destroy with a vengeful grimace. Only one of these happened, by chance, to survive, entitled 'Sons of the Mullah'. It is a prompter's copy, written on wrapping paper. It fully deserves the self-critical attitude of its creator. Two brothers with differing political views arrive in their native *aul* before the February revolution. After various adventures they are reconciled and, on learning of the fall of the autocracy, arrest the local policeman. This takes place to the accompaniment of cries of 'Long live free Ingushetia!' and amidst the enthusiasm of the mountain people, enthusiasm

---

[33] Ibid., p. 154.

[34] Ibid. p. 111.

which apparently had to be clearly conveyed from the stage of a sparsely appointed hall. Approval was sometimes expressed by shots fired into the air. All of this is recorded in *Notes on Shirt-Cuffs* in tones of self-mockery ('You writers and playwrights in Paris and Berlin, just try! Try and write something worse, just for fun! You won't succeed, not even with the talent of a Kuprin, a Bunin or a Gorky. I hold the record! In team work! We were a team of three: myself, the magistrate's assistant and famine. At the beginning of 1921.'[35] From the very start, even at this early stage, cheap writing went against the grain. He was ashamed of it, but force of circumstances demanded utilitarian writing. Hence the feeling of constant irritation which permeates the *Notes*... Everything around Bulgakov upset him; the atmosphere resembled a stifling, tightening hoop, a situation from which there was no way out short of flight.

In the letters to his family written during this period the internal strain is also strongly felt. Bulgakov writes of his literary works. Before 'Sons of the Mullah' he had written a one-act play called 'Self-Defence', which was apparently in the nature of a domestic comedy of manners. In autumn 1920 a local theatre staged 'The Turbin Brothers'. From a surviving review we know that it contained 'domestic scenes from the period of the revolutionary spring of 1905.' Since nothing of the play except the programme has survived we have no way of knowing whether anything more than the title linked it with any later works. Bulgakov also wrote a historical play called 'The Paris Communards' and, according to the author, 'a kind of drawing-room *comédie-bouffe* in three acts called "The Unfaithful Father" (or "The Bridegrooms of Clay")'. This last work was the one which had Bulgakov's highest appraisal. 'The Turbin Brothers' was to him a substitute for something serious which was to deal with matters that were important to him, but which still fell short in the execution, although the play was staged successfully several times. 'In the theatre they called out for the author and applauded wildly,' he wrote in the previously-quoted letter to Konstantin Bulgakov. 'When they called for me at the end of Act Two I went on stage with a feeling of dejection... I looked sadly at the actors' made-up faces and the ecstatic audience and thought: "My dream has come true, but as a caricature of itself: a

---

[35] M. Bulgakov, 'Zapiski na manzhetakh', *Vozrozhdenie*, Moscow, 1923. Reprinted in M. Bulgakov, *Ranniaia neizdannaia proza*, p. 202. Also in *Povesti...*, p. 410.

provincial stage instead of a Moscow one; instead of the play I had cherished about Aleksei Turbin, a hastily concocted, immature work.'"[36]

In truth fate was treating the young writer as if it wished to prepare him in advance for the trials to come. A life of make-believe was accompanied by make-believe writing and make-believe successes. Bulgakov grapples with this. Self-criticism is undermined by a beginner's natural desire to make an impact in the world; fits of despair give way at times to hope for a turn for the better. He sends his plays to Moscow, to various people and to suitable competitions. He asks his relatives to keep an eye on their progress. He foresees that nothing will come of them, so in self-defence he makes light of them and insists that everything be burned. His early pride and self-esteem do not find this easy. The plays are effectively lost from sight in the competitions; possibly some of them simply vanish. For consolation he has only his serious designs, to which he holds; determination and staying power have also been his from an early age; 'I'm now writing a long novel on the basis of "Ill Health",' he informs his cousin Konstantin.[37] 'I'm turning "The Turbins" into a major play,' he tells his sister Nadezhda.[38]

Fate also prepares him for a future defeat. He immediately makes a determined enemy among the local reviewers, one of whom opens fire on 'The Turbin Brothers' with guns of the calibre used six years later against 'The Days of the Turbins'. The play may be make-believe, but the insinuations sound all too serious: Bulgakov is an 'apologist for the bourgeoisie', who 'through his mouthpiece talks sneeringly about the "masses" and the "unwashed" in the first act, of "enraged Mitias and Vanias", saying that art passes over the heads of the crowd.'[39] This is an old ploy but none the more savoury for that: to identify the voice of a character with that of the author. It is sufficient to imagine the political atmosphere in an area where Denikin had carried out a pogrom only a few months earlier. But the situation remains unstable: survivors of the previous regime are still lurking in every corner and the new regime's security organs do not handle them with kid gloves. It is not surprising that Bulgakov remembered the charge of being

---

[36] 'Pis'ma k rodnym', p. 454; also in Mikhail Bulgakov, *Dnevnik....*, p. 12.

[37] Ibid., p. 456; also in Mikhail Bulgakov, *Dnevnik....*, p. 14.

[38] Ibid., p. 459; also in Mikhail Bulgakov, *Dnevnik....*, p. 21.

[39] V. Chebotareva, 'K istorii sozdaniia *Beloi gvardii*', *Russkaia literatura*, No. 4, 1974, p. 148.

a 'supporter' and cited it in *Notes on Shirt-Cuffs*. It is clear that the incident was not an isolated one. From the *Notes...* and the later story 'Bohemia' [Bogema] we can see that again and again the writer made enemies. For a while he was extremely active in various cultural areas: writing feuilletons, giving talks and lectures, introducing plays. He had the gift of dealing with opponents briskly and wittily, upholding a cultural tradition in the face of nihilistic attacks. His defence of Pushkin must have seemed particularly impressive; Bulgakov and Slezkin wrote it together.[40] But at the same time some individuals and offices must have been greatly incensed. Inevitably the future was already being rehearsed; from Bulgakov's texts it is apparent that denunciations had already begun, along with threats and innuendo in the press. No doubt there were also clashes with the local Cheka. In the end Bulgakov and Slezkin were both sacked. Sources of supplementary earnings dried up. It is no exaggeration to say that the ground was burning under his feet. In *Notes on Shirt-Cuffs* Bulgakov's last weeks in Vladikavkaz are described in even more desperate and anguished tones than before. At intervals eloquent allusions to emigration appear, encoded as 'the Golden Horn', accompanied by a series of dots. There are many of these and their date of origin is not always known. Bulgakov was probably even then indicating that he could not say everything he wanted. His correspondence with his family also gives the impression that he is frequently resorting to hints. In addition, it was sent for printing in a form studded with omission marks (...). As we do not know what was missing, there is all the more reason to pay attention to the general tone of his literary works, because from the beginning that tone told the truth.

What we hear is panic. The *Notes...*, 'Bohemia' and his letters are in full accord as to the nature of his departure from Vladikavkaz at the end of May 1921: it looks like an escape from all too real dangers and the impossibility of leading a normal life.

'To flee! To flee! For a hundred thousand you can get out of here,' say the *Notes...* 'Onward. To the sea. Across the sea and across France by land to Paris!'[41]

---

[40] *Devushka s gor*, pp. 18, 35; 'Zapiski na manzhetakh', *Nakanune*, 18.6.1922, Part VI, 'Kameriunker Pushkin'. Also in *Povesti...*, p. 400. [In this edition it is Part V. *Trans.*]

[41] *Ranniaia neizdannaia proza*, p. 202: also in *Povesti...*, p. 410.

The first stage of the journey lay through Tbilisi, where the independent Menshevik republic of Georgia was still in being. A letter written to Nadezhda from there ends with the words, 'Don't be too surprised by my wanderings. I can't help it. There is no other way. What a life! What a life!'[42]

From here Bulgakov proceeded to Batum. We may suppose that here again he very likely wanted to emigrate. Again it was not to be. The *Notes...* register the shock of failure, as stunning as if he had struck his head against a rock wall. There are no details, just bitterness and hopelessness.

Tatiana Bulgakova, whose presence is not felt at all in *Notes on Shirt-Cuffs* (nor indeed in *Notes of a Young Doctor*) – yet she was his true and constant companion – arrived in Tbilisi some time after him and left Batum ahead of him. The couple must have been compelled to make some new and final decisions. Since they had failed to leave the country the nomadic life could not continue indefinitely.

Nadezhda Mandelstam wrote in her *Second Volume* [Vtoraia kniga] of the same period in her life:

'We wandered about Georgia like homeless people, alien and misunderstood refugees from a land of beggars to a foreign and indifferent land. The refugees from "Sovdepia" in well-to-do Constantinople probably felt exactly the same. It was then that I came to know the bitter taste of foreign bread.'[43]

Tatiana Bulgakova travelled to Moscow via Kiev. Her husband followed after her. He spent a few days in Kiev, where he saw his mother for the last time. Soon he would remember with pleasure his moments of respite in her house. But there was no thought of staying in his home town. Nothing has survived of his thinking at the time regarding this but it is sufficient to picture the atmosphere of those years to realize that for an ex-army doctor life in Kiev would have been simply too dangerous. A menacing cloud of odium hung over him at that time. Perhaps this was when he tore from his memory several pages from his past.

Many people were drawn to Moscow for reasons such as these, or for other reasons – in order to begin a new life in a place where the pulse of life was beginning to return to normal.

---

[42] 'Pis'ma k rodnym', p. 459; also in Mikhail Bulgakov, *Dnevnik....*, p. 21.

[43] Nadezhda Mandel'shtam, *Vtoraia kniga*, Paris, 1972, p. 77.

Slezkin wrote of his Aleksei Vasil'evich, 'He wanted to sit down at his desk at last, look through his notes, collect his thoughts, collect himself, after being torn into scattered pieces – in the cold, hunger and acute pain of sufferings that interested nobody.'[44]

Perhaps that is how it really was. But again it turned out to be very difficult.

---

[44] *Devushka s gor*, p. 39. The quotation refers to the early period of Aleksei Vasil'evich's sojourn in Vladikavkaz but the mental state depicted here seems to match that recorded throughout the text of *Notes on Shirt-Cuffs* in both the Caucasus and the Moscow periods.

Chapter Two

The Years of Study and Apprenticeship

I. The struggle to survive in Moscow. Work.
II. The curse of the housing problem.
III. *Notes on Shirt-Cuffs* – life and literature.
IV. *Gudok* – gains and losses.
V. *Nakanune* – Moscow journalism.
VI. Various literary efforts.
VII. The writer creates himself; a broad range of possibilities.

I

Bulgakov arrived in Moscow like Balzac's Rastignac in Paris and like all those who have repeated that age-old situation – with nothing, but with hopes of gaining everything.

So it appears from our distant viewpoint, but seen at close quarters there was nothing at all romantic about it. A terrible weariness was dominant, no doubt, as the journey was desperately difficult. He arrived in darkness and on his first contact with the city he was groping through the night. A kind acquaintance gave him a bed.[1] The very next day saw the beginning of the struggle for that chance to

---

[1] See the relevant part of 'Notes on Shirt-Cuffs', *Rossiia*, No. 5, 1923, reprinted in M. Bulgakov, *Ranniaia neizdannaia proza*, Munich, 1976, p. 202; also in *Povesti. Rasskazy. Fel'etony*, Moscow, 1988, p. 412. See also the account of the typist who recopied 'Notes': 'He said very little about his life. Only once he said, without a trace of affectation, that on the way to Moscow he had covered about two hundred versts on foot, walking along the railway line. I actually believe he mentioned this in the first version of *Notes*.' (Marietta Chudakova, 'K tvorcheskoi biografii M. Bulgakova 1916-1923', *Voprosy literatury*, No. 7, 1973, p. 250.)

survive which would be afforded by a home and a job. Tatiana Bulgakova stayed in a student hostel with a friend from her schooldays, Nikolai Gladyrevsky. There Bulgakov also spent his first days in Moscow. Then they both found refuge in a room belonging to his brother-in-law, Andrei Zemsky, the husband of Nadezhda Afanas'evna, who was then in Kiev with their mother.[2] This was a significant address: No. 10, Bol'shaia Sadovaia, Flat 50, a comfortable block of flats, now run down and bearing the name of 'Commune'. The Bulgakovs would live here again later, in Flat 34, and this building would be the starting point for a whole succession of Bulgakov's fantasies.

Mikhail Afanas'evich started work in the familiar LITO, except that this was its Moscow office, the literature department of Glavpolitprosvet, one of the agencies of the People's Commissariat for Education, which, following its recent reorganization, had acquired a much more complex structure.[3] This was a semi-fictitious position and poorly paid. Besides, galloping inflation gave the transitional 'sovznaki' currency a purely symbolic value. Bulgakov began a feverish search for other openings. He tried everything; his letters of this period resemble dramatic battlefield dispatches. He worked as compère in a small theatre, correspondent for the newspaper *Rabochii* [The Worker], head of the publications department of the Air Force Scientific and Technical Committee (there he enjoyed the patronage of Andrei Zemsky's elder brother Boris), and reporter and columnist for *Torgovo-promyshlenny vestnik* [Commercial and Industrial Herald]; he also had hopes of a job in the flax trust. In all of these he was frustrated. LITO fell victim to budget cuts; *Vestnik* closed down; nothing came of the job in the flax trust.[4] But by dint of feverish efforts and desperate activity it was possible to stay alive. It was a difficult life. Later Bulgakov would call it drudgery, say that he loathed it and recall the period with a grimace of distaste. For the moment, however, he was glad just to be able to keep his head above water, and he wrote in a letter to his mother, 'I arrived in Moscow six weeks ago with just the clothes on

---

[2] See the introduction by E. A. Zemskaia to M.A. Bulgakov, 'Pis'ma k rodnym (1921-1922)', published by E. A. Zemskaia, *Izvestiia AN SSSR. Seriia literatury i iazyka*, Vol. 35, No. 5, 1976, pp. 425, 460, 462.

[3] These matters are discussed in Sheila Fitzpatrick's thorough study, *The Commissariat of Enlightenment*, Cambridge, 1970.

[4] 'Pis'ma k rodnym', p. 453; Chudakova, 'K tvorcheskoi biografii...', pp. 246-48.

my back and I think have done about as much as I could have done in that time. I have a job, which isn't the most important thing, it's true. You also have to be able to make money. I'm managing to do that as well, although in tiny amounts. But this month Tasia and I are somehow managing to eat; we have a store of potatoes; Tasia has had her shoes mended; we're laying in a store of firewood etc.

'We have to work not in any normal way but like mad things, from dawn till dusk, every day without a break.

(...) 'The direction and the trade I mapped out for myself back in Kiev have turned out to be exactly the right ones. It would be impossible to work in any other. It would mean starvation rations at best.

'The end of November and December will be hard. That's when I'll be moving into the private sector. But I'm counting on a huge number of connections and on the energy I've perforce had to show, – and I know now that I can count on it. I have a lot of contacts – journalists, writers and simply business contacts. This means a great deal in Moscow today, as Moscow is making the transition to a new form of life, such as it hasn't had for a long time, a life of fierce competition, feverish activity and initiative etc. Without it life is impossible, you would simply go to the wall. And I have no wish to be among those who go to the wall.

'Tas'ka is looking for a job as a shop assistant, which is very difficult as all of Moscow is still barefoot and threadbare. Everyone's dealing in something at every opportunity, using his own initiative and limited manpower. Poor Tas'ka has to make huge efforts, mill rye grains with the back of an axe-head and produce meals from anything she can find. But she's a wonderful woman! In brief it's quite a struggle to survive. The main thing is to have a roof over one's head.'[5]

Making allowances for the note of bravado which had to be injected to comfort his mother, it can be seen that Bulgakov was again confronting a new and difficult situation. The period of his medical apprenticeship was being repeated. Pavel Popov would later find a precise description: 'Bulgakov was lent wings by the very hopelessness of the situation.'[6] He experienced again the building of

---

[5] 'Pis'ma k rodnym', p. 459-60; also in Mikhail Bulgakov, *Dnevnik. Pis'ma 1914-1940*, Moscow, 1997, pp. 26-28.

[6] The quotation is from Pavel Popov's biographical sketch of Bulgakov, perhaps intended for some planned posthumous edition which did not materialize. The text is in Institut russkoi

everything from scratch, which was very much harder than it had been five years earlier because Mikhail Afanas'evich was outside all conventional frameworks, alone in the face of his own self-imposed requirement, unswervingly pursued, to find his feet in a new career. Moreover he was no longer a youngster. But it is clear that his choice of career was irrevocable. On sober reflection it would seem that medicine would have provided a surer foothold in the seething life of Moscow than the uncertain threshold of literature. The more so as he had medical acquaintances close at hand: one friend and two uncles. Before long, in *The Heart of a Dog*, Bulgakov would describe approvingly the secure position of neutrality afforded by high standing in the medical profession. Perhaps even with envy. Yet there was no going back to the medical profession. He took the line of greatest resistance, accepting the risk. Staking all on the card of talent and determination, Bulgakov wished, as he wrote in the same letter to his mother, 'to make my *idée fixe* a reality: getting back to normal within three years – a flat, clothes, food and books. As to whether I can manage it – we'll see.'

Boris Zemsky, who gave Bulgakov much help during this period, seemed to have no doubt that he would manage it. 'Misha amazes me with his energy, industry, enterprise and spirit. (...) I can state with assurance that he will find his way, his target won't elude him,' he wrote to his brother.[7]

II

'The main thing is to have a roof over one's head.' 'Any little room, and good health.'

Jobs might have been scarce, but it was the housing problem that nagged at Bulgakov for a longer period. It is not surprising that his letters, memoirs and reportage from this time deal with this theme above all others, or that his second volume of collected prose works should have the title 'Treatise on Housing'. The title has its facetious tinge but Bulgakov was an expert in this field, being almost the chronicler of the great Moscow housing crisis.

---

literature (IRLI; Pushkinskii Dom) in St Petersburg, Fond. 369. It was made available to me with some other Bulgakov materials, for which I am grateful.

7 'Pis'ma k rodnym', p. 453

The time was the beginning of NEP, the rush to the capital which was bursting at the seams. A tide of socially-promoted parvenus and new arrivals armed with warrants, orders and unchallengeable new rights to accommodation beat at apartment doors. Property-owners performed miracles of ingenuity and precautionary thinking in order to mislead inspectors, prove their own social usefulness and avert eviction with déclassé status or having to double up with new tenants. Whole campaigns were fought, with surprise attacks and prolonged sieges, feints and flanking manoeuvres, strategic withdrawals and ingenious deceptions; with allies enlisted and desperate fencing with warrants and counter-prohibitions that changed hands again and again. Recounting these battles with the passion of a less than impartial observer, Bulgakov summarized them as follows:

'Let us get one thing clear once and for all: housing is the cornerstone of human life. We can take it as axiomatic that man cannot exist without housing. Furthermore, for the benefit of all who live in Berlin, Paris, London and elsewhere, I can add that in Moscow there are no flats.

So how do people live there?

They manage somehow.

Without flats.

What is more – the past three years in Moscow have made it absolutely clear to me that Muscovites have forgotten the very meaning of the word "flat" and naïvely apply it to anything.'[8]

Here the writer is thinking of the one thing which formed a depressing part of his life and with which the very fabric of his works of this period and many later ones is imbued – the coexistence of random groups of tenants in flats given over to multi-family tenancy, i.e. the so-called 'communal flats'. This was one of the greatest curses of post-revolutionary life, officially proclaimed for some time in collectivistic architectonic thinking as an element of 'socialization'. It remained the housing norm right up until Khrushchev's day. Future studies will demonstrate the dreadful destruction wrought by the communal flat on the human psyche and how it imprinted itself on the mentality and habits of whole generations. For the moment Mikhail Afanas'evich was living in its initial, spontaneous phase, when the new community felt the pain all the more keenly because it was taking shape in old

---

[8] M. Bulgakov, 'Traktat o zhilishche', *Nakanune* (under the title 'Moskva 20-ykh godov'), 27.5.1924; also in *Povesti...*, p. 108.

apartments in no way adapted to their new role. Might, based on plebeian origins, was usually right and triumphed easily here, citing the demagogic slogans of class vengeance, especially as the norms of custom and community life had been shaken, even to a degree negated. The privacy of life became a fiction. People made one another's lives miserable unconsciously or deliberately, wearing one another down, driving one another to distraction or to serious crimes. Intimate life was laid bare and exposed to the attacks of indifference, boorishness or plain ignorance. One's own room ceased to offer protection, and the kitchen, bathroom or corridor became cause for great distress.

It is not surprising that the constantly recurring 'housing problem' became Bulgakov's sorest point. By the very act of writing he would gain control over the situation, distance himself from it, disarm it with his irony, even – as can be seen in the foregoing quotation – make a jocular generalization about it, as if to show that he was above it all. But again and again a spasm of desperation, genuine despair, a crisis of endurance broke through these defences. It was on this basis that, with a slight modification of the contours of reality, his phantasmagorical visions were hatched and in moments of despondency the most venomous destructive thoughts were nurtured, including even pyromania; and it was no accident that the satanic black-magical powers of Woland (how convenient it is to have one's own devil...) were capable of making a communal flat non-dimensional and inaccessible to all earthly powers.

These are not the exaggerations of some spoiled scion of the bourgeoisie. The court records, the press and literature of the period, as well as memoirs, provide a surfeit of similar material. Many writers were grappling with such problems, finding shelter in corners or travelling in from outside Moscow, especially as royalties were still very low and NEP prices high.[9] Bulgakov was writing not only about himself, and what he wrote was fully convincing in what it said about the abnormality of life. If the 'housing problem' is what he felt most keenly, this is most likely because his home in Kiev was the House – a safe haven

---

[9] These problems were not, of course, restricted to Moscow. Note the significant fact that Mikhail Zoshchenko, who was extremely tactful and circumspect, wrote from Leningrad to Gorky in Italy begging him to intervene with the housing administration. (His intervention bore fruit.) See *Literaturnoe nasledstvo. Tom semidesiatyi. Gor'kii i sovetskie pisateli*, Moscow 1963, p. 159.

and refuge, a bedrock of stability for him and the world. That world had vanished, but now there was hope for a new stabilization, doggedly won – and a new home should undoubtedly lie at its basis. And so it would be in the future: amidst changing and usually unfavourable circumstances a fortress with four walls would provide Bulgakov with a much needed anchor-point and refuge. As yet, however, there was nothing of this. On the contrary, the struggle for survival continued in his own flat. The refugee and wanderer had doubtless developed immunity to many things, but it is clear that he found this more wearisome than tramping the streets of Moscow seeking advertisements for *Vestnik* ('Is there anywhere I haven't been? In Miasnitskaia Street hundreds of times, in Varvarka – in the Trade Building in Staraia Square, in the Co-operative Union, I've called into Sokol'niki and had to visit Maiden's Field. I've chased the length and breadth of our vast and strange capital, driven by one desire – to find something to live on').[10] He did this in a thin coat that no longer offered any resistance to the winter frosts, which Mikhail Afanas'evich tried to cheat by walking sideways ('For some reason the draughts get in on the left side,' he wrote to his mother).

Dealing with the management of the housing 'commune' at 10 Sadovaia Street, who demanded the eviction both of Andrei Zemsky, with his long-term absences, and the Bulgakovs, must have been even harder than coping with winter. The matter was eventually resolved favourably, but housing administrators henceforth became one of Bulgakov's pet targets; few people were so systematically exposed to the jabs of his pen, or for so long. The building was home to the most varied collection of individuals, all thrown together in the chaos of the post-revolutionary period; cheek by jowl with the remnants of the old world were arrivistes from the lower classes, NEPmen and representatives of the arts,[11] and much of what took place was recorded directly or indirectly in Bulgakov's writings even as late as *The Master and Margarita*. The greyish-yellow pile, distinguished by its size, not yet overwhelmed by any neighbouring structures, had its own character, and it is no accident that, in addition to passing mention

---

[10] 'Traktat o zhilishche', pp. 4-5; also in *Povesti...*, p. 107.

[11] An interesting account of this by V. Levshin 'Sadovaia, 302-bis' appeared in *Teatr*, 11, 1971, pp. 110-120. The veracity of some details was challenged by the writer's second wife, Liubov' Belozerskaia-Bulgakova. See *Neizdannyi Bulgakov. Teksty i materialy*, Ann Arbor 1977, pp. 22-24.

elsewhere, it was the subject of a work specially devoted to it, 'Number 13', in which descriptions of past domestic splendour are accompanied by the narrator's exclamations of mock delight.

Today it is a typical central Moscow building, with a high arched gateway and enclosed courtyard, where Bulgakov's two rooms, one in Flat 50 and the other in Flat 34, lay opposite each other on the fifth floor. In keeping with the purpose of the building at the time of its construction, the stairwells are austere and somewhat cathedral-like. The ceilings are high and the even rise of the white stone steps, hollowed in the middle and polished by many years of wear, seems like mute evidence of the passage of time.

That is the impression today. But what of Bulgakov's day?

'At seven in the evening I snatched Natasha from the clutches of her husband Volodia, the baker. ("Don't you dare hit me!!.. She's my wife!" etc.).

At eight, when a rousing sailor's dance started up and Annushka started dancing, my wife rose from the couch and said, "I can't stand it. Do what you like but we've got to get out of this place."

"My dear," I answered in despair. "What can I do? I can't get a room. A room costs twenty billion; I get paid four. Until I finish my novel we can't expect anything. You'll have to be patient."

"It's not me I'm thinking of," she replied. "You'll never finish that novel. Never. There's no hope. I'll take some morphine."

At that I felt I had turned to steel. When I spoke there was metal in my voice: "You will not take morphine because I won't let you. I will finish my novel and I can tell you it'll be so good it'll light up the sky."

Then I helped my wife into her coat, locked and padlocked the door, asked Dusia (who doesn't drink anything except port) to see nobody broke the lock, and took my wife off to her sister's in Nikitskaia Street for the three days of the holiday.'[12]

III

The sky would be lit up, of course, by that most important work, long cherished and gradually approaching its final form; by 'the great novel written on

---

[12] M. Bulgakov, 'Samogonnoe ozero', *Nakanune*, 29.7.1923; also in *Povesti...*, pp. 219-220.

the canvas of "Ill Health" [Nedug]', which Slezkin's Bulgakov double 'will write, you may be sure'; by *The White Guard.* For the moment it still bore a different title. It took shape at night, in the hours snatched from sleep and free from feverish activity, when the hubbub of the communal building died down. Time was always short and Bulgakov was always tired; this is the constant refrain in his letters to his family. Sometimes a note of resignation creeps in: 'I've given up on everything. I'm not thinking of writing at all. I'm only happy when Tasia is brewing some hot tea'. Or: 'Of course, with the exhausting job I have I'll never manage to write anything worthwhile...' – but mid-way through this sentence his will to endure again gains the upper hand: '... but it's nice to have a dream and work on it, at least.'[13]

To work on a dream. A well-chosen phrase, dropped in passing but fully appropriate. Dreams were plentiful and the work moved forward despite his doubts. 'At night, when I can find the time, I'm writing "Notes of a Country Doctor".[14] Perhaps something worthwhile will come out of it,' he wrote in a letter to his mother. In the same letter, in an added note to his sister Nadezhda, we read: 'I cherish the notion of writing a long, five-act play by the end of 1922.'[15] Evidently it would deal with the events of 1916-17, as he asked his sister for material about the murder of Rasputin, among other things. Perhaps his later story 'The Fire of the Khans' would be a by-product of this interest. An announcement in the journal *Novaia russkaia kniga* [New Russian Book] in late 1922 stated that, 'Mikhail Afanas'evich Bulgakov is preparing a complete bibliographical dictionary, with literary profiles, of contemporary Russian writers and requests that suitable material be sent to him.'[16]

No doubt this is the insatiable literary novice sounding out all avenues at once, seeking his place in the profession and trying his own strength. It is also clear that from the beginning Bulgakov liked the feeling of having several projects on the boil at once. He himself took on a demanding regime of self-imposed obligations. He was very hard-working and able to push himself forward.

---

[13] 'Pis'ma k rodnym', p. 461.

[14] Ibid.; also in *Dnevnik...*, p. 28. [At this stage Bulgakov refers to this work as *Zapiski zemskogo vracha - Trans.*]

[15] Ibid.

[16] *Novaia russkaia kniga*, Nos. 11-12, 1922.

Some projects fell by the wayside. It was the most accessible one that naturally came to the forefront: an intimate biographical record, setting out his own experiences. It is an unfinished but eloquent account, taking snapshots of the remnants of a world smashed to smithereens. Such is the form of *Notes on Shirt-Cuffs* – fundamentally formless and therefore of course ambiguous: chaos may be described chaotically, but the recreated chaos will then have a certain order. However, Bulgakov probably did not realize all this at the very start. He selected a certain natural mode of expression, similar to that of a diary, the poetics of a page from a notebook, of the immediate private record, of the crib-notes for a life submitted to examinations much more demanding than any school exams. Hence, no doubt, the schoolboy reflex that shows in the location given in the title: 'on shirt-cuffs'.

The world had been shattered. Form had disintegrated. Of course it had all been rehearsed in literature. The tradition of stylistic contrasts, of sharp clashes between loftiness and earthiness, of the natural interweaving of melancholic reflection into descriptive passages traced its origins in Russia back to Bulgakov's master and teacher, Gogol. Dostoevsky had succeeded in infusing a subcutaneous thrill to his narrative, bringing it to near fever pitch and creating that duality of description which at once conceals and reveals, pretending and being surprised at his own pretence. Leskov had pioneered the unlimited possible ways of stylizing an utterance, of playing with words, words imbued with the characteristics of the narrative persona. In this way narrative had been honed and given maximum elasticity and sensitivity by many great pens, making possible new experiments, sounding its depths to discover a second and third level. New explorations had been conducted by modernist art, understood as the personal manifestation of the artist whose language does not have to be subject to the dictates of meaning – with the polished rhythmic and musical constructions of Bely, with Remizov's somnambulist logic, different from that of daily life, and the fantasy of dreams, and, by contrast, with the cold, precise, prose edifices of Zamiatin, conscious of the durability of his verbal material and new techniques in architecture.

In the hands of their imitators and less gifted brethren, susceptible to influence and inclined to creeper-like clinging to the bodies of innovative works, these discoveries became a set of devices, absorbed, passed on and widely disseminated. There appeared a colloquial verbal impressionism, an easy fissuring of the unity of impressions, fracturing the flow of narrative and producing a mood of disorientation well suited to the *fin de siècle* and reproducing it. The doyen of pre-revolutionary journalists, Vlas Doroshevich, introduced the short sentence, dividing his sentences into smaller units marked by full stops. This turned out to match exactly the spirit of the times, and he swiftly forged a career. This was also the style of Iurii Slezkin, the gifted literary technician whose meticulous care and precision in stage-setting Bulgakov seems to respect and would later praise as 'cinematographic'. This epithet itself reminds us that the language of the cinema, then in the process of discovery, also exerted an important influence on prose-writing technique.

The events of the revolution and civil war, perceived by many observers as a cataclysm sweeping everything away, galvanized these powerful processes. A feeling of lost equilibrium took hold, of astonishment, of a journey into the unknown, of unfamiliar perspectives. All this needed to be recorded in exclamatory, immediate and tangible forms. Harmony seemed to be in conflict with the nature of current reality; the horror of some and the delight of others were spasmodically externalized. At first poetry, with its immediate reaction, held total sway over prose, and when prose recovered its breath it could at first manage no more than a poetic treatment of the world, apprehended in fragmentary fashion, in loosely shifting forms and liberally adorned by the emotional attitudes of the author. Thus the prose known as 'dynamic', 'ornamental' or 'neo-realist', which mostly occupied a place in the broad expressionist current, utilized methods close to poetic representation, capturing a moment, a detail, a colour, a state of mind. The methods of the traditional epic appeared to have been exhausted for the moment; a crumbling world could not be embraced; one could only record snapshots of isolated elements of it. This widespread belief was precisely expressed by Evgenii Zamiatin:

'What is needed today is motor cars, aeroplanes, speed, flight, dots, seconds, dotted lines. The old, lumbering, leisurely descriptions belong in the past: instead we have succinctness, but with an enormously concentrated charge and high voltage in every word. We have to pack as much into one second as we used to fit into a minute of sixty seconds: syntax too is becoming elliptical and fleeting; complex prose pyramids are dismantled into the stones of individual phrases. All that was long accepted and habitual eludes the eye in this rapid movement: hence the unfamiliar and often strange symbolism and vocabulary.

Images are sharp-edged and synthetic, containing only one basic feature, one which can be seen from a moving car.'[17]

Zamiatin's taste for technology expresses indirectly the fact that the accelerated rhythm of prose had been coupled by numerous transmission belts to the leap taken by civilization in the twentieth century. Owing to the backwardness of Russia, however, this leap remained for the moment in the sphere of pious hopes and, if it had any effect, it was more like that of a magic incantation in which few had any belief. The decisive accelerating factor was the sense of a historic watershed – with an emotional plus or minus sign – as, in Andrei Bely's words, 'a hurricane sweeping away form'.

This hurricane also blows right through Bulgakov's *Notes*. Their fragmented, lapidary nature is probably a result of his own emotional state and the coarse prose of life, in which he lacked even a desk to write on, superimposed on the trends of the era and the consequences of historical and literary processes. The overlay produced a perfect match. It is no accident that the novice writer should start out this way. As we shall see, he had command of a variety of styles from the start; this particular one was the most direct, the closest to his feelings and best suited to the conventions of the diary or to works imitative of the diary. Thus 'The Unusual Adventures of a Doctor' might have been the beginning of the *Notes*, just as 'Bohemia', with its somewhat slower pace, could successfully have become the twelfth episode – merely a row of dots in the editions we know – logically preceding the flight to Batum and, in thought at least, the attempt to emigrate. But there are several more 'dotted' episodes, and there is also reason to believe that the original text of the *Notes* was substantially longer.[18] Given their formless nature,

---

[17] E. Zamiatin, *Litsa*, New York, 1955, pp. 254-55.

[18] The manuscript of *Notes on Shirt-Cuffs* has not survived; from the information carefully gathered and analyzed by M. Chudakova it is clear that the surviving fragments can be only a small part of the whole (M. Chudakova, 'K tvorcheskoi biografii...', p. 246 ff.). The fragments were printed in *Nakanune*, 18.6.1922 (an abridged version of the first part), the almanac *Vozrozhdenie*, 2, 1923 (an expanded version of the first part), and the journal *Rossiia*, 5, 1923. It was subsequently reprinted in different forms; the fullest version to date is in M. Bulgakov, *Ranniaia neizdannaia proza*, but this does not include all available fragments. At the time of writing of the first draft of the present book, I used the complete set as compiled by the

however, every arrangement can be seen as forming a kind of whole – always by nature open.

The *Notes* divide into a Caucasus part and a Moscow part, not only on grounds of content. The part set in the Caucasus is entirely in the manner of loose pages torn from under the pen-nib by the gale of the epoch. The writing works more like a broken contour line than a definite shape, a blot rather than a spectrum of colours. It vibrates with pathological fever and frantic activity, which contrasts with a state of dazed inertia and slowed reactions. The outlines of reality assume a fantastic quality; chains of abbreviations whirl round the damaged psyche of the narrator ('Foto. Izo. Lito. Teo. Izo. Lizo. Tizo'), along with vignettes from his work in the semi-real literary sub-section, with battles over the classics culminating in the new director's declaration: 'We don't need none of this pornography no more! None of them Gogols and moguls! We'll write our own plays', with threats, fears, hopes and older fellow-writers who arrive via Vladikavkaz and are still viewed with the unmistakable admiration of a novice looking up from below. Disjointed expostulations are punctuated by frequent exclamation marks. He is kept from final desperation by the creative act – by recording the collapse of a world – and secondly by self-mockery, by giving vent to his emotions; the narrator feels sorry for himself, but laughs at his feelings at the same time; the apparent anarchy of form, when we look at it closely, is kept in check by self-criticism.

The chopped, disjointed narrative from the Caucasus becomes rather more fluent in the Moscow part, although the nervous tension remains. This is a consequence of the narrator's psychological situation; the chain of hopelessness has been broken, a fragment of stability has appeared, a basis for positive action. This is the Moscow LITO, the literature section of 'Glavpolitprosvet', the Central Directorate of Political Education, where Bulgakov worked briefly as secretary. A struggle with the absurd takes place – a situation so very typical of this writer. To anyone with such a lively imagination the reality of post-revolutionary chaos coupled with the dead hand of the bureaucracy is fertile ground. The building which houses the office, like the office itself, becomes a phantasmagoria, an illusion, a conundrum. Before anything rational can happen it is first necessary to fight off nonsensical ordinances from above and secure the right to exist, with

---

Manuscript Department of the Lenin Library in Moscow and made available to me along with some other Bulgakov material, for which I am grateful.

staff, resources and a payroll. Bulgakov wrote his 'bureaucratiad' by fits and starts, touching up his raw material only slightly. The literature of that period has shown us many similar institutions, highlighting the curious basis of their existence: people who barely acknowledged the new regime were compelled to go to it for employment and they pretended to work, and the regime had to tolerate this while being incapable for the time being of assuring these half-working workers even a subsistence wage. In the Commissariat of Education this general oddity was further complicated by the consequences of much restructuring, by demarcation disputes, ill-defined areas of competence and modes of operation, and even by constant changes of address. Little exaggeration was needed – in *Notes* and in *Diaboliad*, which picks up the theme of the absurdity of institutional life yet again – to create the vision of the pursuit of a vanishing institution, a pursuit subject to the whims of informants and peppered with quotations from Gogol. At the same time but *à propos* of something quite different, in his theatrical feuilleton Vsevolod Meyerhold was making the same point in the language of the sober columnist when he wrote of 'looking for an office in the corridors of the reorganized Commissariat of Education', exclaiming:

'How many central directorates are there? How many centres? We used to have just one TEO, MUZO, IZO, LITO and one KINO, and now there are as many as there are central directorates, as many as there are centres. According to the People's Commissar himself it used to require a lot of effort to obtain the addresses of all departments and sections before he toured his whole fiefdom. But now any provincial official visiting the capital on business will probably have to spend six months in the lofty labyrinth of power before coming across anybody who might be able to give him the address of the organization he has been sent to visit.'[19]

So it is in Bulgakov's *Notes*: he searches six stairwells of a 'dreadful building' before finding LITO, which has been moved at somebody's whim. Immediately after this it falls victim to the next bout of restructuring and ceases to exist:

'I was the last to leave, like the captain of a sinking ship,' Bulgakov concludes his story. 'I ordered all the files – Nekrasov and The Reformed Alcoholic, the Famine Fund collection, the poetry, the instructions to local LITO offices – to be collected and handed in. I put out the light and left the building.

---

[19] V. Meierkhol'd, *Stat'i, pis'ma, rechi, besedy*, Part 2 (1917-1939), Moscow, 1968, p. 24.

And at once it started to snow heavily. Then came rain. Then something that was neither one nor the other clung to my face from all sides.

'On days of staff-cuts and closures and in this sort of weather Moscow is horrible. And this was another closure. Other people had also been evicted from flats in that dreadful building.'[20]

Thus ended a clash with the absurd: indecisively. One of life's opportunities – a short-term opportunity perhaps – had been lost. But the absurdity had been overcome. A chance had arisen to do something meaningful, a chance that meant so much to Bulgakov, the kind of chance he so eagerly sought throughout his life in the worst situations. A chance to do what he could as best he could, without feeling any affront to his dignity. Since LITO existed it might as well serve some useful purpose. Let it, in Bulgakov's description, 'swim with the tide', find a place in the scheme of things, strange though this scheme may be. Let it give a modicum of support to the people who work in it.

Such are the perceptible foundations of a somewhat firmer balance. In the Caucasus the narrator had been a piece of flotsam in a heavy sea; now a little oil had been poured onto the billows. Not much help, perhaps, but it was better than nothing.

And the final, again self-mocking stylization of the sacked official, in the spirit of the law of the sea, has a discreetly serious undertone. It is the mini-heroism of everyday life, whose authentic flavour is familiar to many generations of ordinary twentieth-century working people.

A Polish poet said in their name:

> To storm life's impregnable fortress
> we go out day by day.
> And often we're struck by sabres
> lunging to right and left,
> in our struggle for basic staples
> like meat, firewood and bread.[21]

---

[20] 'Notes on the Cuffs', *Rossiia*, No. 5, 1923, p. 25; also in *Povesti...*, p. 429.

[21] from Konstanty Ildefons Gałczyński (1905–53). 'Pieśń cherubińska.'

IV

When it became apparent that Bulgakov would survive after all amidst the perils of Moscow, when he had caught his second wind and secured a firm foothold, and the initial struggle for 'staples like meat, firewood and bread' was behind him, the writer recalled his 'most fantastic jobs, which went galloping like consumption to a speedy end.'[22] One of them, however, lasted longer than the others. This was with the newspaper *Gudok* [The Whistle] where, as can be seen from the material he published in it, he worked for more than four years, most probably from spring 1922 to summer 1926, that is, almost until the time when the royalties from the staging of his two plays began to provide a measure of stability.

The trade newspapers of that period had not yet been destroyed by centralist templates and forced to become a pale shadow of the central press. *Gudok*, the organ of the Railwaymen's Union, had its own personality and it had ambitions; it dispatched its own foreign correspondents and took an active part in domestic politics and Party matters. Contact with the profession was based largely on incoming reports from a network of 'rabkory', correspondents in the field. Their raw material was then passed on for sub-editing. For this purpose the paper employed a group of young literary apprentices, some of whom were later to shine. Bulgakov at first had the function of 'obrabotchik', or sub-editor of correspondents' reports. This was drudgery, of which the author wrote in the autobiographical fragment 'To a Secret Friend', 'I've never done a lousier job in all my life'.[23] After a while he was offered the task of writing feuilletons. This genre gave just a little more latitude, but it too relied firmly on reports from the field, sometimes only slightly altered, sometimes providing a basis for leaps of

---

22 'Traktat o zhilishche'; also in *Povesti...*, p. 107.

23 'To a Secret Friend' is a large fragment of a never-completed autobiographical piece dating from September 1929 and written for Bulgakov's future third wife Elena (see M. Chudakova, 'Arkhiv M. A. Bulgakova. Materialy dlia tvorcheskoi biografii pisatelia', in *Zapiski Otdela rukopisei Gos. Bibl. SSSR im. Lenina*, Moscow, 1976, p. 81 ff. The text is held in the Lenin Library. A small part, the source of this quotation, was published by L. Ianovskaia in *Nedelia*, No. 43, 1974. [It has since become available in at least two published versions: *Novyi mir*, No. 8, 1987, in which this line is on p. 172; and *Dnevnik...*, in which this line is on p. 603. – *Trans*.]

imagination which could build hyperbolized micro-scenes onto the infrastructure of reality. A writer of Bulgakov's stamp, with serious works already well advanced, could find little profit in this;[24] he applied no more than a fraction of his creative powers to this work, and then only fleetingly. Sometimes that was enough for an original scenario or a good joke; sometimes practice and a skilled hand made possible a deft use of well-rehearsed devices and assured a reasonable standard, showing the hallmarks of Bulgakov's inventiveness. At other times he must have been simply bored and scarcely able, with the greatest effort, to produce even the equivalent of moustaches and beards added to serious photographs.

There were about a hundred of these feuilletons, some written under various pen-names, not all of which have been deciphered for certain, so the actual number is still unknown.[25] They dealt with everything the correspondents wrote about: poor provision of supplies, badly organized retailing, the presumption of authority, abuses of power, tedious meetings and vacuous speeches, graft and peculation, ignorance and soullessness, and again and again the constant theme of drunkenness, which was becoming society's greatest scourge, as well as quite trivial matters: slippery steps, a school situated next to a church and Tsarist-era official forms which were still in circulation. Writing of this nature could clearly lead to sterility and dissipation of talent, but not for Bulgakov. For him this was certainly just one strictly utilitarian form of writing, to be treated as a craft, an exercise in technique, not to be confused with the creative work for which he jealously cherished the moments snatched from sleep.

Did he really gain nothing at all from the experience of this paper, to which he gave so little of himself? It would be an exaggeration to suppose this were so. There are hardly any simple discernible links between the feuilletons and what he

---

[24] Here M. Chudakova seems much nearer the mark than V. Chebotareva. Chudakova writes, 'What might have been and indeed was good training in literature for beginners was something quite different for the kind of writer Bulgakov was by the early '20s,' ('Arkhiv...', p. 37). Chebotareva arbitrarily asserts, '... in his ideological development and grasp of the full complexity of historical events (sic! – A.D.) he was helped by his work as a journalist and by the literary milieu around him in the editorial offices of those Moscow newspapers.' (V. Chebotareva, 'K istorii sozdaniia *Beloi gvardii*', *Russkaia literatura*, No. 4, 1974, p. 151.)

[25] Besides his surname and initials, the following names appear: M. Bull, Tuskarora, G. P. Ukhov, F. S-ov, M. Neizvestnyi, Mikhail, Emma B., M. Oll-Rait, F. Skitaikin and others.

would go on to write later, but indirect connections may be found. What Bulgakov was doing was varnishing the raw factual material. Often the spontaneous grotesque component in it, the inimitable absurdity of life, shone through unaided. The varnisher was able to appreciate it and point it up occasionally with a flash of colour from his imagination. The rest would have to be laid away in storage, awaiting its chance to be revealed. At this time life's experiences bore in on Bulgakov from all sides. He collected them by simply living and had no need to seek second-hand experience. However, when all that he had known in those years later found its way, having settled and been filtered, into the dense and tightly woven fabric of *The Master and Margarita's* social satire, the *Gudok* material would probably have a part to play.

Bulgakov – it would soon transpire – was possessed of a Gogolian imagination, with a rich strain of the fantastic, given to producing sudden disruptions of the normal course of events and observing what came out of them. It was a perverse kind of conceptualism. On this subject Gogol himself had written, 'For my own amusement I imagined the jolliest things that I could. I thought of the funniest of characters and placed them in the most comical situations, not for a moment stopping to think why I was doing it...'[26] Bulgakov did what he did – this time – with the aim of earning money, but at the same time reality taught him an important lesson: nothing is impossible and there is practically no limit to arbitrary authoritarian caprice. Imagination could only accentuate the contours, develop and take to the point of absurdity things that were already replete with nonsense.

It turned out, for example, that the boundary between life and death was fluid. Somebody can call in two weeks after his death to collect a belated referral from a slothful medical orderly and quite naturally receive a travel warrant 'to Moscow from Zernovo for skeleton so-and-so' accompanied by the injunction, 'Put the coffin in the baggage van!'[27] Somebody wishes to obtain a funeral allowance and claims that his son has died. When the supposed deceased is seen in

---

[26] N. Gogol', 'Ispoved' avtora', *Polnoe sobranie sochinenii*, Vol. 4, Moscow 1874, p. 805.

[27] M. Bulgakov, 'Prikliucheniia pokoinika', *Gudok*, 27.6.1924. Reprinted in M. Bulgakov, *Ranniaia nesobrannaia proza*, Munich, 1978. This is the first collection in book form of the Bulgakov material published in *Gudok* and other periodicals of the period. 'Prikliucheniia pokoinika', is also in M. A. Bulgakov, *Sobranie sochinenii*, Ann Arbor, 1985, Vol. 2, p. 99.

good health he declares, 'Yes, he got up and came back'.[28] To make things easier for the medical orderly, somebody comes to collect his own death certificate in advance of his death the next day, provoking the following exchange:

'A right one you are! Why come before time? If you'd waited till tomorrow afternoon they'd have brought you along anyway.'

'It's like this, Fedor Naumovich. I'm all on my own with nobody to bring me here. My neighbours said to me, "Pafnut'ich, get along and see Fedor Naumovich in good time because tomorrow nobody'll give you the time of day. And you won't last more than a day anyway."'

'Hmm. All right then. I'll put tomorrow's date on it.'[29]

Bulgakov also collected other examples of the limits of the possible being pushed back; a local activist drawing up the minutes of meetings before they have taken place; a manager demanding that none of his subordinates marry without his consent; a chief of railway police requiring his men to catch four criminals per month:

'What the Hell do you think they pay you for? [...] A station this size and no felonies?'

'What can we do about it? It's not like making babies...'

'You'll make 'em if you have to! Violate the laws of nature! Open your eyes! Look sharp! If you see somebody walking along the tracks you march right up to him and say: Right, tell us what you're thinking! And never mind if he looks as sad as Hell and has eyes like a teacher's! He's probably just thinking how he can strip all the lead out of a carriage. Putting it simply, it's like this: in our Soviet state every bugger has a quota to meet and that includes you! I want each one of you to bring me four criminals a month!'[30]

Only time would show what an abyss Bulgakov had glanced into, *en passant* of course, and by the merest chance. He was unable for one moment, for all his imagination, to imagine the theory of the intensification of the class struggle

---

[28] M. Bulgakov, 'Kogda mertvye vstaiut iz grobov', *Gudok*, 8.8.1925. Reprinted in *Ranniaia nesobrannaia proza*. Also in *Sobranie sochinenii*, 1985, Vol. 2, p. 277.

[29] M. Bulgakov, 'Mertvye khodiat', *Gudok*, 25.9.1925. Reprinted in *Ranniaia nesobrannaia proza*. Also in *Sobranie sochinenii*, 1985, Vol. 2, p. 296.

[30] M. Bulgakov, 'Okhotniki za cherepami', *Gudok*, 18.6.1924. Reprinted in *Ranniaia nesobrannaia proza*. Also in *Sobranie sochinenii*, 1985, Vol. 2, p. 95.

and its practical consequences. However, he did know what he was talking about when he marvelled at the magic power of official documents – a theme to which he would return more than once and which taught him that appearances can be truer than the truth if conditions are favourable.

Certain columnists' devices already point towards *The Master and Margarita*. A factory committee, doing its best to entice unionists to a meeting, makes the meeting sound like a concert, at which a report will be delivered 'to the accompaniment of a funeral march by Comrade Chopin', while at a railway station, to boost business, a mammoth restaurant is set up with the slogans 'No service to Smolensk – have some fresh lobsters!' and 'To Hell with the mail! Pancakes today!' The meeting-to-music, the station without trains and the living dead are all sallies, as yet covert sallies, in the direction of the main work still to come, which will show the world of inverted values and compulsory cant as the filtered product of Bulgakov's own bitter experience. But before he accumulates this experience, we find in *Gudok* a feuilleton displaying a situation, sentence structure and inflections which are reproduced exactly in *The Master and Margarita*. It bears the title 'Mademoiselle Zhanna' and tells the story of a pseudo-medium who uses a 'hypnotist' as her prompter to announce to her audience details of the private lives of some spectators.[31] The link with the end of the performance at the Variety Theatre, the unmasking of the chairman of the Acoustics Commission and the beating he receives with an umbrella from his quick-tempered cousin is obvious; Bulgakov is quoting himself. It is typical, however, that the quotation involves a trivial episode. In important matters the writer quickly shows the permanence of a figure and a connection with well-defined motifs, which he then refers to and plays on without repeating them word for word.

To return to the original question: the feuilletons would have their uses, although Bulgakov may not have realized it immediately. From the start he formed himself as a genuine writer, and for writers of this kind there is no such thing as a situation void of literary possibilities. The gains were laid in storage, at the meeting point of subject and object, the point where everything that defined Bulgakov's individuality and world-view met everything that this world itself disclosed to view. This may have produced significant lessons for the future.

---

[31] M. Bulgakov, 'Madmazel' Zhanna', *Gudok*, 25.2.1925. Reprinted in *Ranniaia nesobrannaia proza*. Also *Sobranie sochinenii*, 1985, Vol. 2, pp. 219-221.

Whether Bulgakov liked it or not, the discipline of the feuilleton was most probably also valuable practice; it developed his powers of invention and speed of reaction, as well as that feature of his imagination which may be described as natural stage writing and which relied on ease of refashioning every situation into the form of a playlet, the form of living dialogue, psychologically plausible and consisting of lively exchanges.

None of this can alter the fact that Bulgakov did not enjoy this period of his life. He felt that he could make better use of his time. He regretted the time wasted on the newspaper. He worked quickly, but his section editor wanted his staff to be there all the time. 'As for me,' we read in 'To a Secret Friend', 'there was only one thing I wanted: to get home from that office to the room I loathed with all my heart, but in which lay a pile of closely-written pages. I really had no reason to stay in the office. It was a waste of time. I would start wandering from section to section, bored stiff, chatting with my colleagues, exchanging jokes and endlessly smoking. Eventually, after an hour or two, I would go home.'[32]

This peevish tone may have been imposed partly with hindsight, from the viewpoint of 1929, because other memoirs of the editorial office show a lively atmosphere, due in large part to Bulgakov's contribution. At the same time the paper was joined by some energetic and jolly newcomers from Odessa, who brought much stylistic verve and astute observation of life: Valentin Kataev, Evgenii Kataev and Il'ia Fainzil'berg, later known as Il'f and Petrov, as well as Iurii Olesha, the star of *Gudok* and author of topical rhyming feuilletons signed 'Zubilo'. From other rooms in the large building of the 'Palace of the Press', which housed a large number of editorial offices, other members of the literary and journalistic fraternity would look in to swap gossip, jokes and conversation and poke fun at one another in convivial contests of wit. Bulgakov is usually remembered as keeping a certain distance, which could be felt in his studied old-fashioned elegance. His splendid comic gift was usually concealed behind this reserve, until it manifested itself without warning in well-aimed repartee. When he wanted, he could be the life and soul of the party. Could it be that at all such moments he was revealing only part of himself, while the greater part remained in that room with the 'pile of closely-written pages'?

---

[32] M. Bulgakov, *Dnevnik*..., p. 604; also in *Novyi mir*, No. 8, 1987, p. 173.

Be that as it may, having set aside everything else until a later time, he eventually abandoned the genre of the feuilleton with relief. It was to serve him well again for purely temporary purposes when in 1926, at the peak of his success, he published a volume entitled 'Rasskazy' in a series published by the humour magazine *Smekhach* [The Wag].[33] He offered a number of items from *Gudok*; others came from other magazines or were written specially for this volume. Some were attributed to a fictional 'rabkor' named Kaportsev, a plain-minded provincial whose comically clumsy utterances were imitative of the well-known raw material in *Gudok's* dispatches from the field. Bulgakov continued to make use of this raw material while at the same time taking his facetious revenge. He parodied it and bade it farewell, closing the *Gudok* chapter of his life.

In the same way 'Antosha Chekhonte' had once been renounced in favour of 'Anton Chekhov'.

A similar decision must have been taken by Iurii Olesha; his 'Zubilo' enjoyed great success, but the author of *Envy*, wishing to be a serious writer, put his opportunistic verse-mongering behind him. The situation of Il'f and Petrov was simpler in that the two satirists were able to remodel their feuilleton material directly into the qualitatively superior material of a novel. The highest quality was achieved by Mikhail Zoshchenko, whose comic tableaux encapsulated a society which had destroyed its social norms and whose citizens were floundering helplessly in a void of cast-off criteria and their own ignorance. From the standpoint of later years Zoshchenko appears as a first-rate writer from a time of shattered lives, who wanted to instruct his readers and to give a warning while smiling, but who was seen as a jester. It was he who raised the vulgarized devices of the feuilleton to the status of real art; it was in this genre, if anywhere, that Zoshchenko's creative power reached its zenith.

For Bulgakov, however, it was a purely utilitarian tradition, made loathsome by the fact that it he was forced into it. He worked within it when he had to and abandoned it as soon as he could. His path lay in a different direction.

---

[33] M. Bulgakov, *Rasskazy*, Moscow 1926.

V

'So, my friend, I have lived a triple life,' the writer confided to his 'Secret Friend'. 'One life at the newspaper office. Daytime. Pouring rain. Boredom. [...] I would go home with my head a pounding void.

'My second life began when I left the paper and dragged myself to the offices of the magazine *Sochel'nik* [Christmas Eve]. I preferred this second life to the first.'[34] 'Sochel'nik' is the transparent pseudonym of *Nakanune* [On the Eve]. It was published in Berlin, receiving Russian material twice a week from its Moscow office. The paper had links with the 'Smena vekh' group,[35] which favoured the ideological compromise of that part of the émigré community which was prepared to accept Soviet power as a *fait accompli*, a *de facto* form of Russian statehood. Without going into any assessment of the mechanisms which might have operated here, or the differences between those who were active in 'Smena vekh', we may point out the view – then quite widely held not only in this milieu but in large sections of the intelligentsia – that a mellowing of the radical Bolshevik formula in favour of something more traditional was inevitable. NEP looked like the beginnings of this evolutionary process. While acknowledging deeper motives, we may see here some justification for co-operation with Bolshevik rule, from which the majority of the intelligentsia at first distanced themselves, to say the least. Bolshevik rule had stabilized and become the main employer, if not yet the only one, and in the conditions it had created, if you had not left the country, you had to live. There was now recognition of what it had done to curb the chronic anarchy of recent years, impose some basic order, unite a shattered country into a single organism and tackle the reconstruction of the economy. This at least seemed to merit acceptance on purely patriotic grounds and in order to unify disparate forces, regardless of their differences. This attitude is concisely expressed in poetic form by Maksimilian Voloshin:

---

[34] M. Bulgakov, *Dnevnik...*, p. 604; also in *Novyi mir*, No. 8, 1987, p. 173.

[35] The name is derived from the keynote collection of essays, *Smena vekh* [Change of Landmarks] (Prague, 1921), which in turn alludes to the pre-revolutionary collection *Vekhi* [Landmarks] of 1908.

Москва сшивает снова лоскуты
Удельных царств, чтоб утвердить единство.
Истории потребен сгусток воль:
Партийность и программы - безразличны.[36]

As we know, Bulgakov was no ideologue, but he was a patriot. In his day-to-day life he sought opportunities to work for his own benefit and that of others, no doubt feeling that a certain natural order and equilibrium is part of the nature of the world. He was disinclined to attempt any deeper analysis of meaning or reason; but like others he had been appalled by the anarchy – the antithesis of order – which he had witnessed. He therefore did not look out of place in the *Nakanune* circle, even if there were clearly defined limits, then as later, to the compromises he found acceptable. The unpleasant surprises to come were difficult to foresee, and we should not be surprised at the widespread hopes – based on still unquestioned logic – that a continuing process of evolution would lead to something linking the old with the new. This was the period of NEP, and Lenin, the head of the new government, had stated that this policy had been introduced in earnest and for the long term.

According to the account of Emilii Mindlin, secretary of the Moscow office of *Nakanune*, Bulgakov quickly became a highly valued contributor.[37] Besides him, the leading young writers of the day worked for *Nakanune*, including Esenin, Mandelstam, Vsevolod Ivanov, Kataev, Fedin, and among the second-rankers Bulgakov's friend Slezkin, to whom we owe his portrait. As it turned out, the apprentice writer, who had yet to publish a book, did not sink in this company; on the contrary, he found his own firm place both in the newspaper and its weekly literary supplement.

He found his place as a chronicler of Moscow life. The feverish struggle to earn a living, 'the most fantastic of jobs', the business of collecting advertisements, the enforced contact with varied classes of people – all of this was quickly turned to account. Bulgakov had every justification to write later, in 1924, 'I know

---

[36] [Moscow is again patching together the shreds/ of appanage kingdoms, to reassert its unity./ History requires a concentration of will:/ Party-mindedness and programmes are of no account.]
from M. Voloshin's poem 'Rossiia', *Stikhotvoreniia i poemy v dvukh tomakh*, Vol. 2, YMCA-Press, Paris, 1982, p. 349.

[37] Em. Mindlin, *Neobyknovennye sobesedniki*, Moscow 1967, p. 116.

Moscow of the '20s inside out. I have explored every corner of it and intend to describe it. But when I do I want to be believed. If I say this is the way things are, that means they really are that way. For the future, when distinguished foreign guests start visiting Moscow, I shall have the profession of guide to fall back on.'[38]

In fact he had become a guide already, at a distance, for those émigrés who were watching and waiting expectantly. He undoubtedly had a thorough understanding of their psyche as he had himself spent some time in a quasi-émigré situation and had recently experienced the feeling of entering an unknown world when he had come to Moscow. His news reports, dispatches and feuilletons, showing a flair for the comic and observation of manners, as well as the intermediate genre, between essay and reportage – known in Russian as the *ocherk* – are clearly animated by a wish to give an honest account to Russians outside Russia of what is happening and how things appear. At the same time, however, Bulgakov is giving an account, for his own benefit and theirs, of himself, taking stock of the first stage of his Moscow adventure and finding his bearings in it. The personality of the writer comes through in the verve and dash, the very opposite of the note of disorientation which can be heard in *Notes on Shirt-Cuffs*. This is entirely natural and may be believed no less than the descriptions of Moscow life, in which 'if I say this is the way things are, that means they really are that way', for Bulgakov is genuinely glad to have been equal to the challenge and to have kept his head above water; he has a sporting satisfaction at having won the first round of his contest with fate. He already has a habit which will help him through life; he detaches himself as easily as one can in literature from the trials of life; in Freud's words, he 'adopts a humorous attitude towards himself, in order to avoid possible suffering.'

Sketches of Moscow life predominate among the twenty-odd pieces published by Bulgakov in *Nakanune* in the years 1922-24. This then was a slightly different way of approaching real literature from that of the prose then being written: by way of intermediate genres, semi-journalese genres, which offered plenty of room for manoeuvre. It is not surprising that Bulgakov preferred this 'second life' to his day-labour at *Gudok*, where the editors, it seems, imposed fairly rigid utilitarian guidelines. He himself soon hit on the idea of what he called

---

[38] M. Bulgakov, 'Traktat o zhilishche'; also in *Povesti...*, p. 108.

'an artistic feuilleton about Moscow'; in January 1922 he asked Nadezhda Zemskaia to support the idea of regular dispatches of a type published in one of the Kiev papers.[39] He already had the professional eye of a writer who is able to use his personal impressions as raw material, to see their value and potential.

In his writing he noted above all that NEP had awakened Moscow from its lethargy and given it the rhythm of renewed life, that shop windows were full, that prices had picked up, that speculators and black-marketeers had appeared, that money had regained its value and that those who had it immediately gained self-assurance. The speed of this relative normalization, after the enforced austerity of recent years, came as a shock to many. In literature there were shrill cries of alarm, predicting that the ideals of the revolution would be lost in the bourgeois mire. Critics spoke of the 'NEP disease'; its symptoms may be seen in Leonov, Maiakovsky, Bagritsky, Aseev, Svetlov and many others. It later transpired that the thing that many feared and the thing they wished to protect were not quite what they seemed, and that only the fear was authentic. But the non-revolutionary Bulgakov had no reason to feel any fear for the fate of the revolution. He was concerned for his own chances in the new situation, which he saw as normal and inevitable. In his sketch entitled 'Forty times Forty' he describes his vision of Moscow from above, from the roof of the so-called 'Nirnzee House', in Gnezdnikovsky Lane, where *Nakanune* had its offices, and the thoughts he shared with his friend:

"'Moscow seems to be buzzing,' I said uncertainly, leaning over the railing.

"That's NEP," said my companion, holding on to his hat.

"Come off it!" I replied. "NEP's got nothing to do with it. It's just life. Moscow's coming to life."

There was fear mingled with joy in my heart. Moscow was coming to life, that was clear, but would I survive? The times were still hard. You couldn't be sure what would happen tomorrow. But at least we weren't living on porridge and saccharin. We had meat for dinner. For the first time in years my shoes weren't "allocated" to me – I bought them. And they weren't twice my size, but only two sizes too big.

---

39 'Pis'ma k rodnym', p. 463. See also the commentary by M. Chudakova, 'K tvorcheskoi biografii...', p. 253.

Life down below was interesting and a little frightening. NEPmen were riding in cabs the length and breadth of Moscow and behaving boorishly. I looked upon them with horror and shuddered at the thought that Moscow would soon be full of them, that they had gold coins in their pockets, that they might evict me from my room, that they were strong and malicious, with big teeth and hearts of stone.

Descending into the thick of things from the highest point in the capital, I began to live again. They did not evict me, and I am confident they will not.'[40]

Bulgakov's NEP is far from idealized. The proletarian writer is horrified by the greed of the *nouveaux riches*, and he will continue to lampoon short-term millionaires with relish and venom. But after being battered by a harsh period of instability he wishes above all for order. And order is now taking shape. The Moscow sketches record its symptoms with child-like joy. The boarded-up shops disappear, along with the crowds milling about at the stations, the roadways littered with cherry stones, the homeless children selling saccharin. The lifts begin to work. Private offices take the place of phantom state organizations. Advertising signs light up. The hurried repair of streets and interiors gets under way. Policemen control traffic and drivers willingly comply. You can be fined for throwing away a cigarette end. Passengers with sacks are not allowed on trams. The newspapers carry advertisements.

The very ordinariness of everyday life – so desperately yearned for – seems stunningly extraordinary. The sketch entitled 'The Supernatural Boy' shows with suitable hyperbole the astonishment produced in a Moscow street by the sight of a boy who is neither selling nor begging, 'a real cherub in thick gloves and felt boots', who 'is on his way to primary school. That's all. Full stop.'[41] Another sketch, 'Russian Life. Travel Notes', expresses delight at the new-found normality of a train journey to Kiev: you can buy a ticket at the ticket office, the seat-covers in the compartments are clean, a waiter invites you to the dining car, policemen see off the last of the hawkers from the station.

---

[40] M. Bulgakov, 'Sorok sorokov', *Nakanune*, 15.4.1923. Reprinted in *Moskva*, No. 5, 1963 and in M. Bulgakov, *Ranniaia neizdannaia proza*; also in *Povesti...*, pp. 59-65. For this passage see *Povesti...*, p. 61.

[41] M. Bulgakov, 'Stolitsa v bloknote', Part II, *Nakanune*, 20.1.1923. Reprinted in *Ranniaia nesobrannaia proza*; also in *Povesti...*, pp. 47-48 [as Part III in this edition – *Trans.*].

'This, Comrade Berliners, is how things are,' Bulgakov concludes one of these descriptions. 'And you keep saying "Those Bolsheviks, oh those Bolsheviks!" I love order.'[42]

Elsewhere he says, 'Give us a firm basis in the form of order and we'll move mountains.'[43]

Many of his like-minded contemporaries imagined this order on American lines, holding out the promise of a sudden leap of civilization and lending something of that outward style to the trappings of contemporary life. In those days the fashion for heightened combat readiness, the austerity of the Komsomol, the songs about 'the world-wide conflagration', the paramilitary uniforms and the parades with puppets of bourgeois figures coexisted incongruously with elements of the ultra-modern American world, with jazz, a taste for the technical, the cult of Hollywood stars, labour-saving programmes and stylish clothes. The process reached further than this: in Moscow the first buildings in the constructivist style were being erected, glazed and spare in form ('the Berlin-American style', as Evgenii Zamiatin facetiously dubbed it). There was talk of applying the methods of the capitalist technological revolution, without their ideological underpinning, and the so-called Constructivist Literary Centre would soon announce in all seriousness the requirements for the technicalization of art.

Bulgakov was evidently also counting on these trends enduring. Soon, in 'The Fatal Eggs', he would fantasize about a joint Soviet-American building concern which would erect skyscrapers all over Moscow, 'solving once and for all the absurd and terrible housing crisis which so irked the people of Moscow in the years 1919-1925'.[44] In the meantime, however, he could see the real complexity of the situation. He was not blinded by his enthusiasm. He took sober note of the friction and conflict between the co-existing systems. Under his pen the opposition between two Bolshoi theatres took on almost symbolic significance: the one austere and ringed by a Red Army cordon, serving for official congresses, and the other

---

42 M. Bulgakov, 'Stolitsa v bloknote', Part IV, *Nakanune*, 1.3.1923. Reprinted in *Ranniaia nesobrannaia proza*; also in *Povesti...*, p. 55 [in Part VIII in this edition; for 'Travel Notes' see *Povesti...*, pp. 74-76 – *Trans.*].

43 Ibid.; also in *Povesti...*, p. 59.

44 M. Bulgakov, 'Rokovye iaitsa', *D'iavoliada*, Moscow 1925, p. 47; also in M.A. Bulgakov, *Povesti...*, p. 468.

traditional, alive with light and sound, filled during performances with the audience of NEP. Contrast became in many cases the key to his vision. He interleaved parades of high-spirited NEPmen with a May Day demonstration and a large protest procession following the murder of Vorovsky; a display of private signs with those of state-owned trading enterprises; the revels of the *nouveaux riches* with showings of newsreels from the civil war. But at the same time his Moscow world was not divided simply into two equal parts. He showed what a mixture it was: students sold cigarettes to earn money, while illiterate peasant women sold newspapers; the mothers of Komsomol girls visited fortune-tellers, while at the mention of Christ someone would call out dogmatically, 'He never existed! Never!' In this something can be glimpsed of the initial idea of his major work, as yet far in the future. People might have forgotten what a flat was, but they wanted to enjoy themselves and make up for lost time; women chase after knick-knacks, and a man wears tails to the theatre.

All of this found in Bulgakov a sensitive and conscientious chronicler, even propagandist. Never before or since did he draw so close to the new order in the belief that it actually was order. He provided a detailed account of the first economic exhibition, relishing it in four successive reports. He picked out colourful details of the new life, glad to see it surging ahead; he measured the pulse of day-to-day life, not hiding his deep involvement in it and concluding, 'I don't share the certainty they have in Berlin that Russia is finished. Moreover, the more I observe the kaleidoscope of Moscow, the surer I feel that "everything will settle down" and we will be able to live quite well'.[45] Further on, in the same cycle of fragments entitled 'The Capital in a Notebook', he writes:

'Moscow is a cauldron and the new life is being cooked in it. It is a difficult process. We have to stew ourselves. Among the country girls and illiterates a new organizational framework is taking shape, one that penetrates every corner of day-to-day life.'[46]

Nakanune, however, was not the only forum in which Bulgakov addressed matters relating to the new form of government. In 1923 he contributed to *Golos rabotnika prosveshcheniia* [Teacher's Voice], publishing four reports on teachers'

---

[45] M. Bulgakov, 'Stolitsa v bloknote', Part IV, *Nakanune*, 20.1.1923. Reprinted in *Ranniaia nesobrannaia proza*; also in *Povesti...*, p. 56 [in Part IX in this edition – *Trans.*].

[46] Ibid.; also in *Povesti...*, p. 59.

qualifications, the harsh conditions of student life, on children generally and schools. He wrote objectively and absolutely seriously about the difficult beginnings of Soviet education, the hard life of those who worked in it and the new educational methods. It was typical of Bulgakov, a traditionalist in social matters, that he nonetheless saw benefits in the new experimental educational methods as they fostered the free development of a child's imagination, initiative, sense of responsibility and independent thought. He enjoyed lively gatherings and took the same warm interest in children as a group as he did later in his own step-children. Children were always small people to be taken seriously, and they appreciated this. Often quizzical, ironic and self-mocking, his tone changed completely when he wrote, for example, at the end of his report entitled 'At the "Third Internationale" Settlement School':

'Much has been written about the situation of schoolteachers. I have read much myself and taken no notice. But their threadbare, shiny elbows and worn felt boots speak all too eloquently. Measures must be taken to provide at least basic aids to teaching staff, if they are not to melt away, devoured by consumption, leaving nobody in the classrooms of the school of the "Third Internationale" Settlement to fill the cropped heads of our Soviet children with knowledge.'[47]

For many years, both during his lifetime and later, Bulgakov had the reputation of a cynic who mocked absolutely everything associated with the October revolution. Indeed he did make fun of many things and had good grounds for doing so. But from the beginning he tried to find in the new system evidence that it was rational and offered a chance for human order. In this he set great store and he was prepared to use his pen to promote and nurture these things. There are probably few such objective, detailed and approving pictures of NEP anywhere as in his Moscow sketches. His critics were able to disregard this. Even today, when the opposite extreme is dominant and much eloquent evidence of his loyalty is held against him, material as plain as his sketches in *Nakanune* is unaccountably still barred from Soviet publication.[48] Evidence of how desperately he wanted to be loyal is clearly still unwelcome.

---

[47] M. Bulgakov, 'V shkole gorodka III Internatsionala', *Golos rabotnika prosveshcheniia*, No. 4, 1923.

[48] I am referring of course to selections in book form, such as that first made by V. Levin in the Munich edition cited earlier (M. Bulgakov, *Ranniaia neizdannaia proza*). In the USSR there have

VI

Bulgakov's chronicles of the life of the capital, his sketches of the face of NEP and descriptions of his own accommodation problems form the bulk of the material he published in *Nakanune*. The other works are very varied. The newspaper became something of a testing ground for Bulgakov's experimentation with different literary options.

At an early date, the end of 1922, two works appeared which have already been mentioned. They are important both as biographical sources and as indicators of future motifs in his writing. The works are 'The Night of the Second',[49] setting out the experiences of Doctor Bakaleinikov and alluding clearly though indirectly to people close to Bulgakov, and 'The Red Crown',[50] in which matters of the greatest moment are drawn together and set forth: guilt and punishment, responsibility and ethical memory, and thus conscience; the torments of that conscience, cowardice and solidarity. The hospital setting is also important here, and special significance is attached to the gathering dusk – 'that frightening and momentous time of day' – and a cluster of references to the family situation; in fact all that this short, carefully crafted story contains is important. Its themes were taken up again in *Flight*, and later, in many different manifestations, in *The Master and Margarita*. It was striking that in 'The Red Crown' the writer's style was quite different from any he had used before; in place of the vibrancy of *Notes on Shirt-Cuffs* and the fluent eloquence of the Moscow sketches a hard, heavy-footed, somewhat rhythmic phrasing appeared, with a jerky movement – the language of serious matters, matters considered many times over and irrevocably decided. This too was a herald of things to come, of the new style which would emerge in the story of Pilate and Jesus, even if this story would be different again, distilling the quintessence of the writer's artistic experience.

---

been only a few single publications in the literary press. The position with regard to Bulgakov's *Gudok* feuilletons is much the same. [With the advent of *glasnost'* in the second half of the 1980s, this deficit was made good. – *Trans.*]

[49] *Nakanune*, 10.12.1922; also in *Povesti...*, pp. 189-201.

[50] *Nakanune*, 22.10.1922; also in *Povesti...*, pp. 183-186.

Until *The White Guard* Bulgakov probably wrote no more significant work than this.

Under the title 'An Evening with Vasilisa' he published in *Nakanune* the scene from *The White Guard* in which the Turbins' neighbours are robbed, in a version differing only slightly from that in the novel.[51] He also published a selection from his *Notes on Shirt-Cuffs*. His variations on Gogolian themes, 'The Adventures of Chichikov', brought the hero of *Dead Souls* to Soviet Russia and made him a speculator fit for the scale and conditions of NEP. But this was done only as a joke, though with great stylistic verve, and beyond the jocular replaying of traditional motifs it led to nothing more serious.[52] The critics would later hold these mischievous pranks against him. The grotesque fantasy 'The Crimson Island' was also in the nature of a stylistic game; recent revolutionary events were translated into an allegorical language imitative of Jules Verne and ascribed to him. All of this, in a slightly different way, was reused later in the play of the same name.

Bulgakov gave a very interesting demonstration of his powers in the lyrical story entitled 'The Psalm', written in the form of pure dialogue.[53] Dialogue was a speciality of his and from the very start he had used it widely for satirical purposes, skilfully saturating it with the full range of features of colloquial speech. Here, however, he guided the conversation along a very fine line, in a serious vein. First the narrator talks to the child of a neighbour, then to the neighbour herself. The reactions of the child, the hesitation of the narrator, the subtly erotic scene – all this has a mature precision and forms a unique kind of psychological eroticism. 'The Psalm' is also partly set among the realities of the communal flat, and things which were usually set out in exaggerated form, with heightened colours and satirical over-statement, were this time transposed into a very different key.

---

[51] *Nakanune*, 31.5.1924. Also in Mikhail Bulgakov, *Belaia gvardiia. Kiev-gorod*, Kiev, 1995, pp. 57-68.

[52] If only at a purely formal level, certain devices later deployed in *The Master and Margarita* are anticipated, e.g. the supernatural mode of action of Chichikov, which then completely loses its supernatural quality; his behaviour is also, with some exaggeration for the sake of satire, firmly set in the speculatory context of NEP.

[53] *Nakanune*, 22.9.1923; also in *Povesti...*, pp. 227-331.

Nakanune also published a courtroom report. Though modest in scope, it was significant in that – as with a feuilleton in *Gudok* about the compulsory handing over of criminals to the authorities – Bulgakov had touched on a menacing phenomenon. This report, under the title 'The Komarov Case', dealt with the trial of a notorious murderer, a Moscow cab-driver who enticed his victims with the promise of commercial transactions, killed them, robbed them of small sums and disposed of the bodies with fastidious care.[54] Bulgakov took great care to garner all the facts, trying to clarify in his own mind what had happened before proceeding to his explanation. The point was that Komarov appeared to be 'completely normal', with 'an ordinary face, not an animal's', and he 'killed meticulously and methodically,... without mercy, but without hatred either'; he killed 'for gain, but modest gain.' The former doctor meticulously traces the symptoms of a previously unknown illness, wanting to diagnose it correctly and brushing aside journalese phrases such as 'the beast in man' ('an empty, meaningless phrase'). Bulgakov's intuition and perspicacity do not let him down: the symptoms and characteristics of evil are pinpointed and described. His conclusion, 'a hollow man', hits the mark. The mental aggression, the protracted self-analysis and apparent self-doubt – all this was correct, and this fact was pregnant with consequences. This is a highly dramatic moment: the moment of transition from the nineteenth century to the twentieth. A mind formed in an inherited humanist tradition, in which human evil – whomever on earth or in Heaven is blamed for it – is seen as an occasional aberration upsetting the natural order of things, is astounded at the sight of evil which is quasi-rational, accepted by choice as a gainful or necessary mode of life. Komarov, with his 'meticulous butchery' as Bulgakov called it, paves the way for the planned human butchery of Auschwitz and Kolyma. The writer would be spared the full knowledge of these, but what he sensed was horrifying enough.

Gudok, *Nakanune* and *Golos...* were not the only periodicals to which Bulgakov contributed during his first four years in Moscow. Others were *Krasnaia niva* [Red Cornfield], *Krasny zhurnal dlia vsekh* [Red Magazine for All], *Rupor* [The Mouthpiece], *Krasnaia gazeta* [Red Gazette] and a little later *Meditsinsky rabotnik* [Medical Worker], in which *Notes of a Young Doctor* would appear in 1925-27. It is possible that other publications are yet to be discovered.

---

[54] *Nakanune*, 20.6.1923

Of the works printed in these journals, those which are important for the reconstruction of his biography are 'The Unusual Adventures of a Doctor', which is close to his *Notes on Shirt-Cuffs*,[55] and 'Bohemia',[56] as well as the one work published in *Gudok* which is completely different from everything else he printed in that paper in that it is mature artistic prose. This is the story 'The Raid', with its important scene showing Petliura's brutal violence in the treatment of a Jewish sentry and his companion, so sensitively described that it must have been experienced or witnessed.[57]

The story 'The Fire of the Khans' is also significant.[58] In its genealogy two lines may have crossed: one of them, as already mentioned, derived from the idea of a play about Rasputin and the end of the empire, and took shape in the palace of Arkhangel'skoe, the residence of Rasputin's murderer Prince Iusupov, which Bulgakov had visited. The other may have been the product of talk which apparently took place among his editorial colleagues about the need for a clear focus on narrative and plot in Russian prose, a matter much discussed at the time. Bulgakov, a born weaver of plots, is said to have had great success – as was his wont – with an improvisation of a carefully constructed story called 'Saint Anthony's Fire', exploiting the double meaning of the Russian term 'antonov ogon''.[59] Nothing is known about this story. However the work known in Russian as 'Khansky ogon'' [The Fire of the Khans] tells how the last descendant of an aristocratic clan, Prince Anton Ivanovich Tugai-Beg, returns incognito from exile to set fire to his palace, which has been turned into a museum. The similarities are obvious and it is more than likely that this is how the idea at the

---

[55] *Rupor*, No. 2, 1922. Reprinted in *Ranniaia nesobrannaia proza*; also in *Povesti...*, pp. 153-163.

[56] *Krasnaia niva*, No, 1, 1925. Reprinted in *Ranniaia nesobrannaia proza*; also in *Povesti...*, pp. 256-262.

[57] *Gudok*, 25.12.1923. Reprinted in *Ranniaia nesobrannaia proza*; also in *Povesti...*, pp. 232-238.

[58] *Krasnyi zhurnal dlia vsekh*, No, 2, 1924. Reprinted in *Ranniaia nesobrannaia proza*; also in *Povesti...*, pp. 239-255.

[59] It can also mean 'gangrene' (cf. the French 'feu Saint-Antoine' – ergotism, and the English 'Saint Anthony's fire' – erysipelas).

basis of 'Saint Anthony's Fire' was developed.[60] For the initiated, there is a veiled hint in the fact that the Tugai-Begs are of Tartar origin in the story. The same origin is ascribed to the Bulgakov-Turbin family, on both the spear and distaff sides; and in 'Notes of an Autobiographical Nature', beside a sketch of the genealogical tree, Popov wrote the hyphenated surname 'Orda-Turbin'.

If the 'Tartar' element itself plays what is unquestionably a secondary role in the story, there is no doubt – especially in view of *The White Guard*, which was then in gestation – that this form of fanatical attachment to one's native home, which was also 'The House' for the last of the Tugai-Begs, has great importance. The extended descriptions of the interior of the 'palace of the Khans' – palpable, savoured, slightly archaized, in which Bulgakov demonstrates a new artistic skill, the ability to reconstruct suggestively the material nature of the world via the richness of its forms – are in the same affectionate, even loving key as the enumeration of domestic objects, vibrant with nostalgia, so well remembered by readers of the novel: 'The tiled stove; the furniture covered in old red velvet; the beds with their shiny brass knobs; the worn carpets and tapestries, some plain red, some patterned, one with a picture showing Tsar Aleksei Mikhailovich with a falcon on his arm, another showing Louis XIV reclining beside a silken lake...'[61] All of this deeply-felt inventory, more real than reality itself, is negated in one controlled spasm, by a cruel obituary sentence: 'The walls would crumble, the startled falcon would fly from the white gauntlet, the flame would gutter in the bronze lamp, and "The Captain's Daughter" would be burnt in the stove.' And this sentence may well be connected to 'The Fire of the Khans' by some concealed spiritual conduit. Bulgakov understands and sympathizes with the inner drama of the arsonist prince who has lost his ancestral home, but emphatically rejects his destructive act. *The White Guard* demonstrates that he is able to be objective even in spite of himself. The story also weighs the situation carefully: the Tugai-Beg palace serves the people; it houses a museum and will have a library; it itself will be the object of scholarly studies. Bulgakov can live with this aspect – let us call it the educational and cultural aspect – of the new order. And he emphatically inverts the

---

[60] The story also contains what may be called a tangential allusion, in no way developed, in the form of one of the visitors whose name is Antonov, whose back is covered in a 'chronic, brownish rash'.

[61] M. Bulgakov, *Romany*, Moscow, 1973, p. 15.

roles: the destroyer and the destroyed change places. The 'rabble' cherishes and preserves that which the previous owner destroys. Here too the writer allies himself with the newly-created order. Not out of opportunism, which is never part of his make-up (except perhaps at the very end of his life); on the contrary, out of integrity. But also sobriety.

Prince Tugai-Beg stands at the beginning of a very important line of Bulgakov's heroes, seen at moments of crisis and critical decision. But here the prince is a negative principle, a negative character. As we shall see, Bulgakov's future heroes will be able to throw off the bonds of a fatalistic determinism, free themselves from it by an act of will and find freedom in opposition. The prince is not one of these; by setting fire to his own home he indeed does violence to his own nature, but does not free himself from it; he remains to the end a possessor by nature.

Here we must add that the very act of arson, as the inception of a theme, has importance for the future. It is an act to which Bulgakov attaches particular significance.

VII

Thus Bulgakov finds his way into his chosen and intended profession via both the drudgery which he hated and 'work on his dream'.

The years 1920-24 were Bulgakov's 'years of study and roaming', of learning his trade. By the end of this period, still on the threshold of literature as he had yet to publish any novel or book, he had demonstrated that he had mastered the necessary skills. The range of his ability turned out to be very wide. It spanned the stenographic record of a disturbed state of mind in *Notes on Shirt-Cuffs*; the unlimited stylization of forms of colloquial speech and the creation on the spot of dialogue scenes in his *Gudok* feuilletons; reportage and sketches in *Nakanune*, with the author present as compère; a whole gamut of characteristic playlets drawn from life; effective stylizations in the spirit of Gogol ('The Adventures of Chichikov') and Verne ('The Crimson Island'); the stylistically and psychologically polished dialogue of 'The Psalm'; the synthetic, multi-layered 'Red Crown', so saturated with multiple meanings; the solidly traditional 'Fire of the Khans', written in accordance with all the rules of narrative development; fragments drawn from a full-length novel which was ready for publication; short stories and the *Diaboliad* collection, which we shall come to shortly; and even an inconsequential experiment, a drawing-room comedy in a popular vein mentioned by his third wife, Liubov' Belozerskaia-Bulgakova, which shows that Bulgakov was already capable of any kind of professional literary work, for it must be assumed that it too was written with all professional skill.

There were no miracles and no revelations, only the first tentative attempts at writing, which he destroyed as though to demonstrate his own sober view of himself, but to the regret of later commentators. There was persistence and hard work based on talent. By the work of his own hands the writer created himself.

Chapter Three

An Essay in Satire

I. Second marriage. Changes of address. Prechistenka. Friends and acquaintances. Finding a personality, outlook and way of life.
II. *Diaboliad*.
III. 'A Chinese Tale'. 'Number 13'. 'The Fatal Eggs'. First critical responses. Attitude to satire. *The Heart of a Dog*.
IV. *Notes of a Young Doctor*.

I

As things turned out, Bulgakov's contacts with *Nakanune* were to affect his private life. As the 'Smena vekh' episode moved towards its close, some of the émigrés returned, among them the well-known journalist Il'ia Vasilevsky, who wrote under the pseudonym of Ne-Bukva, and his young wife Liubov' Evgen'evna Belozerskaia. The newcomers, among whom the leading figure was Aleksei Tolstoi, who had edited a literary supplement to *Nakanune* in Berlin, were warmly welcomed by the literary milieu. The atmosphere of one such meeting would later be accorded a lavish description in *A Theatrical Novel*. At some social occasion Belozerskaia and Bulgakov were introduced to each other and after a while this acquaintance came to be of importance to both. They decided to leave their current partners and join their lives to each other. The circumstances were later vividly described in Liubov' Belozerskaia's memoirs.[1]

In this way the chapter of Bulgakov's life with Tatiana Nikolaevna was concluded. As can be seen from the tone of her diaries, a sense of bitterness at this would stay with her for a long time. She had gone through great hardships with him and was frequently mentioned in letters to his family, though hardly ever in his writing. Since things were different with his subsequent wives, this must have had

---

[1] L. E. Belozerskaia-Bulgakova, *O, med vospominanii*, Ann Arbor, Michigan, 1979.

some significance. We can discover nothing for certain and perhaps we should not even try, since Bulgakov – 'the most private of people', as Liubov' Belozerskaia wrote – preferred to keep his intimate life to himself. What is certain is that this part of his life was very important to him. He liked women and had the ability to attract them. Tatiana Nikolaevna, to judge from a few photographs and memoirs – slim, erect, stern, silent, modestly dressed and slow to smile – was by her own admission 'putty in the hands' of her husband, for all that she tried to be firm. With her constant 'absent presence', she now appears, with the benefit of hindsight, almost a shadow of Bulgakov, with all that this implies. 'He always visits us without her,' wrote Levshin, their neighbour, in the memoirs cited earlier.

Marriages could be ended and entered into easily in those years. The registration procedure made everything as simple as possible. There remained the acute housing problem. Again the young couple were helped by Nadezhda Zemskaia, who let them use the staff room of the school at which she was headmistress. Later they found a shabby room in the attic of an old wooden building in Obukhovsky Lane (later Chisty Lane), Number 9. From here the Bulgakovs moved to a small house on the corner of Maly Levshinsky Lane and Prechistenka. Like all the houses before it, this house was overcrowded even by the standards of that period.[2]

This topography seems to have more significance about it than merely mechanical or arbitrary movement. Bulgakov settled and lived not simply in Moscow as a city, but also in well-defined districts of it: between the outer circle of the segments of Sadovoe Ring and the inner circle of the boulevards. Within this range he zigzagged from one flat to another; here he had relations and friends; here were the places which would be important to him in the future. These were also places which had their own specific atmosphere inscribed in the history of Russian culture, embodying the genealogy of the Russian intelligentsia. Bulgakov could cross the Arbat and head towards Prechistenka. The associations of those symbolic names had not yet been lost. In the picturesque, winding alleys, with constantly changing perspectives and rippling wrought-iron railings, stood little houses in the undemonstrative Moscow empire style, which held memories of Pushkin, Gogol and Griboedov, and little onion-domed churches with resonant names recalling society weddings. This was where the spiritual pulse of the city could be felt, in

---

[2] Ibid., p. 12.

spite of the general impoverishment and the mass migrations of people. In any case the closed patriarchal order in which everybody knew everybody had already been upset at the turn of the century by the advance of a wealthy merchant class which had built more and more tenement buildings; but, despite this, newcomers were quickly assimilated and as late as the great destruction wrought by the town-planning of the 1960s – questioned only too late and allowed to continue at length – the symbolic word 'Arbat' stood for a definite pattern of accommodation, for continuing traditions and the resulting social psychology.

The name 'Prechistenka' had slightly different connotations, especially in the '20s. Along and around this street, in the past the site of boyars' homes and the residences of the *oprichniki*, where once a wayward stream known as the Chertor'e flowed, a sizable part of the intellectual elite now resided: philologists, philosophers and liberal-conservative art historians clustered around the State Academy of the Arts, founded in 1922, utilizing their highly-developed scholarly abilities to protect their relative spiritual neutrality.

Bulgakov was drawn to Prechistenka and lived close by for a while. He clearly enjoyed the dignity of it, occasionally recalling with pleasure the views it afforded and the Cathedral of Christ the Saviour which then dominated it. And at the same time he drew close to the liberal-intellectual 'Prechistenka' spirit. Less a traditionalist by nature than a devotee of the archaic, though an artistic innovator, he was entering literature at a time of a violent anti-traditional convulsions, when many of his contemporaries were trying to believe that everything in cultural life would begin again from nothing once the rubble of the shattered past had been cleared away. He did not share such beliefs and was more likely to find support for his views in academic circles than in the literary market-place. Prechistenka also cultivated a high level of professionalism, a broad outlook and a European intellectual culture. Bulgakov, it is fair to say, never became part of it – he had too much inner independence.

He did, however, make good friends here, particularly with Professor Pavel Sergeevich Popov (1892-1964), the philosopher, historian and logician who was married to a grand-daughter of Lev Tolstoi, Anna Il'inichna. In times to come Popov would assume the role of commentator and biographer; when Bulgakov's diary was confiscated during a search and he decided he would no longer keep one, his letters to Popov became a conscious substitute for a diary and a vitally important source, unfortunately so far published only in fragments.

The writer also made friends with Nikolai Liamin, an expert on western European literature, and his wife Natalia Ushakova, an artist. He maintained close relations with the painter Sergei Topleninov, the writers Sofia Fedorchenko, Natalia Venkstern and Sergei Zaiaitsky, and a number of other people. Some of them lived nearby, along Prechistenka Boulevard and the crooked little lanes that ran fitfully down to the Moscow River. Here the newcomer from Kiev could find something of that domestic stability which he so valued; this is why this district received so much loving and detailed description and the features of some buildings will later be found in *The Master and Margarita*, in the Master's real yet fantastic flat.[3]

His other circles of close friends included Iurii Slezkin, his companion in misfortune in Vladikavkaz, Valentin Kataev and Iurii Olesha. With the first two, however, there would soon be a parting of the ways.[4] In the case of Kataev this may have been because of Bulgakov's younger sister Elena, who had moved to Moscow.[5] But it may have had more to do with Kataev's opportunistic willingness to adapt to circumstances – something Kataev always proclaimed publicly as a philosophy to live by. This was an attitude which Bulgakov always found repellent, and the departure from his circle of fellow-writers who chose an official

---

[3] For a penetrating study of Bulgakov's connections with Prechistenka and individual representatives of it, see M. Chudakova, 'Opyt rekonstruktsii teksta M. A. Bulgakova', *Pamiatniki kul'tury. Novye otkrytiia. Ezhegodnik*, 1977, Moscow, 1977, esp. p. 100 ff. Relying on the account of Bulgakov's third wife Elena Bulgakova, the author reports that 'in the 1930s Bulgakov had the idea of writing a novel entitled "Prechistenka", in which a group of "children of old Moscow" are shown in much the same light as in *A Theatrical Novel*.'

[4] It is true that Bulgakov wrote a foreword to Slezkin's *Roman baleriny* [The Romance of a Ballerina] (Riga, 1928; this is Bulgakov's only known work of literary criticism). However, it shows a certain coolness towards the author. There seems to be justice in A. C. Wright's view that Slezkin's refined old-worldliness was alien to Bulgakov and that he saw in it 'an example of the path he might himself have taken in literature [...] but unlike Slezkin he turned his back on it'. (A. C. Wright, 'Mikhail Bulgakov and Yury Slezkin', *Etudes slaves et est-européennes*, No. 17, 1972, p. 90). Further light is shed on this matter by *A Theatrical Novel*, in which Slezkin is the prototype of Likospastov.

[5] Traces of this may be seen in some of Kataev's writing, especially 'Almaznyi moi venets', *Novyi mir*, No. 6, 1978, in which Bulgakov appears in the guise of 'Sineglazyi' [Blue Eyes].

career came to be a regular occurrence. In general he was extremely circumspect and demanding of those he chose as friends. Soon he would find himself surrounded by young actors from the Moscow Art Theatre (MAT), but as they began to win fame that circle would be dissipated and by the 1930s only a small group of truly close friends would visit him.

Bulgakov kept up with the surgeon Nikolai Gladyrevsky, and both his Pokrovsky uncles, Nikolai and Mikhail, the first of whom kept open house and was a determined individualist. Another such individualist was Evgenii Tarnovsky, a relative of Liubov' Belozerskaia. These people would also be important as prototypes of Bulgakov's characters.[6]

At the same time Bulgakov was making a gradual entry into the literary market-place, speaking at literary gatherings, at his own home or in his friends' flats, giving readings from his works, in accordance with established Russian practice. This was a time of heightened publishing activity. True, the high point had passed by 1922, but quite a number of publishing initiatives were still in train. Among publishers, Bulgakov had much respect for Nikolai Angarsky, the editor of the almanac *Nedra* [The Bedrock], which published his 'Diaboliad' in March 1924 and 'The Fatal Eggs' in February 1925. He was a despot by nature, but an able supporter and genuine lover of good literature. Among those associated with this almanac, Bulgakov got to know Vikentii Veresaev, an older writer with a medical background, later Bulgakov's co-author *manqué*. Their collaboration led to much bad blood on both sides, but their friendship endured. [7]

Such was Bulgakov's environment. But what about Bulgakov himself? His youthful figure remained unchanged. A tendency to stoop checked his habit of truculently tossing his head, as if throwing down a challenge to the world about him. 'Irregular features,' wrote his second wife, '... but an attractive face, a face

---

[6] Professor Persikov in 'The Fatal Eggs' shows features of Tarnovskii, and Professor Preobrazhenskii in *The Heart of a Dog* has features of Nikolai Pokrovskii. See Belozerskaia, pp. 22-23.

[7] On Bulgakov's work for *Nedra*, see M. Chudakova, 'Arkhiv M. A. Bulgakova. Materialy dlia tvorcheskoi biografii pisatelia', in *Zapiski Otdela rukopisei Gos. Bibl. SSSR im. Lenina*, Moscow, 1976, p. 37 ff. This extended account casts a particularly interesting light on the figure of Nikolai Angarsky, about whom little has yet been said. For a briefer treatment see Belozerskaia, pp. 25-26.

of many possibilities. I mean a face able to express the most varied of emotions.'[8] The expressive power of Bulgakov's face and gestures are stressed by almost everybody. He had the vocal range of an actor, was a superb story-teller and could be the life and soul of a party. But he was also able to withdraw suddenly into himself, appear absent or distant; his figure would stiffen and his eyes turn cold. He had developed a posture of aggressive defence, most likely as a result of the difficulties of his entry into Moscow society and the fury of the initial struggle to survive. The most visible element of this posture was his fastidious attention to his appearance. The times did not favour this: people wore whatever they had, in whatever style; manners were coarse; the fashion was for the plebeian or a revolutionary asceticism. Bulgakov, however – perhaps for this very reason – paid attention to form and good manners, held well aloof from any familiarity and consistently maintained his own sartorial style. For him this was an accessible kind of link with the past, a way of maintaining continuity through detail. At the worst of times he managed to be elegant – his only shirt impeccably ironed, his trousers threadbare, but clean and with perfect creases. It is no accident that Maksudov, his near double in *A Theatrical Novel*, is much put out by a stain on his jacket. He also adopted mannerisms which at the time were blatantly provocative: he wore a bow-tie and a monocle and flaunted an old-fashioned repeating fob-watch. Photographs exist of him in bow-tie and monocle facing the camera with the same defiant look he wore in that earlier photograph in which he was smoking his post-matriculation cigarette. It is not surprising that he was stunned by the sight of a man in tails at the opera, as described in a separate section of the sketch 'The Capital in a Notebook':

'That tail-coat intrigued me so much that I couldn't listen to the rest of the opera.

'The question that arose in my mind was, "What does this mean?" Either it was a museum piece amidst the service jackets of Moscow in 1923, or the wearer was sending a kind of signal? As if to say: "How do you like it? In six months we'll all be wearing these!"

---

[8] Belozerskaia, p. 10.

'So you think this is a silly question? You don't say.'[9] In the original Russian the last sentence reads 'ne skazhite', a classically Bulgakovian, playful expression, said with a perceptible tilt of the head and archly naïve surprise. But for Bulgakov the question really was relevant: that tail-coat had meaning and could have meant much more – just as his own old-fashioned attire, so carefully premeditated, had meaning and was intended to say something. 'It had to do with my character,' says Bulgakov in one of his accounts. 'The fob-watch and the monocle were just badly selected accessories to overcome shyness and express my independence.'[10]

And independence was a serious matter. In Bulgakov's milieu the art of compromise was being widely practised. From the beginning he had evidently marked out its boundaries for himself, and left himself a narrow margin. He had great ambitions and attributed the greatest importance to his art. But he did not wish to make it publishable whatever the price. In *Notes on Shirt-Cuffs* he wrote in desperation, 'Needing money for food I took my top hat to the market. Some kind people bought it to use as a chamber pot. But I won't take my heart or mind to sell in the market. I'd sooner die.'[11] When it was suggested that he write a 'lachrymose letter' to the highest echelons in order to ensure publication of *The Heart of a Dog*, he underlined the word 'lachrymose' four times, placed two exclamation marks in the margin, and of course did not write such a letter.[12] His sense of independence made it impossible. But at the same time he was no abstract maximalist. He soon felt the tightening grip of the new times and the unevenness of his chances. Then and later he was prepared to parley and concede, as long as his concessions did not touch what was essential, the point at which he might have said, in Luther's words, 'Here I stand and can do no other.'

A sentence from a letter written to his sister from Tbilisi, referring to *The Turbin Brothers*, is thoroughly typical: 'I'm not very keen to make revisions,

---

[9] 'Stolitsa v bloknote', M. A. Bulgakov, *Sobranie sochinenii*, Ann Arbor, Michigan, 1982, Vol. 1, p. 284; also in M. A. Bulgakov, *Povesti. Rasskazy. Fel'etony*, Moscow, 1988, p. 52.

[10] Sergei Ermolinskii, 'O Mikhaile Bulgakove', *Teatr*, No. 9, 1966, p. 94. The author was one of Bulgakov's closest friends in his last years.

[11] M. Bulgakov, 'Zapiski na manzhetakh', *Povesti. Rasskazy. Fel'etony*, Moscow, 1988, p. 408.

[12] see Chudakova, 'Arkhiv...', p. 45.

except small ones perhaps' [Ne ochen' soglasen, ... na nebol'shie razve].[13] These few casual words would turn out to have binding force throughout a harsh life, experienced as a series of attempts to find an honest way out of each situation as it arose.

He worked, in his own words 'fitfully', but the abundant results of his nocturnal efforts are evidence of systematic determination – at the same time he was earning his keep as a journalist during the day. Perhaps Bulgakov still felt he was not being systematic enough; he had his own scale of values and was in the habit of being very hard on himself. It is no accident that on one occasion at home he again applied to himself the word 'milksop'.[14] His health was never robust: throughout his life he was troubled by crises of nerves, insomnia, headaches and fatigue; true to his principles, however, he did not complain to all and sundry, admitting the truth to only a few. To casual acquaintances he showed an untroubled face. In his writing he usually followed a precise plan, of which, however, there is little recorded evidence. In his archive, properly maintained only from 1929 by his third wife, there are few rough drafts except for those of his main work, *The Master and Margarita*.[15] From the very beginning he schooled himself to accept the bitter disappointment of rejection. Even in Vladikavkaz he had tried to take comfort in the idea that it was because his writing was immature. But in Moscow he searched long and hard without success for a publisher for *Notes on Shirt-Cuffs*.[16] Perhaps in his readers' minds the book blended in stylistically with the mass of similar 'ornamental' and 'dynamic' chronicles by young writers then flooding the market. Later, in his autobiography, he wrote: 'The Berlin publisher *Nakanune* bought the

---

[13] M. A. Bulgakov, 'Pis'ma k rodnym (1921-1922)', published by E. A. Zemskaia, *Izvestiia AN SSSR. Seriia literatury i iazyka*, Vol. 35, No. 5, 1976, p. 459; also in Mikhail Bulgakov, *Dnevnik. Pis'ma 1914-1940*, Moscow, 1997, p. 21.

[14] 'If I were a man, not a milksop, of course I would throw Ivan Sidorych out of my room.' 'Samogonnoe ozero', M. A. Bulgakov, *Sobranie sochinenii*, Ann Arbor, Michigan, 1982, Vol. 1, p. 343; also in M. A. Bulgakov, *Povesti. Rasskazy. Fel'etony*, Moscow, 1988, p. 218.

[15] For a thorough treatment of his archive and his method of writing, see Chudakova, 'Arkhiv...'.

[16] See the previously cited account by the typist I. S. Raaben, who transcribed Bulgakov's early texts: 'When he had finished his "Notes", for a long time he could not publish them. He fell into despair, saying nobody would accept them.' Quoted in M. Chudakova, 'K tvorcheskoi biografii M. Bulgakova, 1916-1923', *Voprosy literatury*, No. 7, 1973, p. 250.

book from me, promising to publish it in May 1923. And they never published it at all. At first I felt quite hurt, but later developed a feeling of indifference.'[17] There is no doubt that this 'feeling of indifference' was really his spiritual stability, self-imposed and hard won. Almost all those who remember him agree that Bulgakov was just as sensitive as he was ambitious. He felt deeply all opinions expressed about him or his work, and a single thoughtless word could hurt him so deeply that he would be unable to forgive it even from his best friend. At an early stage, however, he had to acquire the ability to protect his sensitivity against innuendo, slander and denunciations, which he had already met with in the Caucasus; against the simple-minded obduracy of the converts to the class struggle, whom he exasperated by his manners and his prose; against glibly lavished epithets such as 'not one of us', which could have very far-reaching consequences.

So much for his 'indifference'. When he sent his sister in Kiev his feuilleton about Nekrasov, soon after he had arrived in Moscow, he wrote, 'I know in advance that either the journal won't appear, or at the last moment somebody will say it's unsuitable...'.[18] Eighteen months later he confided to Slezkin, 'I've finished "Diaboliad", but it probably won't be accepted anywhere.'[19] This turned out not to be the case, but the vicissitudes of *The White Guard* and the stormy career of *The Heart of a Dog*, with its confiscation during a search, were grounds enough for his forebodings.

And all this was only the beginning.

II

In the meantime his belated début as a published author of books finally came to pass. In May 1925 the 'Nedra' publishers issued a collection of his stories, *Diaboliad*, with the sub-title 'Stories'. In addition to the title story it contained the novella 'The Fatal Eggs' and the short stories 'Number 13' and 'A

---

[17] M. Bulgakov, 'Avtobiografiia', in *Sovetskie pisateli. Avtobiografii*, Vol. 3, Moscow, 1966, pp. 85-86.

[18] *Pis'ma k rodnym*, p. 462; also in *Dnevnik. Pis'ma*, 1997, p. 30.

[19] Quoted in V. Chebotareva, 'K istorii sozdaniiu *Beloi gvardii*', *Russkaia literatura*, No. 4, 1974; also in *Dnevnik. Pis'ma*, 1997, p. 126.

Chinese Tale', as well as Bulgakov's grotesque variations on a theme by Gogol, 'The Adventures of Chichikov'.

'Diaboliad' (the story) was another experiment in the Gogolian vein, but this time less superficial. The creator of 'The Overcoat' had been the first to give Russian literature the prototype of the petty *chinovnik*, locked into the mechanism of the office and the great city which seems to magnify it, while growing ever more fantastic, eroding contours in a mist of ambiguity and releasing hidden surprises. The clerk's mouse-like scurryings are at the same time a struggle to achieve a modicum of humanity. From this tradition Bulgakov's experience could build a bridge directly to the second part of his *Notes on Shirt-Cuffs*. He makes intensive use of Gogolian changes of key and inflection, balancing on the boundary between the prosaic and the fantastic. He proves a most apt pupil, perhaps partly because what for others in different circumstances might have been one choice among many possible conventions became for him the best key to the interpretation of his own experiences.[20] As a Russian intellectual with a good classical education, brought up in a cultured family, he was no doubt accustomed to treating literature as a permanent element of reality. He was therefore able to use Gogol in a natural way to clarify for himself the half-real world of 'Glavpolitprosvet', which was changing before his eyes and subject to more and more new experiments. Then he applied Gogol – for a moment, just as long as was necessary to imprint him superficially upon the plot – to his 'Adventures of Chichikov', possibly partly for his own amusement, for the variations on the theme have the air of a gratuitous joke. In 'Diaboliad', on the other hand, he follows his master deeper into the heart of things. In this process he follows the path mapped out in *Notes on Shirt-Cuffs* and it is quite certain that a factor here is Bulgakov's experience of the uncertain life of the *chinovnik*, filled with essentially grotesque attempts to impose order on great disorder. But this time the autobiographical basis could not be discerned with the naked eye. The author stood behind his material, objectivizing it. This was reflected in the style of 'Diaboliad', which is not a fragmentary stenographic record of the feelings of the writer's wounded ego but an expression, in clear and precise narrative form, of the fragile and fundamentally unclear structure of the world as he

---

[20] At the time it was fashionable to borrow themes from Gogol. See for example M. Barkanov's 'Povest' o tom, kak pomirilsia Ivan Ivanovich s Ivanom Nikiforovichem' (1927), 'Chudasia, ili Mefistofel' v stolitse' by the brothers Tur (1929), and others.

saw it, in other words, order imposed on disorder, clarity on a lack of clarity. This is an important defining characteristic of Bulgakov's writing, which would later enable him to achieve uncanny effects in making the most fantastic visions seem real.

The narrative technique of 'Diaboliad' is rather like a carousel being set in motion, gradually building up speed, then with increasing acceleration reaching a kaleidoscopic whirl of alternating situations all containing the seeds of the final disaster. First the unassuming secretary Korotkov clashes with his new boss. Then he receives his pay in kind, as was common at the time – in this case matches produced at the factory where he works. Their uncertain flickering casts an ambiguous light on everything.[21] Finally he is dismissed and takes up a struggle for his official existence, a struggle which lends him greatly increased, indeed terminal, impetus. In a sharply cut sequence he pursues his superior and tormentor through the phantasmagorical chambers of some supernaturally proportioned offices, tumbling into absurd situations at every turn, losing his documents and then his sense of his own identity. As the man he is pursuing changes his form, turning into a large black cat at one point, it becomes clear that, in pursuing the petty *chinovnik*, Korotkov is actually pursuing the Devil and, given the endless whirling motion, is at the same time being pursued by him. Only a slight shift of the imagination is required to see the strangeness of post-revolutionary institutions as a fantastic labyrinth in which space and form are relative; after all, in *Notes on Shirt-Cuffs* the narrator who is trying to 'get LITO started' is told in all seriousness, 'We didn't think you existed.'[22] This sentence could serve as the leitmotif of 'Diaboliad'.

Hence the Devil is in us but here he reaches a little further into the senselessness of existence. This is precisely that 'diabolus minor', that lesser demon of the title; the dazzling moment of Bulgakov's perception, the riddling nature of the world, made incarnate in that demon. 'The Adventures of Chichikov' had its origin in the author's dream: 'In the kingdom of darkness, over whose entrance a lamp bearing the words "Dead Souls" burned constantly, it seemed as if Satan the practical joker had opened a door.'[23] In that story this meant no more

---

[21] The smell of sulphur is also ambiguous, at once suggesting matches and hell.
[22] *Povesti...*, p. 419.
[23] *Povesti...*, p. 171.

than a daring stylistic flourish. In 'Diaboliad' the pursuer-and-pursued Korotkov-Kolobkov falls helplessly into a swirling vortex, and the stock phrases 'chert poputal' [the Devil of a mess], 'chert voz'mi' [the Devil take it] and 'poshel k chertu' [go to the Devil] are fully reified – to the death.

Except that here death is not yet an altogether serious matter. 'Diaboliad' is the work of a young writer. The time he lives in is also still young, and this allows certain hopes to prosper. Bulgakov lets loose his servant of the shadows into everyday Moscow life, but this is not yet *The Master and Margarita*. There is still much gratuitous fun here, much piling up of effects, a wish to dazzle by the power of invention and show off the potency of his imagination. Daring sequences of scenes sweep us over the surface of things which other twentieth-century writers would treat as particularly important: such as the depersonalization of man shown as the plaything of nameless forces, lost in a maze of Castles and Offices. Bulgakov also enjoys the fact that his hero is merely an appendage of his identity papers, and when he loses these he cannot prove his identity or even undertake a search for his lost self; he makes great play too with an accidental mistake in Korotkov's name which turns the hero into someone else (some years later Iurii Tynianov would use the same idea for a horrifying study of the workings of a soulless state machine in *Lieutenant Kizhe*); at the same time he gives a wink to the reader, hinting in his sub-title that the superior whom Korotkov is pursuing has not divided into two people at all, – he merely has a twin brother. Thus Korotkov is driven to insanity by an entirely natural phenomenon.[24] To a greater extent than 'The Fire of the Khans', in which the traces of the original idea were obscured, 'Diaboliad' is a juggling act of literary devices. It is no accident that it was executed at precisely the time when Lev Lunts, Viktor Shklovsky and many others were calling for greater 'fictionalization' in Russian literature, criticizing it for being amorphous and unpolished.

This aspect of the story was noted by one of Bulgakov's first critics, Evgenii Zamiatin, when he wrote, 'The author is no doubt following the right instinct in selecting his compositional principle: a fantasy firmly rooted in everyday reality, rapid, cinematic changes of scene – all this is one of the few ways our recent times, the years 1919 and 1920, can be encapsulated. The adjective "cinematic" is all the more fitting as the story is flat and two-dimensional,

---

[24] The sub-title of 'Diaboliad' runs 'The tale of how two twins proved the undoing of a clerk'.

everything is on the surface, the scenes are totally lacking in depth. (...) The absolute value of Bulgakov's story – which is somehow very light-weight – is not great, but it looks as if good work may be expected of this writer.'[25]

This 'extravagant work', though clearly written with an eye to the tradition of Gogol's 'Overcoat' and 'Diary of a Madman' and Dostoevsky's 'Double', in fact makes sparing use of that tradition. As the hero of 'Diaboliad' flies into his final abyss we sense that he might at that moment wake from a nightmare, like the narrator of 'The Adventures of Chichikov', before whose eyes 'life in its everyday form began to flaunt itself anew.'[26] For this reason the death of Korotkov has an air of unreality about it; it is the device to end all devices.

And yet it is still death. The Devil is invoked half in jest, but also half seriously. And the serious half emerges as the more important.

III

Diaboliad (the collection) expresses surprise at the demonic fickleness of life no less consistently than the title story. 'A Chinese Tale' departs a little from the pattern of consistency: it is a fairly realistic portrait of a Chinese coolie who supports the revolution for purely material motives, knowing only a few words of Russian, including a demotic expression referring to the reputation of a person's mother, and unintentionally dies a hero's death without rising above a condition of prosaic primitivism. The disproportion was intended to smack of the grotesque, but in the end the author did not go beyond a description of a phenomenon. Could this have been a fragment from some wartime observations at the front? The impression it made was of a fortuitous work, although the suggestion was heard that it might be a veiled polemic with the well-known motif of the worthy Chinaman Xin Bing-wu in Vsevolod Ivanov's *Armoured Train 14-69*. But the evidence for this is insufficient.

'Number 13' concentrated the torments of the housing problem and gave vent to them in a cathartic firework display. Here again it is very likely no accident that 'a fiend disguised as a blizzard rages and howls round the metal gutters,' as the vision of the house is lent a clear demonic slant. The stylistic gusto, which reaches

---

[25] E. Zamiatin, 'O segodniashnem i o sovremennom', in *Litsa*, New York, 1967, p. 217.

[26] *Povesti...*, p. 182.

its onomatopoeic and visually imitative apogee in the scene of the fire, brims over with personal rancour, of course; these flames have about them something of the fires of Hell that consume the Sodom and Gomorrah of the accommodation offenders. A fire did indeed occur, but on a much smaller scale than the one the vengeful author shows us in a spasm of pyromanic delight. Again the effect of the stage-management diminishes somewhat the horror of the situation, turning it into a macabre joke, a play of pure fantasy and a display of stylistic instrumentation. Seen from this angle, rather than actually tackling the things that matter to Bulgakov, 'Number 13' hints at them. As observed earlier, it records the act of setting fire to a building, in this case by accident. An allusion to matters of substance lies in the hidden struggle for the very existence of the house, waged by El'pit, the dispossessed hereditary owner, represented by the hard-driving house-manager, a 'servant of two masters', incidentally an authentic figure. This was a kind of inversion of the plot of 'The Fire of the Khans', as the former owner clutched desperately at his property in the hope of repossessing it. His dead hand was even less appealing to Bulgakov than the destructive passion of Prince Tugai-Beg, as he felt that greed could not have the dimensions of drama. He therefore regarded El'pit without the slightest sympathy.

On the other hand, against the background of other works, there was significance in the words said at the end by the unwitting culprit, Annushka, who is also taken from life and vindictively preserved for future works: 'We are poor benighted people. Ignorant people. Somebody ought to teach poor fools like us.'[27]

We will not investigate the justice of this formulation; the story was intended as a kind of act of revenge, and the narrator's pleasure at achieving this can be heard in his voice throughout. Had it been otherwise, he might have heard Annushka say something different, for example: 'Poor fools like us ought to study.' There is something else that matters more: here we seem to catch the very moment at which faith in the new order *as a form of order* begins to waver.

Annushka's cry also forms a natural link with the most important work in the *Diaboliad* collection, 'The Fatal Eggs'.

This is a key point in Bulgakov's biography as a writer; the autobiographical umbilical cord snaps and falls away. He takes on a contemporary

---

[27] 'Nr 13. Dom El'pit-Rabkommuna', in *Povesti...*, p. 209.

theme in the form of pure fantasy situated in the near future. Of course the background is constructed from the well-known rich material of Bulgakov's own experience. It is significant that he sees the future as an uninterrupted continuation of NEP. The year 1928 has an even more swashbuckling rhythm and Americanized exterior than the preceding years. The quest for enjoyment surges on, with the pursuit of sensation, the advertising, increased motor traffic, and Russian-American joint construction. Electric headline billboards are in style, along with ray guns and if not tail-coats, at least dinner jackets. This forecast turned out to be most painfully wide of the mark, as was hardly surprising. But there is no doubt that this particular year was chosen at random, and it was only fate that decreed that this should be the year of the sudden end of NEP, the 'Shakhty' trial, the announcement of the tragedy of collectivization and the intensification of the class struggle. Nevertheless, by a capricious logic, Bulgakov's tale also has as its focus a blow of fate, fierce and cruel in its consequences, so, seen from a slightly different angle, 'The Fatal Eggs' also matched the spirit of the times.

Bulgakov's blow, however, had about it the smell of sulphur, demonic intervention, and the insertion of a hoofed and furry leg into the sequence of cause and effect. In this story a famous biologist discovers a 'ray of life', which accelerates the process of maturation to a fantastic rate. Before he has time to investigate it thoroughly, his discovery is appropriated by a typical representative of the new caste of professional functionaries with a mad passion for experimenting. Then, when parcels get mixed up in the mail, the life-giving ray is administered to the eggs of vipers, pythons and crocodiles instead of chickens. The apocalyptic vision of a plague of reptiles moving in vast droves across a panic-stricken land allows Bulgakov to show off the best of his dark, visionary qualities. But the idea – one of those which benefits from being fantastic yet driven by realistic motivation – lacks the impetus to last to the end. The outcome is decided by a sudden midsummer frost, a relatively crude device which constitutes one coincidence too many.

This matters little, however.

Motifs of fantastic adventure seasoned with naïve scientism are extremely widespread in Soviet literature of the period. They usually serve fairly crude didactic ends, however, reifying the inevitability of conflict between the Bolshevik state and its capitalist neighbours. But at the level of the writer's workshop this meant – in a simplified way – the implementation of the aforementioned 'fictionalization' of prose. All of this is in accord with what might superficially be regarded as the spirit of the times: Russia, 'flung into the incredible',[28] is seen as Gogol's hyperbolized troika hurtling we know not where and traditionally providing no answers, while the reality of civil war had supplied plenty of examples of dramatic clashes and entangled human destinies. The surging imagination of writers was already dispatching their characters to distant planets, where they made up a technological lag by sheer enthusiasm in order to carry revolution into deepest space (Aleksei Tolstoi's *Aelita*); it was weaving a vision of the extinction of Europe and the coexistence of America with a NEPized Soviet Siberia (Ehrenburg's *Trust D.E.*); it was dreaming up 'current inversion machines' to magnetize the world's armaments and make it impossible for the capitalists to wage war (V. Kataev's *Master of Iron*); or on the contrary telling readers to see in extraordinary inventions a threat to the very existence of socialism, a threat happily averted, it is true (*The Garin Death-Ray* by Aleksei Tolstoi, and others).

In all these and many other works of fantasy an automatic mental reflex invariably operated: inventions were a good thing when they served the cause of communism, and they always did serve communism when they were in the hands of communists.

Bulgakov disrupted this artless pattern, linking fantasy with elements of social satire and creating an inventor's anti-utopia which is the work of inventors. Professor Persikov's discovery has the potential to do good but is turned into a tool of mass destruction by an ignorant arbitrary act. We have only to observe the element of coincidence, by whatever name we choose to call it – including that of the Devil. A blow of fate is the catalyst of misfortune. More precisely, it is the hero of the story, but not the only one; the other is stupidity. More precisely yet, stupidity that wields power.

It is personified in the chairman of the model 'Red Ray' collective farm, Aleksandr Rokk. Bulgakov likes invented surnames. He plays with them and enjoys exploiting double meanings; as Russian 'rok' means fate, predestination, the chairman is a kind of malformed fate, orthographically hobbled and essentially grotesque (this also provides the word-play of the title 'Rokovye iaitsa', and the

---

[28] From Valerii Briusov's 'Tovarishcham intelligentam', *Stikhotvoreniia i poemy*, Leningrad, 1961, p. 483.

basis for some rather schoolboyish humour).[29] Rokk's dress and mannerisms are also grotesque, being relics of the days of War Communism. 'This man,' Bulgakov writes, 'would have looked absolutely right in the streets of the capital in 1919 or even early 1924. But in 1928 he looked odd.'[30] Nevertheless Rokk wins the right to make use of Persikov's invention. This right is granted by the highest authority. The anachronistic Rokks, always dilettantes aflame with zeal and ready to apply their ignorance to new challenges, are clearly still the instruments of the regime. The results are disastrous; chance is all it takes.

Such is the uncomplicated meaning of a work to which we should not try to ascribe great depth. 'The Fatal Eggs' in a way follows a tradition of creative fun, of playing with the imaginative possibilities. Here the author takes great satisfaction in exploiting his journalistic experience; he also enjoys private allusions for the initiated, transparently distorting surnames, jabbing in a malicious needle here and there. One of these in particular, a splendid dig at Meyerhold, 'who, as we know, perished in 1927, while working to stage Pushkin's *Boris Godunov*, when a trapeze-full of naked boyars snapped', cut deep and was not forgotten by the victim. Certain features of the period are enthusiastically parodied: 'an emergency troika comprising sixteen comrades', 'the GPU "Red Raven" publishing house' and the accepted style of current 'ornamentalism *a là* Isaak Babel': 'and he hurled himself into the open sea of war and revolution, exchanging his flute for a sinister Mauser'. Here he is playing with conventions, for example with the stereotype of the scientist, which he reanimates with ease and imagination in the figure of Persikov, here and there adding features of a real figure[31] and constantly winking at the reader to remind him not to take it too seriously.

The story is lightly told in the form of light-stepping, elongated, flowing sentences – more so than in 'Diaboliad'; this is the style of his *Nakanune* feuilletons and sketches. But serious fears still come through. As we know, lightness is Bulgakov's natural mode in literature; writing is a way of shedding life's heavy cares. It also becomes a way of charming away fears and disarming them. In 'The Fatal Eggs' he writes lightly, even archly, of the GPU and the fear it evokes; thus it

---

[29] In addition to the play on 'rok', mentioned by Drawicz, Russian 'iaitsa' [eggs] also doubles as a vulgarism for 'testicles' – *Trans.*

[30] 'Rokovye iaitsa', in *Povesti...*, p. 500.

[31] See Note 6, this chapter.

will remain to the end, to the dream of Nikanor Ivanovich in *The Master and Margarita*,[32] where the stark injustice of authentic confiscations is magically turned into a jolly spectacle, and it is easy enough to see how much this lightness counterbalances the weight of everyday horrors.

'The Fatal Eggs' is a lightweight anti-utopia, or, in Zamiatin's phrase, 'a social fantasy with a minus sign' – in outline. It is original, since the other anti-utopians, including Zamiatin in his novel *We*, tended to fear the opposite, an excess of order, the dead hand of unbending regulations. Bulgakov was afraid not of uniformity but of untamed anarchy. It turned out, however, that these were but two sides of the same coin and both warning lines converged in historical space. They also clearly intersected in the work of Andrei Platonov. This outstanding writer sounded a clear warning against both the arch-bureaucrats whose ideal was total immobility and those demented sectarians who would change everything including the laws of nature.

Bulgakov feared the latter most of all, along with those who came behind them – the legions of Annushkas with their aggressive ignorance. We have seen how he tried his best to lend his support to those things that inspired hope. But one of the unchanging features of his creative personality was a kind of twofold vision: while being receptive to something, his eye would light on some feature of it which fired his satirical imagination. This was a consequence of the integrity with which he treated his calling as a writer. His integrity made him alert to danger signals, while his Gogolian satirical vein fixed them in hyperbolic form. The idea of 'The Fatal Eggs' was partly borrowed – with the source acknowledged – from H. G. Wells's *Food of the Gods*.[33] But Wells shaped his humanist musings on the future of the species into an abstract fictional form, so to speak, and gave them a good conclusion, if artistically less convincing. Bulgakov used the same idea

---

[32] M. A. Bulgakov, *Romany*, Moscow, 1973, p. 576 ff.

[33] See Persikov's conversation with his assistant, Ivanov: 'Vladimir Ipat'ich, Wells's characters are nothing compared to you... And I thought it was all just fairy tales... Do you remember *The Food of the Gods*?

    'Do you mean that novel?' asked Persikov.

    'Yes, of course. It's very well known!'

    'I don't remember it,' said Persikov. 'I remember reading it, but I've forgotten it.'
'Rokovye iaitsa', in *Povesti...*, pp. 475-476.

diagnostically and to sound definite warnings, and concluded his story with the death of his scientist, who falls victim to the blind vengeance of the mob. Set against the light structure of the work as a whole, this ending carried weight.

Later Bulgakov would write much more ambitious works on a much grander scale. Next to these 'The Fatal Eggs' and 'Diaboliad' would look like youthful exercises, pieces of sensationalist prose written with skill and zest. But there was more to them than this, and events would quickly show what they really were: in the same year in which Bulgakov's fanatical dilettante destroys Russia by causing his reptilian invasion, the ruler whose dictatorship was now approaching full strength set about breaking the backbone of the Russian village, dealing the country a far more terrible blow than any literary imagination could have foreseen.

'The Fatal Eggs' also established Bulgakov as a presence on the review pages. He was noticed when the story was published in *Nedra*. At first there was no indication of the storms which would shortly break. The reviews were patronizing but relatively kindly: 'silly, ... but witty and stylish';[34] 'this comical, parodic, sometimes ambiguous, but always delightful tale is characterized by its improbable pace, charm and tension';[35] '"The Fatal Eggs" is a successful attempt to show Soviet reality on the fantastic canvas of a Wellsian plot'.[36] The last reviewer also noted, without disapproval, that, 'Bulgakov is setting out to be the satirist of our age', which some time later took on a bitter taste for Bulgakov. Viktor Shklovsky, with his usual peremptory casualness, made light of the story, seeing the writer merely as an imitator of Wells: 'I do not mean to say that Mikhail Bulgakov is a plagiarist. No, he is a capable writer who is using *The Food of the Gods* for his own modest purposes. Bulgakov's success is the success of an apt quotation'.[37]

However, it was not long before the so-called 'Na postu' critics, the later RAPP group, the most aggressive and sectarian literary grouping, entered the fray. The year 1925 was the high point of the advance of the 'Na postu' far Left: Vardin,

---

[34] N. Korotkov, *Rabochii zhurnal*, No. 3, 1925.

[35] G. Borsh, (name of publication unknown). Like the foregoing reference, this review may be found as a cutting in the album of press notices which Bulgakov maintained. It is held in the Lenin Library.

[36] A. Pridorogin, *Knigonosha*, No. 6, 1925.

[37] V. Shklovskii, 'Zakrytie sezona', *Krasnaia gazeta*, 30.5.26.

Lelevich and Rodov. Their extremism was, it is true, repudiated by a famous decision of the Communist Party (Bolshevik faction) Central Committee and they themselves lost their positions of power, but the spirit of their efforts proved to be enduring. Lelevich, who saw the Bulgakov case as part of a trend, was the one who stated that his stories were 'the most typical examples of [...] a neo-bourgeois literary offensive'.[38] At the same time Leopold Averbakh, the future head of RAPP and the most agile spokesman of literary intolerance, spoke out and set the tone for Bulgakov's critics for years to come:

'Mikhail Bulgakov's flair cannot be denied. He writes with ease and fluency, sometimes interestingly. So the question "how?" can be answered: "not badly". But *what* does he write!

'(...) Should Bulgakov continue to enjoy the hospitality of our publishers and be viewed with favour by Glavlit?

'(...) We need satire. But that satire should be imbued with all the passion of our cause. Soviet satire can only issue from the pen of a writer who lives for our struggle and understands it. Great social sensitivity is needed if one is to avoid sliding from satire and denunciation into mockery and malice. Bulgakov's stories elicit suspicion and concern. Here is a writer who does not even dress in fellow-traveller's colours. Not only our critics and literary scholars need to be vigilant, but Glavlit above all!'[39]

In those years literary custom was still in its formative stage and public denunciations disguised as reviews had not yet become general practice, so it is entirely possible that this was an early signal which Bulgakov remembered well and which produced the idea of the assault on the Master unleashed by the suggestively named critics Ariman and Lavrovich. However, as usual in Bulgakov, this vein of *The Master and Margarita* is also not a straightforward copy but a cross-fertilized synthesis of what had occurred in different versions and in different settings and circumstances. What is striking about Averbakh's comments, however, is the fact that Bulgakov has been emphatically expelled even from the fellow-traveller class, that is, from the literary purgatory where the categorical and demagogic 'Na postu' taxonomists placed most of those writers permitted the satellite status of

---

[38] G. Lelevich, 'V preddverii "literaturnogo sezona"', *Izvestiia*, 30.5.26.

[39] L. Averbakh, *Izvestiia*, 20.9.25; partly in *Dnevnik. Pis'ma*, 1997, pp. 119, 124. For more on Glavlit, the Central Administration of Literary and Publishing Matters, see Chapter Five, II.

accompanying the truly 'proletarian' artists. Being a fellow-traveller meant having promise. Fellow-travellers were there to be won over; during the sharp clashes of the time some of them found protection in Aleksandr Voronsky's *Krasnaia nov'* [Red Virgin Soil].

Once having lost this status, Bulgakov could not count on any support, even in a relatively pluralistic range of groupings, and effectively he had none. From the start he was completely alone. Sectarian logic was the strong point of RAPP: they hardly ever confused the boxes into which writers were sorted. Thus three years later, when Averbakh was at the peak of his power, he consistently consigned Bulgakov to the category of 'neo-bourgeois' and 'internal émigré' writers, and this label also stuck.[40]

It is true that Bulgakov also heard expressions of recognition, but with the exception of the banal phrases cited above, these came mostly in private correspondence. 'The Fatal Eggs' was very much to the taste of Gorky, who mentioned it several times in his letters.[41] But at this time Gorky's status as resident abroad meant he had little authority. Veresaev, the joint editor of *Nedra*, praised the story highly. He would write of this to Gorky and pass on Gorky's view to Bulgakov ('As for the campaign unleashed against you, you will be glad to hear that Gorky, who wrote to me last summer, has taken a close interest in you and has a high opinion of you.')[42] This was a nice friendly gesture, but no more.

---

[40] L. Averbakh, 'O klassovoi bor'be', *Zvezda*, No. 1, 1929.

[41] Bulgakov is first mentioned in Gorky's letter to M. Slonimsky dated 8.5.25; 'I'm very fond of Bulgakov, but he has concluded his story ['The Fatal Eggs' – A.D.] badly. The reptilian march on Moscow is not exploited, and you only have to think what a fantastically interesting scene this is.' *Literaturnoe nasledstvo. Tom semidesiatyi. Gor'kii i sovetskie pisateli. Neizdannaia perepiska*, Moscow, 1963, p. 389. On the same day Gorky mentioned the story again in a letter; a week later he wrote to L. Demidov: '"The Fatal Eggs" is wittily and adroitly written' (Ibid. p. 152); and in a letter to Romain Rolland, dated 10.9.25 and containing a brief run-down of young Russian writing, Bulgakov's stories, with the works of Babel, Leonov and Zoshchenko, are described as 'books which will enter the history of literature'. *Cahiers Romain Rolland. Correspondance entre Romain Rolland et Maxime Gorki*, préface et notes de Jean Pérus, Cahier 28, Paris, 1991, p. 165.

[42] Letter dated 28.9.25. By 'campaign' Veresaev probably means the articles by Averbakh and Lelevich.

For many years the official comment on Bulgakov's work consisted of not only the view but also the style of RAPP, one of abusive, denunciatory accusation, a style polished and successfully applied even after the organization itself had disappeared.[43] This continued despite the fact that the story makes clear that Bulgakov is not saying all is lost: the story is a warning, an expression of fear concerning certain potential dangers, and thus an act consistently animated by the hope that the order he had so enthusiastically welcomed would have a chance of enduring.

The critics did not notice these subtleties.

This was partly a result not only of the 'Bulgakov case', for which a body of evidence was already beginning to accumulate, but of an ambiguous attitude to satire in general. There were many who declared that satire was redundant in Soviet conditions, and that instead the 'appropriate bodies' should be informed of shortcomings and abuses. An ardent proponent of this view was Vladimir Blium, one of the most determined opponents of Bulgakov's plays.[44] His views were not seen as binding; in many discussions and official pronouncements satire's right to exist was clearly spelt out. It was recognized as having its uses as long as it was subordinated to well-defined ideological demands and as long as it was useful in the struggle against external and internal enemies. There was also theoretical recognition for its important role in exposing the shortcomings of the new order,

---

[43] Some classical examples of the denunciatory style can be seen in some of the statements published twenty years after the writer's death: 'M. Bulgakov's phantasmagoria ["The Fatal Eggs" – A.D.] is a pamphlet directed at the new Russia. There are no characters in the work. Humour is replaced by taunts and dreary mockery. [...] Bulgakov attempts to ridicule and discredit his times, in which he sees only turmoil, general confusion and petty, futile scurryings [...]. Relying on a sense of life elaborated by Gogol as total disarray and a comical blend of the absurd and the real, of fantasy and reality, he mechanically transferred into his stories the principles of Gogol's satire and world-view in order to lampoon the ways of the Russia of his day.' L. Ershov, *Sovetskaia satiricheskaia proza 20-kh godov*, Moscow-Leningrad, 1960, pp. 213, 215, 216.

[44] See Blium's statements: 'The satirical tradition has been terminated', 'Art should now cast off its satirical mission', 'There should be no place for satire during the time of the dictatorship of the proletariat', quoted in A. Boguslavskii and V. Diev, *Russkaia sovetskaia dramaturgiia. Osnovnye problemy razvitiia*, Moscow, 1963, p. 220; see the same source for an account of some of the debate and argument over the legitimacy of satire.

and the names of Gogol and Shchedrin were cited. However, this sounded increasingly like so much cant at a time when actual practice among publishers and censors was everywhere placing more and more constraints on domestic satire and when all the more important works of this type had to fight ever harder to break through the limits, if they were not to succumb to them. And after publication, demagogic sleight of hand with pseudo-criteria such as 'one of us' and 'not one of us' was sufficient to place the satirists under suspicion of wrecking, slander and sabotage on behalf of the enemy.

But if the RAPP school of reaction to 'The Fatal Eggs' may be seen as thoroughly unjust, matters were different with the next work, the novella, *The Heart of a Dog*. Here Bulgakov's doubts form themselves into clear certainties; if in the earlier work he was still an anxious onlooker, supporting the new regime while delivering a warning to it, he now joined the opposing camp. The story was read carefully and well understood, in accordance with the criteria that now prevailed. And its author was treated accordingly.

The Heart of a Dog is the story of a failed experiment, picking up the age-old theme of the homunculus, the test-tube human. Professor Preobrazhensky, a distinguished surgeon, grafts a human pituitary gland onto a dog. This operation has limited aims but results in the mongrel turning into a human, who, however, inherits the worst features of the alcoholic donor. The former Sharik, later Poligraf Poligrafovich Sharikov, finally becomes so intolerable when his primitivism is crossed with aggressive demagogy that there is nothing to be done but operate on him to return him to his original state.

This time, then, it is not coincidences or any misapplied techniques that Bulgakov regards as disastrous – it is the discovery and the experiment itself. The act of human interference in the laws of nature and the violence done to them, which upsets the evolutionary order of things, is a catastrophic error. In fact experiments of this type were then considered possible and desirable; it was even fashionable to predict unlimited transformational possibilities in the near future.[45] But there is no doubt whatever that this story is not about science. Very graphically, clearly with the aid of his medical experience, Bulgakov constructs a

---

[45] For some interesting information on the atmosphere of sensation and facile belief in the limitless possibilities of experiments in 'rejuvenation' and allied fields, see M. Chudakova, 'Arkhiv...', pp. 43-44.

vision of a surgical operation with all its paraphernalia, but these carefully-tailored technical trappings undoubtedly form an allegory and, for Bulgakov, a fairly direct one. It is a fundamental vote of no confidence in the great social experiment, the Bolshevik revolution, carried out in a backward country and having the effect of unleashing the baser instincts. It is a fundamental crisis, if not the end of hope for a chance of order. In it one senses the accumulation of many of life's blows, a concentration of sorry experiences producing some measure of bitterness: the story manifests the same element of contempt for the 'plebs' as was shown in Annushka's sentence. Such was the diagnosis of Doctor Bulgakov at the time.

In addition to its central allegorical plot line, *The Heart of a Dog* contains other uncompromising elements. In the very clear outline of Professor Preobrazhensky, who, unlike Persikov, is not merely the product of Bulgakov's play with the conventional figure of the scientist, the aforementioned element of disaffection claims the foreground. The Professor dislikes the system and says so openly, because he is an eminent scientist and can afford to. Bulgakov clearly finds his attitude appealing. Apparently modelled on Bulgakov's uncle, Nikolai Pokrovsky,[46] Preobrazhensky is presented with obvious sympathy: he is entertaining, charming and commands admiration. An important place is also occupied by the malicious and intrusive housing administration which Bulgakov cordially loathed, and traditional aspects of the housing problem – with the degradation of the building and the neighbours singing in chorus. Set against these is the agreeable, orderly, traditional nature of the flat itself, which here takes on the role of the House. All of this forms a picture rich in meaning and unambiguous in its diagnosis, especially since, unlike 'The Fatal Eggs', there are fewer in-jokes and no echoes of the feuilleton-writer at play.[47] *The Heart of a Dog* is firmly set in NEP-period prose, it has many impressive flourishes (above all the dazzling reconstruction of the psychology of a dog and the perception of Moscow from a canine point of view), but at the same time the writing is more ambitious, with firmer contours, more compression and concentration, and more precision in its

---

[46] See Note 6, this Chapter.

[47] Except for such details as, for example, the first name and patronymic of the writer Il'ia Arnol'dovich Il'f, given to Preobrazhenskii's assistant Bormental'. The choice was most likely a form of friendly greeting to Il'f. (The basis for this suggestion is slightly flawed. The assistant's name is Ivan [not Il'ia] Arnol'dovich Bormental' – *Trans.*)

structure. It is satirical prose of high quality. This sharpens its bite and makes the cutting sarcasm of Bulgakov's splendid humour doubly incisive.

It cannot be ruled out that with time a different view of this story may come to dominate: the scientific anti-utopia may move into the foreground and emphasis may shift to such problems as upsetting the balance of nature, or the cluster of legal and ethical questions about organ transplants, or others concerning the relation between inherent and acquired characteristics. Today's atmosphere of civilization in crisis tilts *The Heart of a Dog* towards this cluster of meanings. But the Wellsian aspect – if we may call it this – constantly gives way in certain areas to others more coarse and primitive. They may be thought to be an imprecise balance – *The Heart of a Dog* is the expression of a very 'Prechistenka' figure, with everything that this implies[48] – but chemical precision in weighing out the meanings is not compulsory in satire.

For all this, let us repeat: the story was well understood. It was first accepted for publication by *Nedra*, but after considerable efforts this proved to be out of the question. In March 1926 Bulgakov signed a contract with MAT for a stage adaptation; a year later the contract was annulled.[49] It is probable that the arrival late one evening of some GPU operatives with a search warrant at the attic flat in Obukhovsky Lane came soon after this. After an all-night search, *The Heart of a Dog* and the writer's diary were confiscated. The manuscript of the story, we learn from Liubov' Belozerskaia-Bulgakova's memoirs, was returned to the author two years later thanks to Gorky's intervention;[50] Bulgakov never resumed his diary. Its place was partly taken by his letters to Popov, and his third wife Elena Sergeevna kept a diary.

Thus the waywardness of literature collided with the straightforwardness of power. The difficulties he had encountered in Vladikavkaz had found their Moscow sequel. His attempts to cast spells with the light touch of his 'Fatal Eggs'

---

[48] To be fair we should add that, side by side with the anti-plebeian feeling, *The Heart of a Dog* shows much warm fellow-feeling for social pariahs, for example in the descriptions of the sufferings of the scalded dog or the harsh life of 'ninth-grade typists'.

[49] See Chudakova, 'Arkhiv...', p. 45. Chudakova also attempts to establish dates, showing that the story was probably finished in February 1925 and that moves to secure publication lasted until October of the same year.

[50] Belozerskaia, p. 29.

and dispel the already deepening fear of the secret police proved to little avail, but were clearly vital to Bulgakov, since he persisted. But his free will as a writer and his sense of decency were unacceptable in the context of the time. The road that led that way, the road that might lead to publication, was barred and Bulgakov must have realized this only too well. What he went on to do and what became his life's work was what he did for himself and for posterity. In the meantime, as so often later, he tried to find his way round the blind wall of impossibility.

'Diabolus minor' turned out to be a worthy servant of his master – in literature. Here be it noted in passing that both professors, Persikov and Preobrazhensky, often invoke the name of the Devil, in completely mechanical and habitual fashion, of course. However, when Persikov learns of the cataclysm caused by his ray of life he repeats 'My God!' three times and does not use the Devil's name again.

This splendid stylist of everyday speech surely did not apply such effects in random fashion. Did he believe that the Devil's name should not be taken in vain? Or was he thinking of the folk expression which says that in some situations 'sam chert nogu slomaet' (literally: 'the Devil himself could break his leg')?

IV

His attempts to by-pass the wall of impossibility took various forms; most began with a strategic withdrawal into the past. This manoeuvre was familiar to many writers.

Notes of a Young Doctor, written in 1925-1927 and published in the professional journal *Meditsinsky rabotnik* [Medical Worker], took him back to the recent past.[51]

The writer who scoffed and jeered at the dangerous experiments of the present immediately became utterly serious on the firm ground of the past tense. His *Notes of a Young Doctor* had an autobiographical basis, but beyond the title they had practically nothing in common with the vibrant and quickened pulse of *Notes on Shirt-Cuffs*. This should not surprise us, since the author was now

---

[51] Of the nine stories which comprise *Notes of a Young Doctor*, six appeared in an edition in book form in 1963 (Ogonek Library edition), and later in *Izbrannaia proza*, Moscow, 1966. The title of the collection first appeared in the Ogonek edition.

writing of himself in stable and rational surroundings, filled with purposeful activity. Here too there were plenty of difficult experiences, as we know, but he was able to keep his balance. In any case he could now see it all from the distance of a decade, enclosed in the traditional formula of the short story based on specific episodes. The narrator admits openly to moments of weakness and is unsparing in his self-mockery, describing successes and failures by turns. Perhaps the complete lack of experience he shows at the beginning is partly a device, for if Doctor Bulgakov had served previously at the front this meant that he had some solid medical practice behind him.

Two works from this cycle seem to have greater importance than the rest. One of them is the story 'The Murderer', a new account of the doctor-narrator's enforced mobilization into Petliura's army and the atrocities he witnessed against innocent civilians. The ending here differs from that in other accounts: the narrator kills the colonel-executioner and flees. We are probably entitled to see this variant as the most fictional construction, the most compensatory almost, in relation to actual events, a kind of 'wishful writing'.[52] Doctor Bakaleinikov, the 'intellectual louse',[53] changes here into Doctor Iashvin, who is capable of desperate acts. It may therefore be no accident that the autobiographical traces have been partly erased – by introducing a different narrator. In the second of the stories the author also covers his tracks and does this even more artfully, but the artfulness itself gives some pointers for indirect deduction. This story is 'Morphine', with its seismographic, pitilessly analytical diary of a drug addict (it is noteworthy that he is saved – though not completely successfully – by a woman...). Like 'The Unusual Adventures of a Doctor', the diary is framed in the quotation marks of artifice: it is a text sent to the narrator after the death of the addict. But the quotation marks this time are doubled, for the narrator has a fictional surname. The impression is given that Bulgakov wishes to distance himself carefully from the subject matter and find a counterweight to the powerful immediacy with which the tale is told. But being an ingenious inventor of names, which are just as often the product of cross-fertilization as his characters, he may have deliberately left a curious trail to be followed. The unfortunate addict bears the name 'Poliakov', while the narrator is 'Bomgardt'. By transposing syllables we get the surname 'Bomgakov'. Is this not

---

[52] In English in the original. *Trans.*

[53] In 'The Night of the Second', *Povesti...*, p. 201.

a transparent truncated pseudonym for his own situation? Though himself an addict, the author also emerged the victor over it; so he was able to describe his experiences as a body of *faits accomplis*; furthermore he could, and perhaps had to, put to death his alter ego hero, who really had ceased to exist.

These two stories are chronologically the latest and the most 'literary', departing from unadorned autobiography. For reasons unknown neither of them was included in the first edition in book form of the *Notes*, which appeared in 1963, or in the second in 1966.

Thus the medical chapter of Bulgakov's life came to an end in literature too. But the most important part of the experiences of the author and those close to him became the raw material for the book which was both his first novel and one of his two major works – *The White Guard*.

Chapter Four

An Essay in Honest Reporting

I. *The White Guard* and the experience of the author and his family; the Kiev background.
II. Guilt and punishment. Understanding the causes of the cataclysm. Historicism. The novel as a field of conflicting forces.
III. The spirit of the epic as the spirit of irony. Tradition as a point of departure.
IV. The novel as a stylistic laboratory. Variety of means of expression. Instrumentation. Centripetal focus on the House. The role of the commentator.
V. Difficulties with the novel. Theft and abuse of copyright. Critical opinion. The 'differentness' of *The White Guard*.

I

The main character of *The White Guard* is a moment in history; the overthrow of the world order and its equilibrium, taking place, in Bulgakov's earlier phrase, 'amidst unheard-of horrors' and bearing with it an inevitable crisis of values.

It is a novel about history, which, from being perceived in the remote category of the pluperfect tense, separated from us by the barrier of decades, has become the very stuff of the everyday experience of all.

When it came, this moment, though it had been the subject of many presentiments and prognoses, stunned everybody by its drastic nature; so much so that as soon as the first shock had passed there was a rush to examine it, and then to proceed from partial formulations to the first syntheses.

We already know of Bulgakov's partial formulations. At various levels and in varying keys they reflected his experience and that of those close to him. The writer approached *The White Guard* by way of 'The Red Crown', 'The Raid', 'The Night of the Second' and 'The Unusual Adventures of a Doctor'; he drafted various versions, considered them, set them aside and began again.[1] We can clearly sense how much this novel mattered to him at the time of its conception. In an autobiographical note recorded by Popov we read, 'I regard the novel as a failure, although it stands out among my other works since I took it very seriously.'[2] We may grant the author the right to be self-critical, even if we might think he invokes it too often. The last part of his sentence is frequently repeated.

The crystallizing moment that apparently set the inner wheels in motion was the death of Bulgakov's mother on 1st February 1922. Bulgakov himself spoke of this.[3] At almost the same time came the news that his younger brothers were safe and well abroad.[4] Perhaps that was when he felt the collapse of the self-contained organism which had been the House as final and irrevocable. We do know that the order of that House was a projection of a world order which had passed. In this way we can come closer to the psychological key to the work and at the same time to the system of its fundamental oppositions: the House versus the City; and the City versus everything which lies outside it.

It is not surprising that the novel should open with the death of the mother. We find ourselves at once at the very core of Bulgakov's system, in which factual elements are mingled, shifted and lent new meaning. In reality, in 1918, when the main action of *The White Guard* takes place, Varvara Mikhailovna had merely left

---

[1] See the account by the typist, I. S. Raaben, who retyped *The White Guard* at least four times: 'It was a very big job. (...) In the first draft Aleksei was killed at the school. So was Nikolka, – I don't remember whether that was in the first draft or the second. Aleksei was an officer, not a doctor, then that changed. Bulgakov was dissatisfied with the novel. Besides the cuts proposed by the editor, he himself wanted to rewrite it... He would pace up and down the room, sometimes he would stop dictating, say nothing, and think... I well remember that the novel was called *The White Cross*. I recall that somebody suggested a change of title, but in my time it was not *The White Guard*; I first saw that title when the novel was in print.' (Cited by M. Chudakova, 'Arkhiv M.A. Bulgakova. Materialy dlia tvorcheskoi biografii pisatelia', in *Zapiski Otdela rukopisei Gos. Bibl. SSSR im. Lenina*, Moscow, 1976, p. 35.)

[2] *Zametki avtobiograficheskogo kharaktera* , as recorded by P. Popov; Manuscript Department of the Lenin Library, Fond 218.

[3] 'Mother died in 1921 [scribal error: in fact she died in February 1922, A.D.]. This was a powerful, indelible stimulus. The plan for the novel arose in 1922.' (recorded by P. Popov).

[4] See M. Chudakova, 'Arkhiv...', p. 48.

the family home to live close by after her second marriage. She had, however, physically departed, which was something of a shock in a household like hers, and given the sort of mother she was. On the other hand, his mother had died before the writing of the novel began, so, measured by the time-scale of its creation, his mother died at the beginning of *The White Guard*. This lends to experience a kind of dual identity.

The connections between many characters in the novel and their prototypes are no less complex. When questioned by Popov the author explained: 'Nai-Turs is a generalized, abstracted figure. The ideal of a Russian officer. (...) Lariosik combines images of three people, one with a Chekhovian element. Shervinsky has a definite prototype (...). Myshlaevsky is an invention, although based on the image of a certain officer.' An added note reads: 'The names are invented, but based on the names of the prototypes.'[5] All this has made it possible for Bulgakov's commentators to guess who the prototypes are or might be with a large measure of plausibility, although there is no agreement, for example, as to whether the Elena of the novel is simply a portrait of Varvara Afanas'evna or, as seems more likely, a distillation of the three elder sisters. Of course identification such as this will bring nothing new to our reading of the novel today, important though it is as confirmation of the author's method: he shied away from direct representation of reality in favour of often ingenious artifice. An example is the Talberg of the novel, who received the surname of a former pupil of High School Number One, a lawyer, who died in 1910. By the situation he is seen in, rather than by his character, he corresponds to Bulgakov's brother-in-law Leonid Karum, Varvara's husband. Another is Studzinsky, given the surname of another former pupil, a doctor who died in 1916, but the Christian name and patronymic of a professor of literature, Aleksandr Bronislavovich Selikhanovich.[6] These composites of very disparate elements seem like a clear warning from the author not to try and overburden what is already realistic enough with intrusive trivia, and not to reduce a work of art to the level of social or family gossip.

---

[5] Popov.

[6] These figures were identified by A. Burmistrov in 'K biografii M. A. Bulgakova, (1891-1916)', *Kontekst 1978*, Moscow, 1978, pp. 254, 256. For other facts related to the prototypes, see M. Chudakova, 'Arkhiv...', p. 49, as well as her 'K tvorcheskoi biografii M. Bulgakova, 1916-1923', *Voprosy literatury*, 1973, No. 7, p. 235.

This applies even more to the hero, Aleksei Turbin, who we know in advance has both concealed and unconcealed links with the author.[7] Both returned to Kiev some time before the events described, both have been demobilized, but only one speaks of his service in the active army, which may be – but need not necessarily be – an intimation of Bulgakov's own situation. Both were in private practice and specialized in venereal diseases. Their domestic circumstances are clearly very similar, although Turbin's immediate relations have been reduced to just two, just as we know that the house, in both cases, is Bulgakov's House. We also know that Bulgakov experienced situations 'very like those shown in the novel', and that, besides the account in the novel, there is the semi-grotesque, self-mocking version of the doctor's flight from Petliura's men in 'The Unusual Adventures of a Doctor', which in turn is close to *The White Guard*, but not identical. Here too the contours are shifted and some traces slightly obscured for reasons known to the author and no doubt deliberate, since he already has an extensive armoury of literary devices at his disposal.

Subjected to the laws of literature, the destinies of some characters have been placed in an authentic setting whose reliability has been attested from various angles. Karol Wędziagolski, for example, a Polish witness of the events, recalls them as follows:

'The last Hetman of the Ukraine, Pavlo Skoropadsky, left his homeland by train in a hospital carriage of the German high command, wearing a hospital gown and a bandage on his head as disguise. At the same time the forces of Ataman Petliura were threatening the capital on all sides from the steppe. The order to defend the city was issued to Russian volunteer formations under the command of the Volunteer Army on the Don. It soon transpired that these monarchist units, whose mission it was to bar Petliura's way to the city in the name of a "single and indivisible Russia", were too small and ill-equipped, made up mostly of students and schoolboys, and uncoordinated by any strategic design or battle plan. These defenders of Kiev were given to understand that they were the advance units of some powerful force which in reality did not exist.

In practice this meant that a few hotheads, perhaps a dozen, opened fire with rifles or in exceptional cases machine-guns on the approaching Ukrainian

---

[7] The name and patronymic Aleksei Vasil'evich, for example, correspond to a literary representation of Bulgakov in Iu. Slezkin's *Devushka s gor*.

units, only to perish minutes later under concentrated enemy fire or the bayonets of the furious enemy soldiers. The staff officers melted away to safety while the heroic youngsters were condemned in advance to extermination.

Many perished and there was nobody to keep the record of their deaths, of their heroism, or the despair – worse than death – of their last moments, as faith was lost in their leaders and in the purpose of the sacrifice extracted from their childish submissiveness.'[8]

This sounds like a premeditated summary of *The White Guard*. It is noteworthy that the observer, a Russian officer of Polish extraction, – and only later a Pole by choice – , picks out in his last sentences the same nerve which pulses so strongly in the novel. In his traditional Great Russian version the defenders of the city, raised from childhood to believe in values like honour, duty and loyalty to their vows, experience in their dying moments the cataclysmic sundering of the world they have formed part of and whose permanence they never doubted. Their superiors, 'melting away to safety', repudiate these values by their cowardly retreat. Their adversaries, possessed of overwhelming force, deny these values any meaning, and, by hunting down the vanquished in the streets, usher in the rules of total war.

This is the very stuff of history, combined with the fissuring of the earth's tectonic structure in all areas at once, ripping man out of his spiritual surroundings and suspending him in a void between two widely separated shores, just as Boris Pasternak so splendidly put it:[9]

История не в том, что мы носили,
А в том, как нас пускали нагишом.

Anatolii Al'tshuler, the author of a valuable study of Bulgakov's early work, draws attention to the significance of the contrast between Aleksei's dream in Chapter Five and his younger brother Nikolka's descent into the morgue in Chapter Seventeen. Aleksei dreams of a legend of chivalrous knighthood as his comrades-in-arms ascend to Heaven, bonded with their foes in the brotherhood of shed blood. Nikolka descends into the hell on earth of mass extermination, where the victims of

---

[8] Karol Wędziagolski, *Pamiętniki*, London, 1972, pp. 346-47.

[9] [History lies not in the clothes we wore, but in the fact that we were sent forth naked], from the poem 'Spektorskii', in B. Pasternak, *Stikhotvoreniia i poemy*, Moscow-Leningrad, 1965, p. 336.

battle and terror lie naked, stacked in piles amid the stench of death. Aleksei sees the brave Nai-Turs, the colonel of the Hussars who burrs his 'r's in speech, as a knight of the crusades bathed in a heavenly aura. Nikolka pulls Nai-Turs's body out, suppressing the urge to vomit, from a pile of naked and defiled corpses so that the remaining last rites of mourning, snatched from the new order of nameless mass graves, can be performed: a soldier's burial, as an individual, mourned by his nearest and dearest.[10]

Such is the span of tribulations visited upon the main characters and the degree of shock they are subjected to. It is no accident, then, that Bulgakov chose precisely this moment from among numerous others in the rapidly changing situation in Kiev. In addition to the post-mortem perspective, mentioned previously, the choice was motivated by a feeling that this was the moment when the earth's structure changed. Subsequent changes of government might be even more drastic and bloodier still, but they could no longer be anything new. In any case their consequences seemed to give the people of Kiev a degree of psychological immunity, permitting them to view the uncertainties of their own fate from a certain distance.

If we are considering the shaping of life by literature, it is characteristic that Bulgakov's choice is the one which has come down to later generations, thanks to the great artistic quality of *The White Guard*. Now as they read it they experience most forcefully something that for many eye-witnesses – albeit not the defenders of the city – was not the most memorable experience of the period. In the accounts of other observers, almost the same episodes as those shown by Bulgakov were trivial, as if seen through inverted binoculars. Ehrenburg wrote, 'Petliura's troops moved down the Kreshchatik merrily, harming nobody. The Moscow ladies who

---

[10] A. Al'tshuler, *Dni Turbinykh' i 'Beg' M. Bulgakova v istorii sovetskogo teatra 20-kh godov.* A dissertation presented for the degree of Candidate of Art History, Moscow, 1972.

[The passage in Chapter Five was omitted from the English translation by Michael Glenny, *The White Guard*, Collins, 1971 – to my knowledge the only English version of this novel to date. The omission was made good much later when the omitted pages appeared in Glenny's translation as an appendix to Lesley Milne's *Bulgakov: A Critical Biography*, Cambridge, 1990, pp. 263-267. The revised paperback edition of *The White Guard* published in 1993 by Harvill (an imprint of HarperCollins Publishers) finally incorporates this scene. – *Trans.*]

had not had time to flee to Odessa were filled with admiration: "Aren't they nice?" The White officers were rounded up and locked in the Pedagogical Museum (no doubt because of its dimensions rather than any thought of pedagogy).'[11] Paustovsky recalls, 'I was sickened by the military and political farce and my anger was stronger than any sense of danger. I walked through the column of Petliura's troops in my greatcoat without epaulettes and was struck only twice, fairly hard, by a rifle butt in the back. Knots of worthy Ukrainian folk here and there along the roadside cheered them on and looked at me with loathing.'[12]

There are as many truths as points of view, but we should note that even Bulgakov, in 'The Unusual Adventures of a Doctor', leavened the tragedy with irony and even comedy. Of course, Ehrenburg's and Paustovsky's memoirs were written much later than *The White Guard*, which came hot on the heels of the events. But even as eye-witnesses both writers were able to follow events without the grimace of tragedy: to the Russian-Jewish schoolboy, leftist conspirator and Bohemian artist, as to the half-Polish conscript pressed into service in the Hetman's bodyguard, one pseudo-government with the trappings of comic opera was being replaced by another, just as alien and not wholly serious.

However, all three authors do have one thing in common: all are equally distant from the Ukrainian national cause then represented by Petliura. It is sad that even Paustovsky, one of the most enlightened men of his time and a staunch defender of basic humane values, could not refrain from mocking the 'worthy Ukrainian folk'. Was he yielding to the limitations of his point of view, or to his in-built censor? Most likely both. Whatever the case, this demonstrative Russianness – be it Tsarist or Bolshevik – certainly caused pain to Bulgakov's Ukrainian readers, and continues to do so. For them the entry into Kiev of Petliura's powerful army was the high point of a surge of hope for the rebirth of an independent Ukraine.[13]

---

[11] I. Erenburg, *Liudi, gody, zhizn'*, Vol. 2, Moscow, 1966, p. 288.

[12] K. Paustovskii, *Nachalo nevedomogo veka*, Moscow, 1966, pp. 781-82.

[13] 'The Ukrainian movement during 1919 and the following year was associated almost exclusively with the name of Simon Vasilievich Petliura (...) His enemies, including Soviet historians, have called him a bandit; (...) Enemies of the Soviet Union who have acquired enough knowledge of Eastern European history to know of Petliura's existence, have regarded him as a

Let us note, however, one point in Bulgakov's favour. In *The White Guard*, as will shortly be seen, he did a great deal to give an honest account of the objective background to the events. In doing so, it is true, he reached a certain limit beyond which he was unable to go; perhaps because of the psychological scars left by traumatic personal experiences. But if he managed to go against his sympathies in his writing, he did not go against his principles, and this must be respected. Secondly, he did not set out to write a historical novel about Kiev, but a novel about history unfolding in Kiev in a new form, as experienced by a certain milieu for which the unfolding was a matter of life and death. No more, no less. His talent made the great generalization possible.

II

As we have said, the main character of *The White Guard* is history; people and human affairs are secondary characters. Of the human affairs, the problem of guilt and punishment, the dominant issue in all post-revolutionary settling of accounts, claims first place.

In the aforementioned shorter genres and fragmentary pieces leading up to *The White Guard*, apart from 'The Red Crown', an emotional register predominates. In the novel too there are plenty of emotions, but they are curbed by a passion for analysis. Bulgakov does not merely tell of what happened and how it happened, but states why it had to happen as it did. He analyzes the events experienced as a cataclysm, and rationalizes his vision in this way. Above the characters, with their limited grasp of events, stands a narrator who knows and understands more than they do and who takes the floor again and again.

The characters – the circle of residents of the House and their friends – live in a thickening atmosphere of premonitions held at bay in thoroughly Bulgakovian fashion by a front of unconcern, by rather forced humour, by Nikolka's strumming on the guitar, by vodka and cards. The more 'menacing and bristly' the times become, the more important the Fortress-House, with stability made flesh and durable in its furnishings and the fragile screen of its dainty cream curtains. They

---

hero, while Ukrainophobes have branded the national movement as "Petliurism".' J. S. Reshetar jr., *The Ukrainian Revolution 1917-1920*, Princeton, New Jersey, 1952, pp. 263-64.

all hasten to it to be closer to one another. Here they feel 'peace in the objects and disquiet within themselves', as succinctly stated in a draft fragment.[14]

Around them is the city,[15] alive with hysteria, with the self-deception of the newspaper reports, the quickened pulse of a life of make-believe, greedy consumption of life's pleasures, the will to believe in the possibility of maintaining the tottering old order, with endless, improbable rumours and vengeful dreams of a punishing knout and the volleys of firing squads. Of course, there are thousands of different reactions, but as a whole Sodom with its sinners and its righteous citizens does not understand what confronts it, and still less why.

The narrator does understand, and this knowledge, accumulated over five hard years, accompanies his *alter ego* in the novel like a shadow. He reels off, in terse, journalistic fashion, the mounting peasant anger as rumours spread of agrarian reform, the fuel added to the flames by the Hetman's and German repression, the attraction of the Russian revolution just over the border and the work of its agitators, the alienation of the moneyed classes and the discrediting of one form of government after another, and finally the German defeat and the general collapse of German authority. The national cause is hardly touched upon, it is true. The Russian intellectual cannot be much concerned by it. On the other hand he is very much aware of the pressure of social issues; he feels the weight of that 'twisted peasant fury'.

The voice of the narrator as he begins the novel is tuned to the dignified tone of the *byliny* and folk legends: 'Great was the year and terrible was the year of our Lord nineteen hundred and eighteen...'.[16] This opening is preceded by two epigraphs, both highly eloquent; one, drawn from the Bible, speaks of the dead being judged 'according to their works'; the other is from Pushkin's 'Captain's Daughter' and speaks of an oncoming snowstorm, clearly perceived as a synonym for a historical tempest. The Bible speaks directly of responsibility; 'The Captain's

---

[14] 'V noch' na tret'e chislo', *Nakanune*, 10.12.1922; also in M. A. Bulgakov, *Povesti. Rasskazy. Fel'etony*, Moscow, 1988, pp. 189-201.

[15] In the novel it is not called Kiev but 'the City'; the names of certain streets have been slightly altered (e.g. Alekseevsky Hill in place of Andreevsky Hill, Malo-Proval'naia instead of Malo-Podval'naia); others have been preserved; the topography of the part of the city in which the events take place is described very precisely and may easily be rediscovered.

[16] M. Bulgakov, *Romany*, Moscow, 1973, p. 13.

Daughter', with its celebrated admission of fear of 'senseless and pitiless' Russian revolt, stands as a warning to each generation of Russians. We need to remember that the hero of that story is drawn into the orbit of rebellion and teeters on its edge, repelled by its brutality while drawn to the generous leader. In this astonishingly perceptive story is a sentence worthy of genius: the condemned Pugachev, being led to his execution, recognizes the hero and 'nods the head which minutes later is shown to the people, bloodied and lifeless.' The message of that gesture, with its horrific compression, reached down to the descendants of Grinev a century and a half later, and Bulgakov realized its significance.

Bulgakov, then, could see guilt and punishment in their historical perspective, even if this perspective was limited to certain signals. These signals are sufficiently clear for a Russian reader to pick up their meaning. They set in motion the appropriate series of associations. For the writer of a literary work this is enough. He does not undertake any purely intellectual investigation but nonetheless presents a valuable kind of intellectual sobriety. The fatalistic grimace, which he must have seen as a form of spiritual clowning, is alien to him. He is distinctly ironic at the expense of Nikolka, who, 'did not know yet that everything happens as it must, and everything is exclusively for the best'.[17] The masochistic spasm of Blok is most unlike Bulgakov. Blok saw in the revolution an act of supreme historical justice, and in his readiness to accept in full both good and evil disarmed in advance both himself and that part of the intelligentsia which was subject to his influence. It is by no means clear whether evil perpetrated in response to evil may have a positive value, especially when historical retribution crushes many innocent people and the majority receive from the hand of fate precisely what they least deserve.

Above guilt and punishment in the novel stands hope. It emerged spontaneously from the structural features of Bulgakov's 'natural' world-view, which Pavel Popov described as follows:

'Mikhail Afanas'evich believed that life would always reclaim its own. Even in the event of catastrophe, people would remain... people with their likes,

---

[17] Ibid., p. 14.

dislikes and initiatives, and if those people retained truly human feelings there would be some way out.'[18]

And at another point: 'images of gloom were lightened by his characteristically optimistic view of human nature.'[19]

This nature is manifested in the naturalness of human adaptation, in spite of everything. 'Walls will crumble... the bronze lamp will gutter, and "The Captain's Daughter" will be burnt in the stove,' but the question posed on the same page of the novel, 'How is one to live? How is one to live?', with its dramatic repetition, demands an answer. Life goes on. The Turbin brothers, having narrowly escaped oppression with their lives, lose their heads, figuratively speaking, to the dear souls they meet in dramatic circumstances. Bulgakov had actually intended to go further in this direction. A fragment some tens of pages long, probably from one of the drafts of *The White Guard*, has survived, in which Nikolka dines with Irina Nai, the sister of the dead hussar; Aleksei becomes the lover of his rescuer Iuliia Reiss; Aniuta is made pregnant by Myshlaevsky, and Shervinsky pays much more energetic court to Elena.[20] All of this is present in latent form in the final text, but Bulgakov evidently realized in time that such a development would have lent the novel a different generic character, turning it towards the genre of 'the story of a family'. Whereas in a novel about history, such as this, the role of the denizens of the House comes to an end at the moment the eye of the historical cyclone shifts.

Hope shines through, however, even without this ending, from beneath all the layers of meaning contained in *The White Guard*. There are many of these, all jostling with one another and thus creating a field of great tension. A fervent confession of faith in the charmed circle of inviolable domestic peace – the near-mystical belief in the House – clashes with an apocalyptic vision of ineluctably oncoming destruction. This vision in turn has a rational and analytical strain running through it, which extracts from the apocalypse a historical kernel of cause

---

[18] From Popov's letter to Elena Bulgakova on the occasion of the staging of *Days of the Turbins* at the Stanislavskii Theatre in Moscow. The letter, in an album with clippings, is held in IRLI, in the Bulgakov collection, Fond 369.

[19] P. Popov.

[20] This fragment was preserved in the Bulgakov family archive. [It was published in *Novyi mir*, No. 2, 1987, pp. 138-180, with an introduction by Marietta Chudakova and commentary by V. V. Gudkova – *Trans.*].

and effect; and the determinism which emerges here is called into question by an act of free will at the critical moment by Colonel Malyshev, who goes against the pressure of traditional imperatives and disbands his troops (Bulgakov attaches particular significance to self-liberating gestures of this nature). At the very end, however, this tangle is unravelled in characteristic fashion. Petliura's army quietly slips out of the city; on the other side of the river a Bolshevik armoured train is already waiting,[21] and a Red Army sentry, fighting off the numbing cold and dozing off in it, brings back to us in his dream the earlier dream of Aleksei Turbin: each of them dreams of the fallen Sergeant-Major Zhilin. The coincidence is important. The surroundings are the very opposite of the House: ice-bound, harsh, jagged-edged, austere and exhausted, with the menacing silhouette of the train against a pre-dawn sky. This is an unambiguous vision of the ineluctably advancing force to which the future belongs. But the sentry dreams of domestic warmth, and the red star on his cap reflects the twinkling of both warlike Mars and gentle Venus; their opposition, so clearly stamped in the beginning of the novel, is now blurred – to produce a glimmer of hope...

This too is drawn into a clash of meanings, for this scene gives way to another in which a vision of a new life is cited by the poet Rusakov and a vision of death is seen in Elena's dream. There is also the joy experienced by little Petia and the menacing vision of the cross of Saint Vladimir changing into a sword. This polished structure of alternating meanings seems to have no bottom in *The White Guard*. And yet, beneath all these depths, there is one: it is provided by the belief in the possibility of some sort of earthly harmony, the belief that, whatever may happen, everything will come right.

During the period when *The White Guard* was being written, hope could still be found. Later, however, the harsh weight of the words 'suffering and death', used at the beginning of the novel, tipped the scales. The new harmony was not earthly, and many people from Bulgakov's circle of friends met violent deaths, Father Glagolev was exiled, the churches of the neighbourhood were demolished or converted into warehouses; the walls of their house did not crumble, it is true, but it ceased to be the House, and Bulgakov never set foot in it again on subsequent visits to Kiev.

---

[21] At the end of a sketch describing a journey to Kiev such a train, probably actually seen, is glimpsed fleetingly. 'Putevye zametki', *Nakanune*, 25.5.1923; also in *Povesti...*, pp. 74-77.

And yet, in spite of everything, hope remained, except that it was turned in a different direction.

III

'Der epische Kunstgeist ist der Geist der Ironie,' wrote Thomas Mann, clearly having in mind a profound irony produced by contemplating the world in a ceaseless play of contrasts, from the viewpoint of one dwelling at a crossroads of epochs.[22]

Bulgakov's characters – the Turbin family and those close to them – find themselves in a situation which is supremely ironic. Whereas the omniscient narrator understands the meaning and the scale of the events, the characters grope clumsily for a meaning, bumping into the sharp corners of reality. Mann goes on to say, 'Die epische Ironie ist vielmehr eine Ironie des Herzens, eine liebvolle Ironie.'[23] This is also appropriate, even if a melancholy sarcasm sometimes surfaces in the contrasting arrangement of scenes. The denizens of the House are subjectively 'right' in terms of the author's own feelings and conscience. But being 'right' in this way places them at odds with the workings of history; action eludes the participants between intention and fulfilment, with the ironic result that the cynical opportunism of Talberg and the cowardly prudence of the staff officers who flee the sinking ship triumph over the decency of the Turbins: the chivalrous gesture will be empty if it turns out that there is nobody to defend ('Defend a void? The echo of footsteps?' thinks Aleksei in the deserted school building). The best solution then will be to throw down in haste the arms taken up with such *élan*, as defensive action would ultimately mean guarding the gains of their neighbour, the hoarder and philistine Vasilisa.

The main framework of the ironic structure is buttressed by many lesser ironies. If the macrostructure of *The White Guard* is based on the dynamics of conflicting tensions, on the intersecting vectors of opposing forces, the novel's microstructures share this same dynamic, contrastive and therefore ironic nature, owing to the clash of opposites. This may involve whole scenes, like Aleksei's

---

22 [The spirit of the epic is the spirit of irony], T. Mann, 'Die Kunst des Romans', *Gesammelte Werke*, Vol. 10, Oldenburg, 1960, p. 353.

23 [Epic irony is much warmer-hearted, more generous], Ibid., p. 353.

knightly dream, referred to above, set against Nikolka's descent into the Hades of the mortuary. There is a melancholy irony in the juxtaposition of the call for volunteers and the burial of the first defenders of the city at the same time; in Aleksei's late arrival at the assembly point, his noble gesture frustrated by something as prosaic as sleep, so that all his actions are in vain. Irony lurks even in the flight of the elder brother for his life, when, as it turns out, he is hunted on account of his officer's cap badge – a scene of the highest drama, and most personally felt; and in the very similar flight of the younger brother, who blunders into a courtyard brawl with a caretaker, taking part in the only real combat fought that day and evading death like a schoolboy playing truant. At other times the contrast is limited to the interplay of text and sub-text, of foreground and background, of a word and the preservation or puncturing of a scene by a single well-chosen detail; thus the belligerent mood evident at supper in the House evaporates in an alcoholic stupor; Talberg's farewell to Elena shows its ambiguity to the strains of the aria from *Faust*, against words that beg for pity for a sister, and Colonel Malyshev's headquarters are located in the back room of a dressmaker's shop; the bullets that fell Nai-Turs also bring down a sign with a funny name on it, and the façade of the school which Petliura's forces break into bears the slogan, 'For the Edification of the Russian People'. Irony emerges from repeated gestures which assume a parodic nature: the old caretaker Maksim becomes a grotesque version of Malyshev when he evinces a wish to defend to the last 'a void' and 'the echo of footsteps' in the abandoned building; Lariosik's delight at the cosiness of the House mocks by its naïveté the real feelings of those who live in it.

Bulgakov spares neither himself nor those close to him; the irony is a function not only of his talent, which perceives the world in terms of contrasts and surprises, but also of his decency. When Nikolka, breathless after his narrow escape, draws near his home, a boy he meets informs him, 'Our lads are giving the officers what for. Serves them right. There are eight hundred of them in the city and they've been asking for it. Petliura's come with a million men.'[24] It would be hard to find a more painful note of self-criticism, in which irony verges on sarcasm. It is not surprising then that this whole world of endeavours mocked by fate bears the title – like a cap that is an officer's but with just a suggestion of the dunce – *The White Guard*, which clearly and challengingly brings the official name

---

[24] *Romany*, p. 157.

of the whole movement into collision with the fragility of its declared purpose. This was a late-coming title, selected after many other experimental titles, all of which sounded unambiguous and serious. Perhaps that is why they were rejected.

In his book Anatolii Al'tshuler draws attention to one more highly significant ironic juxtaposition: in the Alexander I High School, beneath a portrait of its patron wreathed in the smoke of Borodino, Colonel Malyshev's company prepares for the battle which is not to be. Here there is an unconscious attempt to emulate the sterling exemplars of the past and the hope of finding a place in the annals of Russian arms, and of expelling the latest usurper. Aleksei Turbin, who in this scheme of things comes to resemble Andrei from *War and Peace*, speaks of this directly: 'Will you, Tsar Alexander, save this doomed building with your regiments from the field of Borodino? Breathe life into them! Lead them down from your canvas!'[25] But history does not repeat itself. As he orders his men to disperse Colonel Malyshev does not permit them to set fire to the building, so any potential analogies are stifled at birth and the deeds of the ancestors prove too great for their descendants to emulate. Thus does tradition too become drawn into the framework of ironies.

There are limits, however: this is precisely where the boundary of ambiguity lies. Tradition shows up the irony, but it is not subject to that irony. In a world in which order is tottering, tradition remains as a stable underpinning. The characters of *The White Guard* are shaped by this tradition – above all, literary tradition – to a degree which is probably rare outside the milieu of the Russian intelligentsia. They think in literary analogies, read Bunin, Dostoevsky and Pushkin, and treat the world of fiction as a form of higher reality which lends shape to the reality of everyday life. They tend to interpret life by means of books, just as Bulgakov himself interpreted it through Gogol and, while writing this novel, also through Pushkin and his Pugachev. The dramatic question mark hanging over the physical existence of the Turbins' world applies equally to spiritual values. What chance do they have? This is a question many creative artists have pondered and the range of answers is broad: from extreme pessimism to buoyant optimism. Here Bulgakov seems to place his trust in the natural order of things and hold out hope for the salvaging of at least the spirit of culture, if not its material substance, for, as his

---

[25] Ibid., pp. 100-01.

commentator says, '*Faust*, like the Shipwright of Saardam, is absolutely immortal.'[26]

Tradition, then, is simply a part of life, and life will go on. This no doubt is the reason Bulgakov looks askance at all artistic extremes which have made a point of breaking with tradition. He was concerned not only about art, but about life itself; it is no accident that his own mode of life and his attitudes were deliberately and provocatively old-fashioned in spirit. To him the destroyers were bent on kicking away one of the few firm supports. This is why Bulgakov in *The White Guard* so savagely mocks the 'phantomist-futurists', who are strongly reminiscent of the (spatially transported) Moscow imagists, the spokesmen of eccentricity in poetry, fond of shocking their readers with ostentatious blasphemy. Bulgakov could rub shoulders with them even in his own home, Number 10 Sadovaia Street, which was visited by poets of that circle and housed their editorial supplies.[27] He may even have developed a certain obsession, since he associated slovenliness in poetry and in attitude, to say nothing of primitive blasphemy, with sickness, degeneracy, mental instability and the operations of under-cover agencies. Years later, in his main work, he was to treat the nihilist poet with more subtlety, but both Rusakov in *The White Guard* and Bezdomny in *The Master and Margarita* would be granted the chance to come to their senses, and both would take it. In one way or another, in Luther's famous words, here he stood and could do no other.

Thus the limits of the crisis of values were marked out, drawn from the hope that 'life always reclaims its own' and from 'an optimistic view of human beings'. Literary plots might be subjected to irony, but not literature itself; the historical vagaries of human destinies, but not historical tradition. The narrator of *The White Guard* could make a melancholy joke of a life subjected to the blind play of chance, when life or death hinge on the order in which documents are pulled from a briefcase – but the 'tired notes of immortal Faust' find confirmation of their everlasting durability in the carefully chosen word 'sovershenno' (absolutely),

---

[26] Ibid., p. 34. Among the many pieces of music present in some form or another in Bulgakov's writing Gounod's *Faust* plays a particularly visible role, being connected in various ways to the House. It also appears in *Adam and Eve* and *The Master and Margarita*. Note also, 'Listening to music is something I need to do. I could say that I adore good music. It is an aid to creativity.' (Recorded by Popov).

[27] Cf. the account of V. Levshin, 'Sadovaia 302-bis', *Teatr*, No. 11, 1971, p. 212.

surprising in context and therefore doubly expressive. But the same supremely confident description would also be applied to the motif of the Shipwright of Saardam, Peter the Great, and thus, as this mental abbreviation may be interpreted, to the Russian national tradition.[28]

For other reasons there is no irony in the presentation of the political situation and the disposition of real forces beyond the author's immediate milieu. At the sight of Petliura's forces that spasm of impotent rage and horror at innocent suffering, which is almost certainly autobiographical, must have taken hold of him. Bulgakov did his best to understand everything, but at this point experience got the better of his rational reflections. The very fact that he does not show Petliura himself has about it something of the popular fear of vampires, which must not be mentioned by name. The very heart of darkness must be avoided. In the early sketch 'The City of Kiev' the author pierced its memory with the aspen stake of the words of vengeful relief, 'and may the memory of Petliura fade away'.[29] There is no justice in this, for at the time lawlessness was all-pervasive. It is possible, however, that Bulgakov, conscious of the limits imposed by censorship, was deliberately applying the principle of synecdoche. If so, Petliura's reign would stand only for the quintessence of revolutionary anarchy. It is not surprising then that the Bolsheviks are awaited in the novel as the hoped-for lesser evil, a hope tinged with bitter fatalism. This may well have been the case, and there was no need for Bulgakov to distort the true mood of the period. The hope that Bolshevism would remain a Russian form of order, if a radically different one, was still alive at the time of the events of *The White Guard* and at the time of the genesis of the novel.

Here too we may perhaps perceive another irony at a still deeper level: the main characters, so bellicose at the beginning, calling for a march on Moscow, are

---

[28] In a more prosaic dimension, the huge tiled stove which heats several rooms in the House is called 'The Shipwright of Saardam'. This double meaning also found its way into *The White Guard.*

[29] 'Kiev-Gorod', *Nakanune*, 6.7.1923; also *Povesti...*, pp. 77-86. [This line concludes the story. *Povesti...*, p. 86 – *Trans.*]. By not showing Petliura as a mythic figure, Bulgakov even at this stage had the artistic instinct to sense the import of a presence off-stage, acting as it were from a distance, and manifesting himself in his actions and his relation to other characters. This method was exploited to the full in *The Last Days.*

sidelined and can only look on as spectators while the forces of evil fight it out with those of even greater evil. It is possible that in the deeper sub-text of this story of a great defeat lay Bulgakov's reflections, on a small scale, on the choice he himself had made, on his own moral worth, on possible alternatives, and the fate of his brothers compared to his own. We will probably never discover the nature of all the links between fact and the fiction which became the new and more important fact, where life ceased and literature began, and vice versa. There is method in the way Bulgakov so artfully rearranged everything. And only the great bitterness, shown earlier, of 'The Red Crown', the tension of the torment displayed in it, which is given the name of madness – rightly or not, it matters little – forms perceptible inner links, difficult to reproduce today, with *The White Guard*.

IV

The period of the genesis of *The White Guard* was a time of great stylistic orgies and general destruction of form, a consequence of a sense of having been plunged into something which beggared all belief. Emotions are expressed in rhythmic, staccato writing, with mingled structures and clashing contrasts, a conscious loosening of composition that approaches amorphousness, and with extensive use of dialect. It was sometimes said that life itself had accelerated the destruction of classical narrative forms. Also significant was the destabilization – still clearly felt – in which all criteria seemed unstable and unclear, and this placed a highly specific stamp on the atmosphere of literary life. In this context a fragment from a letter to Gorky from Konstantin Fedin, who was then still very sensitive to atmosphere, is characteristic of the time:

'... it is difficult to write. Not because you have to spend all your life studying, of course, but because the whole of life is filled with the influence of schools of thought, theories, styles, and of living people. You need something like the Great Wall of China to protect your heart, mind and soul from these influences. Not everybody is capable of resisting them, and sometimes nobody can resist them (...). Everybody is in a hurry, leapfrogging over others, snatching words, titles, devices and styles from one another. The boundary between the permissible and the impermissible has disappeared...'[30]

Bulgakov inhabited the very hub of this heightened pace. Moreover, his own past had made him susceptible to it. It had affected *Notes on Shirt-Cuffs*, 'Diaboliad' and 'The Adventures of Chichikov' as well. It meant running with the literary pack – with Pil'niak, Vsevolod Ivanov, Vesely, Malyshkin, Gladkov, Lavrenev and many other lesser figures. 'The Fatal Eggs' and especially *The Heart of a Dog* represent a slackening of tempo, a search for his own pace, and a clear unwillingness to keep in step. In *The White Guard* Bulgakov moves right away from the pack.

The novel has a premeditated wealth of means of expression. It is a great stylistic laboratory from which the author constantly takes new utensils and applies them to the organic fibre of his work. This can be seen from the very beginning. The biblical and bardic overture, with the epigraphs, defines the scale of the work, prepares the reader for the depth and seriousness of Bulgakov's design, and signals the meaning of the various oppositions – between Venus and Mars, the House and its surroundings, the sun and the snowstorm. The entry into the House then takes place to an elegiac commentary on the Turbins' family situation, rather as a camera zooms in after panning slowly over much-loved details. Immediately after this, in the description of an evening *en famille*, the technique becomes lighter, impressionistic, composed of rippling light, the strumming of a guitar, anxious expectation, disjointed phrases uttered amid eloquent silence and given emphasis by the distant artillery fire. Here Bulgakov is a meticulous designer of atmosphere, in which the weightlessness of spiritual states becomes as dense and almost palpable as in Chekhov's plays, where the pauses between words and the coded spiritual gestures are no less important than the words themselves. Moments later the tension is broken in confusion as Myshlaevsky arrives, followed by Talberg, and a scene of nervous drunkenness ensues and untoward thoughts are shouted down, drowned beneath torrents of words. Here Bulgakov's ability to capture the living structures of colloquial speech in all its naturalness and varied, lifelike intonations comes to the fore. The technique that had served in his feuilletons for the needs of the moment is elevated in the novel to the level of an accepted artistic device. This

---

[30] *Literaturnoe nasledstvo. Tom semidesiatyi. Gor'kii i sovetskie pisateli. Neizdannaia perepiska*, Moscow, 1963, pp. 470-71.

was, incidentally, a very popular device. N. Dragomiretskaia, the author of an interesting study of style in early Soviet prose, correctly observes that, with regard to the constant acceleration in pace and the fragmentation of narrative continuity broadly applied by prose-writers, 'the pinpointing of a voice amidst a multiplicity of voices, or the insertion of direct "human speech" becomes a convenient shorthand device for the building of characters.'[31] Bulgakov, to whom all the characters except the main ones in *The White Guard* are types or forms in which the central figure, time, is imprinted, applies this method successfully. Here lies the promise of his potential as a dramatist.

A shift of the lens of the author's vision to the floor below, to the neighbour's flat, brings with it a change of perspective: the lively emotion of the descriptions of family scenes gives way to the cold precision of balanced sentences with measured orderliness, barely concealing a veiled sarcasm and a sense of hostile distance. Close by and in other scenes we find the ragged and phantasmagorical poetics of dreams ('dreams play a particularly important role for me,' Popov recorded), which form a contrapuntal commentary to the words and deeds of the characters. Further on the narrator speaks in the voice of the lyrical chronicler of the history of the city and at the same time that of a columnist and ubiquitous reporter who seems to project the bustle of the streets of Moscow into Kiev's past, while both these intertwining threads are erased again and again, dissolving in the amorphous crowd reactions, the hubbub of gossip and the fluctuations of collective moods. Bulgakov is a virtuoso at lending shape to shapelessness; he can reproduce a crowd like Ursus in Victor Hugo's *L'Homme qui rit*. Here he comes closest to the widespread stylistic trends of the period, with their 'dynamism' and 'ornamentalism'. He is alert to shouted slogans, like Serafimovich in *The Iron Flood;* he brings together clashing proclamations, tracing in them a projection of reality, like Fedin in *Cities and Years* or Vesely in *Russia Bathed in Blood*; using the method later dubbed by the critics 'orthoepic recording', he tries to set down in words the raw material of sound, the rumblings and inarticulate voices of the crowd – like Malyshkin in *The Fall of Dair*. But ornamentalism is only one of the techniques which, as we know, Bulgakov had thoroughly mastered, and he has many others ready to deploy, as many as there are

---

[31] N. Dragomiretskaia, 'Stilevye iskaniia v rannei sovetskoi proze', in *Teoriia literatury*, Moscow, 1965, p. 161.

strands, spheres, kinds of situation and angles of vision in this novel. And they are applied with dazzling rapidity, now in succession, now at once in varying combinations, like the colours blended by an experienced painter.

The White Guard is orchestrated throughout by various means; it may even be over-instrumented in places, which is also in keeping with the spirit of the period. It has its own musical score, in which importance is given to the nervously casual strumming of the guitar against the background of the measured ticking of old grandfather clocks; the bird-like twitter of telephones resounding with bad news; the futile appeals of voices half-lost in the wires, as if the oncoming destruction had found material form; the unthinking bravado or the inappropriate sentimentalism of soldiers' songs,[32] which give a false impression of strength when sung in full voice; the passage in sound from the hallucinations of Karas' as he falls asleep to the thundering church choirs, and the constantly changing intonation, the individually contrasted sounds inserted like one trying his voice or tuning his instruments.

The novel has a highly complex visual scenario in which people and scenes appear out of the darkness as if picked out by a spotlight only to fade straight back into it, and in which long panoramic shots turn in an instant into huge close-ups. Images sometimes have the precision of realism and sometimes a measure of hyperbole. At times their contours are blurred in the rapid sequences; at others their slowed, solemn movement bespeaks a deeper symbolic meaning. Bulgakov is skilled at selecting the fleeting, telling detail in which a central meaning is focussed: Myshlaevsky's hand touching the tiles of the stove and concealing a light-hearted inscription, his face with its weak chin, 'as if the sculptor modelling an aristocratic face had got carried away in a flight of wild fancy and bitten off a lump of clay';[33] the face of Colonel Malyshev, on which Aleksei suddenly notices that there is no moustache; the droplets of spittle flying from Aleksei's lips as he delivers an impassioned tirade; the 'fox-like right eye and narrow lips not completely closed' of the absurd Hetman Skoropadsky. These are the brush-strokes of a skilled portrait artist who can exploit a detail to produce an impression of the whole.

---

[32] See Popov: 'It was important to me that the cadets should sing songs with utterly inappropriate lyrics.'

[33] *Romany*, p. 23.

The novel attempts to capture time, which arises before us in all its elusive and changeable forms, with its absence of finality. This is a period of great destruction, appropriately presented in a loose, shifting structure of images that seems to be sliding down a slope, and in a descriptive texture as fragile and tottering as the crumbling world order itself. It is therefore a conscious sequel to the technique of *Notes on Shirt-Cuffs*, now, however, without the spontaneity. The author's design keeps constant watch over the whole; the old naturalness of expression has now become a finely worked plan; the friability now has binding elements; the fragments cluster, when necessary, round fixed points and form hard, compact structures. The dynamics of opposing forces colliding and maintaining equilibrium reach into this area too. Besides the composition of its plot, *The White Guard* also has its internal structure, which is its own kind of solar system. At its centre is the House, – tangible, substantial, and unmoving, with 'stillness in its furnishings and disquiet in the hearts' of its occupants, – surrounded on all sides by the seething unrest of the city. The city in its turn, internally disunited but still existing as a structure, is surrounded by the accumulated 'twisted, peasant fury' of the Ukraine. The magnified centripetal weight falls on a small oasis of order and this pressure is felt physically in the novel; the bonds holding the Turbins' world together crack, but they still hold, so that hope need not be extinguished. They hold in the period we are shown, but we know from the beginning that 'the walls will crumble...' and so hope clashes and grapples with the irrevocability of that verdict.

The design may be interpreted in this way. But that is not yet all. The complex work of art that is *The White Guard* also has its autobiographical element built in. The tottering equilibrium affects the author himself and finds expression in the stance of the narrator. For most of the time-span of the novel he remains in the shadows, but slight inflectional overtones seem to betray his constant presence – like a man listening in to a telephone conversation and occasionally giving himself away. He is like a skilled impresario, who not so much links and announces scenes as reveals the action of creation, intervening in the very fabric of events. Such a narrator, in the precise definition given by Maksimilian Voloshin, is 'an accomplice of Fate in shaping the design of the play.'[34] But intervention from

---

[34] The position of the omniscient narrator should not be confused with the disjointed fragments of narration by other characters used as a form of 'skaz'. This especially concerns Nikolka, whose

another dimension is fundamentally impossible. Though all-powerful with regard to the world of his novel, its creator remains powerless with regard to his own past, and this powerlessness can be heard in the voice of the narrator. For all his appeals he can change nothing; exclamations like 'Never remove the shade from the lamp' and 'What are you showing them, Iakub Grigor'evich?' will not prevent anybody from leaving the house or avert innocent deaths. It is like the chorus in a classical tragedy; it is further confirmation of the cruel fate encountered by his main characters as they are dragged under the wheels of history. The narrator is fully aware of the deep irony of the situation, an irony which permeates and determines the behaviour of the characters, but again his hindsight can do nothing to help them. He too is therefore in an ironic situation; and the design of the work, carried into effect at all levels, comes full circle at this point.

Here Bulgakov gave a new function to a device which claims descent from Gogol. It was the author of 'The Fair at Sorochintsy' who taught Russian literature how to make a natural transition from descriptive passage to lyrical commentary and back, without disturbing the harmony of the narrative but instead endlessly extending its range; how to be at once inside the work and outside it, permitting the reader to sense the living breath of the author behind the voices of his characters. Bulgakov's narrator assumes his normal literary obligations, but beyond that, by his double presence in life and in the novel, 'there and then' as well as 'here and now', he gives further evidence of how difficult it was to live through the great crisis.

V

The novel which meant so much to the author, written with difficulty and at length in hours snatched from his night's rest in the years 1922 to 1924, had a troubled history. We know of this from documents and from two accounts given by Bulgakov. Of these *A Theatrical Novel* must be considered only a partial account, having been fictionalized, but no doubt authentic above all at the psychological level. The autobiographical sketch 'To a Secret Friend', however,

---

voice, identified by his characteristic 'ekh, ekh' in the Russian text, is heard for example on pp. 14, 21, 229 of *Romany*.

was written with the clear intention of giving an accurate record of events. In all essentials the accounts coincide.

The difficulties with *Notes on Shirt-Cuffs* and the final fiasco of its publication in book form were early signs that *The White Guard* would not have an easy passage.[35] However, the novel captured the interest of Isai Lezhnev, the editor of the journal *Rossiia* [Russia], which had printed an excerpt from *Notes* in early 1923 and in which Bulgakov had earlier received praise. The journal had had a stormy career; its earlier incarnation, *Novaia Rossiia* [New Russia], had become a bone of contention between the local Petrograd authorities and the Politburo, and owing to this the editorial offices had been moved to Moscow.[36] Here the journal appeared irregularly from 1922 to 1925, occupying an editorial position close to that of the 'Smena vekh' group. The energy and skill of Lezhnev, who persistently sought compromise formulae between the standpoint of the authorities and that of a substantial section of the intelligentsia, publishing Pil'niak, Remizov, Bely and Voloshin, among others, were dismissed by Bulgakov with the words, 'a great career clearly awaits Lezhnev as an editor and publisher.'[37] The prophecy was accurate, for the editor of *Rossiia* later forged a classically Stalinist career, based on the despot's whim. Before this, however, following the publication of two parts of *The White Guard* in numbers four and five of the journal for 1925, the monthly was finally closed down and Lezhnev and the publisher, Zakhar Kagansky, left the country. This so amazed Bulgakov that the idea of possible demonic intervention seemed the most natural thing in the world;[38] but this was only the beginning of a

---

[35] The novel was offered to the almanac *Nedra*, but rejected by N. Angarsky. (See the account in Chudakova, 'Arkhiv...', pp. 50-51, and the fragment there cited from a letter to Angarsky from Voloshin, p. 55: 'I am very sorry you decided against publishing *The White Guard*, particularly now that I have read an excerpt in *Rossiia*. One sees a text more clearly in print than in manuscript.')

[36] For an account of this interesting episode in the cultural policy of the period see Roy Medvedev, *Kniga o sotsialisticheskoi demokratii*, Amsterdam-Paris, 1972, pp. 223-24.

[37] Quoted in V. Chebotareva, 'K istorii sozdaniia *Beloi gvardii*', *Russkaia literatura*, 1974, No. 4, p. 152.

[38] In the autobiographical sketch 'To a Secret Friend', the narrator hears that the disappearance of Rudolf and Rvatsky (representing Lezhnev and Kagansky) is due to the expiry of a pact with the

long series of sudden disappearances and transpositions which always surrounded the writer and for which it was difficult to ascribe responsibility to any traditional devil. The fact that *The White Guard* entered the world of letters in incomplete form was also damaging in the extreme; the novel was both in that world and outside it, which was unambiguously disadvantageous to the author, for as late as the '60s all assessments of *The White Guard*, particularly the extreme views expressed during discussion of *The Days of the Turbins*, were based on an incomplete text, lacking the dénouement of the plot concerning the main characters, together with the crucially important concluding play of text and sub-text, dreams and fragments of reality.

This was not all. Kagansky, once abroad, announced that he held the rights not only to the novel but also to *The Days of the Turbins*, completed a short while later. Bulgakov, the victim of both moral and material injustice, issued a sharp protest, to no avail.[39] The upshot was that in 1927 a German edition of *Days* appeared in Berlin, made not from the final version of the play but from an earlier draft.[40] This was evidently also the version which found its way into the hands of émigré publishers in Riga, where a unique Russian version of *The White Guard* appeared in the same year.[41] Having to hand the greater part, but not the whole of the text, an anonymous compiler fashioned an ending from the fourth act of a draft of *The Days of the Turbins*. In doing so he rewrote much of the stage dialogue as

---

Devil. The sinners have been dispatched to Hell. *Novyi mir*, No. 8, 1987, pp. 164-201; also in *Dnevnik. Pis'ma 1914-1940*, Moscow, 1997.

[39] See the account in S. Liandres, 'Russkii pisatel' ne mozhet zhit' bez rodiny', *Voprosy literatury*, No. 9, 1966, p. 135. Bulgakov also had well-founded complaints against Lezhnev, as can be seen from, inter alia, his submission to the 'Conflict-Resolution Committee' of the All-Russian Union of Writers, in which he writes that, after the closure of the 'Rossiia' publishing house, Lezhnev had retained the conclusion of his *White Guard*, to which he had no right, and would not return it. He also requests that the matter be considered and his interests protected. (TsGALI, Fond 341, Part 1, ed. khran. 257; for this document I am indebted to Bulgakov's late translator Witold Dąbrowski.)

[40] M. Bulgakow, *Die Tage der Geschwister Turbin. Die Weisse Garde*. Autorisierte Übersetzung. (Bulgakov described this 'authorization' as a 'spurious statement'.) V. K. Rosenberg, Berlin, 1927.

[41] M. Bulgakov, *Dni Turbinykh*, Riga, 1927.

prose, adding such modified stage directions as 'Lariosik bridled', 'Elena backed away', and 'Shervinsky made a face'. Aleksei Turbin, who survives in the novel but perishes in the play, could therefore have nothing Bulgakovian to say, so he is silent, only occasionally borrowing phrases from Shervinsky or Myshlaevsky. The beginning and end of this part were now given a pseudo-atmospheric commentary, in trite and banal language, about the fate of the city. The product might be interesting as an example of a phenomenon rare in the history of literature, of the readaptation into prose of a work adapted from prose, were it not for the violence perpetrated upon the helpless author, violence, moreover, cynically masked by his name, since the preface, written by the émigré critic and writer Petr Pil'sky, says not a word about the procedure.

The nature of the fraud was made public only in 1929 in the introduction to the Paris edition of the novel, based on the full text and published with the author's consent.[42] In the same year the authentic version of the fabricated ending was published separately in Riga.[43] In the meantime, however, the fraudulent version, by right of being the supposed first edition, had been widely distributed and had begun to propagate itself in translations. Later, with time, the whole matter was lost to public view; and as late as 1966, when the full text was published for the first time in the Soviet Union in the volume *Izbrannaia proza* [Selected Prose Works], it was common to hear erroneous statements about the 'first version' or the 'variant' of *The White Guard*.

---

[42] M. Bulgakov, *Dni Turbinykh (Belaia gvardiia)*, Paris, Vol. 1 – 1927; Vol. 2 – 1929. The Introduction states, 'The Riga publisher "Literatura", which published Bulgakov's novel – without any permission from the author – had only that part of the novel which had previously been published in Russia. The publisher, however, undeterred by such a trivial obstacle as the absence of the authentic text, entrusted the editing of the first volume and the completion of the second to some deputy of "Count Amari", or possibly to the Count himself [a reference to Mikhail Tsetlin, 1882-1946, a poet, editor and publisher who used the pseudonym "Amari" – A.D.]. The "Count" discharged his commission conscientiously, leaving Bulgakov's novel in three parts, the first extraordinarily ineptly abridged and the third – the last 38 pages – having nothing in common with Bulgakov's text and entirely invented by a hack.' [The last statement is inexact, as the 'hack' was following the text of the play. – A.D.]

[43] M. Bulgakov, *Konets 'Beloi Gvardii' (Dni Turbinykh)*, Riga, 1929.

As if he did not have enough trouble and bad luck in his own country, Bulgakov therefore had to go to court to uphold his good name and his own rights in countries he would never set eyes on.

In the Soviet Union the fact that the novel was not known in complete form made it scarcely visible. Its unusual critical 'career' would begin shortly, when *The Days of the Turbins* came under heavy fire. *The White Guard* would then become useful as an additional point on the charge sheet, evidence of Bulgakov's incorrigible 'objectivism' and other grave, reactionary sins. One of the few early appraisals reads calmly, though with a deprecating slant:

'Bulgakov writes in a light and interesting manner... But – I hesitate to say this, though I believe it is true – it is first-rate refugee writing. (...) Everything is recounted in a very lively, vivid, "objective" fashion. The fact that the author does not show the White cadets as criminals, but as ordinary youths from a particular class milieu who are defeated along with their aristocratic officer-class "ideals", cannot be held against him. But the author, who published his work in *Rossiia*, lacks something important, a world-outlook closely bound to a well-defined social stance. Without this any artistic work is, unfortunately, emasculated.'[44]

Very similar accusations had once been laid at Chekhov's door, and Bulgakov could have replied using Chekhov's words: 'Conscious life without a well-defined world-view is not life but a terrible burden.' The burden of his spiritual boldness clearly weighed on him, and plenty of terrors lay ahead. This was not an exchange of views, however, but a case of the critic and the author speaking different languages. The critic's voice still sounded very restrained. His successors would deploy the usual invective and – drawing practical conclusions from the difference in language – would no longer permit the author the right of reply.

The demands of a time not very distant from the Civil War period required that enemies be shown without mercy, according to established class criteria. Such an approach was utterly alien to Bulgakov. He wrote of almost intimate matters, drawn from the circle of people close to him, knowing how complex these matters were. He tried to weigh them up and treat them fairly, even when this was painful, casting aside sentiment ('Enough of sentiment. We've over-sentimentalized our

---

[44] N. Osinskii, 'Literaturnye zametki', *Pravda*, 28.7.1925.

lives. Enough!' says Aleksei Turbin in a voice that is clearly Bulgakov's.)[45] He wanted to be loyal; occasionally he made minimal concessions, recognizing the reality of the censorship. He did not, however, adopt the conviction typical of some of his confrères that an attachment to a traditional hierarchy of values, to a firm system of ethics, was 'the cross of the intellectual', deserving to be trodden underfoot with a spasm of masochism in the name of the spirit of the new times. It was this spirit that he tried to capture and portray in its nascent state in this book. Against it he set his characters, battered but unbowed, defending what they saw as right. And he did not condemn them. On the contrary: he offered hope. Most of the critics did not read the ending of the novel, but of course they would have been confirmed in their reproaches if they had reached the author's last look towards the stars, when the reality of the book freezes into the crystal of a frosty night. Here a state of transparent saturation and balance of meanings is reached on the frontier of time, in the way the novel reaches out to the impending change and in its higher truth of dreams and reality. Everything is subject to catharsis, everything is spiritually cleansed under the high sky of Tolstoi's Austerlitz and Blok's 'Retribution', which Bulgakov will make his own. The glance towards the stars will be followed by a flight towards them – at this point the two novels come together.

Indeed, what kind of 'world-outlook closely bound to a well-defined social stance' emerges from this? Only a human one.

Bulgakov simply avoided the demands of the time. He could probably repeat after Pasternak, who wrote to Gorky when he sent him his poem '1905', 'the revolution should be seen historically, as a chapter among other chapters, as an event among other events, and given a palpable, non-sectarian, all-Russian dimension.'[46] He himself sought such a dimension, subsuming his experiences into the history of his country and its literary tradition. But all about him he could already hear the grinding of sharpened criteria. Intellectuals shown against the background of the revolution had to be shown confronting typical conflicts and divisions, so that, in the best case, chided and edified by right-thinking proletarians, they could meekly give their approval to phenomena which were bigger than they were. It is no surprise that sharp criticism was levelled at

---

[45] *Romany*, p. 101.

[46] *Literaturnoe nasledstvo*, Vol. 70, pp. 297-98.

Veresaev's *In a Blind Alley*, in which the Civil War is shown as a chain of mutual wrongdoing, each act giving rise to another act of bloody revenge, and in which an elderly Russian intellectual fails to see the logic of existence in the new situation. A suspicious view was taken of the protagonists of the first part of Aleksei Tolstoi's *Road to Calvary*, who tried to protect themselves by their feelings from the mayhem and remove themselves from the battleground of opposing forces. The incorrigible, inveterate intellectual was supposed to suffer a spectacular downfall, as happened with Pil'niak's inwardly divided heroes, harried by the consequences of their weakness, with Fedin's Startsov in *Cities and Years*, with Lieutenant Govorukha-Otrok in Lavrenev's *Forty-First*, who receives a bullet from the hand of his beloved as the final proof that 'being determines consciousness, even if the heart is no servant', and with Fadeev's Mechik, who at the moment of truth lets his comrades down. A chance was granted only to the penitent intellectual who bowed before historical inevitability in good time. In the course of time such heroes became much more numerous, but in spite of their waverings and uncertainties they were increasingly illustrative of attitudes; in the later works of Fedin, in the further parts of Tolstoi's trilogy, in Lavrenev's and Trenev's plays and many other works the movement of the characters became increasingly linear. Equations appeared with unknowns which only *seemed* to be unknown.

All of this ceased to satisfy in the atmosphere of partially rehabilitated historicism of the '60s, when matters of intellectual perspective and development were handled with a slightly greater degree of verisimilitude. It then emerged that Bulgakov had confronted these concepts and gone beyond them. His humanistic universalism had been borne out in life. Today *The White Guard* speaks to us of the scale of great historical changes and tells us how difficult it is at such times to preserve one's dignity and one's life at the same time.

'If the works of Andrei Platonov and Mikhail Bulgakov had appeared at the time when they were written,' Paustovsky once asserted sadly, 'the generations of today would enjoy far greater spiritual wealth.'[47] This is undoubtedly true, but it is no accident that *The White Guard*, though published in part, remained out of sight for many years. It was condemned to anathema and consigned to profound silence. The book's accents came too soon and were non-conformist, and therefore undesirable.

---

[47] K. Paustovskii, 'Budushchee nashei literatury', *Novy mir*, No. 11, 1967, p. 228.

All these factors came even more prominently to the fore during the period of the campaign unleashed around *The Days of the Turbins*.

The turn towards recent history thus proved just as difficult for Bulgakov as the attempt to penetrate the present. It is clear that he attached the greatest significance to that recent history. He wanted to investigate the most important matters, in the circle closest to him, against the background of his city, the House, the country of his childhood, among his close relatives, at the time of those events which had sucked him in and shocked him. He sought vitally needed answers to his question concerning the meaning of the choice he himself had made – or failed to make. As is clear from a number of statements, this was probably to have provided a theme to be developed in subsequent books.[48] But those books remained unwritten. It soon became clear that that route too, roundabout though it was, offered no honourable way out.

In his later writing, however, several strands from *The White Guard* reappear. We have only to recall the rescue of the hero by the prayers and pleading of a woman, or even women – Aleksei's life being saved by Elena; the conversion of the blasphemer; the meaning of those experiences which demonstrate that the traditional evil spirits whose advent is foreshadowed by Rusakov at the end of the novel pale beside human hell; as well as the higher truth of the starry night, whose light shows us the true order of things, and that last questioning look towards the sky.

As happens with the first major works by writers of great talent, *The White Guard* suffers from a certain *embarras de richesse*. Bulgakov deployed everything that he knew about writing, and the result was a degree of stylistic overloading of the material, a degree of over-instrumentalization. This too may have played a tangential part in the muted reaction to the work when it appeared in incomplete form. His readers' sensitivity had been dulled, assailed by the noisy and flashy effects of ornamentalism, and a work which seemed at first sight like yet another

---

[48] See Iu. Slezkin: 'The novel *The White Guard* is the first part of a trilogy. It was read by the author in three evenings at the Green Lamp literary circle.' (Nakanune, 9.3.1924, quoted in Chudakova, 'Arkhiv...', p. 52; see the same source for details about the literary circle, which was intended to be a forum for 'fantastical writers', and for another account in which 'the action of the second part was to take place on the Don, and in the third Myshlaevskii would serve in the Red Army'.)

variation on familiar themes in a familiar register may have made little impression. In reality the novel was above all different from its context, but this became clear only some time later, and only Maksimilian Voloshin wrote astutely and with little exaggeration in a letter that 'as the début of a beginner this can only be compared to those of Dostoevsky and Lev Tolstoi.'[49]

---

[49] M. Voloshin, letter, 25.3.95, in Chudakova, 'Arkhiv...'.

Chapter Five

An Essay in Recovered Dignity

I. Bulgakov the born thespian.
II. Pre-Bulgakov history of MAT. First contacts. Work on the stage version of the novel. First and second versions of the play. Imposition of the third version. Premiere of *Days of the Turbins*.
III. The nature of the play.
IV. The appeal of *Days*. A concert of 'second generation' MAT actors. Audience reaction.
V. Critical counter-attack; devastating criticism.
VI. Restrained criticism. Stalin's letter. No holds barred. The ban on the play.

I

Bulgakov was by nature a theatrical man of many parts.

He had received his initiation in opera and theatre in Kiev and had even dreamed of a career as a singer. He had performed improvisations for his family and friends and cruelly parodied his teachers. He combined a taste for fun and make-believe with the verve of an illusionist who sought to elude familiar modes of classification, baffle the outside world by the sheer variety of new incarnations and relish the pleasure of adopting new guises. As an adult he would use his gift for acting a part to amuse himself and others. He could be a little *chinovnik* from a story by Gogol or Chekhov, paralysed by respect for authority; he could be a government tax inspector, the terror of society of that time, imposing surtaxes without pity; he could be a little lost German with no knowledge of Russian, and, as Paustovsky recalls, 'all the guests who did not know him were quite convinced they were talking to a young German, and a complete idiot to boot.'[1] In reality

---

[1] K. Paustovskii, 'Bulgakov i teatr', *Mosty*, No. 11, New York, p. 385. Also in *Vospominaniia o Mikhaile Bulgakove*, Moscow, 1988, p. 103.

there were times when there was something of the *chinovnik* about him, and he had had his difficulties with inspectors. He was also familiar with situations of complete alienation. By acting these parts he could take his revenge for those moments when he himself was the victim; he could liberate himself from the roles earlier thrust upon him by voluntarily adopting a role of his own choosing, framing life in the quotation marks of make-believe. As we know, in his formal interactions, he was also in the habit of assiduously – even exaggeratedly – observing form, assuming the guise of a gentleman of the old school, though among his friends he would normally be livelier, wittier and at times even impetuous. His manner was half playful, a kind of pose, but of the best kind, based on his innate independence of spirit and a perverse determination to impose his own mini-order upon the world about him. On the larger scale, when he ceased to be a doctor he broke sharply with his own chosen vocation and transformed himself into somebody else. He changed his role in life.

But this brought out only one dimension of his theatrical nature, though perhaps the deepest. Apart from this he gravitated to the theatre as the home of art. He loved the magic that he felt on entering a theatre in the evening, between brightly-lit columns; he loved the expectant hubbub in the house, the mystery of the curtain, the holy of holies beyond the footlights, the dimming of the house lights before the play, the ambiguity of the wings and the dazzling power of acting talent. Here he was in his spiritual element; it is sufficient to immerse oneself in the passion and anguished pleasure with which Maksudov discovers for himself the world of the theatre in *A Theatrical Novel* to realize that Bulgakov must be writing about himself. Theatricality also lay close to the very essence of his talent, which was by nature the talent of a stage manager. Being the product of a world which had been destroyed, he liked the solidity of good theatrical realism, even verism, even conventional operatic excess. He gave sensitive descriptions of the Bolshoi, enjoyed the operettas of Grigorii Iaron, and poked fun at Meyerhold. In prose Bulgakov would have some innovations to his credit, but he preferred to see the theatre as a bastion of tradition.

There was also a third dimension – the creative dimension. From the very beginning there was a dramatic nerve pulsating in his early writing. He saw the world as a series of scenes, and characters manifested themselves to him through action and were defined in their words. Every piece he wrote for *Gudok* could easily be translated into live dialogue; the life of Moscow in the NEP period shaped itself into finished sketches. Earlier, in the Caucasus, his first literary attempts had been attempts at writing for the stage. The results were clumsy or conventional, but he was already trying via this form to approach the most important themes of his mature years.[2] *The White Guard* had almost classical unity of time; its main events take place in the space of twenty-four hours, and its structural symmetry held the possibility of shaping the action into scenes and acts; its crowd scenes, with pronounced vocal identification of individual figures and a series of short episodes, were essentially dramatic.

Pavel Markov, the veteran literary director of MAT, probably came closest to the core of Bulgakov's theatrical gift when he wrote, 'It is no surprise that he dreamed of being a director or actor, but the characteristics of his directing and acting were different from those required by the stage. He was the director and actor in his own works, and his imagination knew no limits.'[3] At another point Markov writes, 'If asked to act a play he had written, he would perform the whole thing, one role after another, and do it to perfection.'[4]

At the beginning of 1925 the idea of returning to theatrical work evidently became irresistible.[5] In *A Theatrical Novel* there is a well-known and oft-quoted account of Maksudov's first attempts at play-writing.[6] The account exudes such a spontaneous and naïve need for stage performance that it too must have some connection with the life of the author. Popov's notes also contain the characteristic admission, 'As for the question of which is more important to me – fiction or drama, as I see it, in the sense of setting one against the other, there is no

---

[2] In addition to this he was also master of ceremonies at a small Moscow theatre (see Chapter Two), but detailed information is lacking about this period, except for a mention in a letter to his sister Nadezhda (M. A. Bulgakov, 'Pis'ma k rodnym 1921-1922', published by E. A. Zemskaia, *Izvestiia AN SSSR. Seriia literatury i iazyka*, Vol. 35, No. 5, 1976, p. 543).

[3] P. Markov, 'O Bulgakove', in *Pravda teatra*, Moscow, 1965, p. 227.

[4] P. Markov, 'Istoriia moego teatral'nogo sovremennika', *Teatr*, No. 5, 1971, p. 80.

[5] See Bulgakov's handwritten note on a draft dust-jacket for an edition of *The White Guard* which in the end was not published: 'I began drafting the play *The White Guard* on 19th January 1925.' Quoted in L. Ianovskaia, 'Mikhail Bulgakov datiruet *Dni Turbinykh*', *Voprosy literatury*, No. 7, 1976, p. 315.

[6] Mikhail Bulgakov, *Romany*, Moscow, 1973, pp. 307-308.

difference; the two forms are bound together, just like a pianist's left and right hands.'[7]

At this time Bulgakov's freedom of movement as a writer of fiction clearly had perceptible limits upon it. The decision to turn to drama, a decision which was to determine a substantial part of his fate as a writer, may therefore have had to do with his spontaneous predilections and an attempt to find a way out of a difficult situation. Yet another change of roles came about, the adoption of another new identity. An opportunity appeared via a change of genre to find a way through the blind wall that barred his way.

It is curious that the finality of this decision should be underlined by an outsider, Boris Leont'ev, a member of the editorial staff of *Nedra*. In a note left in Bulgakov's flat in early May 1926, asking for a copy of *The Heart of a Dog*, he wrote, 'I beg you not to refuse at the moment your publishing affairs are coming to an end and you are moving into theatre. Let's part as friends.'[8] These words turned out to be disastrously prophetic: in this year Bulgakov's 'publishing affairs' did indeed come to an end – for the rest of his life.

A little earlier it had transpired that, without knowing it, Bulgakov and the Moscow Art Theatre were moving towards each other.

II

Bulgakov was ready for the meeting, while MAT was moving towards it at its own pace. In the third decade of its existence the splendid theatre was in deep crisis and was experiencing great difficulties in finding its place in the changed conditions. This was above all a crisis of attitudes among the intelligentsia, whose position MAT reflected and whose souls it had possessed for so many years. But it was also a crisis of established methods linked to a definite repertoire; a crisis in the repertoire itself and an organizational crisis, for in 1919 the civil war had cost the theatre part of its troupe.

---

[7] *Zametki avtobiograficheskogo kharaktera* (as recorded by Pavel Popov), Manuscript Department of the Lenin Library, Fond 218.

[8] Quoted in M. Chudakova, 'Arkhiv M. A. Bulgakova. Materialy dlia tvorcheskoi biografii pisatelia', in *Zapiski Otdela rukopisei Gos. Bibl. SSSR im. Lenina*, Moscow, 1976, p. 46.

The difficulty was compounded by sectarian attacks aimed at closing the theatre down. A theatre of this type presented a convenient target, although on the other hand some politicians and public figures (among whom Lunacharsky was especially active) tried to make it easier for the theatre to find its own *modus vivendi* under the new regime. In 1920 MAT became an academy theatre and two years later set out on an extended tour abroad. On its return in 1924 the question of establishing its identity became an urgent matter, essential for its continued existence. The management tended towards the stance of a group of promising young actors from student troupes. At that time they could have parts in plays in which the MAT veterans took precedence – those of the generation of Moskvin, Kachalov and Olga Knipper. While having an almost worshipful respect for their elders and for the hierarchy, the younger generation yearned for independence. They set about urgently developing a repertoire, and to this end formed what was called the youth repertoire collegium. When it became clear that there was a shortage of ready material for the stage, they turned their attention to the most interesting prose-writers, among them Leonov, Vsevolod Ivanov, Kataev and – Bulgakov.[9]

It was Boris Vershilov who brought news of *The White Guard*. In April 1925 he had written Bulgakov a short letter very like the one Maksudov receives in *A Theatrical Novel* from the director Il'chin, inviting him to come to the theatre.[10] Like his hero, Bulgakov may have been astonished to find in MAT a haven of a particular, almost mystical style, but the sedulously cultivated manners and climate of high culture, like the cult of tradition, must have been to his liking. It was no accident that, while dealing with other theatres, this was the one he singled out and, although in the longer term he did not find complete creative satisfaction in it, he at least found a starting point.

At first everything looked very promising. The young writer found himself dealing mostly with even younger actors. To judge from the reminiscences, he

---

[9] For a description of this period see Markov, 'Istoriia...', p. 77 ff.

[10] This letter appears in Ianovskaia, pp. 312-313. The author also cites an account by Pavel Antokol'sky – not confirmed in other sources – indicating that the Vakhtangov Theatre also approached Bulgakov and proposed *The White Guard*.

won them over immediately.[11] They sensed a fascinating personality and appreciated his imaginative talent and sense of humour. And it was not difficult to discern the dramatic potential of *The White Guard*. A decision was taken to have the author undertake the work of adapting it. This would be easier for him as he had already done some work towards it, although the theatre probably did not know that it was dealing with a dramatist as well as a writer of fiction. Work on the adaptation, which must have been extremely time-consuming, lasted throughout the summer of 1925. It resulted in the first stage version (under a different title), in five acts and sixteen scenes, which was offered to the theatre in September.[12]

In this version Bulgakov remained fairly faithful to the structural skeleton of the novel, leaving out only some of the secondary characters and lending the play something of the aura of a dream. This was achieved especially by making some scenes emerge from the darkness and fade back into it, and also by setting all the action in a frame provided by Nikolka and his guitar, also illuminated then swallowed up by the darkness. But all of this seemed too large and anti-theatrical for a theatre which was accustomed to classical settings. This was apparently successfully conveyed to the author, while at the same time there was a feeling that it was worth proceeding with, and, as Markov recalled, 'Bulgakov's supporters, who had already appeared in the theatre, would not give up hope of seeing *The White Guard* staged. Before long Bulgakov himself realized that a literal adaptation had poor prospects and set about a fairly radical recasting that affected the characters of his novel... In this he had the support of I. Sudakov, above all.'[13]

Some sense of the agonies of adaptation is conveyed in *A Theatrical Novel* in psychologically credible fashion, but with the necessary distance and with

---

[11] See for example E. Kaluzhskii, 'Chelovek i drug', in *Neizdannyi Bulgakov. Teksty i materialy*, ed. by E. Proffer, Ann Arbor, 1977, p. 48. Several other contemporary accounts may be found in a volume of memoirs about Bulgakov prepared some time ago for the Iskusstvo Publishing House. [This collection was eventually published by Sovetskii pisatel' in 1988, twenty-one years after it had been compiled: *Vospominaniia o Mikhaile Bulgakove*, compiled by E. S. Bulgakova and S. A. Liandres, Moscow, 1988. *Trans.*]

[12] For the first detailed description of the play as it took shape and its relation to the novel (then still not published in full in the USSR) see Ia. Lur'e and I. Serman, 'Ot *Beloi gvardii* k *Dniam Turbinykh*', *Russkaia literatura*, No. 2, 1965, pp. 194-203.

[13] Markov, 'Istoriia...', p. 80.

changes to some elements. As for Il'ia Sudakov, he was a product of the so-called Second Studio, linked to MAT, and was blessed not only with directorial talents but also with exceptional energy and the will to surmount obstacles. When appointed to direct the future play in place of Vershilov, who had originally been expected to do it, he mapped out a path which from the beginning was not going to be easy; both the author and the theatre well understood the reality they lived in. The nature of Sudakov's ingenious manoeuvres becomes clear when we compare some of the documents which have survived. In a letter to Bulgakov dated 5th October 1925, Sudakov invites him to the theatre and reports that rehearsals will begin soon and that 'after reading three acts, A. V. Lunacharsky said to V. V. Luzhsky [a member of the theatre management staff – A.D.] that he thought it an excellent play and saw no obstacles to staging it.' However, Lunacharsky's letter to Luzhsky, dated a week later, tells a rather different story. It is true that the People's Commissar for Education finds in the text 'nothing that is impermissible from a political point of view,' but, although he calls the author 'a very talented man', he regards the play as 'exceptionally inept except for a moderately lively scene showing the Hetman's departure', and he sets forth this view in no uncertain terms.[14] Of course, having finished reading the play – in its first version – , Lunacharsky could have changed his view. In the complex situation which arose later, he did develop a more subtly nuanced view. Besides this, either the theatre or Sudakov personally might have ventured a kind of bluffing tactic – as we might call it – of providing incomplete information to the author in order to encourage him to work on it further, in the belief that things would somehow sort themselves out. Whatever actually happened, the play, while still in its infancy, was evidently becoming the subject of exploratory, safety-oriented consultations, horse-trading and hedging.

But this was only the prelude.

In autumn and winter 1925 Bulgakov was working on a new version. It was presented to the theatre in January 1926.[15] It consisted of four acts and twelve

---

[14] This correspondence is held in the MAT Museum. Both letters are published in *Neizdannyi Bulgakov*, pp. 75-76. Unfortunately this edition, like many other Ardis publications, does not state the source of the material.

[15] A very perceptive analysis of the evolution of the final text of *The Days of the Turbins*, listing many importance sources, is given in Lesley Milne, *The Emergence of Mikhail Bulgakov as*

scenes and had gained in ease and elasticity compared to the prototype. There had also been a marked shift towards classical dramatic structure and the method of psychological realism, which was close to the MAT tradition. The blurred outlines and the dream-like quality had been deliberately toned down. A scene with clear echoes of Dostoevsky, in which Aleksei is tormented by a nightmarish apparition, expanded from a scene in the novel, disappears in this version.[16] This new incarnation of the Karamazov demon revealed to the hero the scene in Petliura's headquarters as a new dimension of Hell, and this device was very important to Bulgakov. Nevertheless he abandoned it. He also made fundamental changes to the role of Aleksei by having him absorb Malyshev and Nai-Turs to become the central figure who perishes in the culminating scene of Act Three. This in itself substantially altered the configuration of the cast as given in the novel, as *The White Guard* had no classical central figure. In the new version, Lariosik, the cousin from Zhitomir, arrives at the beginning and not only relieves the tension by providing a lighter, humorous treatment of life, but also introduces an important motif: a naïve belief in the magic power of the House. In Act Four, on the eve of Epiphany, the protagonists who gather after the death of Aleksei place rather less emphasis on their state of loss and their unclear prospects, while declaring their loyalty to Russia as the last lifeline of psychological salvation. Vasilisa, however, the neighbour from the downstairs flat, continues to have a role, and in the Petliura scene the torture of the innocent Jew is included – the trace of something which had clearly dealt the author a brutal psychological blow.

This version went to rehearsal at the end of January.[17] It was mature as theatre and at the same time faithful to the spirit of the novel, in spite of certain insignificant cuts. From the beginning Bulgakov was a difficult partner. In October 1925 he demanded that the management put his play on the main stage,

---

Dramatist, a dissertation submitted for the degree of Ph.D., University of Cambridge, 1975. The author was kind enough to make her work available to me, for which I am grateful.

[16] The apparition utters some lines which originate in Dostoevskii's *Devils* and are included in the novel *The White Guard*: 'Holy Russia is a wooden country, beggarly and... dangerous, and to a Russian honour is no more than a useless burden', see F. M. Dostoevskii, *Sobranie sochinenii*, Vol. 7, 1957, pp. 388-89.

[17] See Milne, *The Emergence...* A fragment of a record of rehearsals, from the MAT museum, has also been published in *Neizdannyi Bulgakov*, pp. 77-79.

not, as originally planned, on the smaller stage, that the play be produced in the current season, and that any changes that might be proposed be not of a fundamental nature. His first and last demands were accepted by the theatre,[18] but soon the problem of changes moved beyond the framework of the agreement between the two interested parties. The third factor was the censorship of the day, the so-called Repertoire Control Committee, known by the Russian acronym Glavrepertkom. This agency was officially subordinated to the People's Commissariat for Education (Narkompros), but this was a fiction from the very beginning. What determined the character of Glavrepertkom, as of Glavlit (the Central Office for Literature and Publishing), which was the senior body, was the fact of the presence in all such agencies, enshrined in law, of representatives of the NKVD and GPU.[19] This gave the censorship agencies a particular tone and scale of operation and allowed them to take little notice of their official superiors from Narkompros. The result was that Glavrepertkom implemented its own cultural policy and opposed the staging of almost all the outstanding plays of the period, including some of the quality of Vsevolod Ivanov's *Armoured Train 14-69*, Konstantin Trenev's *Liubov' Iarovaia*, Maiakovsky's *Bath-House*, and even Lunacharsky's play *Bears' Wedding* – which lends an added piquancy to the picture of this hierarchical system.[20] These plays were only staged after fierce

---

[18] Milne, *The Emergence...*, p. 264.

[19] See L. Fogelevich, *Deistvuiushchee zakonodatel'stvo o pechati*, Moscow, 1927, pp. 43-44. See for example, '2. The Repertoire Control Committee consists of three members: a chairman, appointed by the People's Commissariat for Education... and two members, one of whom is appointed by the People's Commissariat for Education and the other by the People's Commissariat for Internal Affairs (NKVD). For the consideration of general matters, a council comprising representatives nominated by the People's Commissariat for Education and the State Political Administration (GPU) is attached to the committee' etc. etc. A clear illustration of the true role of Glavrepertkom, which was designed to act as a preventive censor, is provided in this statement by a one-time functionary: 'The ideological and artistic guidance, for example, [of theatrical and concert performances – A.D.] was totally concentrated in the hands of Glavrepertkom' (O. Litovskii, *Tak i bylo*, Moscow, 1958, p. 324).

[20] See the material in A Lunacharskii, *Neizdannye materialy* (*Literaturnoe nasledstvo*, Vol. 82), Moscow, 1970, p. 387 ff., 394, 408 ff. Here the Commissar for Education is highly critical of Glavrepertkom and even speaks of the possibility of disbanding it. In reality, however, this body

battles, and who can say that the fiercest of them was not waged on behalf of *The White Guard*?

The theatre must have known of this in advance. This play was very important to it, and finding compromise formulae was no less important. In late March 1926 two acts of *The White Guard* were shown to Stanislavsky, who gave it a very high appraisal and at once suggested possible further changes to Bulgakov. In April, as a result, the scene in Vasilisa's flat was removed. But the pressure on the author clearly must have been constant. Only isolated traces of this can be seen, mostly in the rehearsal record (only part of which is published), but the drama of those few months may still be sensed. What emerges is a kind of play surrounding a play – and perhaps the larger drama should also be staged, alongside *The Days of the Turbins*.[21] Flattered at being singled out by this great theatre and offered the chance to have his most cherished dreams come true, Bulgakov, who was uncompromising in matters of principle but pragmatic in matters of detail, by permitting alterations 'if they're minor ones' gave way little by little, with the greatest reluctance. 'He could change a detail,' Markov recalls, 'only when he had finally become convinced that the change was essential.'[22] No doubt the most determined efforts were made, using arguments that had nothing to do with art, to persuade him of the need – but on this Markov is silent. On 3rd June Stanislavsky again considered the results of Sudakov's work. Direct evidence of the nature of the suggestions which emerged is contained in a letter written a day later by Bulgakov to MAT's board of management:

'I hereby have the honour to declare that I do not agree to the excision of the Petliura scene from my play *The White Guard*.

The reason for this is that the Petliura scene is an organic part of the play.

Nor do I agree to a change of title by which the play will be known as "Before the End".

Nor do I agree to the change from a four-act play to one of three acts.

---

does not seem to be under the control of his ministry. See also the mention of an incident involving Lunacharskii's own play, p. 381 of the same volume.

[21] For the sake of clarity it needs to be stated that the stage version of the novel *The White Guard* eventually went into production as *The Day of the Turbins*, a title foisted upon a reluctant author, who would have preferred to retain the title of the novel – *Trans*.

[22] P. Markov in *M. Bulgakov, P'esy*, Moscow, 1962, p. 8.

I agree to discuss another title for *The White Guard* with the theatre's board of management.

If the theatre does not accept the content of this letter, I request that *The White Guard* be withdrawn forthwith.'[23]

On 25th June the play, which had already been seen by a Glavrepertkom delegation, was discussed in that agency with MAT representatives present. The impression received was formulated in unambiguous terms: '*The White Guard* is a blatant apologia for the White Guards; from the scene in the high school to the death of Aleksei it is utterly unacceptable and cannot be staged with its current interpretation.' The theatre delegation signalled its willingness to make concessions. A list of these was dictated by Orlinsky, a member of the committee. Above all, 'the scene at the high school should be presented in such a way as to discredit the whole White Guard movement, not to show any White Guard heroics.' There was also a need to 'show the White Guards' relations with other social groups, with servants, janitors etc.' and 'to show some of the White Guards and representatives of the nobility or the bourgeoisie in Petliura's ranks.' A suggestion by Sudakov was also accepted, according to which, 'Nikolka, being the youngest, could become the spokesman of a turn towards the Bolsheviks.'

There was also discussion of technical questions, but it is not possible to ignore a parenthetical matter which came through at the end. The chairman of Glavrepertkom inquired 'whether the theatre accepted the corrections indicated by Comrade Orlinsky and whether these corrections compromised the theatre's integrity.' From the minutes it is clear that the MAT delegation avoided giving an answer to the latter question, declaring only that it was 'fully prepared to rework the play.'[24] To borrow Leskov's well-known description, police-censorship factors here demonstrated their 'administrative charm' in the very best spirit of times to come, when the victims of injustice would be obliged to make public statements about the justice of all that was happening to them.

The perversity of this blackmail would have appealed to Bulgakov's imagination, if he had found out about it, but certain specific matters no doubt appealed to it more directly. He was being asked to spoil his play. The spoilage

---

23 Text in MAT Museum; published in *Neizdannyi Bulgakov*, p. 80.

24 All quotations taken from 'Vypiska iz protokola soveshchaniia Glavnogo repertuarnogo komiteta s predstaviteliami MKhAT 1-go', *Neizdannyi Bulgakov*, pp. 81-82.

took place, though to a limited extent. The published excerpts from the rehearsal record provide minimal, but sufficiently clear evidence of the way this process was conducted. In the entries for late August and early September the words 'insert', 'cut' and 'amendment' occur repeatedly. The victims are above all the high school scene and the ending; it is not Nikolka but Myshlaevsky who declares his willingness to collaborate with the Bolsheviks. Various commentators from the early period and later do nothing to conceal the fact that the theatre exerted very heavy pressure on the author.[25] They even emphasize the extremely active role played by Stanislavsky in this procedure; this is quite probable, but caution must be exercised in the use of this evidence as it originated at a time when the view was being energetically propounded that in 'radicalizing' the play MAT did it a favour in spite of the author.

The writhings of the theatre and the author in the stranglehold of their Glavrepertkom controllers are a dramatic illustration of the cultural life of the period, though only one of many. Many elements remain unknown to us; only when the archives are opened will it be possible to arrive at a fair appraisal of the nature of the concessions, the opportunities to resist, the measure of responsibility, guilt and merit.

Whatever the case, in September events gathered pace. On 16th September the difficult matter of the title was resolved, to make it less meaningful, more neutral, and to suggest that it shows only a fragment of a larger picture. The next day the dress rehearsal took place with representatives of the public and of Glavrepertkom in attendance. The latter declared, '... in this form the play cannot be staged. The matter of permission remains to be resolved.'[26] Six days later the rehearsal record indicates that the scene showing the Jew being tortured had been removed and that the Internationale, which was played at the end, did not fade but grew louder. A sense of desperation is palpable here, of staking everything and clutching at almost desperate measures. Right up to the last moment it was not known whether anything would help. It is clear from various accounts that lances were being broken over *The Days of the Turbins* even within Glavrepertkom, as

---

[25] See for example N. Gorchakov, *Rezhisserskie uroki K. S. Stanislavskogo*, Moscow, 1952, pp. 323-324 and E. Poliakova, *Teatr i dramaturg*, Moscow, 1959, p. 43 ff.

[26] This quotation and the following one are from the rehearsal record as given in *Neizdannyi Bulgakov*, p. 77.

well as between it and other very important bodies.[27] The supporters and opponents of the play deployed stratagems and pressure, the complexity of which can only be guessed at.

On 23rd September what was probably another dress rehearsal took place, and four days later the decisive showing.

'At today's performance,' the rehearsal record notes, 'it will be decided whether the play can run or not.

The play is being performed with the latest cuts and without the "torture" scene.

Initially the first half of the first scene was very coolly received; then the audience was won over, the actors began to play with greater conviction, more boldly, and the audience reaction was wonderful.

At the end A. V. Lunacharsky expressed his personal view that the play could and most likely would run.'[28]

And so it was. The premiere performance took place on 5th October.

'Congratulations on your triumph!' wrote Meyerhold to Stanislavsky loyally and generously on the occasion.[29]

But the battle was just beginning.

III

The play which opened at the Moscow Art Theatre on 5th October was a theatrical work of high quality, though deliberately vitiated at certain points.

Like many other plays of this period (Lidiia Seifullina's *Virineia* and Leonid Leonov's *Badgers* before it and Vsevolod Ivanov's *Armoured Train 14-69* after it,

---

[27] See for example a fragment of Isidor Shtok's story 'Muzyka': 'The day before yesterday the dress rehearsal of *Days of the Turbins* in its revised form took place. The repertoire committee again banned the play. The Central Committee approved it. The members of the repertoire committee resigned. A meeting at the People's Commissariat for Education went on for two days. They argued till they were hoarse.' (I. Shtok, *Prem'era*, Moscow, 1975, p. 78.) The information about the meeting is confirmed by what Lunacharskii said at a party conference on theatre matters (See note 44).

[28] *Neizdannyi Bulgakov*, p. 77.

[29] V. Meierkhol'd, *Stat'i, pis'ma, rechi, besedy*, Vol. 2, Moscow, 1968, p. 103.

to name only the most important), *The Days of the Turbins* derived from a novel. Unlike most of the others, however, its genesis in fiction did not adversely affect the dramatic form. All the basic rules of drama are observed, so that it can be considered independently of its prototype. Its four-act structure make it a sequential whole. Act One sets forth the situation, introduces the characters and establishes the atmosphere in the House, the relationship between the residents and the visitors, the uncertain climate of expectation and Talberg's rat-like desertion. Act Two widens the horizon, replying to the Turbins' uncertainty with a picture of the contending forces: those of the Hetman and Petliura. Act Three, drawing together some scattered scenes from the first version as well as a number of characters from the novel, focusses attention on the figure of the hero, who resists the pressures put upon him; in the dynamic high school scene Aleksei Turbin dismisses the battalion and perishes. Finally Act Four, departing from the unity of time observed until this point, shows the characters in a situation like that at the beginning, but they are no longer all present, and they have changed.

At a time when an amorphous quality of dramatic form was seen as almost a requirement (if not a virtue) – the product, as in fiction-writing, of a sense of being jolted by seismic shocks – a theatre steeped in the classical dramatic conventions was the recipient of a play which seemed so professionally crafted that it might be the subject of a seminar study in the poetics of drama. It respected the rules of exposition, development, culmination and dénouement, with fully-rounded characters, and with dialogue that was organically attuned to the action on stage, furnished implicitly with a clear vision of the actors' movements and stripped of the rhetoric that was then so widespread.

Owing to this form and as a result of departing from the original dreamlike atmosphere, *The Days of the Turbins* necessarily lost the alternation of levels and meanings which was present in the novel, just as in places it lost its charming and sometimes exaggeratedly flickering forms, the density and depth of structure and the particular prerogatives of the narrative position. There also had to be a marked shift of emphasis: instead of a change in the course of history materialized as a catastrophe, the play personalized that change in terms of human destinies – manifesting this, of necessity, through the characters. The profoundly Bulgakovian motif of the individual enmeshed in adversity and driven to tragic action comes to the fore: the tragedy is fully played out, but the individual achieves the dignity of resistance. Colonel Malyshev's decision in the novel gains in significance many times over in its dramatic reprise by being taken by Colonel Turbin.

The conditions of censorship, however, placed their stamp on these organic features. Bulgakov knew very well what he was doing when he fought long and hard to preserve the scene in which the Jew is tortured to death; above and beyond his own most intimate experience, this scene provides a vital balancing element, in emotional terms. Without this scene the Petliura episode holds relatively little menace and might become a stock genre tableau which would not bring out the threat of extinction hanging over the world of the Turbins. The words pressed into Aleksei's mouth in the high school scene about the end of the White movement are totally lacking in psychological plausibility ('There on the Don, if you reach it, you'll find the same thing. You'll find the same generals and the same pack of headquarters rats. [...] They'll force you to fight your own people' etc.).[30] It is clear that a professional officer at the end of 1918, when the outcome of the civil war was by no means a foregone conclusion, would be more likely to use Colonel Malyshev's cautious phraseology ('...I think the best that each of you [...] can expect is to be sent to the Don') than the loud declarations that belong in some quite different psychological reality.[31] Moreover, according to a statement made several years later in all honesty by Sudakov, 'the theatre consciously strove to "radicalize" Myshlaevsky, working on the assumption that by doing so it would lend the play more acceptable political undertones.'[32] The result of this 'work' and of Bulgakov's fairly substantial concessions was an ending in which most of the characters, led by Myshlaevsky, place certain hopes in the Bolsheviks. This is eloquently accompanied by the strains of the Internationale, which, as we know, 'do not fade but grow louder'. This was a mechanical transplant of a piece of propaganda tissue, which, if it managed to take hold in the living body of the play, did so thanks to the professional skill of the author and the talent of the performers. A trace of the anxiety this must have caused Bulgakov may be heard in the suppressed sarcasm in his words, 'There was no music when Petliura's men and

---

[30] *P'esy*, 1962, pp. 88-89.

[31] *Romany*, p. 108

[32] I. Sudakov, 'Rezhisser i avtor', *Teatr i dramaturgiia*, No. 3, 1934, p. 37.

the Bolshevik forces entered Kiev. The march and the Internationale were my own invention.'[33]

One of the epigraphs of *The White Guard* speaks of the dead being judged 'according to their works'. Any judgement of the concessions to the authorities made in Bulgakov's day must be tempered by an awareness of the actual conditions in which they were made and how far they went. The concessions made by the author of *The Days of the Turbins* were relatively modest. In a more detailed analysis the direction they followed should be carefully traced and they should not be confused with the changes imposed by the demands of the stage. His concessions did indeed go some way towards upsetting the complex of meanings which *The White Guard* presents in such polished fashion and which Bulgakov wished to preserve. According to the original design, the cataclysm which sweeps over the characters leaves them nothing at the end beyond their faith in the course of life and the belief that 'everything will find its place.' The changes which were imposed instructed the denizens of the House to 'grow' to accept the incoming regime, which, thanks to the sedulous efforts of its propagandists and censors, was in this way constructing for itself a false genealogy. The result was that *The Days of the Turbins* was shifted closer to other works which employed examples from the intelligentsia to illustrate the functioning of Marxist determinism, though fortunately this play maintained its distance from the simple-mindedness of most of them.

In the first fifteen years of the life of the play this levelling and skewing of its meaning were masked by its qualities. In this sense we may cautiously state that the concessions forced upon the author 'paid off', in so far as this was the price paid for the very existence of a play which for its time was unusual: it was a valuable antidote in the consciousness of its audience, something which could profoundly reshape that consciousness. But only the author himself could rule on the matter of whether and how far such a compact with one's conscience is permissible. It is clear, however, that today *The Days of the Turbins* should be staged not according to the final and officially published version, but following the so-called second redaction, the one presented to the theatre in early 1926, as this is

---

[33] *Zametki...*

the fullest embodiment of Bulgakov's design.[34] Some decisive action towards this end would be of benefit both to the play and to the memory of its author.

IV

The play which began its run at the Moscow Art Theatre on 5th October was more than a well-crafted play. It was also a daring challenge, and this despite all the losses it had suffered.

Bulgakov threw down the gauntlet to the hitherto dominant stereotype of the opponent, questioning, as I. Nusinov wrote indignantly, 'the attitude to the Whites which has rightly prevailed and which has made the words "Denikinite" and "White officer" synonymous with violation, betrayal, destruction and rabid animals.'[35] But since the Turbins' circle was the intelligentsia in uniform, the scale of the matter was broader. The undecided had also earned the right to some dignity; this meant those who had kept their distance, wrestling with themselves and their own doubts. Here the play filled a powerfully-felt social need. There were many who craved such moral rehabilitation. This was the moment when it seemed that the time had come: it was no accident that a year later Iurii Olesha's *Envy* appeared, dramatically posing the question of the uses of an intellectual's spiritual baggage in the new times. Before long the harsh criteria of the intensified class struggle would loom over all this, but for the moment Bulgakov succeeded again in showing the severe loss suffered by people who deserved better, and he did this soberly and fairly. This was sufficient, at such a time, for him to shine like a dazzling new star and also display mature artistic argumentation.

The first to succumb to its fascination were the performers, for whom the play became not merely a great artistic opportunity, but also a means of self-determination. Actors who were, as Markov tells us, 'twenty-five or twenty-seven immersed themselves in what they knew and had experienced; none of them was indifferent to the play.'[36] At first it was expected that the 'veterans' would have

---

[34] The first to state this was Lesley Milne. It is evident that the distortions forced upon the author are an impediment to its current theatrical life and prevent it from occupying the place it deserves in the repertoire.

[35] I. Nusinov, 'Put' Mikhail Bulgakova', *Pechat' i revoliutsiia*, No. 4, 1929, p. 45.

[36] Markov, 'Istoriia...', p. 82.

roles in it, but in the end the play was taken over entirely by the second MAT generation, who made of it a kind of personal manifesto. This had its effect on the fevered atmosphere of the rehearsals, at which everybody was aware of what was at stake; due recognition is also given in the memoir accounts to the part played by Bulgakov himself, who took on some of the duties of assistant director and gave very helpful suggestions to the actors.

'Bulgakov captured the theatre not only by his talent,' writes Konstantin Rudnitsky. 'He also won it over as an ideologue, able to state most forcefully and accurately the Moscow Art Theatre's view of Russian reality. This was the reason why, after long years of artistic stagnation, frustration, squabbles and disputes, an atmosphere of joyful excitement, enthusiasm and creative unity arose during the work on *The Days of the Turbins*.'[37]

As a result, the play entered history – and legend – thanks to the actors' performances.[38] Aleksei was played by Nikolai Khmelev, economically and with careful consideration to detail in gesture and attitude. From the beginning a taut sense of impending defeat undermined Aleksei's resolve and the self-confidence expressed in his reactions and responses. When in the culminating scene he stood still on the high-school steps above the crowd of disorientated cadets – with his left hand in the pocket of his fur jacket and his right thumb hooked on a button, his face expressionless and his erect silhouette bristling slightly – he became the embodiment of the failure of the cause Aleksei served, and at the same time elevated this failure to the status of true tragedy. Mikhail Ianshin as Lariosik established himself for decades in the memory by his natural charm and comical helplessness; but his comic side also had the special warmth of a natural goodness, for which the play and its audience very clearly felt a need. Of several actresses who played Elena the one best remembered was Vera Sokolova, with her particularly captivating feminine charm, vibrant sensitivity and her timid and natural longing for happiness. Opposite her Mark Prudkin played a dashing Shervinsky, an inspired yarn-spinner and ladies' man, who is at the same time a good-hearted person with Khlestakov's way of telling tall stories which he himself believed. Boris Dobronravov was superbly equipped for the roles of convincing positive heroes;

---

[37] K. Rudnitskii, *Spektakli raznykh let*, Moscow, 1974, p. 236.

[38] In a number of accounts of the performance, the following stands out by its precision: N. Zorkaia, 'Dni Turbinykh', *Teatr*, No. 2, 1967, p. 14-21.

his Myshlaevsky was thoroughly plausible, with his spontaneity and the straightforwardness of his enforced 'radicalization' covering the traces of the violence done to the play. As tradition required, the performance was finely honed in every detail of the acting and *mise-en-scène*. In the staging, every effort was made to pick out the internal rhythms and provide counterpoint to the changing mood. Nikolai Ul'ianov, the scenographer, gave the domestic scenes an authentic warmth and cosiness by means of soft pastel colours. The Hetman scene in Act Two introduced some hyperbole, the false pathos of exaggerated gestures, and an element of grotesquery parodying the well-known device of comic changes of clothes. True to its genesis, the Petliura scene had the atmosphere of a sinister nightmare – with spectral figures, much play of light and shade and shrill musical motifs; at the end everything dissolved into darkness. Act Three was propelled along by the surging ebb and flow of a carefully orchestrated crowd, which gradually lost its cohesion and became a mob of refugees; towards the end the spread-eagled body of Aleksei lay motionless on the steps in a last sacrificial gesture of atonement for the sins of all. The return to the House immediately after this, according to one commentator, 'repeated the motifs brought out previously and the features of the characters, encapsulating them in a succinct funereal coda – like the last slowly falling stones as an avalanche comes to an end.'[39] Finally Act Four recalled the framing of Act One, closing the play in a suggestive situational circle: the same people, in the same place and a similar situation, are shown to be somehow different, and here the stage-manager did his best to ensure that, although Aleksei was dead and Nikolka wounded, in spite of everything there were still grounds for hope.

'To the new generation of MAT the *Turbins* has become a new *Seagull*,' wrote Vasilii Sakhnovsky in 1934, looking back from the five hundredth performance and referring to the beginning of the theatre's artistic history, which opened with Chekhov's play.[40]

---

[39] Ibid, p. 20.

[40] Letter to Bulgakov on the occasion of the 500th performance of *Days of the Turbins*. *Neizdannyi Bulgakov*, p. 90. [*The Seagull* was not, in fact, MAT's very first production. This honour is claimed by A. K. Tolstoi's *Tsar Fedor Ioannovich*. It is true, however, that *The Seagull* is widely considered the production with which the new theatre first made its mark. – *Trans.*]

The enthusiasm of the players, despite all the difficulties, communicated itself to the audience, who – by all accounts – were no less enchanted. Apparently the immediate reaction from the audience at the premiere was surprise and astonishment, as might be expected: until now nobody in Russia had spoken publicly of these matters in this manner or language. Then came an outburst of enthusiasm, which became the hallmark of the performances that followed. Very likely because of the extremely tense atmosphere in the wings before the premiere, the author allowed himself a curtain call only after the second performance. The play was at once surrounded by an air of sensation, further whipped up by furious massed attacks by the critics and rumours that it might soon be taken off.

There is no doubt that different spectators viewed the play with different feelings. Large numbers of intellectuals went to the theatre (often saying 'let's go and see the Turbins', to give an intimate emphasis to the importance of the meeting) to reassert their dignity, which had so often been called into question. On stage they saw people like themselves, whose personal values stood in opposition to the mechanistic patterns of class determinants. They saw people who could suffer defeat with honour, with the courage of the decisions they had taken, even with grace. The best of Bulgakov's characters achieved a heroic dimension; the others could at least touch them and evoke sympathy. On occasion, when on stage there was a knock at the door of the House, there came a cry from the audience, 'Open up! We're friends!'[41] At the end there were often cries of 'Thank you!' The degree to which part of the audience identified with the play was extraordinary, even for the Russian theatre, which traditionally is highly charged with emotion.

It is curious that the proletarian spectators, the Komsomol element and even some activists, influenced by the play, found, often to their surprise and horror, that their simplistic pseudocriteria and thought patterns had been called into question. The human thrust of the play had the most direct emotional impact and awakened dulled sensitivity. From this point of view the play's genuinely educational role – in the deepest sense – cannot be over-stated, although it defies accurate measurement. In a way this anticipated the much larger social role being played by Bulgakov's writing in today's struggle to restore normal human consciousness.

---

[41] See e.g. L. Belozerskaia-Bulgakova, *O, med vospominanii*, Ann Arbor, 1979, p. 46.

'We, the audience that came to *The Days of the Turbins* in the late '30s, having come to view the White Guards as degenerate neurotics, drug-addicts and terrorists,' Zorkaia recalls, 'took the Turbins to our hearts and this "contradiction" did not bother us in the least.'[42]

This was, then, an unusual play – and something more than a play. There is a view that it was the Moscow Art Theatre's best play ever, but this is not the sort of thing that can be verified. It is certain that it was one of the most significant events in Russian drama. Among the older generation there are many who saw it a dozen times or more.

V

The theatre and the author had won their first battle when they succeeded in getting *The Days of the Turbins* staged. But the strain of combat did not slacken for an instant, as their adversaries immediately launched a counter-attack. The play surrounding the play entered its second act.

This was a massed counter-offensive. Bulgakov himself spoke of the three hundred reviews and notices preserved in the family archive, of which two hundred and ninety eight were utterly hostile.[43] A study of this archive, carefully compiled by the author, shows that nine tenths of the material derives from the period 1926-1929 and is the result of a press campaign against Bulgakov's plays, of which *The Turbins* was subjected to the most ferocious attacks.

Some of the opponents had their work made easier by the fact that, working in Glavrepertkom and perhaps other more important agencies, they not only edited professional journals and wrote theatre criticism, but also sat on the executive of artistic associations. Therefore the more aggressive they were, the greater the range

---

[42] Zorkaia, p. 21.

[43] See the text published as 'Pis'mo Bulgakova Sovetskomu pravitel'stvu', *Grani*, No. 66, 1967, pp. 154-161. Fragments of this, in a slightly different version, are cited in S. Liandres, 'Russkii pisatel' ne mozhet zhit' bez rodiny', *Voprosy literatury*, No. 9, 1966, p. 138. L. Belozerskaia (p. 99) questions the authenticity of this letter. It is possible that it is a draft or a version of a personal letter. [Also in *Novyi mir*, No. 8, 1987, pp. 194-198 and *Dnevnik. Pis'ma. 1914-1940*, Moscow, 1997, pp. 222-228; in English translation in Lesley Milne, *Mikhail Bulgakov: A critical biography*, Cambridge, 1990, pp. 268-274 – *Trans.*]

of opportunities open to those who were prepared to act in the spirit of the well-known Russian saying 'by drubbing if not by scrubbing' or 'by hook or by crook'. It was none other than Lunacharsky – by no means the most aggressive figure involved – who publicly stated a little later, 'We decided to respond to the play with some degree of criticism.'[44]

And so it was. 'Some degree' of criticism can be seen clearly in the headlines: 'Against Bulgakovism', 'Down with *The White Guard*!', 'Where is MAT Heading?', 'In Judgement on *The White Guard*', 'Four Steps Backwards', 'Citizen Bulgakov's False Coin'. The conclusions drawn were no less categorical. 'What can a Soviet spectator care about the sufferings endured by external and internal émigrés because of the premature death of the White movement?' asked Osaf Litovsky, a censor and one of Bulgakov's most implacable life-long enemies. He answered, 'Absolutely nothing. We do not need this.'[45] Orlinsky, another functionary, concluded that 'the play is a tendentious demonstration of the supposed mass heroism of the Whites. It idealizes the White Guards and essentially distorts the Civil War period.'[46] And Vladimir Blium, the head of the theatre section of Glavrepertkom, roundly condemned by many for his excessive liquidatory zeal but clearly quite influential, an enemy of Chekhov, Tchaikovsky, satire of any kind and therefore of Bulgakov, asserted a year later that by staging *Days* on the eve of the tenth anniversary of the October Revolution MAT was 'taking up a stance outside the joy and triumph of millions of working people.'[47]

The critical functionaries and the critics without official positions were at one in their conclusions, though their views differed as to the details. 'It is no more than a competently made tearjerker' said Litovsky condescendingly.[48] 'There is no art in it whatever, of course, and the theatre's and the author's pitiful wavering between one title and another clearly exposes the artistic worthlessness of the play,'

---

[44] A. Lunacharskii, 'Zakliuchitel'noe slovo', in *Puti razvitiia teatra, Stenograficheskii otchet i resheniia partiinogo soveshchaniia po voprosam teatra pri Agitprope TsK VKP(b) v mae 1927*, Moscow-Leningrad, 1927, p. 232.

[45] *Komsomol'skaia pravda*, 10.10.1926.

[46] A. Orlinskii, 'Grazhdanskaia voina na stsene MKhAT', *Pravda*, 8.10.1926.

[47] V. Blium, 'Nachalo kontsa MKhAT', *Zhizn' iskusstva*, No. 43, 1927.

[48] O. Litovskii, '*Dni Turbinykh* v Moskovskom Khudozhestvennom Teatre', *Glazami sovremennika*, Moscow, 1963, p. 226.

said Blium in the tone that was his trademark.[49] 'The only thing that can justify the play is the acting, which is first-rate and of unforgettable power and talent,' said Litovsky.[50] 'The better they [Sokolova and Ianshin] act, the worse for the author, for the theatre and for these actors themselves,' said Blium.[51] 'It is clear to me now that MAT has a white centre,' said one of the participants in the discussion headed 'In Judgement on *The White Guard*'.[52] 'And yet, even *The Days of the Turbins* is a great step forward for the Moscow Art Theatre,' said Lunacharsky.[53] 'This seems to me a logical and expected culmination: they started with Auntie Manya and Uncle Vanya and ended with *The White Guard*,' wrote Maiakovsky.[54] 'Compared to the White Guards, Petliurovism (which was revolutionary, even if it was petty bourgeois) [...] is closer and more akin to us,' wrote Blium.[55] 'After all, we all know just how revolutionary Petliura's men were. In the play they are brave and dashing Zaporozhians, not even much given to brawling,' [?! - A.D.] said Litovsky.[56] 'The fury with which Bulgakov depicts Petliura's forces is no doubt partly due to his hatred for that armed, rampaging "lout",' said Lunacharsky.[57]

In this contest, then, anything the writers fancy may be used against the author. Orlinsky, the source of the 'corrections' pointed out to MAT at a meeting with the censor, was not slow to return to them yet again, also criticizing the play for not showing 'a single orderly',[58] which this time was seized upon by Blium: 'Indeed: we see the White officers without any orderlies; there is a whole banquet

---

[49] V. Blium, 'Eshche o *Dniakh Turbinykh*', *Programmy Gosudarstvennykh Akademicheskikh Teatrov*, No. 57, 1926.

[50] Litovskii, *Glazami...*, p. 227.

[51] Blium, *Programmy...*

[52] 'Sud nad *Beloi Gvardiei*', *Novyi zritel'*, 13.10.1926.

[53] A. V. Lunacharskii. 'Dostizheniia teatra k deviatoi godovshchine Oktiabria', *Izvestiia*, 14.12.1926; also in A. V. Lunacharskii, *Sobranie sochinenii v vos'mi tomakh*, Moscow, 1964, Vol. 3, p. 338.

[54] *Novoe o Maiakovskom*, Moscow, 1958, p. 40.

[55] Quoted by Zorkaia, p. 19

[56] Litovskii, *Glazami...*, p. 227.

[57] Lunacharskii, *Sobranie sochinenii*, Vol. 3, p. 327.

[58] A. Orlinskii, 'Protiv Bulgakovshchiny (*Belaia Gvardiia* skvoz' rozovye ochki)', *Novyi zritel'*, 12.10.1926

scene, but they have no servants.'[59] The absurdity of this charge even shook Bulgakov's resolve to keep his distance from the campaign: 'even if I had really wished to show those orderlies I couldn't have done, because there weren't any,' said the author in his only recorded public statement during a discussion of the play. 'Moreover, even if I had shown such an orderly, I can assure you that this would not have satisfied the critic Orlinsky. Of this I am quite convinced.'[60]

This last observation hit the mark: the orderlies were not the issue. 'The Turbins' epaulettes immediately drew forth the blind rage of the critics,' wrote Al'tshuler. 'They saw before them an enemy who as yet had neither any precedent in the theatre nor any right to exist – at least not in the aesthetics of MAT.'[61] We may add: they saw an enemy defeated and eliminated from the struggle by proxy, by the hand of Petliura; an enemy who admits defeat and is shown amidst ironic nuances, which the play points up more than the novel.[62] But this was no help. Even in the slightly more relaxed climate of NEP the demands made upon the artist in fundamental matters remained categorical. The play was perceived to be a weapon in the ideological struggle and the artist was required to declare that he was on the right side. Only when he had made this clear did he gain relative freedom to manoeuvre in matters of detail.

---

[59] Blium, *Programmy...*

[60] Quoted in V. Petelin, 'M. A. Bulgakov i *Dni Turbinykh*', *Ogonek*, No. 11, 1969, p. 26. Other versions also exist of Bulgakov's speech during the discussion (of *Days of the Turbins* and *Liubov' Iarovaia* by Trenev at the Meyerhold Theatre on 7.2.27). The account quoted here is based on the stenographic record, held in TsGALI (Fond 2355, ed. khran. 5), which seems the most reliable source.

[61] A. Al'tshuler, *Dni Turbinykh' i 'Beg' M. Bulgakova v istorii sovetskogo teatra 20-kh godov*. A dissertation presented for the degree of Candidate of Art History, Moscow, 1972, p. 14.

[62] The irony is most telling in connection with Lariosik, but not only here. The whole of Act Four, for example, in which an attempt is made to maintain the ritual of observance of the holiday in conditions of great uncertainty, is profoundly ironic – in the Chekhovian sense of 'a conspiracy against Fate' (N. Berkovsky's definition). Conscious references to certain of Chekhov's motifs and situations are clear in the play, and the author introduces deliberate signals (for example, Lariosik carries the works of Chekhov with him), which are partially negated or inverted. For more detail see A. Al'tshuler, '*Dni Turbinykh...*', p. 18 ff.

Bulgakov rejected this enforced subordination to the prevailing ideology and blind acceptance of the *fait accompli*. It was not that he utterly denied that it had any basis. But he reserved for his characters the right to choose, and for himself the right to be an objective witness. He stood above preordained positions. Having the highest respect for the profession of writer he strove to pursue it as the great writers of the previous century had done – as an independent arbiter or, at least, a witness to events, for in this play that essentially Chekhovian stance was closest to him.

Something far more important and profound was therefore at stake than those epaulettes: a question of a public stance. Even at this early stage a stance such as this did not have the right to be publicly proclaimed. Least of all in the theatre, in a dramatic form which made manifest and underscored problems – and supplied an instant audience reaction to magnify them. Least of all in a mature and therefore highly suggestive artistic form. Least of all now, at this distance, with those enemy uniforms that so offended the sight.

Some of the critics of the day were no doubt bedazzled young neophytes, for whom the gleaming epaulettes were more than enough. But others, like Litovsky, upheld the rightness of their position to the end of their days.[63] Some, like Blium or Beskin, were about fifty at the time of the campaign against *The Turbins* and had been writing long before the revolution. It is true that Meyerhold said that Blium was 'basically irresponsible' and Lunacharsky called him 'half-mad'; but his half-madness conformed to the norms of the new times, so there was method in it, and the half-mad knew very well what they did.

The efforts made by Konstantin Simonov are typical. Over forty years later, in a letter to an unnamed correspondent, he explains that 'the problem of *The Days of the Turbins* was very much more complicated than it might appear today,' because '... only six years separated the period from the storming of Perekop and only four from the fall of Vladivostok'; because 'this was a problem related also to the situation of the state, the regime and the party in a peasant country, in which, be it added, a new *kulak* class was then appearing'; and because 'there was also the problem of the absolute, overpowering military superiority of the capitalist

---

[63] See the works cited, *Tak i bylo* and *Glazami sovremennika*, in which the author consistently denies – often distorting or altering details – that Bulgakov's plays have any value.

encirclement.'[64] And so on. In short, the campaign against the play is explained by the circumstances of the state of emergency. It is also true that many decades after the storming of Perekop, after the destruction of the 'new *kulak* class' and after military parity with capitalism – if not military superiority – had been achieved, nothing even remotely approaching the ideological challenge of *The Days of the Turbins* ever occurred in the Soviet theatre. Writing in the same article about *The White Guard* and making a visible effort to find sufficiently balanced epithets, Simonov states that in the novel Bulgakov's position is 'far from generally accepted views.'[65]

A word to the wise. Like *The Heart of a Dog*, *The Days of the Turbins* received the treatment it fully deserved, according to the criteria which applied at the time and thereafter, criteria soon to be enshrined in the succinct formula 'he who is not for us is against us', with all the consequences that flowed from it. The mere fact that it could be staged in these conditions was an extraordinary gift of fate, along with the fact that the campaign surrounding it could take place in an atmosphere of public accountability. The enthusiastic public pressure which countered the verdict of the critics further inflamed their wrath. There was still a remnant of normality in a world from which normality was departing.

VI

Bigoted criticism predominated, but it did not have the field entirely to itself. A restrained position was adopted towards the play by, for example, Valerii Pravdukhin, a well-known literary figure and critic, who wrote that, 'by showing with talent "anti-Soviet" people he [Bulgakov – A.D.] was performing the useful service of depicting reality.'[66] When attacked at once for 'critical colour-blindness'[67] (it should be stressed that by the criteria of the day this charge was also fully applicable) by Grigorii Gorbachev, one of RAPP's most aggressive critics, Pravdukhin upheld his point of view:

---

[64] K. Simonov, 'Razgovor s tovarishchami', *Voprosy literatury*, No. 9, 1968, p. 86.
[65] Ibid.
[66] V. Pravdukhin, 'Literatura signaliziruet', *Krasnaia vecherniaia gazeta*, 27.2.1927.
[67] G. Gorbachev, 'Kriticheskii dal'tonizm', *Leningradskaia pravda*, 20.3.1927

'I said and I repeat that it is to be expected that Bulgakov should be popular and widely read and that his play should unfortunately enjoy the greatest success. All this testifies to the mood of the reader, and by no means only the bourgeois reader.'[68]

A highly ambiguous standpoint was adopted by Lunacharsky, who viewed *The Turbins* from several different angles at once: as a dramatist and critic who practised and advocated a quite different kind of repertoire; as a native of Poltava and former pupil of the same school but with completely different experience; and lastly as a political and cultural figure who, on account of this play, had to wage a complex struggle in a fairly difficult situation. Hence the extremely convoluted course of his arguments. From the beginning he maintained that the play was 'not dangerous..., moreover nothing to be afraid of', that a ban on performance would be 'utterly counter-productive'[69] and that 'the production of plays like it should be greeted with satisfaction.'[70] With time he increasingly emphasized his belief that *Days* had played a positive role in drawing MAT closer to the new reality.[71] It is clear that this is what mattered most to him. At the same time, in giving his view of the play he was competing with the most implacable of critics when he spoke of the 'political idiocy' that typified the characters and their desire for 'petty-bourgeois creature comforts',[72] of the 'atmosphere of canine copulation surrounding the red-haired wife of some friend', of the fact that Bulgakov himself 'like his characters was a political innocent' and 'the central comic figure in his play'.[73] Behind this may lie both conviction and tactics – adopting the style and tone of the extremists the better to guard against their attacks. In this context we should also note the truly masterful piece of demagogy by which, at a party meeting devoted to theatre matters, Lunacharsky went one better than the arch-demagogues of the stamp of

---

[68] V. Pravdukhin, 'Lenivye umy', *Krasnaia vecherniaia gazeta*, 27.3.1928.

[69] Quoted in M. Broide (debate on Lunacharskii's report at a discussion entitled 'The Theatrical Policy of the Soviet Government', held on 2.10.26). *Programmy Gosudarstvennykh Akademicheskikh Teatrov*, 1926, No. 54.

[70] A. Lunacharskii, 'Dni Turbinykh', *Krasnaia gazeta*, 5.10.1926.

[71] See the articles and speeches in A. Lunacharskii, *Sobranie sochinenii v vos'mi tomakh*, Vol. III, Moscow, 1964, pp. 337-338, 345, 483.

[72] Quoted in Broide.

[73] Lunacharskii, 'Dni Turbinykh'.

Blium and Orlinsky by effectively seeking to demonstrate that they were the ones, with Glavrepertkom, who were responsible for staging *The Days of the Turbins*.[74] And he added immediately, 'I don't think we have any other writer so clearly counter-revolutionary as Bulgakov. But he sets an example. Moreover his plays are fashioned with exceptional skill.'[75]

Distancing himself at every opportunity from Bulgakov and seeming to throw him to the wolves of the far Left, Lunacharsky (a relatively liberal politician) showed a good command of one of the norms of the new times which was putting an end to individual ethics, in particular to loyalty.

He had little in common with Bulgakov, and there was much that divided them. But even when writing in connection with *Days* about MAT, which he genuinely loved, he said that 'the degree of intuition and sincerity injected by the performers into the pseudo-positive characters in this play is evidence of the preservation in the theatre of a strong petty-bourgeois intellectual leavening.'[76] It is worth pondering this subtle critical denunciation in order to grasp the fact that the criteria of the period were being formed systematically from the very start and that there is no qualitative difference between this statement by the 'liberal' Lunacharsky and the later, less ambiguous viewpoint of Stalin, who evidently thought that an

---

[74] 'As you know, the most left-wing person here is V. I. Blium. He let *The Days of the Turbins* through, signed the permit, and developed such faith in his own ideological ability and authorial talent that he rewrote or corrected the play with Bulgakov. (Blium: That's not true.) After all, Comrade Orlinskii said that it was the repertoire committee that brought the play to a more or less acceptable state. (Orlinskii: Under our guidance.) Precisely. You thought that by more guidance of that kind you could change *The Turbins* into something that could be accepted. And you granted permission. And when the theatre had sunk several thousand into it and the cast knew their parts you decided to take off a play that had progressed so far thanks to the indulgence of your 'leftist' comrades! What were we supposed to say? That our repertoire committee was useless, that it had allowed *The Turbins* to go to dress rehearsal, and that – disregarding the fact that it would cause great material and moral losses to a theatre of world renown – we should repair the committee's mistake at the expense of the state and the theatre? That was difficult, even impossible. The People's Commissariat for Education debated this matter and concluded that in the circumstances the *Turbins* should be allowed to proceed.' *Puti razvitiia teatra*, pp. 231-32.

[75] Ibid., p. 234.

[76] Lunacharskii, *Sobranie sochinenii*, Vol. 3, p. 338.

actor who could convincingly act the part of a spy must have the innate inclinations of a spy. Nor is it surprising to hear Khmelev's angry protest a few years later, when the criteria were fairly firmly established: 'When people say to me that we play *The Turbins* better and more warmly [...] than *Armoured Train 14-69* because "it is closer to us", I lose my temper and am ready to shout: "It's not true! It's a lie! [...] I'm a Soviet man, I'm young [...]. I don't remember the past and I don't know it.'[77]

In the meantime the play found a very influential backer whose opinion would play an important role in deciding its future. This was none other than Stalin. In reply to a letter from the playwright Bill'-Belotserkovsky, who had appealed to him with expressions of outrage provoked by both *Days* and the preparations to stage *Flight*,[78] he first gave a negative appraisal of the latter, then went on:

'As for the play *The Days of the Turbins*, it is not as bad as all that and does more good than harm. Do remember that the main impression the spectator takes away from the play is one that is favourable to the Bolsheviks: if even people like the Turbins are compelled to lay down their arms, admitting that their cause is finally lost and submitting to the will of the people, this means the Bolsheviks are invincible, that nothing can defeat them. *The Days of the Turbins* is a demonstration of the overwhelming power of Bolshevism. Of course, the author is in no way "to blame" for that demonstration, but why should we care?'[79]

Stalin could be crude, but he was no simpleton. The phrase 'people like the Turbins' expresses some acknowledgement for the characters' qualities – perhaps for their loyal service to a lost cause. Perhaps this tireless theatre-goer, who had seen this same play so many times, derived a perverse pleasure from viewing something that was disappearing into the past thanks to the 'overwhelming power of Bolshevism'. Or perhaps his tired eyes found it restful to gaze on the beloved old ways, on the cut and style of those old uniforms, which – like some other trappings of the defeated regime – would yet come in handy. In Stalin's highly

---

[77] N. Khmelev, 'Rol' pishetsia dlia aktera', quoted in E. Poliakova, p. 61.

[78] The drift of the unpublished letter from Bill'-Belotserkovsky may be deduced indirectly from Stalin's reply, in which he quotes his correspondent's question, 'Why are Bulgakov's plays staged so often?' I. V. Stalin, *Sochineniia*, Moscow, 1949, Vol. 11, p. 328.

[79] Ibid.

pragmatic approach – so like Pravdukhin's assessment – we are struck by the thing that Lunacharsky sought and which was soon to become established practice – the separation of author and work, with all credit going automatically to the theatre. Nevertheless, whatever his reasons, the man who was moving towards the final seizure of all power was an admirer of *Days*. This soon turned out to be as important as everything else Stalin personally touched.

But this letter was written in February 1929 and not officially published until twenty years later; for the moment there was nothing to ease the path of the play. Numerous shrill campaigns were organized then and, increasingly, later but the intensity of this one was unprecedented. Fuel to the critical flames was also added by the play's enormous success, which was such that predictions of a speedy end to its stage life were met with great resistance, as would happen later, when other plays by Bulgakov – *Zoika's Apartment*, *The Crimson Island* – had the chance to run concurrently, and preparations were in train to produce *Flight*. This ephemeral success and the position, briefly held, of darling of theatrical Moscow seemed to mock the aggressors, further inflaming their fury. All of this coincided with an increasingly tense situation in the cultural sphere.

Some elements of the campaign appeared bizarre even then. In addition to much punning, caricature and malice, there was, for example a parody of the play, which, however, was not staged.[80] *Ogonek* printed a photograph of a building used by the Bolsheviks and demolished before the revolution with the caption 'the work of the Turbins.' Finally, Aleksandr Bezymensky in his play *The Shot* had one of his characters give a slanted but heated account of how his brother had been tortured by 'Colonel Aleksei Turbin'.[81] This projection of a fictional figure into the literary works of others creates an interesting literary-historical problem, but at the time what counted was the immediate result.

---

[80] V. Bogoliubov, I. Chekin, *Belyi dom (o chem oni molchali)*, Moscow, 1928.

[81] Note the following excerpt:

Sorokin: I'll throttle him with my own hands!
        Tell me who the bastard was!
All: Tell us his name! His name! His name!
Demidov: Colonel... Aleksei... Turbin.
All: Colonel Aleksei... Turbin.

(A. Bezymenskii, *Kniga satiry*, Moscow, 1956, pp. 233-34).

It was not long in coming. First, efforts to include the play in the repertoire of other theatres came to nothing; it could only be performed at MAT.[82] In August 1927 it was announced that there would be no reprise in the coming season;[83] however, the management of the theatre succeeded, with the support of Lunacharsky, in overturning this decision and gaining permission for the next year.[84] In June 1928 a decision by Glavrepertkom was issued, stating that 'it had been deemed desirable to exclude *The Days of the Turbins* from the MAT repertoire. The play will remain in the repertoire until production of the next play begins.'[85] The implementation of this suspended sentence was announced in March 1929, when MAT staged Vsevolod Ivanov's *Blockade*,[86] and after 289 performances the play was taken off. The press statement by Fedor Raskol'nikov, the new head of Glavrepertkom who still had much influence, 'We cannot permit the staging of *The Days of the Turbins*', became a reality.[87]

It would not be permitted. After two attacks the stormy action of the play surrounding the play was suddenly broken off. But this was only an interlude, not yet the end.

---

[82] There were plans to include it in, inter alia, the programme of the Leningrad Bolshoi Drama Theatre, which announced *Days* in its repertoire plan for the 1926-27 season. See Milne, *The Emergence...*, p. 253.

[83] See Milne, *The Emergence...*, p. 294.

[84] An exchange of letters on this topic between Stanislavskii and Lunacharskii is kept in the MAT Museum and was published in *Neizdannyi Bulgakov*, p. 83.

[85] *Zhizn' iskusstva*, No. 25, 1928.

[86] *Rabochaia Moskva*, 6.3.1929.

[87] Fedor Raskol'nikov, *Komsomol'skaia pravda*, 15.11.1928.

Chapter Six

An Essay in Comedy and Compromise

I. *Zoika's Apartment* and the comedy of manners in the NEP period. The play and the critics.
II. *The Crimson Island* as Bulgakov's 'Impromptu de Versailles'. Its brief stage career.
III. *Flight:* a play that changes course half-way through. The significance of the figure of Khludov.
IV. The campaign surrounding *Flight*; the play's changing fortunes; failure of attempts to support it.
V. All Bulgakov's plays taken off.

I

We are at the summit of Bulgakov's success, even if we can sense the uncertainty of the future. The critical assault on *Days* continued and intensified, but the play continued to run. It was an important event, and since the normal social mechanisms continued to operate, the whiff of scandal only added to the fame of both the play and the playwright. The fireworks of its popularity soared high in the sky – so the darkness that followed would be the deeper. For the moment, however, Bulgakov was lionized and found himself the focus of society fashion. A steady flow of theatre royalties gave him a chance to get his breath back and take a normal holiday in the Crimea or the Caucasus. He was even pestered by small-time confidence tricksters phoning to seek contributions.

On 28th October, three weeks after the premiere of *Days*, another premiere took place. The Vakhtangov Theatre staged *Zoika's Apartment*. Here too Bulgakov had great success, although the scale was different as the calibre was considerably lighter. *Zoika's Apartment* is a comic interlude written with talent and verve, almost pure entertainment, into which Bulgakov injected none of the things that mattered most to him. It is an interlude between serious works. Even the corpse which turns up at the end may be taken more as a device from the inventory of contemporary picaresque comedy, with a vein from the genre of the thriller, while the name given to one of the guests 'Dead Body' reflects a literary-historical joke, an allusion to a well-known story by Vladimir Odoevsky.[1] This play has an easy, relaxed air, which does not conflict with adroit stagecraft. Bulgakov plays with the traditional convention of changing guises, juggled by the jolly scoundrel Ametistov, who is descended from a long line of comic rogues but tinted with the local colour of his time – and who is also a forerunner of Ostap Bender.[2] The author also enjoys parodying the device of deception unmasked, when two lovers bump into each other in a house of assignation. He is a deft creator of colourful characters: the crafty *arriviste* of the title; her wimpish drug-addict consort Obol'ianinov, gifted with nothing more than the manners to impress the *nouveaux riches*; the lyrical embezzler Gus'-Remontny, who has emerged from the lower orders without resisting the temptations of power and money; the brassy housemaid, a new incarnation of the tradition of the pert soubrette. All of this, heavy with the atmosphere of the period and at the same time obeying the rules of comedy, is delivered in showy trappings employing several pretty girls, daring costumes, tail-coats, foxtrots, bluish opium smoke, two lisping Chinamen – *de rigueur* at the time – and a flashing knife. And all of it is concluded by the ritual fall of the arm of justice.

Zoika's Apartment, which was apparently written very quickly,[3] is limited to the space indicated in the title, an enclosed setting, ablaze with the glitter of

---

[1] A tale of some human remains which cannot be identified. [Odoevsky's story is entitled 'Zhivoi mertvets' (The Living Corpse) – *Trans.*]

[2] See the sketch by D. Likhachev, 'Literaturnyi ded Ostapa Bendera', in which he speaks of the closeness of these two figures and of a possible model for both: Jingle in Dickens's *Pickwick Papers*. In *Stranitsy russkoi literatury*, Moscow, 1971, p. 247 ff. On the possible influence of Bulgakov on Il'f and Petrov, see also M. Chudakova, 'Arkhiv M. A. Bulgakova. Materialy dlia tvorcheskoi biografii pisatelia', in *Zapiski Otdela rukopisei Gos. Bibl. SSSR im. Lenina*, Moscow, 1976, p. 46

[3] Apparently in the autumn or early winter of 1925 (see M. Chudakova, 'Arkhiv...', p. 59; see the same source for information on the available typescripts of the play and the difficulty of establishing a definitive text). Until now the following have served as basic published source texts: the version published in the quarterly *Novyi zhurnal* Nos. 97-98, 1969, 1970, familiarly

short-lived prosperity. This little comedy of manners means as much as it says and makes no claim to do anything more. The author's observations of Moscow life during his *Nakanune* period clearly came in handy; now he could make use of the sketches he had earlier discarded, of millionaires, embezzlers and sharp dealers in floor space – as he could of his own housing difficulties, the accumulated source of so many jangled nerves. It is difficult to avoid this conclusion even in the chaotic first scene, when 'the courtyard of the huge building is emitting sounds like a hideous musical snuff-box', producing a vulgar cacophony of various clashing melodies. As can often be seen, Bulgakov is particularly sensitive to the musical accompaniment to life. To his texts music imparts an added and constant ironic commentary – its unchanging motifs underline the fickleness of life, exposing the illusory nature of words and gestures, or supplying a meaningful sub-text to them. Thus it was in *The Heart of a Dog, The White Guard* and *Days* – and so it is in *Zoika's Apartment*, in a somewhat less sophisticated version. It is certain that personal scores are also being settled in the cunning and corrupt Portupeia [called 'Alliluia' in Bulgakov's earlier drafts – *Trans.*], the prying chairman of the tenancy committee, who represents a particularly detested caste.

As for the fundamental idea of the setting – a house of assignation maintained in the guise of a dressmaking workshop – the realities of the NEP period offered plenty of examples. Nor is it surprising that different commentators point to different prototypes,[4] each of whom individually – and all of whom together – could be the real one, for the author was skilled in cross-fertilizing and

---

known as 'the first version' (the publication is incomplete and careless, with erroneous comments), and that in M. Bulgakov, *Tri p'esy: Adam i Eva, Bagrovyi ostrov, Zoikina kvartira*, Paris, 1971, known as 'the second version' and supposedly regarded by the author as final. [A more recent volume, M. A. Bulgakov, *P'esy 1920-kh godov*, ed. by A. A. Ninov, Leningrad, 1989, includes the texts of various redactions of Bulgakov's principal theatrical works, including *Zoika's Apartment – Trans.*]

[4] For example V. Levshin, 'Sadovaia 302-bis', *Teatr*, No. 11, 1971, p. 116, sees Georgii Iakulov's studio at Sadovaia 10 as the model for the flat. L. Belozerskaia-Bulgakova, in *O, med vospominanii*, Ann Arbor, 1979, p. 29, offers a different theory; yet another possibility has been suggested to me by Konstantin Rudnitskii: in 1929 *Ogonek* (No. 10) wrote of the closing down of a thieves' den run by one Zoia Shatova, where Esenin and Mariengof were among those detained.

synthesizing. The atmosphere of the bandits' lair and the criminal milieu is no less authentic; the trappings of the period were far from idyllic.

At the time there were more works in this vein: the comical essence of the situations to which NEP gave rise imposed themselves independently, while certain devices had become current. There are analagous elements in Boris Romashov's play *The Soufflé* (*Vozdushny pirog*, 1925), in which the ruthless *arriviste* Semion Rak also manages to suborn and deprave the respected manager. The hero of Aleksei Faiko's play, *Evgraf the Seeker of Adventure* (*Evgraf, iskatel' prikliuchenii*, 1927), breaks out of the workaday triviality of a barber's shop into the bright lights of the outside world, which – as in *Zoika's Apartment* – take the form of a flashing knife and complicity in crime. In the stage adaptation of Valentin Kataev's *Embezzlers* (*Rastratchiki*, 1927), the head book-keeper and cashier succumbs to the temptation of easy profit, which can only lead to trouble. According to the official line, literature thus exposed the vestiges of the old world, by gathering up 'the dregs of NEP'. With hindsight it is perfectly clear that in the new system graft, fraud and the drive for personal gain by fair means or foul had become even more prevalent and had penetrated even the highest centres of power, to say nothing of the clear and systematic segregation of rulers from ruled in privileged enclaves of private life and entertainment, compared to which the temptations of Zoia Pel'ts's flat are small beer. The trouble was that this subject was by now taboo in comedy.

What Bulgakov showed was therefore directed towards the future, but it would be wrong to credit the chronicler of NEP with any special foresight. He simply showed what he could see: the reactions of people worn down by their recent experience of enforced austerity and eager for bright lights, entertainment, the 'Europe' that inhabits the dreams of several of his characters and which for them found makeshift form in a surrogate venue. Perverse though this may have been, it was natural, the more so as the new system had declared the end of traditional morality, trampled flagrantly upon its standards while offering nothing in return. The authorities also noted 'a mood of decadence' among the young and were concerned about an ostentatious laxity in behaviour, while readily regarding all this as a 'hangover', a 'vestige of the past', and consciously or otherwise avoiding the truth. Among playwrights Nikolai Erdman in his *Mandate* (1925) probably went further than others, showing that in an ethical vacuum the sole criterion is power, gained by finding one's way into the machinery of authority, or pretending to do so. From the start Bulgakov deeply detested time-serving opportunists, but in *Zoika's Apartment* he did not try to settle any serious scores with them. He simply depicted them, without exposing them. Through the hearty fixer Ametistov, an inspired, charming liar, a comic plebeian version of Shervinsky, he mocked the figure of the administrator, with pleasing effect. 'He did not believe,' wrote Rudnitsky, 'that the Ametistovs could triumph where the Turbins had laid down their arms. [...] To him as an outside observer, a contemporary historian of current events – not a participant – the bustle of NEP seemed an amusing absurdity.'[5] But it was not only this. It was also the price he had to pay for the normality he longed for.

The text submitted to the Vakhtangov Theatre in January 1926 was one which would work well as a stage piece and held promise for actors. Aleksei Popov, the director, during rehearsals, held discussions with Bulgakov aimed at making cuts, but must have realized quickly that Bulgakov would not be compliant: in the end, although some cuts were effected, the four-act structure was maintained.[6] Ten years later, in 1935, the play was subjected to some stylistic revision with certain textual changes – including the excision of Ametistov's political jokes. This may have been connected with its staging in Paris at the Vieux Colombier Theatre.[7] On this subject Bulgakov conducted a correspondence with his brother Nikolai, insisting that some of the arbitrary textual amendments be removed. This was done.

The play was a source of much fun for the audience and players alike. Young Ruben Simonov made a dynamic and dashing con-man as Ametistov: 'Just because I was shot in Baku, does that mean I can't come to Moscow? I was completely innocent and they shot me by mistake!'[8] Years later he recalled the winning stage devices hit upon in the course of the rehearsals, which sharpened the

---

[5] Konstantin Rudnitskii, 'Mikhail Bulgakov', in *Voprosy teatra; Sbornik statei i materialov*, Moscow, 1966, p. 134.

[6] A. Popov's letters are held in IRLI, Fond 369. One of his demands was that the play be refashioned into three acts.

[7] See S. Liandres, 'Russkii pisatel' ne mozhet zhit' bez rodiny', *Voprosy literatury*, No. 9, 1966, p. 137. There is no doubt that, from a literary viewpoint, the result of these changes – the 'second version' – is a marked improvement on the first.

[8] *Tri p'esy*, 1971, p. 207.

comic effects especially in the scenes involving Kozlovsky as Obol'ianinov.[9] Boris Zakhava gave a full-blooded performance as the bribe-taking chairman of the tenancy committee. Zoia was played by Vakhtangov's favourite pupil, Tsetsiliia Mansurova, an actress of great temperament with a sense of stage humour which breathed the fullness of life into a character merely sketched by Bulgakov. The set, designed by Sergei Isakov in the spirit of the period, economically evoked the showy style and ambiguous glitter of a den of thieves, exploiting the hallucinatory effects of a mixture of female tailor's dummies and live models. The vigour of the dialogue enhanced by the vigour of the acting and directing must have produced the desired result: the production was a great success.

A great success with the public. The critics greeted it with the full arsenal of well-established anti-Bulgakov prejudice. Thus it was asserted that *'Zoika's Apartment* is written in the style of a collection of petty-bourgeois jokes which might have been topical about three years ago',[10] that it gave a poor imitation of devices used by Faiko, Romashov and Erdman, and that it perfectly expressed the author's tastes and his liking for the kind of world depicted on the stage. There was surprise that a theatre, 'which had made such a good start with *Turandot* and moved on to modern times with *Virineia*',[11] had now descended to a work 'worse than pitiful in its lack of talent and depth'[12] and dependent on 'revelling in piquant situations and fashion shows on stage, displaying ladies' costumes with cut-outs in every possible place: in front and behind, at the shoulders and the waist'.[13] The summing-up was equally categorical and dismissive. 'Bulgakov's laughter is bitter,' said one of the reviewers. 'It is the grim mirth of one confronting his own political death.' And further: 'In a socio-political sense Bulgakov's plays are an attempt by a lost, desperate and unreconstructed adherent of "Smena vekh" to find

---

[9] R. Simonov, 'Moi liubimye roli, sozdannye M. Bulgakovym', in *Neizdannyi Bulgakov*, Ann Arbor, 1977, p. 71.

[10] O. Litovskii, '*Zoikina kvartira* v studii im. Evg. Vakhtangova', *Glazami sovremennika*, Moscow, 1963, p. 229.

[11] Ibid.

[12] A. Orlinskii, 'Zoikina kvartira', *Pravda*, 3.11.1926.

[13] K. Minskii, 'Parizh na Arbate', *Ekran*, No. 44, 14 November, 1926.

a place in Soviet reality with a whole swag of decadence imported from pre-revolutionary days.'[14]

Short, succinct and clear.

Other writers of satire were usually accorded much more indulgent treatment, even kind treatment, but then, none of them had written anything resembling *The Days of the Turbins*.

This time Lunacharsky did not take part in the debate in the press, but in a speech during a discussion of theatre matters he distanced himself fully from *Zoika's Apartment*, stressing that he had protested four times against its being staged and again blaming Glavrepertkom for the fact that it had gone ahead.[15] No doubt this was in accord with his tactics and his convictions, as this time the issue was not MAT.

Yet the playwright who had been so comprehensively condemned to anathema had no thought of repentance. On the contrary, while he still held a bridgehead on the stage he was busy regrouping his forces and preparing a counter-attack.

II

One of the theatrical colleagues who remembers Bulgakov has written that his smile was sometimes more like a snarl. This is hardly surprising, just as it is hard to miss the specifically personal inflection in a sentence in his *Life of Molière* that runs: 'But our hero felt like a lone wolf with the breath of a pursuing pack of hounds on its neck.'[16]

This sentence described Molière's situation when he staged his 'Impromptu de Versailles', a desperate assault on his many avowed enemies. The wolf turned and bared its teeth. In a situation from which there was no exit this itself seemed a

---

[14] V. Bogoliubov, 'Eshche o *Zoikinoi kvartire*', *Programmy gosudarstvennykh akademicheskikh teatrov*, No. 14, 20.14.1926.

[15] A. Lunacharskii, 'Zakliuchitel'noe slovo', in *Puti razvitiia teatra, Stenograficheskii otchet i resheniia partiinogo soveshchaniia po voprosam teatra pri Agitprope TsK VKP(b) v mae 1927*, Moscow-Leningrad, 1927, pp. 232-233.

[16] M. Bulgakov, *Izbrannaia proza*, Moscow, 1966, p. 451.

way out, and we cannot exclude the possibility that as he embarked upon his own 'Impromptu', Bulgakov gave his own wolfish grin.

Bulgakov's counter-attack was called *The Crimson Island* and was based on motifs from the story with this title which had appeared in *Nakanune*. The play was written in 1927 and submitted to the Kamerny Theatre in March of that year. In September, most likely to the author's surprise, permission came for its production.[17] The premiere, however, did not take place until 11th December 1928.

This was a play within a play, set within the frame of theatrical life. A young writer submits to a theatre company the corrected version of his own play, which – since nothing is impossible on the stage – is to be performed at once before the chief censor in a dress rehearsal. Thus in *The Crimson Island* by Bulgakov we see *The Crimson Island* by Vasilii Dymogatsky performed in full. (It is known that Bulgakov was fond of this Russian-doll structure, with its notional distancing effect which allowed him to say 'It's not me' and at the same time 'Of course it's me'; and he even applied it in his most important novel.) At the same time all kinds of theatrical politicking and manoeuvring takes place around it.

This device of the quotation within a quotation effectively dealt a double blow. The play was aimed at the censor and at the same time at hack work in the arts; at the bureaucrats and functionaries, but also at his fellow-writers and theatrical confrères. The wolf had turned.

Hack writing that pandered to the moment is parodied by the play within the play. The story on which it is based is a stylized joke which toys with an allegory of revolution, employing motifs borrowed from Jules Verne. But the meaning of the device is altered: it is less a matter of imitating history than of the manner in which this is done, less of *what* is related, more of *how* it is related; not the revolution itself so much as its treatment by literary con-artists. Reality supplied plenty of material, and Bulgakov filtered it mischievously into a collection of stereotypes and clichés, ready-made schemes and models of class struggle and social disruption, with programmes announced in posters and slogans that perfectly suited the manner of Verne's adventure stories for young readers. Here Bulgakov gave voice to his hatred for sycophantic literature, for those who sniffed out the

---

17 See part of a letter to E. Zamiatin: '*Flight* has been completed and performed, and permission has been given for *The Crimson Island*.' (Quoted in M. Chudakova, 'Arkhiv...', p. 63).

trends of the future and adapted their beliefs to circumstances, for writing that vied for the favour of the powerful. It so happened that at almost the same time Bulgakov's sworn enemies were also alarmed by the phenomenon of hack writing under the cover of revolutionary sloganeering. These included Maiakovsky, who in Act Three of his *Bath-House* created a vicious parody of the schematic allegory, and Vsevolod Vishnevsky, who a year later similarly derided the recycling of operatic clichés when he opened his *Last, Decisive Battle* with a parodic slapstick scene. These two opposed hack work on ideological grounds; Bulgakov on grounds of ethics. In life they were poles apart, but on this they were at one.[18]

The play lashes out at writers. It also lashes out at producers for whom the summit of morality and the end that justifies all means was the salvation of the threatened premiere, those who are prepared to perform the most ingenious acrobatics of opportunism, perjure themselves to the hilt and ruin the material beyond all hope of repair. And yet – and this idea is transparently clear – the main culprit is the censorship, for it is its dead hand that predetermines everything; the terror that it inspires compels submission and produces grovelling liars and lickspittles. Even before he is seen in the theatre, the dreaded Savva Lukich looms large in the director's ploys and defensive manoeuvres ('Oh those allegories! Bear in mind that Savva Lukich can't abide allegories. I know all about those allegories, he says. Allegory on the surface, and underneath it such out-and-out Menshevism that you can cut it with a knife!'),[19] stamping his complacent ignorance in advance on everything he touches. And from the moment of the Ober-censor's solemn entrance all the action serves him and revolves round him, amid manifestations of abject servility.

This even results in a degree of inconsistency, for – as the author suggests at the beginning – Dymogatsky, the author of the play within the play, has spoiled it on the orders of the director, obeying those of the censor. But towards the end Bulgakov makes Dymogatsky speak out loudly in energetic protest. On learning that his play has been banned he rails at his misfortune, sleepless nights and the

---

[18] Maiakovsky, in keeping with the self-imposed maximalism which led him to be aggressively intolerant of many cultural phenomena, fought doggedly against *The Days of the Turbins* at various levels, although he maintained personal relations with Bulgakov. On Bulgakov's relations with Vishnevsky see Chapter Eight.

[19] *Tri p'esy*, 1971, p. 86

slave labour of journalism, and in this an echo of Bulgakov's own voice can be heard. This means that either he is a compliant literary opportunist and hack – as the tawdry product of his endeavours suggests – or a gifted writer brought low by the censorial and directorial grasp. It turns out that he is both. While it is true that life can produce many contradictory phenomena, this play leaves the impression that it is so intent on its main aims that it loses sight of logic and consistency.

During the staging process, the anti-censorship accents of *The Crimson Island* evidently became sharper. Savva Lukich was transparently based on Vladimir Blium. This created an atmosphere of sensation around the play, which was directed by Aleksandr Tairov.[20] However, the theatre soon took fright at its own daring and, shortly after the premiere, whether under pressure from above or not, it dropped the play.[21] All this had about it something of the air of a sequel to the play itself, appended to it by life.

Of the circumstances surrounding this production very little is known. Nor is it altogether clear why Glavrepertkom was so liberal on this occasion. It is possible that internal intrigues played some part, especially as Blium was a rather unpopular figure. Confirmation of this possibility might lie in a somewhat unusual fact: one of Bulgakov's more aggressive critics, Pavel Novitsky, at first gave a highly favourable appraisal of the anti-censorship aspect of the play. He called *The Crimson Island*, 'an interesting and witty parody in which we see the sinister shadow of the Grand Inquisitor crushing artistic creativity, fostering unctuous and sycophantic theatrical clichés and levelling down the individuality of the actor and writer.' 'If such a malign force exists,' Novitsky concluded, 'the indignation and malicious wit of the bourgeoisie's favourite playwright are fully justified.'[22]

The critic did not stand by this rare show of objectivity for long; by the middle of the following year he was writing in the generally accepted tone, that the play 'takes malicious satisfaction in mocking the political dictatorship of the

---

[20] In collaboration with L. Luk'ianova; set designed by V. Ryndin.

[21] 'The premiere was held on 11th December 1928, and immediately after it the theatre's Artistic Council announced that the play would be taken off.' (M. Chudakova, 'Arkhiv...', p. 63)

[22] *Repertuarnyi biulleten'*, No. 12, 1928. Bulgakov appended this testimonial to what may have been a draft of a letter to the government (Chapter Five, see Note 43; hereafter this text will be referred to as 'Draft').

working class and parodying the course of the October Revolution.'[23] In this view the critics were at one, in spite, as we know, of the clearly expressed and reasonably objectivized intention of the author. From now on, everything that Bulgakov would write could be turned against him. The case did not need to be argued. It is no surprise to find that I. Nusinov, the author of a collective accusation against Bulgakov (cited previously), descried a deliberate consistency and premeditation among his many crimes:

'Bulgakov resolutely persists in his division of his own labours: upon one theatre he bestows a satire of Soviet reality, and upon another a play which evokes sympathy for the Whites, for the victims of this Soviet reality.

'If *Zoika's Apartment* shows the demoralization of a responsible Soviet official, *The Crimson Island* shows the decay of Soviet culture; it attacks revolutionary ideology.'[24]

Stalin, who was well disposed to *The Days of the Turbins*, conceded in a letter to Bill'-Belotserkovsky that the staging of *The Crimson Island* 'and other trash of that kind' at the 'truly bourgeois Kamerny Theatre' was one of many errors in the work of Glavrepertkom.[25] The adverse opinion which leaked out from this letter (and those privileged to receive such documents did nothing to conceal them – quite the contrary) clearly counted for more than any favourable views, and Stalin's taste, though not yet the main evaluative criterion, already carried much weight.

To be sure, the task of the critics was made easier in one respect: the play was not a work of the first rank. It had a splendidly witty and pointed setting in theatrical life, presented in a kaleidoscopic torrent of scenes and subjects: the machinations of the manager, the tribulations of the author, the anxieties of the troupe of actors, the lordly posturing of Savva Lukich. Here we sense the experience of an old theatrical hand, who knows its offices, its dressing rooms, its back doors and stage doors. He knows that a collective effort goes into a performance, along with casting intrigues and jealousies, tactical alliances, calculated compromises and competition for the favours of the powerful; behind the bewitching charm of the set he can see the patchwork of improvised props – the

---

[23] *Pechat' i revoliutsiia*, No. 6, 1929.

[24] I. Nusinov, 'Put' M. Bulgakova', *Pechat' i revoliutsiia*, No. 4, 1929.

[25] I. V. Stalin, *Sochineniia*, Moscow, 1949, Vol. 11, p. 328.

volcano fashioned from a decapitated Mount Ararat and the backdrop for *Mary Stuart* patched with a piece of that for *Ivan the Terrible*. In this there is a tenderness tinged with bitterness, and a sardonic smile accompanying the manager's exclamation that 'the theatre is a temple'; there is understanding and sympathy for the hard theatrical life, and there are melancholy jokes at the playwright's own expense, and that of *Days* and *Zoika's Apartment*,[26] as well as an all-embracing and sincere fascination with all of this – good and bad alike – a fascination which forms the truth of his own life and an augury for his *Theatrical Novel*.

On the other hand, the play which Bulgakov places within this setting is such an elaborate allegorical structure that it becomes ponderous. The story of the tyrant Sizi-Buzi, the opportunist Kiri-Kuki, the predatory Lord Glenarvan and their numerous retinue mimics the stereotypes, of course, but the effect remains latent unless brought out in the staging. It depends on this whether the central 'quotation effect', showing imitated follies as parody, will work; if it does not the humour will be problematical.

Recent experience of staging the play indicates, however, that it can be done, that it is possible to bring it to life with outstanding results, and that the allegorical part then resonates with slightly altered meanings derived from later experience of the period of decolonization.

But at the time the hunted wolf could hear the hue and cry ever louder as the pack closed in on him.

III

Bulgakov's three 'theatrical years', 1926 to 1928, were a period of spectacular discharge of accumulated dramaturgical energy. This energy was converted into a wide variety of new forms. But it is clear that *Zoika's Apartment* and *The Crimson Island* are by-products, substantial by-products perhaps, but peripheral to what would come as a sequel to *The Days of the Turbins*. In this

---

[26] See the theatre manager's lines: 'I won't have *Zoika's Apartment* here.' (*Tri p'esy*, 1971, p. 155). 'The author of the play came to see me and – can you imagine – offered me *The Days of the Turbins*! How do you like that?' (Ibid., p. 185). Note also Savva Lukich's line, 'It's a "Smena vekh" play' (Ibid., p. 185); 'But I won't allow your little play to run in other cities... We can't have a play like that permitted all over the place!' (Ibid., p. 190).

direction lay the opportunity to pass through the wall and speak of the things that mattered most.

The design of a new play was conceived at an early date, as the author dated his work on it '1926-1928'.[27] It arose from close contact with MAT. This was the honeymoon of the union between the playwright and the theatre. For Bulgakov the triumph of *Days* was probably compensation for his heartache at having to modify it, while the almost boundless gratitude of the young troupe for the chance to make a splendid start no doubt made up for the unpleasant aftertaste of recent conflicts.

As he wrote, the playwright had certain performers in mind and, as Markov recalls, 'considers their character traits and personalities, as well as the range of their abilities, while not for a moment assuming that they will follow the beaten track'.[28] New variations in acting technique were to emerge from the new characters, their newly-configured lives, a new over-arching idea and a new style. The emerging play took shape as a chronological sequel to *Days*, though a sequel in no other sense, for everything else about it is different. The essential point is that the central characters have had the one constant element in their lives, their anchor point, their House, knocked out from under them; their belief in the permanence of life, their belief that 'a solution will be found', has nothing to hold on to. From the start all this is doomed to defeat. This is a completely new concept. We may state at the outset that the writer makes a significant concession to class criteria and the spirit of historical determinism. To a great extent he steps down from his spiritual independence. It is true, however, that he is saved by the self-liberating gesture of the character most affected by the weight of this determinism, but only up to a point.

Without jumping to conclusions, we may note that homelessness has curious artistic consequences. This applies above all to the first two scenes or 'dreams' into which the play is divided. Its title is *Flight* [Russian 'Beg'], and its epigraph a verse by Vasilii Zhukovsky:

Бессмертие — тихий, светлый брег;
Наш путь — к нему стремление.

---

[27] M. Chudakova, 'Arkhiv...', p. 60.

[28] P. Markov, 'Istoriia moego teatral'nogo sovremennika', *Teatr*, No. 5, 1971, pp. 82-83. Here the casting is foreshadowed: Khludov – Khmelev, Golubkov – Ianshin, Serafima – Sokolova, Charnota – Kachalov, Korzukhin – Ershov (other options are also considered).

Покойся, кто свой кончил бег!...[29]

Both the quotation and the nature of the play indicate that it would be wrong to interpret this title as 'running away'; what is intended has more to with the sense 'run' or 'course', meaning the course and consequences of events, the course of life and human destiny. The situation of 'running' as a state which is by nature fluent and changeable takes us back in the first act to the scenic structure of *The White Guard*, with its fluid and friable downhill movement. Caught off balance, the characters blunder from one episode to another within changing configurations of fate, as shown earlier from the inside, from a different viewpoint, in *Notes on Shirt-Cuffs*. In the first dream their fragile anchorage is a monastery, where they are surprised by an advance unit of Red cavalry and whence they immediately flee. The second dream shows the fall of the next point, the headquarters of General Khludov, the commander of the White front, already breached by the Reds; everything now continues its crumbling downward movement, towards the sea and the ships.

The first two dreams may well be among the best material Bulgakov ever wrote for the stage. Here he is in his element – ambiguity, the Gogolian variability of form, and the natural phantasmagoria of life. Everything looms out of darkness and is exposed in an uncertain creeping light against the background of the singing of the monks, rising from the cellars of the monastery, from the mysterious substrata of existence, amidst refugees and some scrimshankers feigning injury, pretending to be someone else and indeed no longer themselves. Everything is seen amidst changing destinies, when the Reds drive out the Whites only to cede the field to them at once, while the Whites also prepare to withdraw. (Here Bulgakov gives something like a menacingly dramatic reinterpretation of an old comic device.) The second dream is even better: the very moment of destruction itself is made palpable, with its atmosphere of extreme exhaustion tinged with restrained hysteria, with the mechanical motions of sleepwalkers, with senseless acts of despair, brutality and sheer will-power. The characters in this episode speak less to one another than past one another; their utterances only occasionally

---

[29] ['Immortality – a quiet, bright shore/ Our route – a striving towards it./ Rest, who his race has run! ...']. Note Chudakova's percipient remark that 'this motto ... is a programme for the forthcoming plot of *The Master and Margarita*'. 'Arkhiv...', p. 62.

connect; we observe a collapse of logic, a separation of cause and effect, a grotesque confusion of kinds of order collapsing into chaos. Almost everyone is like the stationmaster of whom Bulgakov says, 'he moves and speaks, but he's been dead for twenty-four hours',[30] while the entrances of actual living characters from a different dimension only underscore the nightmarish quality of the vision. In this dream we see a distillation of the very essence of defeat and failure, the end of the world in its purest form – shown as few others have ever managed to show it in literature.

Up to this point the play is first-rate. And therefore the disintegration which sets in immediately after this is all the more apparent. Act Two is set in Sebastopol just before the evacuation and is made up of ordinary scenes which together form something like a sensational melodrama, with interrogations, intrigues and people being imprisoned and set free. It all assumes an orderly form and becomes normal, with a strain of fairly conventional satire – and is consequently banal. Acts Three and Four, on foreign soil, are even more conventional. Here we are offered genre scenes of the émigré's hard lot, a dog-eat-dog life in which the exile can only prostitute himself and lose whatever dignity he still has – or go home. The real tragedy is what they left behind in their homeland; what reaches Constantinople and Paris is part melodrama, part comic farce. The basis for the use of the term 'dreams' now becomes purely notional; the contours of the scenes are clearly delineated and the situations are static and unambiguous. While Act One shows a clear stylistic link with the poetics of *The White Guard*, with its nervous orchestration of sound and alternating light and shade, while we can also sense in it the presence of the half-real packaging of the later *Days of the Turbins*, derived from the first adaptation, in which Nikolka emerges out of the darkness whistling a jaunty air, the subsequent acts, especially Acts Three and Four, are professionally-fashioned, realistic set-pieces.

A number of factors possibly converge here. Bulgakov is simplifying the émigré experience, perhaps in doing so finding support for the decision which fate somehow took without consulting him, ordering him to stay in Russia; perhaps this is a form of subjective auto-persuasion, a voice debating with him and trying to convince him that he has done the right thing. Perhaps too, in basing the foreign

---

[30] M. Bulgakov, *P'esy*, Moscow, 1962, p. 142. Also in M. A. Bulgakov, *Sobranie sochinenii v piati tomakh*, Moscow, 1990, Vol. 3, p. 228.

scenes on the recollections of Liubov' Belozerskaia, whose account he used and to whom he dedicated the play, he also absorbed the emotional climate of those recollections, which must have been quite unambiguous. 'He wrote only about what was close and understandable to him, what he had experienced to the full,' wrote Popov later.[31] But this time he had to rely on second-hand material, without that feeling of closeness, and this must have cramped his pen, inevitably making his scenes look merely illustrative. (This would happen again later.)

Lastly, it is likely that his internal censor played its part. Even the most upright of authors engaged it automatically. The author of *Days* knew by now the limits of the permissible. On the politically treacherous ground he had ventured onto he realized they were even tighter. He therefore accepted significant compromises in advance. He agreed to a paradigm which placed the blame squarely on one side (Voloshin and Veresaev, for example, managed to be considerably more objective in a similar situation). He denied émigrés the chance of a normal life, a chance he had previously granted to people from the Turbins' House. He bade the exiles demonstrate with their own broken lives that life outside Russia was not possible and not worth living; near the end of the play two of the young characters express their spasmodic urge to return to their lost homes. 'I want to go to Karavannaia Street again. I want to see the snow! I want to forget all this, as if it had never been!' cries Serafima, the 'young Petersburg lady',[32] and in her cry we hear the ironic-melancholy ambivalence of Chekhov's heroines, who are determined to 'work' and 'go to Moscow' – but not *too* determined. Bulgakov suppressed the ambivalence. Within the play the only way they can regain their lost equilibrium and find a constant in life is to go to Canossa, prostrating themselves before the victor. Here Bulgakov is playing on powerful emotional registers; on the passionate Russian bond with the homeland and the cruel pull of homesickness in the émigré heart.

Thus *Flight* is a play of conscious half-truths, half-correct and half-tragic, and the artistic consequences of its half-measures are dire indeed: the play divides into two parts.

---

[31] *Zametki avtobiograficheskogo kharaktera*, Manuscript Department of the Lenin Library, Fond 218.

[32] *P'esy*, 1962, p. 213. Also in *Sobranie sochinenii*, 1990, Vol. 3, p. 276.

It is saved from complete collapse and artistic failure by the figure of General Khludov and his cause, which goes some way to restoring its shaky balance.

Khludov, as we know, was modelled on General Iakov Slashchev, a commander as outstanding as he was pitiless, who performed sterling service in the defence of the Crimea following the defeat of Denikin at the end of 1919. By the time of the action of *Flight*, however, he had been relieved of his command. In this situation we can see Bulgakov's typical attitude to his models; the facts are transposed, the externals of a situation altered, but the psychology of that situation is supremely true to life. That this is so is demonstrated by the tone of Slashchev's two books, brimful of bitterness, venom, ambition to command, and a wounded sense of his own dignity, with perhaps also an element of persecution mania.[33] Bulgakov reconstructs this state of mind, while exercising his creative right to give it a slightly different setting. In the second dream, which occurs in Khludov's headquarters, Khludov is assailed by the same sense of the imminent end of the world to which the characters of *The White Guard* fall prey; by defending an idea, he has become a criminal, so the collapse of that idea causes him to feel a terrible weight of responsibility. The disintegration he is witnessing is so suggestive for the added reason that it is inwardly coloured by the general's advancing illness, so it seems the more acute in his fixed gaze, with eyes aching from lack of sleep. The last execution carried out on his orders, of an honest orderly, tips the scales and brings down the whole burden upon Khludov. This is the point where one of Bulgakov's most important motifs is engaged and begins to operate. It is familiar from 'The Red Crown', where a younger brother is sacrificed to an idea in whose name people have been hanged and where visions of the dead cause the narrator to go mad. We remember the question: 'For all I know that man swinging from the lamp-post in Berdiansk, the one with the soot on his cheek, might come calling on you.' And the statement: 'If he does, it's right that we should suffer.'[34]

Khludov takes his justified suffering away with him across the sea, almost exactly as in Aleksei Tolstoi's *Ibikus*; and that description may have exerted some

---

[33] Ia. Slashchev-Krymskii, *Trebuiu suda obshchestva i glasnosti*, Constantinople, 1921; *Krym v 1920 godu*, Moscow, 1924. The first book naturally gives a much more direct record of the author's emotional state.

[34] M. A. Bulgakov, *Povesti. Rasskazy. Fel'etony*, Moscow, 1988, p. 188.

influence on Bulgakov: 'Just this morning the man was a dictator. As a warning to others he ordered the hanging from the arch of a railway bridge of a stationmaster, his assistant and a third suspicious individual with tattoos on his arms – and that evening the same man is huddled with his bundle beside the smokestack of a steamer, glad that it's taking him away – no matter where.'[35]

The unidimensional quality of Tolstoi's pamphlet, towards which some scenes from the second part of *Flight* tend to gravitate, is partially avoided by the tragic nature of Khludov's life, by his unremitting tribulations and his endless trial by conscience, which will come to be so important in *The Master and Margarita*. Around the general a field of real tension is created; there is a concentration of motifs which are very important to Bulgakov, such as 'dusk', 'a terrible and crucial time of day', when the dominant brilliance of the Constantinople sun, shining on a semblance of life, fades and a vision-like reality – one that exposes the essence of things – finds expression. It is Khludov who takes on the anguish of the narrator of 'The Red Crown'. In the deepest sense, it is he who takes responsibility for the murders which somewhere, at some time, certainly filled the author with horror. And it is he who repeats the gesture of Malyshev and Aleksei Turbin – though under greater pressure than these two – and abandons his flight to nowhere, takes control of his fate and recovers his dignity. Slashchev himself had done the same: he returned to Russia. His decision met with approval; the general was pardoned and he went on to lecture at higher military academies until January 1929, when he was killed by a bullet fired by the brother of one of his victims, in a strange kind of distant echo of 'The Red Crown'.

In regaining his own dignity, Khludov at the same time restores the dignity of *Flight*, in so far as this is possible. Everything that had previously – alas – been lowered to the trivial level of the uncomfortable yet comic plight of the vanquished, who had lost their identity outside their homeland, – repeatedly compared in an elaborate analogy to cockroaches drowning in a bucket – takes on a truly tragic dimension, and therefore a human one. This dimension is close to that of Dostoevsky's characters, but Khludov is no Raskol'nikov; the situation has been inverted. The general can kill without placing himself beyond good and evil, but in the name of an idea, and it is the ultimate disintegration of the idea that deprives the killing of all justification. Perhaps Bulgakov consciously selected this particular

---

[35] A. Tolstoi, *Izbrannye sochineniia*, Moscow, 1951, Vol. II, p. 415.

area of the literary tradition with the intention of treating it critically; in *The White Guard* and *Days* Dostoevsky had already been mentioned ironically;[36] this time the patent impotence of a religious stance, the negation of the traditional role of the monastery and the 'wise monk' are characteristic. These elements turn upside down the motifs of the 'shepherd' (when Patriarch Afrikan runs away and abandons his flock) and the 'deluge', and develop an elaborate system of counterpoint with regard to the biblical motifs. If this intention is present, it is not elaborated owing to the unidimensional nature of the play, which does not reach above the level of petty mockery and spite. Not until *The Master and Margarita* would the required dimension be achieved. For the moment there is no attempt – and there could be none in the prevailing climate of half-truths – to take up the central intellectual strands of the great Russian literary tradition. They are barely touched on – and found to be fragile and insubstantial. This is hardly a fruitful way to proceed. This time the pupil of Gogol and apt reader of Pushkin does them little credit.

But the creation of Khludov must tell in his favour.

IV

It is difficult to guess whether or to what extent a MAT production of *Flight* would have respected the original stylistic formula, especially in the first two dreams, with its spectral and somnambulistic realism, its eloquent play of light, colour and sound, and its new contrapuntal musical score, in which a highly intricate role is played by the well-known 'Legend of the Twelve Brigands', for example, forming an ironic backdrop to Khludov's moral dilemmas. With time the

---

[36] Notably in the scene in Act One in which a frozen Myshlaevsky appears. For reasons unknown the text of this scene differs substantially in the editions of 1962 (*P'esy*, Moscow) and 1965 (*Dramy i komedii*). Viz.: 'Vot eti samye bogonostsy okaiannye sochineniia gospodina Dostoevskogo' (*P'esy*, p. 26), and : 'Vot eti samye milye muzhichki sochineniia grafa L'va Tolstogo' (*Dramy i komedii*, p. 26). My attention was drawn to this curious change, introduced without comment, by Militsa Colan. [Editions which follow the 1940 manuscript, such as *Sobranie sochinenii v piati tomakh*, Moscow, 1990, Vol. 3, (p. 11) have: Vot eti samye milye muzhichki iz sochinenii L'va Tolstogo. *Trans.*]

theatre developed the artistic stiffness brought on by age – and, alas, by considerations of expediency – as could be seen in *Dead Souls*.

Meanwhile, however, MAT was delighted to have *Flight*. The play was delivered to the theatre in March 1928, though written earlier and perhaps existing in different versions.[37] On 9th May Glavrepertkom banned the production.[38] In the autumn of that year the theatre initiated counter-measures. The culminating point was reached at a meeting of MAT's artistic council on 9th October, with a number of important and influential guests present. Sudakov, who had been named as the new director of the play, reported on the direction of the changes agreed with Glavrepertkom; these would be aimed mainly at presenting a more favourable picture of the Reds in the first dream and at making the decision by three of the characters to return home look more like a conscious political choice. The minutes of the meeting show that *Flight* was winning influential support. The outstanding critic and editor Viacheslav Polonsky regarded the play as 'one of the best-written works of the recent period', and although he had some reservations concerning the psychological credibility of the figure of Khludov and foreshadowed the need for changes, he judged that Bulgakov should be granted 'the chance to become a Soviet playwright'. Gorky also spoke up, expressing his enthusiasm and taking Sudakov to task for being too ready to make concessions:

'It is a splendid play. I have read it three times and have also read it to Rykov and other comrades. It is a play which has profound and skilfully concealed satirical content. I would like to see it on the stage at MAT [...]. *Flight* is a wonderful piece which will be an outrageous success [anafemsky uspekh], I assure you.'[39]

A. Svidersky, the head of the newly-formed Central Directorate of Art (Glaviskusstvo) within the Commissariat of Education, was another admirer of the play. He was supposed to assume authority over Glavrepertkom but this turned out to be impossible and soon the relatively liberal policies of the new body –

---

[37] See M. Chudakova, 'Arkhiv...', p. 60 on the works entitled 'Rytsar' Serafimy (Izgoi)' and 'Perekop'.

[38] The decision was appended to a letter sent to MAT's management on 18th May. (MAT Museum; first published in *Neizdannyi Bulgakov*, p. 84.)

[39] Quoted in the minutes of the meeting (MAT Museum), first published in *Neizdannyi Bulgakov*, p. 85-87. For another version of the minutes see *Mosty*, No. 11, 1965, pp. 388-390.

influenced no doubt by the affair of *Flight* – came under concentrated fire.[40] Bulgakov now had another opportunity to taste a refined twist of fickle fate: he had found an official protector, but at the very moment when that protector itself was in grave difficulty. Meanwhile Nemirovich-Danchenko, who was to be artistic director of the play, expressed his optimism ('When Glavrepertkom sees the play on stage I don't think it will object to the production'),[41] and Glavrepertkom, according to information made public two days later, 'gave MAT permission to start rehearsing on condition that certain amendments were made'.[42]

The scene looked set for a repetition of the success of *Days*, achieved with so much effort and strain on the nerves. But time had moved on and the fateful year 1928, as foretold in 'The Fatal Eggs', showed itself indeed to be 'more and more thorny and threatening'. The grip that was strangling the wretched remnants of freedom tightened even more and the *Flight* affair was evidently seen as a good enough pretext for a drive to crush without mercy the last vestiges of relative liberalism. Not all the details of the intrigues behind the scenes are fully known, but a few days later permission was apparently withdrawn. On 23rd October a meeting of the council of Glavrepertkom took place with an unusual agenda: Sudakov read aloud the first part of *Flight* and Raskol'nikov, the chairman of the committee, the second. Then there was discussion, in which Sviderskmy, though formally in charge, was in the minority supporting the play, which in the conditions of the time was quite noteworthy. Sudakov's somewhat contorted argument, according to which the production would be 'a victory in the struggle against Bulgakov' found no acceptance. It was decided to uphold the ban but give the theatre a chance to make changes.[43] The same day the consistently ultra-leftist *Komsomol'skaia pravda* carried a whole column with the headline 'The Backward Flight must be Stopped', the tone of which was truculent in the extreme.[44] Three weeks later *Rabochaia Moskva* ran a report on a meeting of the Moscow core committee of Party cultural workers, at which Sviderskky again defended the play;

---

[40] A penetrating analysis of the history of Glaviskusstvo is given in Sheila Fitzpatrick, 'The Emergence of Glaviskusstvo', *Soviet Studies*, 1971, Vol. 23, No. 2, pp. 236-253.

[41] Minutes of meeting, p. 87.

[42] 'MKhAT prinial k postanovke *Beg* Bulgakova', *Pravda*, 11.10.28.

[43] M. Zagorskii, *Spor o 'Bege'*, an album of cuttings, Lenin Library.

[44] 'Beg nazad dolzhen byt' priostanovlen', *Komsomol'skaia pravda*, 23.10.28.

the tone of both the meeting and the reporting of it is clear from the headline and sub-heading: 'Let us Strike a Blow against Bulgakovism' and 'The Spineless Policy of Glaviskusstvo'.[45]

From this time forth the painful and phantasmal half-existence of *Flight* continued on two levels. MAT did not immediately lose hope. 'For two or three seasons,' wrote Markov, 'rehearsals were resumed which promised great success, but, after vain attempts that went on for a month at a time, new and even stricter bans were imposed.'[46] Meanwhile in the public forum a play which nobody knew outside a handful of initiates became at once a butt for critical barbs and a touchstone of ideological orthodoxy;[47] those who had not read it took the authoritative critics at their word, or thought the very name of Bulgakov was incriminating enough, or treated it purely as a pretext for articulating their own stance.

For this reason the arguments themselves had less importance this time. An extraordinary state of affairs simply became more extraordinary. This meant that even half-truths had little chance, being only half acceptable. The mistake of holding a public hearing in which the public participated, as had happened with *Days*, which had been supported by the audience's enthusiasm, was not to be repeated; *Flight* was condemned *in absentia*.

In the criticism we see for the first time a quantitative leap operating automatically: *Days* had been infuriating because it had given the enemy a platform, which of course brought cries of 'rehabilitation'. But in the Turbins' circle the highest ranking officer was only a colonel. In *Flight* a general treads the boards; this was sufficient to allow it to be said that the apologia embraced the leadership of the White army.

The critics must be given their due: at a time of deliberately heightened vigilance they proved to be extra-vigilant and immediately focussed their anger on what really was most important and most menacing in *Flight*: Khludov's decision and his preservation of his own dignity. It was said that he 'returned to Russia for

---

[45] *Rabochaia Moskva*, 15.11.28.

[46] P. Markov, 'Istoriia...', p. 82.

[47] For example S. Kanatchikov, a RAPP activist, was disciplined for stating that he 'could see nothing anti-Soviet' in *Flight*. (see S. Sheshukov, *Neistovye revniteli*, Moscow, 1970, p. 211.)

spiritual self-cleansing, without regarding his cause as disgraced or discredited',[48] and that 'he bears within himself the White standard, unsullied, and with him [...] his White cause also returns'.[49] It was also stated that Bulgakov 'showed not the bankruptcy of the Whites but their human tragedy',[50] creating a 'theatrical memorial service in memory of the White Guards',[51] presenting them in 'an aura of selfless heroism' and elevating his characters 'to an even higher level of intellectual superiority'.[52] Finally it was announced that *Flight* was 'a play in which the leadership of the White army is rehabilitated',[53] 'a new and worse version of *The Days of the Turbins*'[54] and quite simply 'the most reactionary play of our time'.[55]

The situation, then, was the very opposite of the explanation Konstantin Simonov attempted to offer:[56] the further we find ourselves from the storming of Perekop, the harsher the critical language. This despite the fact that we are dealing with a play which is characterized by a spirit of compromise, even political submission. Reading today the critical comment of that time, it is difficult to resist the thought that it precisely foretells everything that came later.

The most highly-placed defender of *Days* agreed this time with the view of most of the critics when he wrote to Bill'-Belotserkovsky:

'*Flight* is an attempt to evoke warm feelings or even sympathy for certain sectors of the anti-Soviet émigré community – and is therefore an attempt to justify or at least half-justify the White Guard cause. *Flight* in its present form is an anti-Soviet phenomenon.

'It is true,' Stalin went on, 'that I would have nothing against the staging of *Flight* if Bulgakov added another dream or two to the present eight to show the social mainsprings of the Civil War in the USSR, so that the spectator could see

---

[48] R. Pikel', '*Beg* – ot kogo i kuda?', *Zhizn' iskusstva*, No. 22, 1929.

[49] I. Bachelis, 'Tarakanii nabeg', *Komsomol'skaia pravda*, 23.10.28.

[50] P. Novitskii, *Pechat' i revoliutsiia*, No. 4, 1929.

[51] O. Litovskii, *Tak i bylo*, Moscow, 1958, p. 234.

[52] Decision of Glavrepertkom, in *Neizdannyi Bulgakov*, p. 84.

[53] I. Kor, 'Udarim po bulgakovshchine', *Rabochaia Moskva*, 15.11.28.

[54] R. Pel'she, 'Itogi teatral'nogo sezona', *Repertuarnyi biulleten'*, No. 5, 1929.

[55] A. Selivanovskii, 'Votchina metsenatov,' *Literaturnaia gazeta*, 23.9. 29.

[56] K. Simonov, 'Razgovor s tovarishchami', *Voprosy literatury*, No. 9, 1968, p. 86.

[57] Stalin, *Sochineniia*, 1949, Vol. 11, p. 327.

that all those "decent" Serafimas and all those private tutors were expelled from Russia not because of some Bolshevik caprice but because they were sponging on the people,' etc. etc.[57]

Fortunately, though no doubt hearing such suggestions from other quarters too, Bulgakov did not write such a play. A few years later he did indeed make a few more concessions to try and make possible a stage-life for *Flight*. He did this specifically in relation to Khludov. But he did not add 'another dream or two', although some of his literary confrères seized on such opportunities.

We do not know if years later, Litovsky, who was already set in his views for life, writing that *Flight* 'could not run because the author refused to make the minimal number of essential corrections which would have made it acceptable', was thinking of Stalin's suggestions.[58] In any case it hardly matters.

V

The scandal surrounding *Flight* was a harbinger of further far-reaching decisions. These were not long in coming. Earlier separate accusations against Bulgakov relating to his political sins in *Days*, *Zoika's Apartment*, *The Crimson Island* and *Flight* were now drawn together and used to support one another. Reaching yet further into the past, clear evidence of a hostile attitude was found in *The White Guard* and 'The Fatal Eggs'. This was the point when the first long critical article about the writer appeared, by Nusinov, who had earlier published an article about him.[59] Both pieces are couched in the style of a speech for the prosecution, gathering the evidence of guilt into one coherent whole.

There were no speeches for the defence; the defenders of Bulgakov were fighting for their own survival, or else preferred to keep silent. The Bulgakov case was seen as lost in advance. The spirit of the times demanded the unmasking of

---

[58] O. Litovskii, *Glazami...*, p. 17. See also this critic's assertion that 'the Paris scenes *chez* Generals Khludov and Charnota... are worthy of an erotic revue' (*Tak i bylo*, p. 233), although Khludov does not even reach Paris and Charnota only plays cards there.

[59] I. Nusinov, 'Put'...'

[60] I. Bachelis, 'O belykh arapakh i krasnykh tuzemtsakh', *Molodaia gvardiia*, No. 1, 1929. In the light of this and similar statements, Bulgakov's decision to conceal his military service (see Chapter One) in the Tsarist and White armies seems to me very far-sighted.

enemies. Nobody filled this role better than the person who, it was stated, was 'a writer with a single theme and a single idea – the White idea'.[60] But a little later the next victims would be found: Boris Pil'niak and Evgenii Zamiatin, who were accused of publishing 'slanderous' works abroad.

Vecherniaia Moskva reported the removal of Bulgakov's plays from production under the headline 'Theatres freed from Bulgakov's plays'.[61] Other statements were in accord, though not full accord, with this position, saying that 'the exclusion of Bulgakov's plays from the repertoire has not been easy. The theatres put up stiff resistance and used some cunning and endurance before agreeing to take them off.'[62] *The Days of the Turbins*, however, was allowed to run until the end of the season. *Zoika's Apartment* probably had about two hundred performances altogether; *The Crimson Island* had the shortest run of all; the last chance to stage *Flight* finally disappeared in late January 1929, although hope seemed to revive a few years later.

It is characteristic that news of the plays being taken off, in March 1929, almost coincided with Lunacharsky's resignation from the Commissariat of Education.

'We do not wish to suggest by this [the removal of the plays – A.D.] that the name of Bulgakov has been erased from the annals of the Soviet stage',[63] – wrote one of the reviewers. This, however, was a conventional formula, a kind of ritual gesture.

The period of Bulgakov's half-life had begun.

---

[61] 'Teatry osvobozhdaiutsia ot p'es Bulgakova', *Vecherniaia Moskva*, 6.3.29.

[62] *Novyi zritel'*, quoted in A. Al'tshuler, *Dni Turbinykh' i 'Beg' M. Bulgakova v istorii sovetskogo teatra 20-kh godov*. A dissertation presented for the degree of Candidate of Art History, Moscow, 1972, p. 33.

[63] R. Pikel', 'Pered podniatiem zanavesa', *Izvestiia*, 12.11.29.

Chapter Seven

The Crisis, and Essays in Recovery

I. The fickle drama of a writer's fortunes. The flat in Bol'shaia Pirogovskaia Street. The difficult summer of 1929. The application for permission to emigrate.
II. Defence with the aid of literature. The sketch 'To a Secret Friend'. The beginnings of a novel about the Devil.
III. *A Cabal of Hypocrites* and the cabal surrounding the play.
IV. An act of desperation. The letter to the government. The telephone conversation with Stalin.
V. Work in TRAM and MAT. Adapting *Dead Souls*. The day-to-day duties of an employee of MAT.
VI. *Adam and Eve*.
VII. Adapting *War and Peace*. A new season for *The Days of the Turbins*.

I

The drama of Bulgakov's fortunes had a more elaborate structure than any of his plays.

Having started with a bold leap into the unknown, with a romance with literature, he continued the assault on his new profession with a period of determined journey-work, which, however, was good training, a way of getting his hand in until he achieved something close to all-round proficiency. Neither his character nor his circumstances made life easy for him; at an early stage he learned all about collisions with impossibility and lessons in enforced compromise, the dead hand of the censor and plain dishonesty. Much of what he managed to do did not pay off. But he was determined and prepared to take risks; he regrouped his forces, concentrated on the theatre and achieved great success. But each achievement which contributed to that success called forth increasingly furious counter-attacks from the hard-liners who were gradually taking control over cultural policy. Bulgakov's stance, and later his very existence as a writer, offended them deeply. As a result, after ten years' work, the writer was crossed out of cultural life. It was worse than returning to square one, because he was at a lower point, with all exits blocked. A blind wall surrounded him on all sides.

But the desperate lament of Dymogatsky did not burst from his creator's lips. He continued to dazzle with his defiant elegance, although there was no doubt that his vision of tail-coats being generally accepted had faded forever, together with NEP, which had been cut off in mid-stride. He assumed a proud stance that accorded with his image as a 'neo-bourgeois writer'; and this is how he was remembered years later by Ianshin, who interpreted his attitude as saying: 'If you want to see me this way, go ahead! Here you have me. At your service!'[1] He diligently cut out the bloodthirsty reviews, underlining the most savage lines and only occasionally putting question marks in the margins, and hung them on his wall. This was his way of maintaining his challenge, drawing the fangs of the attacking hounds, using humour to deflect threats of danger. It was also his stubborn way of finding domestic refuge, in a home of his own at last, a refuge that he could shape as he chose. While enjoying a wave of success and a surge of royalties, the Bulgakovs had bought a tiny but fully self-contained flat at 35A Bol'shaia Pirogovskaia Street, in a district of medical clinics, right beside a noisy tram depot but also close to the Novodevichii Monastery. This time the writer moved outside the magic circles of central Moscow, though not for long... The interior consisted of small rooms on different levels, which were gradually filled with comfortably antique furniture bought as and when the opportunity arose. In his study, which one entered via two steps, stood a weatherbeaten but handsome desk with two old candlesticks on it, as Bulgakov liked to work and receive guests by candlelight; there was also a lamp with a shade on it, and a bust of Suvorov. Behind the desk stood a book-case, and photographs show mostly the spines of old books; this was a good collection of Russian literature of the nineteenth century, in addition to dictionaries, encyclopedias, manuals, books on the theory of literature, books with dedications from his fellow-writers and presents from friends, books from various fields which interested Bulgakov or for which he had some special use.[2]

---

[1] M. Ianshin, in *Neizdannyi Bulgakov*, Ann Arbor, 1977, p. 53.

[2] For more detail on Bulgakov's library see M. Chudakova, 'Usloviia sushchestvovaniia', *V mire knig*, No. 12, 1974, pp. 79-81.

The description of the future home of the Master, which was actually modelled externally on the home of some friends, would show features of this interior too. There may also be something of the spirit of the Kiev House about it. Until the spring of 1929 it was lively and jolly, so much so that the householder sometimes took refuge in his study; it is true that not all the regular visitors were more than fair-weather friends. Impromptu plays were put on; the atmosphere was one of merriment and good humour. ('Nobody else could joke like you,' Akhmatova would write after Bulgakov's death.)[3] Mikhail Afanas'evich wrote jocular letters signed by cats, drew his demon 'Horns' wearing a diamond ring, while his friend Natalia Ushakova, the graphic artist, did illustrations of episodes from family life. On the walls, besides the reviews turned into exhibits in his private collection, hung earnest slogans turned into jokes, while a visiting card on the door announced 'Bouton Bulgakov, ring twice', referring to the Bulgakovs' russet spaniel.[4]

All this, then, was an attempt at normality, and Liubov' Belozerskaia's memoirs exude the atmosphere of this interlude of stabilization: tennis, riding, concerts, dreams of owning a motor-car, friends in artistic circles, trips to the south...

The blow of the proscription of his plays, though perhaps not wholly unexpected, was crushing when it burst upon all this. The domestic atmosphere must have been deeply affected. Bulgakov's being struck off the register of creative artists also meant financial ruin, particularly as the tax inspector, a regular visitor, was in the process of levying a substantial surtax based on the indicators of a period of prosperity, and in the autumn MAT would demand the return of an advance for *Flight*, which had not been produced.[5]

The summer of 1929 was a very difficult time. Published excerpts from a letter to his brother Nikolai show Bulgakov's courageous restraint:

---

[3] See Akhmatova's poem 'Pamiati M. B-va', *Den' poezii*, Leningrad, 1966.

[4] For an account of this period with much detail on day-to-day life see L. Belozerskaia-Bulgakova, *O, med vospominanii*, Ann Arbor, 1979, p. 67 ff.

[5] See M. Chudakova, 'Arkhiv M. A. Bulgakova. Materialy dlia tvorcheskoi biografii pisatelia', in *Zapiski Otdela rukopisei Gos. Bibl. SSSR im. Lenina*, Moscow, 1976, p. 85.

'And now I must tell you that my situation is not favourable. Production of all my plays has been proscribed in the USSR and nobody will publish so much as a line of my prose-writing.

'In 1929 my annihilation as a writer has been completed. [...]

'A dark rumour that I am doomed in every sense of the word is already circulating.

'If my request [for permission to travel abroad – A.D.] is refused you can consider the game over, stack the cards and snuff out the candles.

'I shall have to stay in Moscow and not write, since not only my writing but any mention of my name can't be tolerated.

'Without being at all faint-hearted I can tell you that my elimination is only a matter of time. Unless some miracle happens. But miracles don't happen often. Please write and tell me if you can understand what I'm saying in this letter, but don't on any account express any sympathy or consolation, to avoid upsetting my wife.'[6]

The situation looked hopeless. There was no prospect of any improvement, for the struggle with the 'Right' was being extrapolated from intra-Party intrigue into all areas of life. This was the culminating moment of the expansion of the hard-line, dictatorial RAPP, which with the blessing of the authorities and the aid of similar groupings in various spheres of the arts, was dictating the fundamentals of cultural policy. It would do this for the next three years, before being deemed an insufficiently effective instrument. Many a writer would be cowed, crushed and condemned to ideological anathema but few would be so mercilessly robbed of any chance they might have had.[7]

---

[6] Ibid., p. 81; also in V. V. Gudkova, 'Ne vse li ravno, gde byt' nemym; Pis'ma M. A. Bulgakova bratu, N. A. Bulgakovu', *Druzhba narodov*, No. 2, 1989, p. 204-205; *Dnevnik. Pis'ma 1914-1940*, Moscow, 1997, p. 209.

[7] RAPP's negative classification embraced a substantial proportion of the literature of the day and new names were being constantly added. Note that in attacking Bulgakov the critics often placed him in a broader context, juxtaposing with him Leonov and Kataev, and of the classics Chekhov and Dostoevsky (B. Vaks, 'V zashchitu kritiki', *Zhizn' iskusstva*, No. 25, 1929). As a satirist Bulgakov was likened to Ehrenburg, 'a provincial follower of Anatole France', and Il'f and Petrov, 'who trace their ancestry back to Bulgakov's cheap Conan-Doylism' (N. Zubov, 'Satira i iumor v sovetskom teatre', *Vecherniaia Moskva*, 15.10.1931). A 'genealogical tree' of contemporary

It was logical, then, that the idea of emigration should occur; the action he had almost taken once before now looked like the only solution. In the summer and early autumn Bulgakov drafted letters to the government requesting permission to leave the country. Some of these have been published;[8] it is not known for certain which of them are final versions and which are drafts, but all of them reflect his resignation, exhaustion and awareness of his hopeless situation. Gorky was one of those whose help he sought. A letter to him dated 28.9.29 concludes with these words:

'All my plays have been banned; nobody will publish a line that I write; I have no work ready to sell and I receive not a kopeck by way of royalties. No institution or individual will answer my requests. In short, everything I have written in ten years of work in the USSR has been destroyed. All that remains is for them to destroy me as well.

'I am asking for a humane decision: to let me go.'[9]

II

For the moment his cries went unheard. Everything was exactly as Popov said: 'Being in his private life a man of extremes, of profound contradictions and changeable moods, he found relief at this time of defeat in a surge of emotional energy.'[10]

At the darkest moments in his life the writer protected himself with literature, and the worse his situation the more intensely he worked. At his desk at night, by candlelight, with a sheet of paper in front of him, he was master of the

---

literature published in *Na literaturnom postu* placed Bulgakov on the lowest right-hand branch, amongst the 'Bourgeois writers' A. Tolstoi, Zamiatin and Ehrenburg. Beneath him were only the 'living corpses' Akhmatova, Voloshin and Bely.

[8] See the broad selection of Bulgakov's correspondence and related material published by Lesley Milne in 'K biografii M.A. Bulgakova', *Novyi zhurnal*, No. 111, 1973, p. 152 ff.

[9] Ibid., p. 154. Another, shorter, letter about this matter to the same addressee bears the date 3.9.29 (Ibid., p. 153). Both letters are also in *Dnevnik. Pis'ma*, pp. 210-212.

[10] P. Popov, *Zametki avtobiograficheskogo kharaktera*, Manuscript Department of the Lenin Library, Fond 218.

situation. The world was shut out, beyond his window; even the noisy trams, whose rumble usually annoyed him, failed to bother him.

He had recently met a woman who would become an important figure in his life: Elena Sergeevna Shilovskaia. This friendship would be on two levels: one of them official, the other concealed for a long time. This latter level gradually became more important and from his sense of its importance no doubt arose the sketch 'To a Secret Friend', written in the summer of 1929, when Elena Sergeevna was away.[11] This work is a brief summary of the more important moments in a part of his life which had recently drawn to a close. It is a story about himself, for himself and someone close to him, probably set down in order to understand what had happened and to open new ways forward. It is also possible that his incisive pen laid certain ghosts. Whatever the case, he felt this to be a liberating gesture, while feeling a compulsion: his experiences must be digested and set down on paper; a self-declared writer, one who is a writer by choice, is entirely a writer; his writing is his life.

The people, institutions and episodes in this sketch are transparently pseudonymous, but their authenticity is plain. We have here, with certain shifts in the order of events, the well-known peregrinations of *The White Guard*, involving Lezhnev-Rudol'fi and Kagansky-Rvatsky and their disappearance, on which somebody remarks, 'Do you know that your Rudol'fi has been abducted by an evil spirit and so has Rvatsky!' There is a graphic description of wage-slavery at *Gudok* and a mention of *Nakanune*, here called 'Sochel'nik' (Christmas Eve). There are echoes of those Kiev experiences and nightmares – as well as a visit from Rudol'fi, who for the first time appears to the hero as a latter-day devil. All of this will later be taken up again in *A Theatrical Novel*. But in the meantime this is a significant meeting-point of strands and motifs which are important to the author; it represents a door standing ajar and affording a glimpse into his laboratory. There is no doubt that Marietta Chudakova is right to say, in her perceptive analysis of this fragment of writing, that 'in this abstract of a story we find in condensed form the "necessary and sufficient" features of his prose, stripped of all that is "optional", everything that might characterize one work but be absent from another. [...] From this angle Bulgakov's artistic work plots a course in various directions at once. We can see the motifs of a novel he has already written, *The White Guard*,

---

[11] See Chapter Two, Note 23. Also in *Dnevnik. Pis'ma*, pp. 593-614.

those of one that was emerging in that year (1929), then entitled "The Engineer's Hoof", and also of *A Theatrical Novel*. In this unique memorandum prepared for his "secret reader" various ideas are seen in exceptionally close cohabitation; the novel which has already been written appears suddenly in the form of its primary impulses and the contours of one still unfinished are sketched; elements of his personal biography are closely intertwined with others which have been artistically refashioned, and so the story assumes the role of a meta-novel describing the writer's other works (compare the structure of *The Master and Margarita*).'[12]

The interpenetration and overlap of motifs can clearly be seen; and it is no accident that demonic motifs hold pride of place. Through these we draw closer to his main work. It was already coming into existence, probably as early as 1928. It also helps the author overcome despair, though it too soon falls victim – for a time – to this despair.

Diabolus minor was summoned to his greatest task. He had been seen in a comical dream in 'The Adventures of Chichikov', introduced into a Moscow office to confound Korotkov and sow confusion where confusion already abounds, 'disguised as a blizzard' in 'Number 13', and invoked every minute by Persikov – evidently with good reason – and less frequently by Preobrazhensky; he had been seen seen in Aleksei Turbin's dream – less comically this time – and been appealed to time and again by all who gave him a thought. Until now he had fulfilled his usual function, while remaining in the background. Now his hour had struck. Bulgakov resorted to the Devil as a main character. What emerged, according to a description which the author consistently repeated, was 'a novel about the Devil'.

We must thank Marietta Chudakova, who had access to the Bulgakov archive, for a particularly detailed description of the eight successive versions of the novel.[13] At first it bore the title 'The Engineer's Hoof' [Kopyto inzhenera]. By May 1929 at least fifteen chapters were ready. They were partially burned by the author in March 1930, at the point when despair got the better of him.[14]

---

[12] M. Chudakova, 'Arkhiv...', pp. 83-85.

[13] M. Chudakova, 'Arkhiv...', and 'Tvorcheskaia istoriia romana M. Bulgakova *Master i Margarita*', *Voprosy literatury*, No. 1, 1976, pp. 218-253.

[14] When Bulgakov tore out and partially burned some pages, he left evidence of the novel's existence – sufficient to make possible an attempted reconstruction; see M. Chudakova,

Chudakova, however, having the opportunity to compare texts, proposed and carried through a convincing reconstruction of the greater part of the text which had been destroyed. She also researched the author's surviving notes from his source materials.

She established that from the very beginning these materials had dealt with Christ and the Devil above all, and that the strand with which the novel opens, the meeting in the square, the death of Berlioz, the evening at the Variety Theatre and the peregrinations of the people connected with that institution took the same form as in the final version, as did the evening in Griboedov House. The biblical strand remained at this stage enclosed in a single chapter narrated by Woland, with constant emphasis on his presence as narrator. Certain tangential motifs, which later disappeared, were also limned in. Many characters bore different names. Bulgakov always selected names with great care, trying out various versions. Gradually the presence of the Devil's retinue assumed firm shape, as a result of Bulgakov's study of the Brockhaus and Efron encyclopedia and a book by M. Orlov, *The History of Relations between Man and the Devil* [Istoriia snoshenii cheloveka s d'iavolom]. The idea of a witches' sabbath can also be seen, 'perhaps linked in the author's imagination with Satan's ball.'[15] The second draft of the first four chapters, completed at the same time, introduced the Judas strand.

This is how things stood at this point, and an event of great importance had already occurred: into the very heart of everyday Moscow life, at a time close to that of the conception of the novel, a devil or magician had entered as a *diabolus ex machina*, a new incarnation of Bulgakov's conceptual and situational sense of the fantastic, as the unfettered play of imagination applied by a free act of the creative will to a fixed pattern of reality; as a 'what if ...?', and perhaps even as a whimsically literal materialization of the constantly repeated phrase 'to the Devil with it' and 'the Devil take it'.

Who can say whether at some point the pupil of Gogol, having exclaimed in anger, 'the Devil take the lot of it!', did not break off suddenly, listen to his own fading words and think, as he later wrote: 'the Devil take it? That can be arranged'?

'Arkhiv...', and especially 'Opyt rekonstruktsii teksta M.A. Bulgakova' in *Pamiatniki kul'tury. Novye otkrytiia. Ezhegodnik*, Moscow, 1977, pp. 93-106.

[15] M. Chudakova, 'Arkhiv...', p. 77; see this source for information on the nature of the first two drafts (pp. 63-80).

And indeed it could. From this time on, though with interruptions, the novel would be the companion of all his other projects – long kept secret, but occasionally partially disclosed. But we need to bear in mind that at the beginning the demonic visitor does not have sufficient power to provide much protection against life. An invocation by the pen does not always work; the emotional charge will not overcome everything. This is why the moment would come when the hand that had invoked the Devil would consign his novel about him to the flames.

Such acts do not go unpunished.

III

What was it that finally exhausted Bulgakov's powers of endurance on that March day?

It may have been everything taken together, suddenly felt to be an unbearable burden. It may also have been the news from Glavrepertkom that production of the play about Molière would not be permitted.[16] For in the bitter year 1929 the writer had also used this play as a defence. This was a completely natural gesture. He knew the value of what he had already done and was very sensitive about it, while affecting to despise carping reviews. He knew that his actions and his understanding of the role of the writer placed him firmly within a tradition that was both Russian and universal. It was also close to him as an ethical and aesthetic anchor amidst the convulsions of the present, which exceeded in violence even his boldest visions. It is not surprising that among the writers of the past he should discern kindred spirits and wish to investigate the meaning of their experience. He must have felt that this would be of benefit not only to him.

What followed was a new manoeuvre; he would withdraw into himself and into history at the same time. This was an even more determined attempt to by-pass the blind wall, while preserving what was most precious. At that time many writers sought to escape by husbanding their resources in various ways or by

---

[16] See the draft fragment of his letter: 'On 18th May [clearly a mistake – this should read 'March'; A.D.] 1930 I received from Glavrepertkom a document informing me laconically that my play *Molière (A Cabal of Hypocrites)* had not received permission to go into production'. *Grani*, No. 66, 1967, p. 160. [The letter is printed in full in *Dnevnik. Pis'ma*, pp. 222-231. Bulgakov here (p. 227) gives the date 18th March. – *Trans.*]

withdrawing – into history, into children's literature, or into travel to seek new inspiration. Ephemeral genres such as sketches and reportage were popular; some allowed themselves to be recruited for the tasks of the moment. Genuine creative artists were able to extract some benefit even from situations they were half-coerced into; lesser lights were confined to stereotyped illustrations, while the opportunists could tack boldly with the wind. Before long Bulgakov would impale these singers of the praises of 'rosy-cheeked collective-farm girls' on his nib and as long as he lived would not forgive them for besmirching the honour of the profession.

For himself, rebounding from the depths of ill fortune, he now found what would become one of the most important themes of his writing: the fate of the artist confronting tyranny and the spiritual corruption caused by tyranny.

He is supposed to have said that when he died and went to Heaven the first person he would meet would be Molière. He always felt a particular affinity with the author of *Tartuffe*, perhaps sensing certain similarities of character and personality, apart from everything else. The similarities in their careers must have impressed themselves upon him, since both were dependent on the whim of their lords and masters and completely at their mercy. He therefore made a careful study of the life and work of Molière in order to use him, as he used Gogol and Pushkin, to elucidate certain of his own riddles; and conversely, he reconstructed his own 'Molièrade' from elements not only culled from his reading but also proven by experience. This was a kind of dialogue with history, in which he posed questions and sought answers to them. The nature of his immersion in Molière became even clearer in his subsequent book about him.

'For some time,' wrote Popov, 'Mikhail Afanas'evich has talked of nothing but Molière. He collects books about him, visits libraries, explicates his works and tries to understand him from the inside.'[17] The first product of this was the play *A Cabal of Hypocrites*, written between October and December 1928. The 'Molièriana' which he perused in connection with this are reflected in the notes in his archive, but, as usual with Bulgakov, historical truth took second place, after the higher logic of artistic truth.

In its packaging, *Cabal* is perhaps the most traditional of all Bulgakov's dramatic output. It operates with tried and tested devices, stylizing events in the

---

[17] Quoted in *Sovetskie pisateli. Avtobiografii*, Moscow, 1966, Vol. III, p. 98. On his work on *Cabal*, see M. Chudakova, 'Arkhiv...', pp. 85-93.

manner of the period and the literature about the period, and even of a received, popular notion of 'Frenchness', – to produce a classical *pièce bien faite* of the highest order. At the same time, however, it seems to be fully imbued with an awareness of the play of styles; one senses the discreetly placed quotation marks. 'French' material and Bulgakov's material coexist and intertwine. The first comprises love as a ruinous passion, the intrigues of a hooded mafia, musketeering cloak-and-dagger rituals, insults and duels, an eloquence and elegance of gesture, not to mention a rascally servant, an inconstant wife, a treacherous prince of the Church, a mysterious stranger and a swashbuckling duellist; all in all this is much in the manner of Dumas *père*. The touch of Bulgakov's pen may be felt in the atmosphere, the shadow and shading of certain scenes, reminding us that *Cabal* was written after *Flight*; in the play of voices and sounds, the singing of choirs and the winking of lights; in the demonic changes in Archbishop Charron, who at one point, without any additional motivation, becomes a servant of Hades, and in the sinister figure of the nun;[18] as well as in the stage directions, which, as in *Flight*, develop into prose *études* in their own right, establishing a certain mood.

From this material Bulgakov fashions a structure which is very much his own. The theatrical framework is of special importance here; the play opens and concludes with a play by Molière as seen from behind the scenes, showing the nervous ambivalence of the performers and the gilded tinsel of play-acting that is striving for the highest patronage. This is no more than a fragment of a play within a play, unlike *The Crimson Island*; but the theatricality is all-pervasive in the dual nature of the game being played; the stakes being the play itself, and life itself. Hence the brightness of the striking colours, the dazzling effects and dynamic conflicts when the shadows and darkness recede.

The writer selects and alters the historical elements in his presentation of what matters most to him: his hero, devoted to his work, to the exclusion even of moral scruples. *Tartuffe* constitutes Molière's morality; for the sake of his play he is ready to play the part of court eulogist. At first he can carry it off, but fittingly,

---

[18] M. Bulgakov, *Dramy i komedii*, Moscow, 1966, p. 259. These stage directions are, however, absent in the earlier edition (*P'esy*, Moscow, 1962), as is the figure of the nun. The latter edition may have been based on the version censored by Glavrepertkom (see the commentary by Chudakova in 'Arkhiv...', note on p. 92). It is surprising that these editions leave such significant textual disparities without commentary (see also Chapter Six, note 36).

at his moment of triumph, the mocking mask of Charlatan keeps appearing, to underscore the irony of the situation. As we know, collisions such as these are among Bulgakov's favourite effects. The tide of success at once bears with it the germ of defeat; the decision is taken to marry Armande Béjart, who may be Molière's own daughter; the traitor-to-be Moirron also appears. Acts Two and Three paint a picture of a struggle to maintain a position in the face of swelling intrigues, while the king is a cool, aloof arbiter, observing at a distance the contest for his favour, but also wholly convinced of his own superhuman nature. Molière loses this struggle; his opponents deploy blackmail, slander, denunciations, provocation and hired assassins – and Act Four, while repeating the play-acting situation, smacks of defeat.[19]

In this condensation of the case of Molière, a pen quivering with the author's own feelings is apparent. We know that in reality much was different.[20] But the playwright was fully entitled to fashion the historical material into a kind of extended argument about the situation of the writer in an abnormal context. This abnormality is decreed by tyranny, by the concentration of power in the hands of one person, permitting him at the merest whim to preordain the existence or non-existence of people and their works. Molière has many enemies; a cabal of these destroys him, but, just as in *The Crimson Island*, the diagnosis points to the main culprit, the tyrant – all the more dangerous for being so refined. In conditions of tyranny a pretext is sufficient; and perhaps this is the way we should treat the theme of Molière's supposed incest, which is well developed in the play.[21] In a certain atmosphere every element of the royal playwright's disorderly life could be used against him; incest turned out to be the most convenient. Bulgakov leaves no doubt as to what is important to him in the play and what is secondary.

---

[19] This structure, in which the conclusion takes us back to the situation at the beginning but gives it a different meaning, is reminiscent of the composition of *The Days of the Turbins*.

[20] For instance, in reality Louis XIV banned performances of *Tartuffe* only for a while, and not immediately before the death of Molière, who did not die on stage. The Brotherhood of the Holy Writ, shown by Bulgakov, was in reality known as the Company of the Holy Sacrament (though it was indeed derisively termed 'The Cabal of Hypocrites' [La Cabale des dévots]) and was disbanded four years before *Tartuffe* was staged. Some characters had models in life, though Bulgakov subjected them to fictionalization.

[21] Molière specialists regard this matter as unproven.

The play's difficulties also seem to indicate that those who dealt with it understood or sensed what it was really about. At the time of its genesis the contemporary despot was only beginning to set about creating his own cult, but with time the idolatry grew apace. Bulgakov did not write a flat allegory with allusions and winks at the audience. Instead he uncovered features of the past that corresponded to the present and he consciously underscored them. We may exclude all possibility that, in the marvellous scene of the obsequious applause for Louis XIV, he had no one else in mind. The same applies to the draft sketch of Molière's first audience with the king, who toys with his servile courtiers by ordering them to guess his moods;[22] Bulgakov must have known that the new tyrant enjoyed precisely such perverted and humiliating games as this. Delation, without which, in the view of the king's righteous cobbler and court jester, 'the kingdom cannot exist', also had quite an evocative echo, when combined with blackmail, provocation and entrapment of one's nearest and dearest to produce a 'dossier' to be slipped to the supreme arbiter. Bulgakov was aware of the uses of informing and did not lose sight of it. He knew what he was writing when his Molière exclaimed, 'All my life I've been licking his spurs and thinking the same thought: Don't crush me! And he's crushed me all the same! The tyrant! [...] Don't grovel, Bouton! I detest the king's tyranny.'[23] And Bouton, horrified, does his best to drown out his voice with his own cries in honour of the king; this device would be repeated later.

Considering the time of writing, this whole seam of double meanings – or, if you prefer, of enduring and supratemporal meanings – turned out to be extremely prophetic. It must also have spoken eloquently to Bulgakov's contemporaries. But the situation did not permit them to speak of the central issue. This is why around his *Cabal* or *Conspiracy* a new and highly characteristic conspiracy developed; a conspiracy to pretend that this was a play about something entirely different, to

---

[22] See the fragment cited by Chudakova: 'Louis: Messieurs! Are there among you no admirers of the writer de Molière? Speaking for myself, I count myself among them. [Agitation] Courtiers: Magnificent works. Louis: Well, my writer feels oppressed. He is afraid... I shall be grateful if anyone can tell me of any danger that threatens him. (To Molière) To the best of our limited ability we shall protect you.' Chudakova, 'Arkhiv...', p. 90.

[23] M. Bulgakov, *Dramy i komedii*, Moscow, 1965, p. 274.

manufacture a central theme from a peripheral matter and criticize this artificially centred element, in order to push a dangerous object into the furthest background.

And so it happened, in spite of a glimmer of dawn in October 1931, when the censor waived the ban. Gorky was instrumental in this; his succinct and very favourable evaluation of the play has survived, along with Bulgakov's letter thanking him for his help.[24] The road onto the stage seemed to be clear for *Cabal*. But it turned out to be a long and tortuous one.

IV

Meanwhile in March 1930 a ban was imposed. Even before this it was clear that the outlook was grim. Bulgakov had written of this to his brother. In one of his letters we read: 'In unbelievably difficult conditions I have tried to discharge my mission as a writer as I should (...) At night I rack my anguished brain trying to think of a way out. But I can't think of any. Who, I wonder, is there still left for me to turn to?'[25]

It was already clear whom he should turn to and who really decided these matters, but it was necessary to observe the proper forms. No doubt this is why the draft letter cited earlier is addressed to 'the Soviet government'. The spirit of the age was Tartuffian to the core, and the writer's situation was assuming the shape of a sequel to his *Cabal*.

---

[24] 'Of M. Bulgakóv's play *Molière* I can say that in my view it is very good, artfully designed and each part in it gives rich material for the actor. The author has been very successful in this, which again confirms the general view of his talent and ability as a playwright. He has created a wonderful portrait of Molière in his last days, a Molière worn down by both the complexity of his private life and the burden of fame. The Sun King has been rendered just as effectively, boldly, and I would say, nicely, although all parts are well done. I am absolutely convinced that the Art Theatre will produce it successfully, and of this I am very glad. A splendid play.' (From a letter to Bulgakov's Berlin publisher Fischer-Verlag, Gorky's archive. This archive also contains Bulgakov's letter of 25.12.31, saying, 'My *Molière* has received permission. Knowing how important your favourable view of the play was in obtaining permission, I want to thank you from the bottom of my heart.')

[25] M. Chudakova, 'Arkhiv...', p. 92. The letter is dated 21.2.30. Also in *Dnevnik. Pis'ma*, pp. 218-219.

Everything happened at once, possibly even on the same day. An important sequel to the conflagrations in Bulgakov's fiction was suddenly provided by the burning of that fiction itself; the piquancy was shocking. 'Personally, with my own hands' – we sense what this emphasis means – 'I threw the draft of a novel about the Devil into the stove, along with the draft of a comedy and the beginning of another novel called *The Theatre*.' These words come from a draft of one of the writer's letters, written at the same time.[26]

We repeat: we do not know the relation between the draft and the letter. It is highly unlikely that it was identical with it. But the authenticity of the draft is not in question, so it may be regarded as the raw material of the letter. We recognize the circumstances of Bulgakov's own situation. He writes of matters we know of: of three hundred and one reviews, of which three were favourable; of the jibes aimed at *Days*; of the idea that *The Crimson Island* is not a lampoon on the revolution but a pamphlet aimed at Glavrepertkom (referring to Novitsky's favourable notice). The author describes the features of his writing: 'black and mystical colours [...] showing the innumerable deformities of our life, the venom in which my tongue is steeped, a profound scepticism with regard to the process of revolution which is taking place in my backward country and a comparison between this and my preferred Great Evolution, and above all a picture of the terrible features of my people [...], and a consistent portrayal of the Russian intelligentsia as the best stratum in our country.' The conclusion is, 'Now I have been destroyed.'[27] Pikel' and Averbakh are mentioned as proof that the critics give a writer no chance. In closing Bulgakov begs to be 'released' (this fragment was for some reason allowed to be extensively cited in his homeland), or 'given work in a theatre as a director', an extra or stage-hand.

The real addressee responded to one of the letters by telephoning. He liked gestures of this sort, knew what dose to administer and knew their weight. For him this was a fairly difficult moment – one of the last in which he still felt

---

[26] Draft letter to the Soviet government (see Chapter Six, Note 22). [Also in *Novyi mir*, No. 8, 1987, pp. 194-198 and *Dnevnik. Pis'ma. 1914-1940*, Moscow, 1997, pp. 222-228; in English translation in Lesley Milne, *Mikhail Bulgakov: A critical biography*, Cambridge, 1990, pp. 268-274. The authenticity of this document has been confirmed by these later publications. – *Trans.*]

[27] *Novyi mir*, No. 8, 1987, pp. 195-197; *Dnevnik. Pis'ma.* pp. 225-227; Milne, *Mikhail Bulgakov: A critical biography*, pp. 270-272.

relatively insecure – after his article entitled 'Giddy with Success', in which he manoeuvred himself out of the officially sanctioned injustice of forced collectivization. It has also been suggested that Maiakovsky's suicide by shooting on 14th April 1930 may have caused Stalin to be indulgent towards literature. The conversation took place four days later, on 18th April.

Accounts differ in the detail, but the approximate record set down later by Elena Bulgakova is not disputed:

'We've received your letter. My comrades and I have read it. You will receive a favourable reply. Are you really asking to go abroad? Are you so sick of us here?'

'I've been thinking a lot lately about whether a Russian writer can live outside his country, and it seems to me that he can't.'

'You're right. I don't think so either. Where would you like to work? At the Moscow Art Theatre?'

'Yes, I'd like that. But when I raised the matter I was refused.'

'Why don't you apply? I believe they will agree...'[28]

We can hardly assume that Bulgakov, with his acute sensitivity, failed to appreciate the jocular inflection in the last sentence. But the sense of these conversations was fully serious and the surprised recipients of these calls were often at a loss for words. Only later did the jokes and legends which circulate to this day arise. Both testify to the spirit of the time.

Thus it was that the ruler who was then depriving millions of Russian peasants of a chance in life granted one to a Russian intellectual. He offered him his protection. Being fond of historical postures, consciously or not, Stalin to some degree emulated the relationship between Nicholas I and Pushkin, although the result was trivial and bureaucratic, lacking in majesty and grand gestures. The *Cabal of Hypocrites* played on, played by life itself, but life altered the role of Louis XIV in it. Moreover, Bulgakov was not given permission for any *Tartuffe*.

But by a gesture of lordly grace he was granted the opportunity to exist.

As the transcript of the conversation shows, he chose to exist in his own country. Why he did this he alone could tell.

---

[28] Quoted in S. Liandres, 'Russkii pisatel' ne mozhet zhit' bez rodiny', *Voprosy literatury*, No. 9, 1966, p. 139; also in M. A. Bulgakov, *Pis'ma. Zhizneopisanie v dokumentakh*, Moscow, 1989, pp. 173-174; *Dnevnik. Pis'ma*, p. 230.

V

The consequences of that conversation were not long in coming. Bulgakov was visited by a delegation from the Young Workers' Theatre (TRAM). A contract, backdated to 3rd April, for Bulgakov to work as a 'drama-directing consultant' was speedily concluded.[29] This theatre was part of a movement which bore the same name and its speciality was dramatized journalism, so the involvement of this particular writer in it was somewhat strange, but stranger things had happened to him in the past. That summer he therefore set off with them for the Crimea. He was polite with them, though probably always kept his distance, as this tribe was alien to him. He was soon discharging his duties in his usual conscientious manner – when there was work to do it had to be done well. A number of his internal reviews have survived, in which he gives a sober appraisal of the first attempts of some would-be playwrights. For example, he advises one of them, instead of condemning 'the bourgeois way of life', to keep his feet on the ground: 'The snow-white tablecloth of a bourgeois restaurant must be matched by another snow-white tablecloth.'[30] In matters of detail he remained true to himself. He left TRAM after a year, pleading ill health, and indeed the difficult times had taken their toll on his robust health, producing neurasthenia, insomnia, frequent bouts of depression and fatigue.

No sooner had he joined TRAM than in May 1930 he found a more suitable place for himself, perhaps even the best possible position at the time, in the Moscow Art Theatre. His nomination to the post of assistant director formalized a *de facto* connection which had existed until shortly before this; Bulgakov's creative input into the work on his own plays was stressed by all, especially by Stanislavsky, who wrote to the newcomer in August 1930, on his return from abroad:

'My dear Mikhail Afanas'evich,

You can't imagine how glad I am to have you in our theatre! I was able to work with you only on a few rehearsals of *The Days of the Turbins*, but I sensed that you were a director (probably an actor too?). Molière and many others have

---

[29] IRLI, Fond 369.
[30] Ibid.

combined this profession with writing. I welcome you with all my heart. I sincerely believe in our success and would very much like to start work with you as soon as possible.'[31]

This wish was soon to come true, although the realities of co-operation turned out to be different from the pastel vision.

For the moment the future looked bright. As he did not have any play of his own in the theatre, Bulgakov could start at once on the work he felt made for: a play based on Gogol's *Dead Souls*. An earlier adaptation did in fact exist, but the author of 'The Adventures of Chichikov' wrote two years later that at the sight of it he 'saw green'. He added, 'I realized that at the very door of the Theatre I was in deep trouble. I had been assigned to a non-existent play. A good beginning? [...] In short, the writing of it fell to me.'[32]

The new version took shape that summer and autumn, in collaboration with the director, Vasilii Sakhnovsky. The author did his best, of course, to equal Gogol's vision in the things that had always fascinated him: in the combination of pitilessly accurate detail and the disturbing ambiguity of this detail, which commanded the viewer to see in it the surface of an essentially dreamlike world. We know that, according to the original design, events were to be viewed from the perspective of Rome, where *Dead Souls* had first been created, and this distance was a matter of some importance to Bulgakov. It was also to be set in a stylized ornamental frame, to emphasize that it was a dream. The inevitable impoverishment of Gogol's multi-dimensional prose, brought about by translating it into a series of theatrical scenes and shifting the plot into the foreground, would be partly compensated by the introduction of a narrator, to some extent personifying Gogol himself. Not only fragments of the novel are placed in his mouth, but also a meticulously constructed mosaic consisting of a number of different, sometimes minimal fragments of Gogol's texts, to produce the

---

[31] Quoted in V. Sakhnovskii-Pankeev, 'Bulgakov', in *Ocherki istorii russkoi sovetskoi dramaturgii*, Moscow-Leningrad, 1966, pp. 128-129. Note a letter from Bulgakov to Stanislavsky, written a month earlier: 'After the deep sadness I've had about my lost plays, I felt better when, after a long interval, and in a new capacity, I crossed the threshold of the theatre you have created for the glory of the country.' Chudakova, 'Arkhiv...', p. 94; also in *Dnevnik. Pis'ma*, p. 238.

[32] Quoted in Chudakova, 'Arkhiv...', p. 93.

impression of a cohesive whole. In this way the basis of the lyricism of Gogol's prose is preserved. At the end of the adaptation the elements of a phantasmagorical situation are clearly limned in, especially by Korobochka's mechanical questions and by the introduction of the figure of Captain Kopeikin, the crippled brigand.[33]

From Sakhnovsky's extensive account it emerges that this way of seeing and treating the great classic seemed apt and fruitful, although, to Bulgakov's regret, the Roman perspective was soon abandoned.[34] Everything else, however, was retained. His ideas for the staging were taken up and developed in sketches and models by the gifted set-designer Vladimir Dmitriev. A stylized elegance was combined with a disturbing degree of hyperbole in the detail, pregnant with deeper meanings. As usual with Bulgakov, the musical score played an important part, as can be seen especially from the planned conclusion, as described by Sakhnovsky:

'As the bells of Chichikov's departing troika rang out, there came gradually, from various directions, the sound of other bells. These bells grew louder and louder; then came the thunder and rumble of a hyperbolic, rushing troika. Into this sound background blended a voice, singing a coachman's song. Then the song was taken up by a choir with organ accompaniment; the orchestra, choir, organ and drums swelled to *fortissimo* before gradually fading through *diminuendo* into silence. The curtain came down in darkness and when the house lights came up it was already in position.'[35]

The play was developing steadily in a particular direction – until the autumn of 1931, when events took a new turn.

In the meanime, for several months Bulgakov was only feeling his way and finding fulfilment to a limited degree. This was a period of perceptible numbness – rare for Bulgakov – , a kind of semi-paralysis of his creative faculties. He was still suffering from the effects of shock. Motifs of physical indisposition constantly

---

[33] On Bulgakov's design, see V. Sakhnovskii, *Rabota rezhissera*, Moscow-Leningrad, 1937, p. 210 ff., and Lesley Milne, 'M.A. Bulgakov and *Dead Souls*: The problems of adaptation', *Slavonic and East European Review*, No. 128, July 1974, pp. 420-440. [On the subsequent fate of Kopeikin in the adaptation, see Chapter Eight – *Trans.*]

[34] See a letter to Popov dated 7th May, 1932: 'My Rome was eliminated the moment I submitted my general plan. And I'm terribly sorry about it!' Quoted in Chudakova, 'Arkhiv...', p. 94. Also in *Dnevnik. Pis'ma*, p. 274.

[35] Sakhnovskii, *Rabota...*, p. 248.

recurred. 'The cause of my ailment is the hounding I have suffered for many years, followed by silence'[36] runs the former doctor's diagnosis in the draft of a new letter to Stalin, dated 30th May 1931. Again we do not know whether this letter was sent, or in what form. This draft is not the last of those that are known; Bulgakov was clearly trying to turn to advantage the strange situation he found himself in, but who can tell whether the attempt was abandoned before it finally bore fruit? In any event nothing was heard of any new results; his protector was silent. Bulgakov, however, if Paustovsky's memoirs are to be believed, turned his epistolary activity – whether fully realized or only planned – into a joke.[37] This was very like him, even if he did take liberties with facts. In the letter we are speaking of he argues his case for permission to travel abroad 'from 1st July to 1st October 1931'. He explains that he is physically unwell. He lists his works. He gives assurances that he will not settle abroad and asks permission for his wife to accompany him. He also seeks an audience and refers to the earlier telephone conversation in which Stalin himself suggested that he go abroad.[38]

There is in all this a kind of hope of creating a new version of the relationship between Nicholas I and Pushkin. But it cannot be repeated – the material is lacking. Bulgakov's privileged position brings only negative benefits – in the things that he does *not* have to face. He has a minimalist patron. His protector remains silent.

Meanwhile the well-meaning Veresaev wrote to Bulgakov, 'It is quite clear to me that one of the reasons for your severe depression is that you have abstained from writing.'[39]

He emerged only gradually from his state of shock. There were signs of a return to the main design of his novel. This was probably his third attempt. Its known results are fragmentary: the figure of Margarita shines through for a

---

[36] Quoted in Milne, 'K biografii...', p. 155.

[37] 'Bulgakov supposedly writes Stalin long and mysterious letters every day, signing them "Trampazlin".' (In the further development of this theme a supposed meeting between Bulgakov and Stalin is described in the spirit of jokes and stories popular at the time.) K. Paustovskii, *Povest' o zhizni. Kniga skitanii. Sobranie sochinenii v 8 tomakh*, Moscow, 1968, Vol. 5, p. 447.

[38] Milne, 'K biografii...', pp. 154-157.

[39] Chudakova, 'Arkhiv...', p. 98.

moment, with her companion, as yet nameless, and the motif of the final flight of Woland appears. The presence of the narrator is more strongly felt. Some scenes gain new elements. All these are but disconnected fragments. One of the pages bears an inscription resembling the expression of a sigh: 'Lord, help me finish this novel. 1931.'[40]

It was like the days when he was writing *The White Guard*; the time to write had to be stolen from his hours of rest; his working day was filled by the duties imposed by two institutions and the search for supplementary income. His duties were many. In the last letter cited above he lists them: he directs, he stands in for actors missing from rehearsals, he is 'appointed in the Art Theatre to direct all the festive and revolutionary celebrations of the year'.[41] His archive does indeed show much evidence of this last activity. An ironist, he found himself in a supremely ironic situation, doing things to which he was worst suited. But he evidently had a certain debt to work off, and perhaps it was easier to assign to him the chores everybody else avoided. From the minutes of a meeting we learn, for example, of a resolution 'to organize two working parties to be charged with establishing as soon as possible the seating arrangements in the hall on 30th September and 1st October and visiting the mills and factories in question to establish close contact with union branches, party bodies and the editorial offices of wall-newspapers, and to establish which are the most urgent current problems in the enterprises in question.' Further, 'The processing of the material collected by this working party is to be entrusted to Bulgakov, Verbitsky, Livanov, Raevsky, Gorchakov and Markov. Bulgakov to take charge.'[42] There is no shortage of information about the other activities of this MAT worker in connection with public holidays, solemn commemorative gatherings and special programmes; he is also routinely invited to various kinds of training session, celebrations and meetings, whose nature may be seen in the following exhortation, for example: 'Bear in mind that we are competing with the Bolshoi Theatre to achieve one-hundred-percent attendance at the general meeting dealing with the matter of the collective

---

[40] Ibid., p. 97.
[41] Milne, 'K biografii...', p. 156.
[42] IRLI, Fond 369.

agreement!' and in the already obligatory reference two lines further on to 'Comrade Stalin'.[43]

It is possible that these rituals were performed tongue-in-cheek in the temple of high theatrical art, but this was the very period when the theatre was being subjected to tight political control and much had been done to end its formerly privileged position. Stanislavsky, now increasingly ailing and less frequently present in the theatre, and increasingly circumspect in everything he undertook, could do little about it. There were attempts to turn the theatre into a kind of agency of RAPP and its playwrights.[44] These came to nothing, but as can be seen from the documents already cited, the uniform pattern of the 'literary five-year plan' then being launched in culture, with the euphoria of writers' working parties, field trips, reports and urgent commitments, was being imposed on MAT as well. It is true that it would soon contrive to escape from them, to shed some of the organizational troubles, but the artistic problems would only deepen.

This was the MAT that Bulgakov found himself in after an interval – no longer the theatre it had once been. This was the theatre which became his refuge, still the heir to a great tradition celebrated at every step and embodied in those who carried it forward, but now on the brink of decline. While far from being a quiet haven, it was still very much better than many others. Cultural continuity could still be felt in it. While it was ever more difficult for the theatre to keep up its own best ethical and aesthetic traditions, it could still remember them, refer back to them and at least assure them a kind of presence. And the new assistant director must have valued this presence, even if he was being exploited as general factotum for ideological prescripts. He was already familiar with make-believe working duties, and no doubt was conscious of the strangeness of his new role, in which he was more acted upon than an actor. But at least he had a good stage.

VI

For some time creative work seemed to be pushed aside by other activities. But gradually the numbness passed. In the draft of his letter to Stalin he spoke of

---

[43] Ibid.

[44] See the account in P. Markov, 'O novom v iskusstve MKhAT', in *Pravda teatra*, Moscow, 1965, p. 191.

'ambitious and firm' plans, which had arisen after 'a silence lasting eighteen months'.[45]

It is possible that these plans included the play which came into being in the summer of 1931 in accordance with a contract with the Leningrad Krasny Theatre and the Vakhtangov Theatre. Its title was *Adam and Eve*. After a reading in the Leningrad theatre, when it turned out that it could not be produced, according to the memoirs of the literary director, 'the author was probably less put out than many others; he explained this by saying that, when he had finished writing it, he himself felt that the play would be unlikely to see the stage.'[46]

Reading the play now, one gains the impression that Bulgakov must have felt this from the beginning and that this work was something he had written for his own private use. Perhaps he wanted to arrive at answers to important questions, or reaffirm his beliefs. Or to get his hand in, to test it, to ensure that he was still able to call himself an active playwright, in spite of everything. But it is difficult to see how he could have believed that what he was writing might be performed.

Again Bulgakov bases his concept on a fantastic idea set in the near future, like his satirical tales of the 1920s. This time, however, the fantastic element recalls those politically didactic works of many of his fellow-writers who had been eager to set down their vision of great conflicts between the Soviet Union and the capitalist encirclement. The analogy is self-evident, although gradually it turns out to be superficial. The hostile West has launched a surprise attack on the Soviet Union, using a tide of poison gas, and an invention by the great scientist Efrosimov has rescued a small number of people, who begin a new life in primitive conditions in an unnamed 'City'.[47] The title underlines the deeper meaning of this initiation, although the content does not develop it; this time the Bible provides only a reference point, the source of the idea, without providing an anchor point, as will

---

[45] Milne, 'K biografii...', p. 155.

[46] E. Sheremet'eva, 'Iz teatral'noi zhizni Leningrada', *Zvezda*, 12, 1976, p. 199.

[47] According to Milne, there was a version of *Adam and Eve* in which the City is named as Leningrad and at the end the events described do not turn out to be a fantasy or a dream. L. Milne, *The Emergence of M. A. Bulgakov as a Dramatist*, unpublished PhD thesis, Cambridge, 1975, p. 339. [The text as published in Mikhail Bulgakov, *Sobranie sochinenii v piati tomakh*, Vol. 3, Moscow, 1990, restores 'Leningrad' and does not include the final brief scene in which Efrosimov is shown waking from a dream. – *Trans.*]

shortly be seen elsewhere. Among the initiators are the eponymous young couple, whose personalities are very vaguely sketched;[48] the heroic and orthodox airman Daragan, armoured with revolutionary principles; the careerist writer Ponchik-Nepobeda, and the good-natured lout Markizov, simple-minded, but genuine; and finally the scientist, endowed, like Persikov, with the classic features of the absent-minded professor, but having in addition the role of saying and showing things that are clearly of great importance to Bulgakov. As the action proceeds, the play turns increasingly in a direction which the other fantasy-writers of the day never dreamed of – demonstrating the moral and intellectual superiority of Efrosimov, with his classic liberal and intellectual humanism.

At first the scientist's behaviour and speech emphasize the distance between him and his surroundings, and Bulgakov's own thoughts and even intonations can clearly be heard in them.[49] Gradually Efrosimov gives expression to views which accord perfectly with today's notions of peaceful coexistence:

'The capitalist world is filled with hatred for the socialist world, and the socialist world for the capitalist world. [...] There will be war, because it's so stifling today! There will be war because every day somebody in the tram says to me: "What a hat!" There will be war because when you read the papers your hair stands on end and you think you're having a nightmare. What do they print? "Capitalism must be destroyed". Right? And what do they print over there? "Communism must be destroyed". It's a nightmare! [...] Even girls carrying rifles – girls patrol the streets singing, "Shoot straight, my little rifle; don't spare the bourgeoisie!" Day in, day out! There's a flame under the pot and there are bubbles in the water, so who but a blind man could imagine it won't come to the boil?'[50]

---

[48] There is one curious detail: the young couple's names, Adam Krasovskii and Eva Voikevich, sound one hundred per cent Polish (Adam Krasowski, Ewa Wojkiewicz), but it is difficult to judge whether Bulgakov (who attached much importance to anthroponymics) meant anything by this, and if so, what.

[49] For example, Efrosimov, worn down by Markizov, says, 'My only regret is that the Soviet government didn't witness that scene... so that I could show them the kind of raw material they intend to use to build the classless society' (M. Bulgakov, *Tri p'esy*, Paris, 1971, p. 10). This clearly matches the reflections heard in *The Heart of a Dog*.

[50] *Tri p'esy*, 1971, pp. 14-15.

Things that are obvious today sounded provocative at the time, especially as the professor – a committed pacifist – ostentatiously refrains from evaluating the attitudes of others. When disaster strikes, Efrosimov does indeed prove the unwilling saviour of the group of survivors, but, in accordance with his principles, he declares that he intends to offer his invention, which neutralizes deadly gases, to all of humanity. He also renders harmless the stockpiles of bombs, making retaliation impossible. It is not surprising that Adam and Daragan vie with each other to call him names: traitor, anarchist, benighted dreamer, enemy and fascist. In ideologically-committed writing as late as the end of the 1940s, angry Stalinist salvoes were still aimed at deluded scientists who persisted in the belief that their work would serve the whole world when objectively it served the cause of the enemy.[51] It therefore appears as if Efrosimov is doomed, but it turns out that his intellect is essential and in the closing scene Bulgakov takes satisfaction from placing him opposite the blinkered ideological stalwart Daragan as an equal partner. Furthermore, the beautiful Eve will leave her Adam for the professor, so the configuration of biblical names is modified and a new cycle of human life can be conceived out of reflection and goodness; traditional humane values can emerge victorious from the trial.

Thus does Bulgakov reproduce yet again the complex of his own belief and feelings of consolation and satisfaction. He takes delight in mocking the opportunist Ponchik, who, at the slightest change in the political climate, is prepared to renounce his previous self and carries with him his servile third-rate opus about 'rosy-cheeked collective-farm girls' even after disaster has struck. Bulgakov also gives a chance to the loutish Markizov, who, like the unwitting arsonist Annushka before him, realizes after the catastrophe that he should study. He then places it all in his beloved quotation marks of non-fulfilment by revealing at the end that the cataclysm was all a dream, and adds the musical framework of his favourite 'absolutely immortal *Faust*', an emanation of the creative human spirit which no apocalypse could destroy.

This complex of very simple meanings, rather like a literary postscript to a letter recently sent – with a plea for tolerance for the figure of a highly qualified specialist and the eloquent comparison drawn between him and the disloyal

---

[51] See, for example, Aleksandr Shtein's play *Law of Honour* and Konstantin Simonov's play *Alien Shadow*, both based on such motifs.

opportunists – was most ill suited to the times. It was a time of increasing external threats of war and increasing internal militarization; honest professionals were being terrorized by well-publicized trials while adroit manipulators forged ideological careers. At the same time a clear vision of genocide, even if tempered by the hope of final victory, carried too much menace to be shown to the public. The commander of the Soviet Air Force, when invited to the Vakhtangov Theatre for a reading of the play, stated this authoritatively.[52] The evolutionary pacifist, spiritual brother of Efrosimov, enemy of all violence, friend of animals and citizen of the world expressed his *votum separatum* in *Adam and Eve*; and he gave material form to the latent situational possibilities of his period in a conceptual device, in order to 'create one's own world by a determined act of demonic creative will', in the words of Vladislav Khodasevich, '[53] and to win the battle with reality on the printed page.

This form of artistic revenge for life's treacherous blows would pay off handsomely in the future, but for the moment, if we are honest, its success is questionable. The trouble is that *Adam and Eve* is one of Bulgakov's weakest plays. Whether this is the result of the hackneyed application of scientific inventions and attempts to activate a benumbed imagination, or whether the largely alien raw material offers too much resistance, the fact is that when set next to Bulgakov's earlier writing this play looks like the work of a beginner. The characters are rough-hewn dummies, especially the two ideological protagonists, Adam and Daragan; Bulgakov is so far from having any sense of this kind of psychological make-up that he can reach no further than the technique of the propaganda poster, and, especially in the case of Daragan, he produces a propaganda poster in reverse: the valiant airman is able to do no more than pontificate, denounce, intimidate, breathe hatred and kill. Adam is his indistinct shadow; the beautiful Eve is a conventional symbol of 'the eternal feminine', the point at which male passions intersect, and Efrosimov's reward. Bulgakov's skill with dialogue, depending essentially on making the lines signal the characters' state of mind and having the words form complex relationships one with another, often indirectly, conveying something about the characters' behaviour and providing a

---

[52] See L. Belozerskaia-Bulgakova, p. 121.

[53] Vladislav Khodasevich, from the poem 'Daktili', *Sobranie stikhov* (1913-1939), New Haven, Conn., 1961, p. 197.

multi-dimensional, spiritual set design, is reduced to simple exchanges: cue and response, question and answer, action and reaction. The situations are conventional and inflexible in their structure; the fantastic lacks fantasy. Only Act Two, with its nightmarish vision of a department store into which a tram has crashed, with figures frozen at the moment of sudden death, has the dimension of horror and the power to make us feel uncomfortable. 'In the vast windows of the department store,' say the stage directions, 'there is Heaven and Hell. Heaven is lit up from above by the early morning sun, and Hell is below, illuminated by a dense and distant glow. Between them smoke is rising and in it can be seen a transparent chariot, above the ruins and burned-out buildings.' Act Two ends thus: 'The whole block silently collapses in the window, revealing another colonnade and some horses lit by a strange light.'[54] These are splendid images with more than a touch of surrealism about them; before this there had been no such ghostly visions in Bulgakov's work. Yet they represent a novelist's intrusion into theatrical material which is developed in a far more conventional manner and does not connect with their import.

Perhaps the rigidity of form is also a consequence of borrowing a whole situational model; this time Bulgakov borrows from H. G. Wells, as he did in the case of 'The Fatal Eggs' and *The Heart of a Dog*,[55] and it is doubtful whether a Wellsian-style fantasy may be adapted to the means of expression of conventional drama. It is also possible that this time the writer was not greatly concerned with form, which is treated as the temporary packaging of ideas demanding expression. If this is so, the act of setting them down and confronting them may have given a feeling of fulfilment – so Bulgakov could part with this play with no regrets. Several of the motifs which appear in it would recur later in fuller and richer form: the woman by the side of the creative thinker, rescuing him and guiding him to

---

[54] *Tri p'esy*, 1971, pp. 30, 45. In this vision some of the specifics can be recognized as Leningrad.

[55] On the connection between *Adam and Eve* and Wells' *World Set Free* and *The Autocracy of Mr Parham*, see Christine Rydel, 'Bulgakov and H. G. Wells', *Russian Literature Triquarterly*, No. 15 (1978), pp. 293-391.

eternal rest;[56] the penitent blasphemer, found in *The White Guard* in the person of Rusakov; and the exclamation, 'There are only two forces in the world: dollars and literature',[57] which acquires a sarcastic bite in the major novel when the hard-currency shop and the temple of third-rate literature go up in smoke. Bulgakov's motifs, as we know, constantly migrate, passing through the walls of neighbouring works, dividing and mutating, to disappear then re-emerge after an interval. And, as it would turn out in the end, all these migrations serve a definite, higher purpose, of which the artist, being its implement, knows nothing.

Meanwhile Bulgakov read *Adam and Eve* at the Vakhtangov Theatre and the Krasny Theatre in Leningrad. It was well received in both places, but as a female listener in Leningrad diplomatically put it, 'to our great regret, the theatre was unable to produce it'.[58] The motivation is not stated, but it can easily be guessed. The play was not staged in Moscow either, or in Baku, although a production there was planned.[59]

But perhaps at some deeper level in Bulgakov's creative biography, hidden from public view, *Adam and Eve* played an important role, though one that could not be measured: by shaking him out of his inertia and introducing him to a new rhythm of life, at first slow, but later increasingly intense. Perhaps here, in these hidden depths, is the place where it was staged.

VII

This period, particularly difficult because it coincided with an inner crisis, lasted for two and half years. Bulgakov was also engaged in a stage adaptation of *War and Peace*, commissioned by the Leningrad Bolshoi Drama Theatre. This he carried out thoroughly and conscientiously, in four acts and thirty scenes, but it

---

[56] As well as having 'my favourite dream every night: a black horse, always with a black mane, carries me out of these forests' (*Tri p'esy*, 1971, p. 53); the link with Margarita's nocturnal flights is palpable.

[57] Ibid., p. 49.

[58] E. Sheremet'eva, op. cit.

[59] Chudakova, 'Arkhiv...', p. 100.

was never produced. Bulgakov took on tasks such as this primarily because he needed the income.[60]

An unexpected turn for the worse came when Stanislavsky saw *Dead Souls* as an almost finished play, rejected it, and started work on it all over again, in spite of all Bulgakov had done.

A turn for the better came when Bulgakov managed to obtain agreement for *A Cabal of Hypocrites*, and with it the hope of a stage career for this play.

And finally came cause for a minor celebration. This happened in the New Year of 1932. In mid-January Avel' Enukidze, a senior government figure and a member of a special commission for theatrical affairs, phoned Stanislavsky and asked whether MAT could resume production of *The Days of the Turbins*. There was probably never any doubt that this was Stalin's own wish.[61]

'In the afternoon of 16th January,' wrote Bulgakov to Popov, 'I received a call from the theatre, informing me that *The Days of the Turbins* would be staged again as a matter of urgency. I'm ashamed to admit that this news crushed me. I felt physically unwell. I was overcome with joy, which soon gave way to sadness. Ah, my heart, my heart!'[62]

The play's renaissance was prepared within a month, in an atmosphere of collective satisfaction, but also of tension, due, no doubt, to the pressure of numerous circumstances of which the staff of MAT were aware, for this was an event that had no precedent.[63]

The new 'premiere' of *Days*, with some small changes in the cast, took place on 18th February. 'The actors were so nervous that their nerves infected me,' the author wrote in his next letter. 'They turned pale under their make-up,

---

[60] The text of the adaptation, as yet unpublished, may be found in the Bulgakov archive at IRLI, Fond 369. Besides this, Bulgakov signed a contract on 17th April 1931 with the Theatre of the Institute of Public Health for the production of N. Venkstern's play *Odinochka*; this work was not carried out.

[61] See the account by L. Leonidov in his article written for Stalin's 60th birthday. The author attributes the play's new season to Stalin. L. Leonidov, 'Drug Sovetskogo teatra', *Sovetskoe iskusstvo*, 21.12.39.

[62] Milne, 'K biografii...', p. 163.

[63] On the circumstances of the new production, see E. Kaluzhskii, 'Chelovek i drug', in *Neizdannyi Bulgakov*, p. 50, and F. Mikhal'skii, 'Gody molodye', Ibid., p. 62.

broke into a sweat, and their eyes were tormented, wary and questioning.'[64] This letter contains a splendid description of his own state of mind and the atmosphere of the reborn play as observed from behind the scenes. The two came together eloquently in the conclusion set forth by Bulgakov:

'At that moment there appeared a messenger in the form of a beautiful woman. Lately I have developed the most acute ability, so acute that it makes life extremely difficult, to guess in advance what somebody wants of me. The sheaths of my nerves endings must have been completely worn away, and contact with my dog has taught me to be always on the alert.

'In short, I can tell what people are going to say, and the worst of it is that I know that they won't say anything new. Nothing unexpected can happen. Everything is known in advance. I only had to look at her unnatural smile and I already knew she was going to ask me not to go on stage.

'The messenger said that K. S. [Stanislavsky – A.D.] had phoned and asked where I was and how was feeling.

'I asked her to convey my thanks and say that I was feeling well, that I was behind the scenes, and that when the audience called for me to come forward, I would not.

'You should have seen how she beamed! She said that in K. S.'s view this was a very sensible decision.

'The decision is not really particularly sensible. It's a very simple decision. I have no wish for any tributes, or to be called onto the stage. There's really nothing I want, except to be left in peace, so that I can take hot baths and not have to think every day what I'm to do about the dog when the lease ends in June.

'There's really absolutely nothing I want.

'There were twenty curtain calls. The actors and my friends went on at me afterwards: why didn't I come out? Why that demonstration? It seems it's a demonstration if I go onto the stage and a demonstration if I don't. I really don't know what to do.'[65]

Such were the circumstances and the climate in which the play surrounding the play was resumed. This time there were no dramatic clashes. The play

---

[64] Letter to P. Popov, 24.4.32, in Milne, 'K biografii...', p. 166; also in *Dnevnik. Pis'ma*, p. 269.

[65] Ibid., pp. 166-167; *Dnevnik. Pis'ma*, 270.

resumed its firm position in the MAT repertoire – nobody else's. Apart from sporadic sallies, there was no longer any question of a campaign against it; the times had brought the highest degree of social awareness and it was immediately understood that *Days* had special immunity and protection. A situation which was still deteriorating turned out in this isolated case to be to the benefit of Russian culture and the honest artist.

Such cases were possible.

'How mysteriously does our destiny toy with us,' wrote Gogol in 'Nevsky Prospect'.[66]

---

[66] N. V. Gogol', *Sochineniia v dvukh tomakh*, Moscow, 1965, p. 471.

Chapter Eight

An Essay in Normality

I. The failure of *A Cabal of Hypocrites* in Leningrad. Departures from Bulgakov's version of *Dead Souls*. Bulgakov helps to destroy his own vision.
II. Third marriage and relative domestic stability. Intimations of mortality. Restricted social life. Dropping out of official circles. Practical work. An interlude of acting. Foreign travel planned, and abandoned. Moving house for the last time.
III. Attempts to revive *Flight*. *The Life of Monsieur de Molière*, another failure.
IV. The third version of a novel about the Devil. *Bliss* and *Ivan Vasil'evich*. New hopes.
V. Film work: screenplays for *Dead Souls* and *The Government Inspector*. Plans frustrated.
VI. Difficulties in collaborating with Veresaev; *The Last Days*.
VII. Epilogue to *A Cabal of Hypocrites*. Rehearsals, premiere, an article in *Pravda*. The play is taken off; chain reaction.

I

'For the author of the play,' wrote Bulgakov of the decision to revive *The Days of the Turbins*, 'this means having part of his life restored to him.'[1]

When the decision was announced it was not known how far-reaching the turnabout in his destiny would be. It soon emerged that it really was only a part – and a small part at that – of Bulgakov's life.

A month after the premiere the writer reported to Popov that the Leningrad Bolshoi Drama Theatre had changed its mind about staging *A Cabal of Hypocrites*:

'Molière has been killed off by a private individual, unaccountable, apolitical, primitive and amateurish, for reasons having nothing whatever to do

---

[1] Quoted in *Sovetskie pisateli. Avtobiografii*, Moscow, 1966, Vol. 3, p. 97.

with politics. This individual is a professional playwright, who appeared in the theatre and gave them such a fright that they dropped the play.'[2]

This account was subsequently developed in a cycle of images or metaphors, in a tone of great astonishment. Although he knew from his own extensive experience all about the art of slander and political innuendo, Bulgakov was ill prepared to see it applied so openly and, moreover, by a fellow-writer. He compared this to a stab in the back. He did not name his assailant, but from the description it is not difficult to guess that he is speaking of Vsevolod Vishnevsky, as was actually confirmed in print.[3] This writer was known for his powerful and clearly demonstrated feelings of envy for his fellow-playwrights. It was not difficult for him to lash out at Bulgakov, and it is no surprise that the latter, in a letter dated 30th April 1932, does not beat about the bush:

'All I want to say is that in the form of Vishnevsky a flower has appeared in the past year in the field of Russian drama that not even a botanist such as myself has ever clapped eyes on.'[4]

So apart from *Days of the Turbins* – a single play running in a single theatre – everything remained as before.

The adaptation of *Dead Souls* was taking a turn for the worse. The play was assuming a shape increasingly distant from the adaptor's original design. When he took over direct artistic control,[5] Stanislavsky first of all rejected Dmitriev's set design and entrusted the task of coming up with a new one to Simov. He then dropped the narrator, whom Bulgakov in his text called 'Number

---

[2] Lesley Milne, 'K biografii M. A. Bulgakova', *Novyi zhurnal*, No. 111, 1973, p. 164.

[3] See Chudakova, 'Arkhiv M. A. Bulgakova. Materialy dlia tvorcheskoi biografii pisatelia', in *Zapiski Otdela rukopisei Gos. Bibl. SSSR im. Lenina*, Moscow, 1976, p. 102 for information on Vishnevskii's article, 'Kto zhe vy?' (*Krasnaia gazeta*, No. 266, 11.11.31.)

[4] Milne, 'K biografii...', p. 167.

[5] In October 1931, Stanislavsky had previously rehearsed only individual scenes. A year earlier, in October 1930, the adaptation project was put to Nemirovich-Danchenko, who accepted it, though with great reluctance. (For a detailed account see K. Rudnitskii, 'Mertvye dushi MKhAT 1932', in *Teatral'nye stranitsy*, Moscow, 1979, pp. 145-185, esp. p. 161. For further discussion of these matters see Lesley Milne, 'M. A. Bulgakov and *Dead Souls*: The problems of adaptation', *Slavonic and East European Review*, No. 128, July 1974, and M. Chudakova, 'Bulgakov i Gogol'', *Russkaia rech'*, No. 2, 1979, pp. 39-48.)

One' [Pervyi].[6] He also removed the Captain Kopeikin scene. Essentially he strove consistently to eliminate everything that, in Sakhnovsky's words, 'tended towards hyperbole, fantasy and the grotesque'.[7] In the view of Konstantin Rudnitsky, the author of an extended study of this play, 'Stanislavsky's position in the work on *Dead Souls* emerged most clearly and emphatically... in his wish to give full expression to the comic element, while the lyrical element, so powerfully expressed in Gogol's great epic, was simply expunged.'[8] If the word 'lyrical' is understood in a broad sense, as the author evidently intended, this meant the elimination of everything that mattered most to Bulgakov. And so it was. Stanislavsky's intentions tended towards a play that was purely for actors, static in most of its scenes and performed as a series of acting duets. The renowned director's authority was sufficient to cause both Sakhnovsky and later commentators to assert that this was the only solution that matched the artistic profile of MAT, although this same Stanislavsky in this same MAT had recently been able to create some very dynamic and effective comic performances.

This time too Stanislavsky came up with a superb treatment of some individual scenes for the actors involved. The Art Theatre's old guard – Moskvin, Tarkhanov, Leonidov and Lilina – forged splendid roles, thanks to which *Dead Souls* remained in the repertoire for a long time.[9] At the premiere, however, held on 28th November 1932 after a long and interrupted series of rehearsals, Stanislavsky and those close to him felt that the play was not yet ready. Olga Bokshanskaia, Bulgakov's sister-in-law and Nemirovich-Danchenko's secretary,

---

[6] In the first version there were two narrators: the Reciter and the Admirer (see Chudakova, 'Bulgakov i Gogol''). The text of the role of the former appears in Milne, 'M. A. Bulgakov and *Dead Souls*', p. 432 ff. For the full text of the adaptation, certainly identical with or very close to the version performed on stage after modifications, see M. Bulgakov, *Ivan Vasil'evich. Mertvye dushi*, Munich, 1964.

[7] V. Sakhnovskii, *Rabota rezhissera*, Moscow-Leningrad, 1937, p. 222. Note also: 'The word "grotesque" was not in favour with Stanislavsky at that time' (K. Rudnitskii, *Teatral'nye stranitsy*, p. 153); and a typical line from a letter from Stanislavsky to Il'ia Sel'vinsky, 'Russia is too serious a country for the grotesque' (quoted in O. Reznik, *Zhizn' v poezii*, Moscow, 1967, p. 358).

[8] Rudnitskii, *Teatral'nye stranitsy*, pp. 153-154.

[9] For over thirty years; *Dead Souls* was performed a total of 805 times.

wrote in a letter to her employer that, 'Bulgakov's play as he wrote it is not what is being acted here; however, it is a series of wonderful portraits.'[10]

Without Gogol's and Bulgakov's 'lyricism', without the interweaving of the real and the fantastic, the disturbing play of meanings, the palpable presence of the author in his melancholy reflections, the particular refractions of the perspective of provincial 'Russian-ness' as seen from far-off Rome, and without what Andrei Bely called 'the personification of fiction', that is, the precise, illusive description of situations which are essentially unreal, it could hardly have been otherwise. Gogol was transposed onto the level of a kind of realism of manners and treated as a representative of this genre. What came into being was a cycle of tableaux, executed reverentially and with much attention to historical verisimilitude. This had its own point and charm, even if the episodic impression was overwhelming.[11] But the spirit of Gogol had been banished.

The reviewers were not unfair this time in describing it coolly, saying that it was 'in its way interesting for the viewer, especially for the young, like any nicely executed illustration for a book'[12] and that it would be 'very stodgy fare were it not for the great skill of the performers.'[13] There were also some shriller voices, among which the heated philippics of Andrei Bely in one of his last public statements stood out. Dismissing out of hand the Art Theatre's vision and contrasting it with Meyerhold's *Government Inspector*, Bely wrote that the theatre had 'got lost in a forest of museum details and lost sight of what mattered most', and that Russia 'had been replaced by a gallery of genteel interiors.'[14]

There was a fine demonic irony about this test at the hands of fate: as a conscientious assistant director, present at almost all rehearsals, Bulgakov participated in the demolition of his own design. Evidently, as he always sought opportunities for purposeful action, he wished to convince himself that this too had real purpose, and as he believed in Stanislavsky's creative powers he expected

---

[10] Quoted in Rudnitskii, *Teatral'nye stranitsy*, p. 180.

[11] 'The essential feature of this play was its "concert-like" nature, both in the sense that the actors gave perfectly honed and polished virtuoso performances, and in that it could be broken down with ease into individual "concert numbers"'. Rudnitskii, *Teatral'nye stranitsy*, p. 158.

[12] V. Mlechin, 'Neprochitannyi Gogol'', *Rabis*, No. 1, 1933.

[13] P. Novitskii, 'Mertvye dushi', *Izvestiia*, 22.12.32.

[14] A. Belyi, 'Neponiatyi Gogol'', *Sovetskoe iskusstvo*, 20.1.33.

great discoveries to follow. In an extremely warm letter of 31st December 1931 to his theatrical superior he voiced his genuine admiration for his work and added: 'I have no fears for Gogol when you are at the rehearsal. With you as intermediary, he will come. He will appear in the first scenes amidst laughter and depart in the last scene, veiled in a mantle of profound thoughts. He will come. Yours, Mikhail Bulgakov.'[15]

The actual result was the opposite: Gogol retreated further and further. Even if we had no other evidence, the drama of Bulgakov's career – spanning the full gamut from hope to hopelessness – could clearly be seen by comparing the letter quoted above with one written to Popov four months later, on 7th May 1932:

'*Dead Souls* cannot be adapted. You may take this as axiomatic from a person who knows the work well. I'm told that 160 adaptations exist. The figure may not be exact, but whether it is or not *Dead Souls* cannot be acted...

'So why did I undertake to do it?

'I did not, Pavel Sergeevich. For a long time I haven't undertaken anything, because I am far from being my own master. Fate has me by the throat.'[16]

It is not often that we hear such despair from Bulgakov, but this is authentic despair, the product of his sense of the hopelessness of the situation.[17] All faith in a directorial miracle had evaporated. In his modesty he had seemed to admit the possibility of making some new discovery about Gogol, in some other way. But six months before the premiere it was clear that there would be no discovery. Typically he at first placed the burden of impossibility on the adaptation. This was very much Bulgakov's self-possessed way of taking blame that should rest with others. But either because his pen would not lie or thanks to an oversight, two sentences later he says that '*Dead Souls* cannot be *acted*'. And then the self-

---

[15] Quoted in *Ezhegodnik MKhATa za 1948 g.*, Moscow, 1950, p. 425; also in *Dnevnik. Pis'ma 1914-1941*, Moscow, 1997, p. 259.

[16] Chudakova, 'Arkhiv...', p. 93; also in *Dnevnik. Pis'ma*, p. 274-275.

[17] Note the exclamation with which Bulgakov ends one of his letters to Popov: 'But anyway it makes no difference. It makes no difference. It makes no difference' (quoted in Rudnitskii, p. 161). This forms a clear connection with Chebutykin's words, repeated several times, at the conclusion of *The Three Sisters*.

possession is gone. But in any case Bulgakov plainly needed this correspondence with Popov in order to give vent to feelings which he sometimes camouflaged.

And he was blamed for the faults of others anyway. This was the outcome of the intricate manipulation of the Gogol affair. 'In Bulgakov's treatment,' wrote one reviewer, 'Gogol becomes a distant, detached observer, a genre-bound writer who confines himself to objectively retailing jokey elements of Russian life.'[18] The same charges were levelled at the author of the adaptation, whose name appeared on an Art Theatre poster, during a discussion at a Moscow factory. 'What has happened to all Gogol's lyrical digressions?' asked Bely, demanding that Captain Kopeikin, 'that figure of such stunning symbolic power', should also appear on the stage.[19]

What was the author of the adaptation and assistant director to say to all this, being aware of his own situation and of working practicalities, to say nothing of the concept of loyalty?

He said nothing. After the premiere he said only, 'I wanted to write a play, not a series of tableaux.'[20] As for any further thoughts he might have had, since they were not set down and never made public we can only imagine them.

II

Important changes were coming about in a quite different sphere. For the third and last time it was his private life that was the arena for them. The breakdown of his second marriage had probably been in the making for some time. The presence of Elena Shilovskaia had been becoming more and more important to Bulgakov. Finally they evidently judged that it was no longer possible to keep up appearances.[21] Both of them dissolved their current marriages (Elena Shilovskaia's husband was a staff college lecturer, equivalent in rank to general), and on 4th October 1932 they were married. Elena Bulgakova then moved into the flat in Bol'shaia Pirogovskaia with her younger son Sergei.

---

[18] V. Mlechin, 'Neprochitannyi Gogol''.

[19] Belyi, 'Neponiatyi Gogol''.

[20] Quoted in Rudnitskii, *Teatral'nye stranitsy*, p. 177.

[21] It is possible that Bulgakov's relative financial stability following the resumption of *Days* was also significant.

It seems certain that Bulgakov's last companion was able to give him the reassuring sense of stability that he so sorely needed, in addition to many other things. Bulgakov's life had been far from normal, but Elena Sergeevna clearly had a vision of normality for it – within reasonable limits – as well as the ability to bring this about. A well-run household was part of it, along with an archive maintained in exemplary order, and a diary in which to record precisely the course of his life and art; it certainly also included mental equilibrium and acceptance and recognition of her husband's endeavours. This did indeed provide a particularly good home atmosphere for his last years, although the pressure of circumstances constantly affected his nerves and made him a difficult partner – which, in fact, he always was. He was able, however, to appreciate his home surroundings and made this abundantly clear. Apparently he was also an exemplary step-father to his two step-sons, treating them with serious and indulgent sensitivity; he got on particularly well with the elder of them, Evgenii.

It must also be said that, not wishing to cause pain to anybody who was dear to him, he had a clear sense, which he stressed, of the exceptional nature of this last alliance. Though fond of jocular dedications (when he gave his friends and relations copies of his old books he was able to feel like a *normal* writer, handing out freshly-minted copies) he wrote very seriously on a copy of 'The Fatal Eggs', 'To the secret friend now secret no more, my wife Elena Sergeevna Bulgakova: You will go with me on my last flight.'[22]

The penultimate word in this dedication is as important as the last. Bulgakov already sensed that his life was moving towards its close, although he was only just over forty and as yet there was no serious threat to his health, which was always fragile and aggravated by his nerves. A little later when he wanted to test his luck once again and request permission for a short trip abroad, he wrote to Veresaev and Popov in the same tone – 'if only in the evening of my days';[23] 'strange though it may seem, twilight's coming on!'[24] Before this he would complain to Popov, 'towards the end of my career as a writer I was obliged to

---

[22] The dedicated copy is held in the Bulgakov family archive.

[23] Cited in the almanac *Glagol*, Ann Arbor, 1978, p. 128.

[24] Milne, 'K biografii...', p. 162.

work on adaptations.'[25] When he eventually resumed work on his novel, he would leave a note in the margin: 'I'll finish this before I die!'[26]

From now on his certainty of approaching death would cast a shadow over everything he did – for a living, for the theatre, or for himself. This was not the shadow of resignation – on the contrary: the intensity of his endeavours strains credibility, if we remember that these endeavours were so often frustrated, and that, with the exception of his main work, all his plans led to nothing, as if a spell had been cast on them. And yet his new diary of commitments was crowded; one deadline followed another, one project came on the heels of another. Once his period of mental fragility was behind him, he reacted to the constant grip of the dead hand – relaxed only once to permit *Days of the Turbins* – by working. In spite of everything and against all odds. The foreboding of his imminent demise hurried him on. His face improved with the passage of time, the sharp triangular geometry softened, the corners became rounded and his features acquired more harmony. In later photographs he has a steady calm and looks inward at something inevitable that only he can see. Gone is the quizzical grin; the impish defiance has faded and the mocking tilt of the head, in which you could almost hear his voice saying 'Ne skazhite!' [You don't say!], is a thing of the past. He now has the assured clarity of self-knowledge.

Outwardly he was now rather different, less open to others. His circle of friends and acquaintances narrowed and casual acquaintances were dropped. No doubt this sometimes left a bitter taste. Loyal by nature, he would have felt it deeply when his loyalty was not returned. Some of his friends, no doubt energetically crossing themselves, were able to renounce him with alacrity. Pavel Markov claimed to find 'incorrect material' in *Days*;[27] Stanislavsky in conversations a little later, asserted that the play was marked by 'serious flaws, for which, no doubt, we and the author are to blame... Those who actually made the revolution are not shown'.[28] When Nemirovich-Danchenko sent the theatre a cable of congratulation on the five-hundredth performance of *Days* (while the troupe was on tour in Leningrad), Bulgakov wrote, 'I was sure that not one word of it applied

---

[25] Quoted in Rudnitskii, *Teatral'nye stranitsy*, p. 146.

[26] Chudakova, 'Arkhiv...', p. 112.

[27] P. Markov, 'MKhAT i proletarskaia revoliutsiia', *Sovetskii teatr*, No. 2-3, 1931.

[28] Quoted in M. Gorchakov, *Rezhisserskie uroki Stanislavskogo*, Moscow, 1952, p. 468.

to the author.' And he added, 'I suppose the proper thing is for the author to keep silent. Previously I didn't know that. I suppose I'm not sufficiently well brought up.'[29] Perhaps the letter to Bulgakov from Sakhnovsky on the same occasion, enthusiastic in tone and calling *Days* a 'new *Seagull*',[30] should therefore be treated as an attempt to make amends for Nemirovich-Danchenko's *faux pas*; but it is doubtful whether it succeeded with Bulgakov. Within the Art Theatre, where he was undoubtedly highly regarded, he was generally lauded in private correspondence, in conversation and in the theatre's newspaper; but in the '30s there was a total absence of any trace of support for him outside it, while there is evidence of moves against him. No doubt it was felt that the spirit of those inhuman times demanded sacrifices, and it was relatively easy to sacrifice Bulgakov.

If this was the situation in the Art Theatre, it is hardly surprising that Tairov shunned *The Crimson Island*, while Aleksei Popov, the director of *Zoika's Apartment*, felt it appropriate even thirty years later, in changed conditions, to write that 'the play began to attract audiences of NEPmen', and 'after about a hundred performances the theatre removed it from the repertoire' (both these statements are obviously false).[31] Equally natural at the time was the behaviour of Meyerhold, who, it is true, congratulated Stanislavsky on gaining permission for *Days* and did his best to woo Bulgakov as the author,[32] but having sharply criticized *Dead Souls* he placed the main burden of blame for a bad play upon Bulgakov, although, according to a contemporary witness, 'he knew (he could not help knowing) that Stanislavsky, when he started work on *Dead Souls*, removed precisely those things which were close to Meyerhold's interpretation of Gogol and which were to a

---

[29] Quoted in Rudnitskii, *Teatral'nye stranitsy*, p. 185.

[30] See Chapter Five.

[31] A. Popov, *Vospominaniia i razmyshleniia o teatre*, Moscow, 1963, p. 187. In fact *Zoika's Apartment* was performed about two hundred times and was taken off not by the theatre itself, but by Glavrepertkom. [Popov in fact wrote 'more than a hundred times', not, as Drawicz renders this, 'about a hundred times' – *Trans.*]

[32] See L. Ianovskaia, 'Dva pis'ma Vs. Meierkhol'da', (*Voprosy literatury*, No. 7, 1975, pp. 315-318) for interesting details, including some concerning Meyerhold helping Stanislavsky to select his audience for the decisive dress rehearsal of *Days*. Two of Meyerhold's letters have been published in Milne, 'M. A. Bulgakov and "Dead Souls"', p. 425.

considerable extent inspired by that interpretation.'[33] Consistent with this was his article 'Meyerhold against Meyerholdism', published during the 'anti-formalist' campaign, which was a difficult period for him. The author defended himself by attacking others, calling *A Cabal of Hypocrites* 'ideologically defective material' and criticizing the Satire Theatre because 'Bulgakov, for example, had penetrated it.'[34]

To these moves, not permissible under traditional rules, Bulgakov no longer reacted as sharply as he had to Vishnevsky's intrigues. We only know that he held them in particular contempt. It is no accident that, though Bulgakov shuns bloodshed, it is the professional informer who is subjected to public execution in *The Master and Margarita*; he alone is given no chance to redeem himself. As we know, the author himself had attempted a number of times, and would try several times more, to find some accommodation with reality. The art of compromise was not alien to him. But he never came close to the procedure of accusing himself and others in what was euphemistically known as 'criticism and self-criticism'. Around him this kind of activity was becoming routine; breast-beating and finger-pointing, either in a sincere, self-induced frenzy or with a cold, knowing wink, were coming to be the norm. Collective and individual statements of support or condemnation in the press, imitating 'public opinion' when the signal was given, had become the fashion. There were few in the field of culture who did not write or sign something of this nature, but Bulgakov's signature is nowhere to be found. Protected by the ruler's lordly, if parsimonious grace, he could surely, if he had wished, have made this the stepping-stone to a career. There were plenty of other examples of this. But he did not. He merely drafted letters to his strange protector, and perhaps even posted some of them. One of the surviving drafts is a request to have Nikolai Erdman's case reviewed and permission given for him to return to Moscow (after a three-year term of exile).[35] Erdman really did receive permission, but some time later. It is not known whether this was thanks to Bulgakov, but his active kindness and readiness to provide help to anybody who needed it is remembered by many.

When the rules of the game went by the board he had to drop out of circulation. In the 1930s, apart from brief mentions of forthcoming projects and

---

[33] N. Chushkin, 'V sporakh o teatre', in *Vstrechi s Meierkhol'dom*, Moscow, 1967, p. 420.

[34] V. Meierkhol'd, *Stat'i, pis'ma, rechi, besedy*, Moscow, 1968, Vol. 2, p. 355.

[35] Milne, 'K biografii...', p. 159.

unfavourable notices from the critics, the press was silent about him. He ceased to exist in the literary marketplace, even in 1932-34, when the cultural strait-jacket was slightly relaxed. The realignments and regroupings which took in many of the 'fellow-travellers' passed him by. The First Congress of Soviet Writers not only managed without him, it managed not to mention him; although some very energetic playwrights clashed in this forum in heated debates over style, tradition and innovation, these were people of different background.

It is not surprising that he withdrew into himself, into his home, into a tight circle of friends, into his work, into his self-protective mode of banter and confabulation, and into letters to Pavel Popov, which are evidence of his maintaining contact with someone sympathetic, as well as being a form of creative art and at the same time a protest. 'After all I'm not quite dead yet,' he exclaims in one of these letters, 'and I want to speak in my own words.'[36] In his everyday life he dealt mostly with the words of others, even if they did belong to Gogol. In these he had to seek something of his own fulfilment – this at the prime of his creative life and the summit of his powers. He was generously endowed with life and physical freedom, and allowed to die a natural death, but he was tormented spiritually, although he conducted a determined defence. 'I look at my bookshelves with horror,' he wrote in another letter. 'Whom will I have to adapt tomorrow? Turgenev, Leskov, Brockhaus and Efron, Ostrovsky? Luckily Ostrovsky adapted himself, probably foreseeing what would happen to me between 1929 and 1931.'[37] In the next few years, besides Gogol and Tolstoi, he would interpret Molière and reassemble him in a synthetic, dramatic whole. He would sign a contract with the Art Theatre for the translation and adaptation of Shakespeare's *Merry Wives of Windsor*, but subsequently break the contract. He would produce the dialogue for Erwin Piscator's film *The Fishermen's Revolt*. He would tackle film versions of other works by Gogol. He would try anything that he could do honestly; at one point, as can be seen from an agreement with the Children's Theatre, he was set to undertake 'an unpublished play from the time of the French Revolution', probably

---

[36] Milne, 'K biografii...', p. 163.

[37] Quoted in Rudnitskii, *Teatral'nye stranitsy*, p. 146. Also in *Dnevnik. Pis'ma*, Moscow, p. 273. [Brockhaus and Efron were the compilers of the most famous Russian encyclopedia of the late pre-revolutionary period. – *Trans.*]

his own *Paris Communards*, which dated from his Caucasus period, but again the contract was breached.[38]

He had once fled from medicine to literature, abandoning an earlier version of himself, hoping no doubt for greater freedom. Now he must have known that there was nowhere else to run to. But perhaps for this very reason, as a born actor, he wanted for a moment to change his skin and become a professional actor. Was this a playful way of trying to elude the vigilance of destiny, or merely a wish to experience the life of an actor on stage? Whatever the truth, in 1935 he took on a small role as the judge in Natalia Venkstern's adaptation of Dickens's *Pickwick Papers*, directed by Viktor Stanitsyn. All accounts agree that he played it very well.[39]

At the same time he was again thinking of travelling abroad. 'I ought to see the world, and I have a right to, if only briefly,' he wrote to Veresaev in April 1934, having prepared an application and his documents. 'I keep asking my wife if I have the right to, just to check. She says I have.'[40] He always felt close to French culture, and now he had delved deeper into it, thanks to Molière, and was dreaming of Paris. 'I've already had dreams of the waves on the Mediterranean, the museums of Paris, a quiet hotel where I don't know anybody, the Molière fountain, and cafés, – in a word, of the opportunity to see all this,'[41] he confided to Popov. He relished in advance the thought of what he would write on the journey – and what he would write about the journey – and even dictated the beginning to his wife immediately; typically, this was a graphic vignette of his theatrical travails in Moscow, devoid of any foreign references.[42] He also appealed to Gorky for support.[43]

His application was turned down, although at first the outlook seemed favourable. He may have written to Stalin again. In a draft letter which has

---

[38] Traces of these intentions, in the form of contracts, survive in IRLI, Fond 369.

[39] See for example Vitalii Vilenkin, 'Nezabyvaemye vstrechi', in *Neizdannyi Bulgakov*, Ann Arbor, 1977, p. 55.

[40] Milne, 'K biografii...', p. 161.

[41] *Glagol*, p. 128; also in Mikhail Bulgakov, *Dnevnik. Pis'ma*, p. 328.

[42] Published under the title 'Byl mai...', *Avrora*, No. 3, 1978; also in *Dnevnik. Pis'ma*, pp. 615-616.

[43] See the letter or draft in Milne, 'K biografii...', p. 157-158.

survived he explains that if he leaves the country he will certainly not remain abroad. As proof of his good faith he adduces a range of arguments concerning his family, the theatre and himself, adding, 'I do not understand why anyone should ask for one thing while having some other plan in mind.' This is very much his manner.[44] We can be fairly sure that he would not have refused to return; apart from everything else, his gentlemanly nature would not allow him to deceive anybody – no matter whom.

But again nothing came of it. The ban remained in force and Bulgakov could not have a holiday, or see his brother, or get to know any foreign land. With his keen intuition, he certainly sensed this in advance, often calling Paris 'my unattainable city'. But when he put the matter behind him he did so in very much his own way. A year later, when the latest attempt had also come to nothing, he wrote to Veresaev, 'I've been refused permission to travel abroad (of course you will throw up your hands in astonishment), so instead of being on the banks of the Seine I'm here on the banks of the Kliaz'ma. Well, what of it? The Kliaz'ma's a river too.'[45]

This was Bulgakov all over.

Now he would make only one very short move: to a new flat in Nashchekinsky Lane (later to be Furmanov Street 3/5). The Bulgakovs moved in February 1934. This was the last time he would move house, and at the same time it was a return to his previous home territory of central Moscow – near the Arbat and Prechistenka. From here he could walk to the Art Theatre by way of Sivtsev Vrazhek, dear to Muscovite hearts, and Gogol Boulevard, shaded by lime-trees, where Bulgakov was in the habit of pausing at the statue of his patron and mentor...

The flat was cosy, perhaps another reincarnation of the atmosphere of the House, with the sure and sensitive hands of its mistress in control. 'A splendid house, I can tell you! There are writers living upstairs and downstairs, in front, behind and next door,' he wrote ironically.[46] But he adds with heartfelt

---

[44] Ibid., p. 158.

[45] M. Bulgakov i V. Veresaev, 'Perepiska po povodu p'esy *Pushkin (Poslednie dni)*', *Voprosy literatury*, No. 3, 1965, p. 162. Also in Mikhail Bulgakov, *Pis'ma. Zhizneopisanie v dokumentakh*, Moscow, 1989, p. 346, and *Dnevnik. Pis'ma*, p. 387.

[46] Milne, 'K biografii...', p. 161; also in *Dnevnik. Pis'ma*, pp. 328.

satisfaction, 'I'm glad to be out of that dank hovel in Pirogovskaia. And what a luxury not to have to take the tram!'[47]

Luxuries were few, but the hard-won spiritual equilibrium, once achieved, made it possible for him to relish every turn for the better.

Thus did his strange life take an even stranger course, despite tireless efforts to make it normal, or at least to behave as if it were normal, acutely conscious as he was of the abnormality of the life of an author known for a single play. 'My whole life now hangs by a thread on that play,' he wrote to Popov, 'and every day I pray that no sword will come and cut that thread.'[48]

In another letter he recalled his mother, 'whose only wish was that her sons should become railway engineers.

'I wonder if our late mother knows,' he wrote, 'that her youngest son has become a balalaika-soloist in France, her second son a bacteriologist, also in France, while her eldest chose not to become anything.

'I think she does know. And when sometimes, in my bitter dreams, I see that lampshade, the piano keyboard and her (as I have three times lately; why does she haunt me?), I want to say to her, "Let's go to the Art Theatre and see a play. Will you come, Mother?"'[49]

III

But the resurrection of *Days* could not help arousing other hopes. Again there was talk of *Flight*. In a letter to the Art Theatre management on 27th April 1933, Sudakov reported Enukidze's verbal agreement to the commencement of rehearsals, and a conversation with Litovsky, who stated on behalf of Glavrepertkom that, 'the actual implementation of the proposed [...] changes will make production of the play possible.'[50]

The changes in question, as the letter shows, concerned 'Khludov's line as the bearer of the White idea'.[51] The energetic director, who knew the art of

---

[47] Milne, 'K biografii...', p. 161; also in *Dnevnik. Pis'ma*, pp. 328.
[48] Chudakova, 'Arkhiv...', p. 103.
[49] Ibid.
[50] In MAT Archive; published in *Neizdannyi Bulgakov*, p. 89.
[51] Ibid.

aggressive diplomacy, was evidently able to convince Bulgakov that such changes were necessary, as two days later the theatre signed an agreement with him about the amendments. These were speedily effected and sent to the theatre at the end of June;[52] after this the author still had to do some work on the text. As a result the ending underwent significant changes. Several versions of it have survived.[53] In one of them the young couple, Serafima and Golubkov, decide to stay abroad. In another, described by the author as 'final' and dated 9th November 1934, Khludov takes his leave of his comrades and commits suicide. If this was really intended to be the new version of the play, Bulgakov had made a very important concession by depriving Khludov of his freedom of choice, that is, of the very thing that gave the play its true depth. We might wonder whether the price for this conclusion was too high, or whether it was worth paying, – but for the fact that in the end it was not paid. Once again everything fell through. This may have had something to do with the deteriorating internal situation following the murder of Kirov. Later there would apparently be new hopes of production in 1937, but these were short-lived.

In the introductory fragment of his never-completed travelogue, Bulgakov precisely recorded that particular state of mental incoherence and inner instability at the time when he was revising *Flight*. He receives peremptory instructions ('Act Three needs rewriting. Throw out Act Three, Scene Two and shift Scene One to Act Four') from a friendly playwright who has the combined features of Afinogenov and Kirshon, two spokesmen of the world of official drama who were then at the height of their careers. The know-all playwright is savagely mocked by Bulgakov, who concludes the story thus: 'with a heart-wrenching rumble the scene revolved and I died every day, and then May came round again.'[54] The sequence

---

[52] See Chudakova's account, 'Arkhiv...', p. 105. Note the typically Bulgakovian letter to Sudakov at this moment of new hope on the occasion of the 400th performance of *Days*: 'Times have changed. We're alive and so is the play, and what's more, you're planning to rehearse *Flight*. Splendid! Splendid!'

[53] The versions were made available to me at IRLI, Fond 369. [The versions published at the time Drawicz was writing mostly conform to the text described in Chapter Six. The version published later, in M. A. Bulgakov, *Sobranie sochinenii v piati tomakh*, 1990, Vol. 3, is the one in which Khludov commits suicide. – *Trans.*]

[54] See Note 42; also in *Dnevnik. Pis'ma*, pp. 615-616.

of change in nature and the seasons underscores the immutability of fate; it remains forever unchanging.[55]

But his readiness to try again was also unchanging. Molière's turn had come again. Bulgakov first compiled a work from several separate Molière strands entitled *Half-witted Jourdain*.[56] It was intended for the studio-theatre headed by Iurii Zavadsky. It was not produced.

Another new Molière-related venture was a monograph on his favourite French writer for the series new entitled 'Lives of Remarkable People', which began to appear at the end of 1932. It might have been an extended foreword to *A Cabal of Hypocrites*, although chronologically it was more in the nature of an afterword. Either way the material in it no doubt assisted the actors, who continued, with long interruptions, to work on *Cabal*.

The book is full of sparkle; it is one of Bulgakov's most dazzling texts. His usual eloquence is enhanced here by the 'Frenchness' for which he had such a sure feel and which he imitated so effortlessly. He deliberately displays in the text his role as architect of the material, appearing as a *sui generis* organizer and master of ceremonies, ever present, holding forth like some worldly grandee. *The Life of Monsieur de Molière* has a bravura opening: the narrator talks to the midwife who brings the new-born Jean-Baptiste Poquelin into the world and learns from the narrator's brief lecture whom she is holding in her arms. This opening sets the tone for all that follows. Bulgakov was not interested in the genre of the scholarly study following academic conventions; he was too much the writer and too well aware that Molière needed different treatment. He therefore created something that recalls the technique of modern story-writing, treating the material synthetically, altering the viewpoints and perspectives, including other voices and other evidence, while his own voice remains constantly audible. This polyphony, making for complex yet at the same time very natural structures, sometimes recalls the polished counterpoint of *The White Guard*. With consummate ease, as if executing figures in a stylistic ballet, the author shifts from one key to another; again we can feel that Gogol's lessons have been well learned. The narrator expresses surprise at the

---

[55] A curious fact: a brief fragment of *Flight* was published by the Leningrad *Krasnaia gazeta* (1.10.32). When he submitted the script, Bulgakov, in his usual manner, added the warning, 'But I remind you once again that *Flight* has not been cleared for performance' (IRLI, Fond 369).

[56] First published in M. Bulgakov, *Dramy i komedii*, Moscow, 1965.

fickleness of fate, weighs up the chances of various dénouements, queries accepted views and admits that certain things are unclear. Other things apart, Bulgakov may simply have wanted to avail himself fully of the writer's prerogatives, since he had found it so difficult to apply them profitably anywhere else. There was one further consideration: in Molière he was dealing with a man obsessed with the theatre; the theatre was the stuff of his life, so it could also become the form in which that life was shown and could be set forth in a sequence of colourful scenes with sharply delineated characters.

This was exactly the result: Molière is seen immersed in the hurly-burly of the streets of Paris, amidst the most varied social and family relationships, experiencing the vicissitudes of the theatrical life and the swings of the scales of fortune. It was not difficult for Bulgakov to sense the drama of his predecessor's career – he had demonstrated this in *Cabal*. As his hero learns the art of writing and the theatre, he constantly studies the art of manoeuvre, sycophancy and feigning; he balances on the wobbly ladder of his career, tormented by the fear of losing favour, the envy of his rivals, the hatred of offended potentates and the spectre of financial ruin. But he defends himself by means of his work, while being at the same time in its service, and it speaks for him, outweighing the flaws in his character and the mistakes he has committed. As in *Cabal*, the mechanics of genius are not subjected to observation or analysis, – they represent a given; this is why Bulgakov does not embark on literary analysis or elaborate descriptions of the creative process. What interests him is the formation of a personality at the junction of creative art and life, while engaged in a struggle against everyone else – a struggle whose rules Bulgakov knew well. With understanding he gives perceptible emphasis to Molière's distortion of his own plays, his fellow-writers' envy and the uncertain patronage of the powerful, with the king at their head. With deliberate insistence he asks, 'Who will explain to me why a play which could not be staged in 1664 or 1667 could be staged in 1669?'[57] and describes a certain critic of *L'École des femmes*, by the name of de Visé, 'who wanted above all to prove that the play could not succeed, but was unable to say this because the play was a resounding success. De Visé therefore asserted that the play owed its success to the superb acting, which shows he was not stupid. Then de Visé claimed to be simply disgusted by the excessive amount of obscenity in the play, observing in

---

[57] M. Bulgakov, *Izbrannaia proza*, Moscow, 1966, p. 478.

parenthesis that the plot was poorly constructed.'[58] Compared with *Cabal*, the drama of events in *Life* is somewhat more attenuated, closer to the authentic historical accounts; the plot against Molière assumes less menacing proportions, his enemies are a little less dangerous, the king more genial. But both the manoeuvres of his enemies and the actions of Louis XIV appear to have been verified in Bulgakov's own experience. The king permits some mockery of the aristocracy, because he is accustomed to holding it 'in hands of steel';[59] quietly, waiting for the opportunity, he dispatches those he considers dangerous; he likes to maintain an inscrutable expression while toying with the insecurity of his flatterers...

Based on diligently studied sources, pedantic in the detail, which Bulgakov sought in letters to his brother – from whom he demanded a full description of the Molière monument,[60] – this book is also, in Bulgakov's own fashion, a personal confession of faith and hope. In it we again see his favourite defensive manoeuvre. A lightness of style serves to overcome the weight of destiny; a clarity of tone helps to dispel a lack of clarity in his own circumstances; literature becomes an anodyne for anxiety. Only occasionally does bitterness sound, in a slight quaver of his voice in the last sentence, directed at the monument to his hero in Paris: 'And I, who am destined never to see it, send it my farewell salute';[61] something that would become known only a year later, with the failure of his attempt to travel abroad, is clearly perceived even now. And this is no surprise, since it is the writer's business to know everything, as this book demonstrates. 'I solemnly declare,' the narrator finds it in his power to say, 'that this is highly improbable; as far as I can remember, no priest ever joined the troupe.'[62] So the author has the power to recollect events that happened three centuries ago and more; before long Satan himself would confirm this with his extra-temporal authority.

This Bulgakovian Molière, rather like the Molièresque Bulgakov, could not find fulfilment in print. The rules of the cabal surrounding *Cabal* operated here too; it was clear there were historical resonances in the present, of a kind too dangerous to be named. The editor of the series, Aleksandr Tikhonov-Serebrov, who was

---

[58] Ibid., p. 447.

[59] Ibid., p. 437.

[60] See the lines cited by Vladimir Lakshin in the Introduction to *Izbrannaia proza*, p. 31.

[61] Ibid., p. 504.

[62] Ibid., p. 376.

otherwise well-disposed towards the author and reviewed the manuscript, even stated plainly that *Life* contained 'fairly transparent allusions to our Soviet reality.'[63] Gorky, the founder of the series, is reported to have given a forthright reaction in conversation: 'There's no question about it. It's well written. But if we start publishing books like that there'll be hell to pay.'[64] In a letter to Tikhonov (*verba volant, scripta manent*) his thoughts were reflected in more official formulae: 'this is not a serious work and, as you rightly point out, it will be roundly condemned.' In Gorky's view it was necessary not only to 'fill out [the book] with historical material and enhance its social significance, but also to modify its "playful" style.'[65]

Bulgakov summarized the matter in a letter to Popov in similar 'playful' style to that of *Life* – as this was his natural style – , ending with the words: 'After thinking it over, I decided it was best not to take up the challenge. I bared my teeth over the form of the review, but didn't bite. Essentially, I said: T. [Tikhonov] says that instead of my narrator I should introduce a "serious Soviet historian". I told him I wasn't a historian and refused to rewrite the book.'[66]

Thirty years later the unmodified *Life of Monsieur de Molière* took its place in the series for which it was written.

IV

Work on *Life* had interrupted another project, the most important one. Bulgakov now returned to his novel, for the fourth time. This appears to have been in the second half of 1932. Some time later, on 2nd August 1933, Molière's biographer wrote to Veresaev: 'A demon took hold of me. While still in Leningrad, and here too, sitting in my cramped rooms, I started filling page after page with the

---

[63] Quoted in Milne, 'K biografii...', p. 167.

[64] Quoted in L. Belozerskaia-Bulgakova, *O, med vospominanii*, p. 119.

[65] Milne, 'K biografii...', p. 174.

[66] Ibid., p. 167. See also a fragment of Bulgakov's reply to Tikhonov: 'You understand that having written my book one way I cannot turn it inside out. For goodness sake!' (Quoted in Chudakova, 'Arkhiv...', p. 105; also in *Dnevnik. Pis'ma*, p. 289).

novel I destroyed three years ago. Why? I don't know. For the fun of it! Let it all go hang! I'll probably drop it soon anyway.'[67]

But he did not drop it; the last sentences here sound rather like a way of invoking a defensive spell, of deflecting the attention of fate and making light of what was now the most important thing to him. The whole of the latter half of 1933 was taken up with the novel. It had not yet received a definitive title. The first page of the new manuscript bore several versions: 'The Great Chancellor', 'Satan', 'Here I Am', 'The Hat with the Feather in it', 'The Black Magician', 'He Has Come', 'The Foreigner's Hoof'.[68] This time the idea was carried through, in essentials, to the end, though many elements appeared in note form. The biblical strand was now divided between the contemporary parts. The theme of the lovers assumes definite shape, although the Master does not yet have this name. He is still referred to as 'Faust' or 'the poet', but he has already written his novel. Certain strands and fragments are built up which would ultimately be pared down, like the hero's and heroine's flight from Moscow, which is here accompanied by catastrophe, gunfire, bloodshed and pursuit. The flight itself lasts longer and, at the request of Margarita's lover ('I've never seen anything'), they fly low over several cities of the world. The motif of ultimate forgiveness of sins and liberating compassion is clearly delineated, and it is noteworthy that the author stresses that Woland is merely the agent of the will of a superior power. This emerges clearly from the concluding lines of this draft, for example, where Woland has a conversation with the Master-to-be:

'I've received instructions concerning you. Most agreeable instructions. You are to be congratulated. You've been successful. So I have been ordered...'

'Can you really be given orders?'

'Oh yes. I have been ordered to escort you...'[69]

---

[67] Milne, 'K biografii...', p. 161; also in *Dnevnik. Pis'ma*, p. 301.

[68] Having no access to the original source, I have translated these titles from the Polish rather than Bulgakov's Russian. This list contains some titles which do not figure in the list provided by M. Chudakova in her article 'Tvorcheskaia istoriia romana M. Bulgakova *Master i Margarita*', *Voprosy literatury*, No. 1, 1976, p. 225. – *Trans.*

[69] For an account of this stage of the work on the novel see Chudakova, 'Arkhiv...', pp. 106-112. Also the quotation on p. 111.

Here the manuscript of the third redaction of the novel breaks off. Over the next two years the author worked only intermittently on a number of elements of it, and, as Chudakova writes, 'the new hero of the novel gained increased importance in its structure as the text was refashioned and the Master squeezed out Woland himself.'[70]

'Oh, what a lot of work I have to do!' wrote Bulgakov to Popov on 26th June 1934. 'But images of my Margarita, the cat and flight drift about in my mind.'[71]

The presence of the novel was to become overwhelming, right to the end. But other endeavours did not cease. Instead they overlapped.

In the draft of his letter of March 1930 to the government, he had mentioned, among other things, burning 'the draft of a comedy'. This may have been an early version of *Bliss*. A new version came into being at the end of 1933, according to a contract with the Satire Theatre.

Again the idea was based on science, but this time stripped of the hyperbolized implications introduced satirically into 'The Fatal Eggs' and *The Heart of a Dog*. The basis was not a discovery, but, as in *Adam and Eve*, an invention, and a moderately conventional one – a time machine. An affinity with Wells and his *Time Machine* may be noted, though such devices were present in the atmosphere of the period, albeit largely thanks to Wells. More clearly apparent was a wish to deliver a riposte to Maiakovsky, partly to *The Bedbug*, partly to *The Bath-house*, not on a broad front but on a limited one. Bulgakov clearly did not intend to engage in any serious manner with the contemporary world; he did this in other places at the same time, but this play was designed for practical purposes, – to be staged and to earn royalties. The science fiction theme made it possible to establish the distance required to defuse the issues and avoid conflict.

The distance was almost three hundred years, since the protagonists of *Bliss* – the inventor of the machine, the caretaker-cum-informer and the villain – are transported to the year 2222. A rational and just society of the future awaits them; the title of the work was the name of the district of Moscow in which this vision is set. But this society, for all its creature comforts, is boring in its triviality; even the villainous confidence man Miloslavsky, a reincarnation of Ametistov, appears

---

[70] Ibid., p. 112.

[71] Quoted in Ibid., p. 115; also in *Dnevnik. Pis'ma*, p. 343.

attractive, sympathetic and genuinely human in this setting. In this way Bulgakov could indicate that he remembered *The Bedbug* and that he could overcome what for Maiakovsky was an insurmountable contradiction that upset his play's internal logic. Maiakovsky believed fervently in the future and wanted to compromise Prisypkin, whom he placed in that future; but under his pen the future turned out to be insipid and dry, while Prisypkin, in spite of everything, was closer to him, being normal. Scarcely any production of *The Bedbug* can overcome this structural illogicality, for it too is a product of the divided soul of its author, who schooled himself in maximal passion to the highest degree but, as a true artist, had to be completely honest with himself in the creative act, and what he wanted to feel collided with what he actually felt. Bulgakov had no ideological obligations and no illusions, only the knowledge that this time he must be careful, so he merely outlined the issue, allowing himself only a few lightly-venomed barbs at the 'radiant future' constantly foretold in current propaganda. Against *The Bathhouse*, however, he seemed to mount more determined opposition, by resolving in his own malicious way the heated argument in that play about who is worthy of the Communist paradise and whom the Phosphorescent Woman should take with her. He did this, as in *The Heart of a Dog*, by enlisting chance, with the result that those selected by fate are a petty functionary and an equally petty villain. In this way the writer, like his own Efrosimov, demonstrated 'the material of which the classless society was to be built.'

While writing *Bliss*, no doubt he also had another work in mind: the first great anti-Utopia of the century, Evgenii Zamiatin's *We*. (The two writers maintained good relations; both were being pilloried by the end of the 1920s; both wrote letters to the government and sought Gorky's help; but Zamiatin availed himself of the opportunity to leave the country.)[72] The mention of the Institute of Harmony, whose purview includes optimal selection of marriage partners and the evaluation of individual human worth and which, in the words of its director, 'doesn't make mistakes',[73] belongs in spirit to the sterile, totalitarian 'One State' of

---

[72] A collection of their correspondence, still unpublished, also exists. It continued after Zamiatin had emigrated in 1931. [Bulgakov's letters to Zamiatin may be found in *Dnevnik. Pis'ma – Trans.*]

[73] M. Bulgakov, 'Blazhenstvo', *Grani*, No. 85, 1978, p. 25; also in Mikhail Bulgakov, *Sobranie sochinenii v piati tomakh*, Moscow, 1990, Vol. 3, p. 400.

Zamiatin's novel. But Bulgakov does not explore any of these themes in depth; he only touches on them, making them resonate lightly. He is also able to activate the obverse of these views; the images of the future provide a background on which all that is most detested in the present may be highlighted. This is best personified by the house-manager and former prince Bunsha-Koretsky, with his insincere, inflated servility, his flair for informing and his pose of tin-pot tyrant of the apartment building. The future harmony shows up the absurdity of these features; the denizens of *Bliss* will make nothing of the meaning of the rationing system (introduced in the '30s following the destruction of agriculture). On the other hand, they will wear tail-coats, so dear to Bulgakov's eye and once seen by him as a sign of better times to come.

But even these meanings receive hardly any emphasis; in this play Bulgakov treads gingerly between one sphere and the other. This caution cramps his movements and ultimately gives *Bliss* an inner stiffness, as if it were structurally incomplete and held in check at every moment. It is probable, however, that from the very beginning the work had no clear idea where it was going. Originally it was intended for a music hall; yet from the surviving manuscripts it is known that the figure of the inventor was treated very seriously, even dramatically at first. What finally resulted was amusing in places, but the extended scenes showing the world of the future exuded sheer boredom. Excursions such as this had lost their momentum before the '20s were out. Besides, no writer had succeeded in achieving notable results with positive projections. The imagination evidently could not be deceived. Only anti-Utopias were convincing. Here fate united Maiakovsky and Bulgakov: both writers failed to depict the future. In this they were not alone.

Bliss, like *Adam and Eve*, is among Bulgakov's feeblest works. Similar reasons for failure are not hard to find: the self-imposed constraints and the attempt to write in a cautious and calculated manner. This pseudo-freedom paralyzed the writer's artistic movements. Perhaps he was not yet sufficiently professional and could not yet cope with these constraints. In a deeper sense it would emerge that both these deficiencies were for the best; they compelled him to seek and find his own sphere of fulfilment. Many writers encounter similar difficulties, but few manage to extricate themselves with their talent unimpaired. In Bulgakov's writing, the enduring effects of the crisis he experienced at the end of the '20s can be seen; the early creative sweep of his theatre writing would never return.

No wonder that his reading of the play at the Satire Theatre was unsuccessful. It was justly assessed. 'Everybody liked the first act and the last,' Bulgakov wrote to Popov, 'They all latched onto Ivan the Terrible and fell in love with him. Apparently I've written quite the wrong thing.'[74] He wrote on the same subject to Veresaev, 'They said the beginning and the end were fine but the middle of the play wouldn't do at all. So instead of forgetting all about it I lie in bed with neuralgia wondering whatever good I can be as a playwright. [...] As it is, I can see no end. Yet I have to find one.'[75]

The failure introduced additional tension into deadlines that were already tight enough. On 31st March 1934 Bulgakov had signed a contract for a film-script based on *Dead Souls* which gave him very little time to complete it. This was also the moment when he was also dreaming of travelling abroad. The summer was a difficult one, marred by nerves and intermittent ill health. In October he signed a contract to rework *Bliss*; at the same time he had an idea for a play about Pushkin, work continued on another cinematic project — a scenario based on *The Government Inspector*, and he was still writing his *Story about the Devil*. All this while he was busy with his regular theatrical duties related to the rehearsals of *A Cabal of Hypocrites*. 'Misha gets terribly tired these days. He's afraid he won't be able to cope with the work,' Elena Bulgakova noted in her diary on 28th December 1934.[76]

All this meant that the reworking of *Bliss* was put back to the autumn of 1935. On 2nd October he read the new text to the actors of the Satire Theatre, 'with great success', according to his wife's diary.[77]

In effect a brand new play resulted. In *Bliss*, the figure of Ivan the Terrible had made a fleeting appearance, summoned from the past by the inventor. The Tsar hid in the attic, and at the end was dispatched back to the sixteenth century. Now the time machine was trained on the past and the time-travel presented symmetrically: Ivan is installed in a Moscow flat and Bunsha and Miroslavsky find their way into his court. The Satire Theatre had good reason to 'latch on' to the Tsar, sensing from the start the splendid comic potential. The plot developed using

---

[74] *Dnevnik. Pis'ma*, p. 327.

[75] Ibid., p. 325.

[76] Quoted in Chudakova, 'Arkhiv...', pp. 116-118.

[77] Ibid., p. 120.

the classical devices of the comedy of errors and disguise. The Tsar and the house-manager played opposite each other with inevitable complications and much straightforward comedy. Standing squarely on historical and contemporary ground, without venturing blithely into the rarefied atmosphere of the future, Bulgakov was himself again, to a large degree at least: in his stage sense, in the comic exploitation of local colour, in the fun.

Not that it was all pure fun. *Ivan Vasil'evich* – that was the play's title – contained more pointed contemporary satire than its earlier version. Bunsha-Koretsky was now the heir not only of Christy (from 'Number 13') and Portupeia/Alliluia (from *Zoika's Apartment*), but also of Ponchik-Nepobeda (from *Adam and Eve*). Installed upon the throne, he cannot immediately forget the habits of caretaker and rent-collector, but once he has acquired a taste for the charms of borrowed authority he is ready to renounce his forged plebeian origins with alacrity and admit to having aristocratic forebears. Beneath the layer of gratuitous laughter, there is something disturbing in the ease with which the domestic informer, who poisons the life of the inventor and believes that 'the state will collapse if the tenants stop paying the rent',[78] reclines on the imperial throne, adapting to an atmosphere of oppressive fear and freshly-committed acts of cruelty (even if the mention of skinning and boiling people alive belongs within the conventions of comedy). In this way, if only in passing, Bulgakov demonstrates the continuity of the link between the twin traditions of satrapy and bureaucracy, of which the latter turns out to be the stronger. Bunsha would be set to embark on a long reign and 'begin by setting up house-management boards',[79] if comic convention had not deposed him from his autocratic throne; Ivan the Terrible, on the other hand, with his grandiloquent monarchic gestures, feels completely lost in the role of present-day house-manager.

Again, the moment lent added meaning. At the time of writing, Bulgakov was using *Ivan Vasil'evich* to create for himself his favourite kind of refuge in humour, by applying the fickle concept of the dream framed in quotation marks. (This time, as distinct from in *Bliss*, everything is the inventor's dream.) This was the last moment when it was possible to try to laugh at Ivan the Terrible; soon the tradition of the blood-stained tyrant would be incorporated into a larger framework,

---

[78] *Ivan Vasil'evich. Mertvye dushi*, p. 18.

[79] Ibid., p. 62.

in which references to Russian history would justify the modern tyranny. A pseudo-historical pseudo-nationalism would arise. Bulgakov availed himself of the chance to make comic use of his experience in film-making. Ivan is treated by a contemporary director as an able character actor from a film about himself. Bulgakov also aims a few passing barbs at the widespread phenomenon of domestic informing; in the play not only the house-manager is an informer, but also the neighbour. He mocks arrogant know-all rationalists; just as earlier, in his *Nakanune* days, somebody had called out that Christ 'never existed', so here Bunsha, transported to the Tsar's court, exclaims, 'It's all an illusion. [...] They died a long time ago.'[80] And Bulgakov's main work, being written concurrently with this one, would, as we know, punish the doubter by beheading him. The resourcefulness of Timofeev, the inventor of the time machine, gives a nod in the direction of *The Master and Margarita* when he explains that he wants to 'break through space and reach into the past.'[81]

Bulgakov's own journey into the past again seemed to hold out the promise of change for the better. The play was accepted and the theatre energetically set about rehearsing it. Auguries of renewed hope ushered in the New Year 1936.

V

The excursion into film-making had occurred a little earlier. In the course of 1934 Bulgakov produced three versions of a scenario for *Dead Souls*. The last of these was accepted.[82] But the director of the new film, Ivan Pyr'ev, immediately began to make substantial corrections to it. Preparatory work went

---

[80] Ibid., p. 48.

[81] Ibid., p. 20.

[82] Before this happened, however, Bulgakov had to abandon his plans to follow in the spirit of the original theatrical adaptation, which emphasized the phantasmagorical. See his letter to Popov dated 10th July 1934: 'Everything I liked best about it, the scene with Suvorov's soldiers..., the separate long ballad of Captain Kopeikin, the memorial service at Sobakevich's estate, and above all Rome, with the silhouette on the balcony – all this has been completely ruined. I shall be able to save only Kopeikin, and then only part of him. But – Heavens above! – how I regret losing Rome!' (See Chapter Seven, Note 34 in connection with this last sentence.) Quoted in K. Rudnitskii, *Teatral'nye stranitsy*, p. 184; also in *Dnevnik. Pis'ma*, p. 345.

ahead, and the cast promised to be extremely interesting. As can be seen from the scant published evidence, the author of the scenario felt it necessary to protest against the distortion of his design.[83] The negotiations were prolonged and wearying, without leading to any agreement. Film-work can be difficult and demanding for a writer at any point in the twentieth century and in any part of the world. So it is possible that the insurmountable problems were of a quite ordinary nature, but it is also possible that the critical factors were the limits imposed precisely at this time and place, along with a fear of experimentation. Years later Pyr'ev took it upon himself to explain that he had been alarmed by the so-called 'anti-formalist' campaign in *Pravda*.[84] But this campaign did not begin until January 1936, so the causes of this alarm – if the decision was his – lay elsewhere, unless plain ordinary caution played some part, urging him to worry, just in case.

The surviving script is clearly a serious work, close in its basic lines to the adaptation for the theatre. At certain points Bulgakov exploits the broader possibilities of the cinema, expanding effectively on the fairy-tale quality of the ball given in honour of Chichikov, for example; at moments he gives free rein to his phantasmagorical proclivities, as when he shows Chichikov's dream of holding a roll-call of dead souls, who rise from the grave and line up. But the work as a whole – at least in the screen version which was published – is fairly conventional in nature. It looks as if the author, chastened by his bitter experiences at the Art Theatre and perhaps forewarned, bridles his imagination this time, reluctant to take risks.

Of much greater interest is the scenario for *The Government Inspector*, written for the Ukrainfilm studio with the director Korostin.[85] What proportion of the work is Bulgakov's is uncertain, but the scenario, partly in the manner of silent films, brims over with the sweep of a fertile imagination. The events are placed against the broad background of a small provincial town, peopled by grotesquely menacing figures, whose recurrent similarity to one another produces the effect of a unique mechanical ballet. The rapid changes of scene render the images at once

---

[83] On the circumstances of this see Chudakova, 'Arkhiv...', pp. 114-116, especially p. 115; also Iu. P. Tiurin's introduction to M. Bulgakov, I. Pyr'ev, 'Mertvye dushi. Kinostsenarii', *Moskva*, No. 1, 1978, p. 126.

[84] Tiurin, p. 126.

[85] Scenario published in *Novyi zhurnal*, No. 127, 1977, pp. 5-45.

fluid and synthetic; the film-makers' feel for the camera's potential greatly enhances the effect when the hero tells his most extravagant lies. The additions to the original text of the play are entirely in the spirit of Gogol. Khlestakov visits a number of municipal institutions, all of which share the same prison-like features. Amidst the comic occurrences the real government inspector appears and the point of the scenario is made when he accepts a collective bribe, demonstrating that a fundamentally unaltered way of life will continue. The influence of both Meyerhold's famous stage production and of Kozintsev's and Trauberg's film of *The Overcoat* can be felt. The result makes one wish to see the film which might have been made, and one feels certain that this film would have been true to Gogol.

But no such film exists. History repeated itself, and repeated strokes of ill luck are, as we know, an ever-present part of Bulgakov's experience. In the second half of 1934, concurrently with the brouhaha surrounding *Dead Souls*, there was much activity surrounding *The Government Inspector*, with proposals and counter-proposals, opposition and concessions, new versions and discussions.[86]

'The film directors made a great deal of noise in the flat,' recalls Sergei Ermolinsky, a friend of his later years. 'Both of them, the Kiev and the Moscow directors, wanted active co-operation. But for Bulgakov it was difficult to get used to such a noisy style of work; having been a writer for many years, he was used to a quiet environment.'[87]

The more important issue, however, seems to have been the purpose of the work rather than the style, and the purpose must have become increasingly problematic, being eroded amidst never-ending and fruitless activity. 'All these conversations,' his wife wrote after discussions with the directors, 'have a depressing effect on Misha. They are tedious, unnecessary and unproductive, as they have nothing to do with art.'[88] And a little later: 'I can feel how uninvolved Misha is in the work on *The Government Inspector* and how trying he finds it. It means working with other people's ideas, for money.' If this was the feeling that

---

[86] See the account in Chudakova, 'Arkhiv...', pp. 115-118.

[87] Sergei Ermolinskii, 'O Mikhaile Bulgakove', *Teatr*, No. 9, 1966, p. 89. Ermolinskii's extensive recollections contain many curious facts and debatable interpretations. The author makes very free with chronology, often departing from the known sequence of events.

[88] Quoted in Chudakova, 'Arkhiv...', p. 116.

resulted from his work on Gogol, things really were bad. Even Bulgakov's own mentor could do nothing to help. On the contrary, as we read in the next line of the diary, 'he hampered me terribly during my work on *Pushkin.*'[89] Thus it fell to Gogol, not for the first time, to enter the magic, phantasmagorical circle of Bulgakov's life and complicate it further. A strange and fickle decree of fate.

In the end *The Government Inspector* was dropped, like *Dead Souls*, without reaching its consummation.

VI

'Work on *Pushkin*' began in the midst of other commitments. The idea came to Bulgakov, according to Elena Bulgakova, in early October 1934, and from the start it was intended that the hero should not be physically present.

According to his wife's commentary, Bulgakov felt it impossible to have 'even the most gifted actor appearing on stage in a curly wig and side-whiskers, laughing they way Pushkin laughed, and then speaking the most ordinary everyday language.'[90]

This decision showed his unerring artistic taste. To many it seemed problematical, although its undoubted rightness should have been obvious. Bulgakov's profoundly Russian participation in the cult of Pushkin also found felicitous non-verbal expression. We know that the writer explained his world in terms of Pushkin, that Pushkin was one of his main landmarks between the past and the present. He had defended Pushkin passionately against his detractors in the Caucasus.[91] Pushkin was the one exception to his declared aversion to poetry, as he wrote in a letter to Popov: 'Pushkin is not poetry!'[92] In another letter, already cited, in which he rebelled in astonishment against the intrigue by Vishnevsky, who had barred the way for *Cabal*, he stated sadly, 'A hundred years ago, when the

---

[89] Ibid., p. 118

[90] E. Bulgakova, introduction to M. Bulgakov i V. Veresaev, 'Perepiska po povodu p'esy *Pushkin (Poslednie dni)*', *Voprosy literatury*, No. 3, 1965, p. 151; also in Mikhail Bulgakov, *Pis'ma. Zhizneopisanie v dokumentakh*, p. 332.

[91] In *Notes on Shirt-Cuffs*. See Chapter One.

[92] Quoted in Milne, 'K biografii...', p. 165. Also in M. Chudakova, "K tvorcheskoi biografii M. Bulgakova', *Voprosy literatury*, No. 7, 1973, p. 232.

Commander of our Literary Order was killed, the mark of a serious bullet wound was found on his body. A hundred years later, when people undress the body of one of his descendants before sending him on his last journey, they will find a number of stab-wounds – all in the back. New times bring new weapons.'[93]

These bitter lines provide the psychological key to Bulgakov's latest scheme. As in Molière, so in Pushkin he descried a kindred spirit; he approached him with understanding of the tragedy of his life – perhaps having arrived at an even deeper understanding of his own life. This may have provided a little hard-won comfort. He was not the only one who needed Pushkin: in those years many creative artists turned to him, showing, apart from anything else, a need to maintain the fragile spiritual connection with the past and mark out the authentic spiritual genealogy of the Russian intelligentsia, and perhaps – at a deeper level – to maintain the dignity, so systematically trampled upon, of that intelligentsia. This is the line taken by the works of Tynianov and Leonid Grossman, the Pushkin studies of Akhmatova and Veresaev, and many others.

It was to Veresaev – a kind and close friend, as well as a first-rate specialist in the field, the author of the seminal book *Pushkin in Life* – that Bulgakov turned with a proposal that they work together. The proposal was accepted and it was agreed that 'Bulgakov would deal with the theatrical side while Vikentii Vikent'evich would see to the selection of the material.'[94] Of course, true to his principles of conscientious work, Bulgakov also made a thorough study of the documents and historical accounts, as his archive shows.[95] In December 1934 a contract was signed with the Vakhtangov Theatre, which intended to stage the play on the centenary of Pushkin's death in 1937, when festivities on a grand scale were planned. The Moscow Art Theatre was also interested in the play for the same reason. In May 1935 the authors signed another contract, with the Leningrad Krasny Theatre. By this time the play was ready; it was entitled 'Pushkin'.

The difficulties that followed first arose between the two playwrights. As they recorded these in writing, in letters, the correspondence published by Elena

---

[93] Ibid., pp. 164-165.

[94] E. Bulgakova, *Voprosy literatury*, No. 3, 1965, p. 151; also in *Pis'ma. Zhizneopisanie v dokumentakh*, p. 332.

[95] See for example L. Ianovskaia's publication, 'Mikhail Bulgakov: Iz chernovykh tetradei p'esy *Aleksandr Pushkin*', *Zvezda*, No. 6, 1974, pp. 202-204.

Bulgakova clearly shows the focus of their differences. Veresaev was concerned with the detailed historical truth and with extracting the full social significance of Pushkin's fate. Bulgakov was far from intending to treat historical reality as freely as he had in *Cabal*, but he did seek artistic licence. To him the ultimate criteria were artistic truth and performable theatre. There were sharp differences of opinion, especially when Bulgakov read the play to representatives of the Vakhtangov Theatre. While maintaining the proper decorum, treating each other with all civility, the partners made free with harsh words. 'What you are writing is not a play,' Bulgakov asserted. 'You don't round out the characters and you don't alter them. Instead you transfer fragments of books into the tragedy we have written, with the result that amongst living [...] characters we find lifeless masks bearing the labels "goodie" and "baddie".'[96] 'The fundamental reason for our differences is clear to me,' replied Veresaev. 'It is your organic blindness to the social aspect of the tragedy of Pushkin.'[97] They sought possible compromises with good will, but without success. Veresaev offered detailed new variants; Bulgakov rejected most of them, arguing that they were not stageable or were merely narrative. Finally, after honest consideration, a straightforward solution proposed by Veresaev was adopted; his name would be removed from the title page and *Pushkin* would become Bulgakov's play.

There is no reason to re-examine a matter resolved with such good grace. The presence of Veresaev remained in the play and it is only right that this should be remembered. On the other hand, the play as it stands is of a somewhat illustrative nature, so that it is difficult not to side instinctively with Bulgakov, who did all that he could to move away from the illustrative effect. The decision to name Bulgakov as sole author produced a situation which was probably closest to the facts of the matter.

Pushkin, later renamed *The Last Days*, relies on the audience's basic knowledge of the subject, which may be taken for granted in a Russian theatre, and this knowledge, built into the design, complements the action on stage. Moreover, since the action takes place in the last days of the poet's life and right before his

---

[96] *Voprosy literatury*, No. 3, 1965, p. 166; also in *Pis'ma. Zhizneopisanie v dokumentakh*, p. 350.

[97] *Voprosy literatury*, No. 3, 1965, p. 167; also in *Pis'ma. Zhizneopisanie v dokumentakh*, p. 351.

death, the principal playwright is history itself, to which the writer wishes to remain faithful and must remain faithful. His freedom of manoeuvre is limited by certain facts which are universally present in the consciousness of society. He cannot discover anything totally new, so cannot completely avoid the role of illustrator.

He may, however, select and arrange the material, and in doing so, relying on intuition and invention – which is permissible up to a point – lend it his individual interpretation. As in *Cabal*, Bulgakov is fascinated by the fate of the artist under a tyranny, a fate which leads to the inevitably fatal entrapment of the artist in an environment corrupted by tyranny. To a greater extent than in the play about Molière, there is in *The Last Days* a concentrated sense of an inevitable unhappy ending. This a play about the hounding of Pushkin, not so much about the poet as about the situation of the poet; in this sense his physical absence gains further justification. In Act One, Act Two and half of Act Three, the author conducts a unique artistic investigation, preparing the ground for the tragic dénouement. The basis is personified in creditors, small-time informers, cynical gendarmes, envious literati and an indifferent and spiritually distant wife and her bedazzled admirer. In keeping with the hierarchical structure of the period, but also with the principle of supreme accountability as developed in *Cabal*, this cast of characters is surmounted by the Tsar, a figure who is far from one-dimensional, a man maintaining an assumed inner pose, convinced of the extraordinary nature of his role, inflatedly sentimental and given to prating with conviction about the homeland, honour and love. His statements are contradicted by the very situation of oppressive autocracy to which the Tsar gives shape without, of course, noticing the contradiction; Bulgakov's tyranny is egocentric, and thus blind, and, whatever it may think or say, it is by nature inhuman.

Debates about the historical last days of Pushkin still continue and many things remain unclear. Bulgakov's view was based on the material he could gain access to at the time, of varying reliability, and on his own beliefs, which were also debatable. He may have done an injustice to Benediktov, a poet of great talent (as is apparent from the poem Bulgakov allows him to recite) who is shown as a puppet in the hands of Pushkin's envious foes. Time has also accumulated more arguments for the defence of Natalia Goncharova; on the other hand, Akhmatova's research has demonstrated that the poet's sister-in-law Aleksandra was not nearly as well-disposed to him as the play would have it.[98] Veresaev may have been right to reproach his co-author for lending d'Anthès – in reality a shallow figure – too much psychological depth. But the veiled suggestion of the Tsar's direct complicity in the death of the poet does not seem exaggerated: using conjecture to reconstruct an obscure episode, Bulgakov has Nicholas I suggest indirectly to his gendarmes that they should not prevent the duel; according to recent research the Tsar, who was very well informed, did nothing to prevent the intrigue against Pushkin, which led to an easily predictable tragic outcome.[99] These two views are not very distant from each other and this is not the first time an artist has divined in literature something that is later confirmed by a researcher, or has established his own form of the truth, which soon receives demonic endorsement.

In his theatrical investigation Bulgakov performs a conscientious reconstruction of a picture of the period. Historical figures speak a language based on the evidence which has survived or is thoroughly plausible, and slightly stylized. The etiquette of high society is authentic, as are the forms of current romantic convention; the play evokes the cold, rigid trappings of the reign of Nicholas, which grips the poet in its dead hand. Compared with the emotional expressiveness of *Cabal*, the tonality of *The Last Days* is muted and imbued with the inevitability of misfortune; the slow progression of fairly static scenes measures out the concluding stages of a life. The muted spectrum of colours in the solid interiors blends in many scenes into the darkness, forming a visual metaphor for the atmosphere. Against this background the language of isolated brighter highlights is eloquent and disconcerting: chandeliers, burning brands and lanterns – in addition to sparing musical effects.

If, according to Goethe, a great artist displays his skill when constrained, then Bulgakov, constrained by the need to observe historical truth, here gives proof of true artistry: the play lives, and the drama of the poet is played out authentically, not in merely decorative style. It is typical that only one scene is of a decorative nature: the crowd demonstrates under the windows of Pushkin's home, while Lermontov's poem 'On the Death of a Poet' is declaimed. This is a good illustration of what *The Last Days* might have become but, happily, did not: a kind

---

[98] See Anna Akhmatova, 'Aleksandrina', *Zvezda*, No. 2, 1973.

[99] See for example S. Abramovich, 'K istorii dueli Pushkina', *Voprosy literatury*, No. 11, 1978, pp. 210-228.

of dramatized thesis on Pushkin the 'socially progressive' 'people's poet'. Veresaev evidently sensed this, as he wrote in a letter, 'the scene on the Moika, intended to be central, is terribly dull and I fear it will be the undoing of us,'[100] while Konstantin Fedin who reviewed the play, had good reason to say that the crowd of demonstrators 'recalled the statistical mean between the Decembrists and the "Men of the 'Sixties".'[101]

Also characteristic is the fact that total mastery is also displayed even where there are no constraints: in the creation of characters and invented situations. Bitkov, a watchmaker and agent of the Third Section, is constantly present in the circle surrounding the poet. At first his presence seems merely to set the seal on the persecution of Pushkin. But before Act One is over this plebeian informer, who relishes the charm of Pushkin's poem 'A Winter Evening' – 'A blizzard covers the sky...' –, is seen to have a painfully lyrical nature which wins him some sympathy, even if it is laced with revulsion. This ambiguity is well known to readers of Dostoevsky. At the purely formal level, Bitkov's presence is not trivial, as it provides a frame for the play. When in the closing scene we see a brief halt, in an eerie atmosphere, while the body of the poet is being secretly transported to the monastery of Sviatye Gory, Bitkov, Pushkin's shadow, reappears, and it is apparent from his words that his years of spying have bound him to the 'spied-upon' by a mysterious bond of understanding, sympathy and even a kind of guardianship:

'They didn't let him go anywhere without me. Wherever he went, I went... Never so much as a step away... But that day they sent me somewhere else, on a Wednesday... I sensed something at once. They wanted him on his own! Cunning rogues! They knew he'd go where they wanted by himself. Because his time was up. So off he went to Chernaia Rechka, and they were waiting for him. I wasn't there.'[102]

---

[100] *Voprosy literatury*, No. 3, 1965, p. 163.

[101] Konstantin Fedin, 'Mikhail Bulgakov o Pushkine', in *Sobranie sochinenii*, Moscow, 1973, Vol. IX, p. 547. 'Men of the 'Sixties' is the term used to described the radical intelligentsia of the 1860s.

[102] M. Bulgakov, *P'esy*, Moscow, 1962, p. 358; also Bulgakov, *Sobranie sochinenii*, 1990, Vol. 3, p. 511.

What is more, Bitkov turns out to be infected by Pushkin's poetry, whose meaning he instinctively grasps ('Because of those poems of his, nobody had any peace, ... he himself didn't, the authorities didn't, and nor did I, your humble servant, Stepan Il'ich... Luck was never with him. Whatever he wrote, he didn't harm the people he was aiming at...')[103] and which pierces his heart, like the lines from 'A Winter Evening'. The confessions of a repentant spy, in whom Pushkin's genius fanned a spark of humanity, being truly dramatic, are also a far better way of showing a 'people's poet' than a crowd scene. The informer's troubled emotions have in them a bitter and ambivalent lyrical quality; the hidden, and very Russian, bond between the persecutor and the persecuted, sealing the hopelessness of the victim's situation, carries within it both catharsis and an indistinct promise of hope. In the final scene – the halt at the post-horse station – through the grim situation and the utterly mechanical actions of the gendarmes shine the authentically humane lines of 'A Winter Evening', lingering at length, like the 'absolutely immortal' *Faust* in *Adam and Eve*.

There is no doubt that this is the best scene in the play; by itself it gives a clear idea of the scale of Bulgakov's talent. When the play was finally accepted by the Art Theatre, this was the scene that the theatre threatened to cut. It is probable that in wartime, when sturdiness of spirit was a requirement, this scene was felt to be too pessimistic. Nemirovich-Danchenko, however, who followed the fate of the play and participated in rehearsals immediately before the premiere in March and April 1943, appreciated it and defended it.[104] After the premiere too the ending came under attack, from Fedin, among others, writing in his review that, 'this episode... freezes the action, repeating what we already know from the play.' But subsequent stagings reaffirmed the value of the scene.[105]

---

[103] *P'esy*, 1962, p. 357; Bulgakov, *Sobranie sochinenii*, 1990, Vol. 3, p. 510.

[104] Note his comments: 'There is something tragic about the fact that after we have seen a comfortable apartment, a palace, the opulent Saltykov residence, the play ends in a shabby little room. Here Bulgakov shows extraordinary profundity'; 'I do not understand how the last scene can be cut. Ideologically and politically it is essential, and highly expressive. Because it offers no hope? What hope could there be in the reign of Nicholas I? A great poet is buried in secret. How can that last scene be omitted?' Quoted in L. Freidkina, *Dni i gody Vl. N. Nemirovich-Danchenko*, Moscow, 1962, pp. 579, 564.

[105] Fedin, p. 550.

The stumbling block for many remained the absence of Pushkin. While work was still in hand, Veresaev, who had at first been persuaded that this was right, had doubts about it. During discussions with the Art Theatre, Leonidov categorically demanded a live Pushkin.[106] After the premiere, the absence of Pushkin became the reviewers' main complaint. With time, however, the opposite view began to prevail. Today the matter is hardly discussed. From the time of *The White Guard* Bulgakov well understood the eloquence of apparent absence, giving the effect of ubiquitous presence. In *The Last Days* we see only the poet's shadow and his outline as his body is carried, but everything that happens is directed towards him, happens with him and in relation to him; so he is played obliquely, by the whole cast. The whole play is infused with his poetry, both directly and indirectly. If in *Cabal* he was reluctant to quote Molière's works, this time Bulgakov wished not only to quote Pushkin's poetry, but also to create an atmosphere which we may perceive emotionally as being consonant with his poetry and prose (there are clear allusions to *The Tales of Belkin*, in particular), and he succeeded. In the physical absence of Pushkin there is an additional psychological truth which it is difficult to miss: the victim of an intrigue which seems to develop almost by chance, but nevertheless inevitably, Pushkin is doomed even before d'Anthès fires his shot; there is no place for him in the world in which he is condemned to live. On the other hand, having spiritually survived his own death and rising higher and higher in the estimation of subsequent generations, the Russian genius materializes in the imagination of every reader of his poetry, thus denying physical imitation any real purpose.

This was confirmed by the indisputable failure of such imitations. 'In our theatres,' wrote the critic Vera Smirnova, taking issue with Fedin, who held the absence of Pushkin against Bulgakov, 'there were some attempts later to "put Pushkin on the stage". And with what result? We heard Pushkin speaking in the verse of Globa and the prose of Paustovsky; but even the talented Iakut at the Ermolova Theatre was only able to have us believe for occasional moments that we were seeing Pushkin's shadow. The rest was either disappointment or cause for outright indignation.'[107]

---

[106] See the record of the meeting of the MAT Artistic Council for 24.10.39. (MAT Museum)

[107] Vera Smirnova, *Knigi i sud'by*, Moscow, 1968, p. 433. She refers to Andrei Globa's play *Pushkin* (1937) and Konstantin Paustovskii's *Nash sovremennik Pushkin* [Pushkin, Our

The play was completed by autumn 1935 and the Vakhtangov Theatre began preparations for the staging. Vitalii Vilenkin, a friend of Bulgakov's and a veteran of the Art Theatre, recalls that, 'We at the Art Theatre did not give up hope of doing a parallel production, at least, for the hundredth anniversary of Pushkin's death. There was a copy of the play in the Art Theatre and it was discussed at length. I. Sudakov was longing to direct it. It had the energetic support of Sakhnovsky and the literature department; Nemirovich-Danchenko definitely liked it. Stanislavsky remained cool towards it.'[108]

Other theatres were also interested in *The Last Days*. In the end, however, the premiere of the play took place at the Moscow Art Theatre three years after the death of the author. More immediate plans and projects, while seeming to multiply and develop promisingly, were actually approaching a new and brutal crisis.

VII

'So my Molière days have started!' Bulgakov reported to Popov in April 1933, gaily announcing the failure of *The Life of Monsieur de Molière*.[109]

In fact his 'Molière days' had started, as we know, as long ago as 1929 and lasted, with interruptions, for almost seven years.

In 1934 the career of his *Cabal of Hypocrites* entered a new phase. Hitherto the play had had an existence similar to the life of the author: quasi-real and unfulfilled. While theoretically figuring in the repertoire plans of the Art Theatre, it was constantly pushed into the background. Rehearsals were initiated, then suspended; the members of the cast changed. Work on the play now proceeded in a more consecutive way. Nikolai Gorchakov became the director, but, as Vilenkin recalls, 'it was apparently in the hands of Konstantin Sergeevich [Stanislavsky], although at that time he no longer visited the theatre. Occasionally the actors would be summoned to his presence, with the director... In my view they feared his summonses more than they looked forward to them; Konstantin

---

Contemporary] (1949). In the former, V. Iakut played the title role. It is characteristic that Paustovsky, who turned Pushkin into a conventional figure, years later admitted that Bulgakov's was the superior approach. K. Paustovskii, *Naedine s osen'iu*, Moscow, 1967, p. 159.

[108] Vitalii Vilenkin, 'Nezabyvaemye vstrechi', in *Neizdannyi Bulgakov*, p. 56.

[109] Quoted in Milne, 'K biografii...', p. 167.

Sergeevich had very little to say about the play. They talked more often than they rehearsed. And it already seemed too late to just talk.'[110]

As the published records show, meetings were held in March, April and May 1935.[111] At the first of these Stanislavsky fundamentally queried the nature of the play and demanded that it show the scale of Molière's genius. 'In front of the actors (after four years)' Bulgakov wrote to Popov, 'he started telling me that Molière was a genius and how I should describe this genius in my play. The actors gloated and started asking for bigger parts for themselves. I was filled with rage. I felt like throwing the script away and saying to all of them: "You can write about geniuses and non-geniuses yourselves! It's no good trying to teach me, because I'll never be able to! And I'll act instead of you." But I couldn't, I couldn't do that. I stifled the impulse and tried to defend myself.'[112]

The new drama surrounding Bulgakov's drama was set down in polyphonic minuted records. These have considerably more plausibility than Gorchakov's earlier account, based on them, in his book *Stanislavsky's Lessons in Directing*, in which many statements are simply distorted.[113] This book was written during a difficult period and is decidedly hagiographical in nature. But in spite of this it failed to conceal the disintegration of the great director's creative personality. It is a painful spectacle, for the processes of advancing senility are pitilessly clear, and under the humble adoration and subservience of the troupe it is not difficult to detect that all are fully aware of the position.[114] We are already close to the sarcastic scenes of *A Theatrical Novel*, with the theatrical rehearsals depicted in it. It transpires that this time there was little need for exaggeration or embroidery; grotesque reality is but a step away from the grotesque in literature. If we are to believe Gorchakov, in granting permission for rehearsals Stanislavsky was offering only conditional approval: as a way of convincing Bulgakov that he

---

[110] *Neizdannyi Bulgakov*, pp. 55-56.

[111] Ibid., pp. 91-132.

[112] *Glagol*, No. 2, p. 129; also in *Dnevnik. Pis'ma*, p. 363.

[113] M. Gorchakov, *Rezhisserskie uroki Stanislavskogo*, Moscow, 1952. On *Cabal*, see pp. 540-563.

[114] In the records one can sense the psychological ambivalence with which the actors treat the terminology introduced by Stanislavsky; it is rather like another form of play-acting – in addition to the central one – and would be savagely mocked later in *A Theatrical Novel*.

should change the direction of his play to give a historical view of Molière.[115] To the author, however, this was unacceptable. Conscious of the complexity of the situation, he agreed to some minor modifications. 'I sit over a copy and can't lift my hand,' he wrote in the same letter. '[...] It's like stitching green patches onto black tail-coat trousers! The Devil only knows what I should do!'[116] As co-director he was again expected to co-operate in the destruction of his own original design. Except that by now he most likely had no illusions. He had seen Stanislavsky following his whims, stunning all by his arbitrary decisions, being side-tracked into non-essential matters, promoting peripheral activities and celebrating minor acting études. While behaving like this, Stanislavsky apparently still hoped that the author would make concessions. In the meantime, he recommended rehearsing the play in fragments and by its central scenes, in order to reconstruct the pattern. This idea did not work in practice and was soon abandoned.[117] According to Vilenkin, in the theatre, 'there were whispers about "the old man" being displeased, about Gorchakov's intricate policy of manoeuvring between three fires (Stanislavsky, the cast and the author), and about the absence of prospects. There was very serious talk about the lack of direct contact between Bulgakov and Stanislavsky, and what a tragedy it was for the theatre that Konstantin Sergeevich could not take on the long-overdue rehearsal of scenes.'[118]

The outstanding characteristic of Stanislavsky's actions in his late period was his extreme caution. He could not fail to be aware of the rich meaning of the statements contained in Bulgakov's text. In demanding 'historicism' and a tighter biographical approach, he may have been trying to steer the play towards safer ground or simply playing for time. It was not difficult for him to imagine a new critical assault on this author, since only one of his works enjoyed immunity. Moreover the thrust of the play tended in the direction of none other than the provider of this immunity, in whose honour paeans of praise and tributes were now

---

[115] Gorchakov, pp. 541-544.

[116] *Glagol*, No. 2, p. 129; also in *Dnevnik. Pis'ma*, p. 364.

[117] See Gorchakov, pp. 542-543, and the same author's *Rabota rezhissera nad spektaklem*, Moscow, 1956, pp. 49-50, where Stanislavsky renounces his own idea.

[118] *Neizdannyi Bulgakov*, p. 56. Note also similar statements in K. Rudnitskii, 'Mol'er, Tartiuf i Bulgakov', *Nauka i religiia*, No. 1, 1972, pp. 84-90; and M. Ianshin, 'Dni molodosti – *Dni Turbinykh*', in *Neizdannyi Bulgakov*, pp. 52-54.

being widely composed, and who had favoured the Moscow Art Theatre with special attention. It is possible, therefore, that at rehearsals the ailing grand old man of the Russian theatre used words that partially concealed or disguised his thoughts. From a purely human perspective, this is fully understandable. The tragedy of the Art Theatre, whose downfall would soon establish a new pattern and whose values would be exploited for the worst possible ends, was already assuming definitive shape.

But at the same time this meant that the cabal surrounding *Cabal* continued, along with the author's travails. At the very first trial run he said plainly to Stanislavsky, 'This has been going on for five years. I've had enough.'[119]

The situation was coming to a head. At a rehearsal on 17th April 1935, at which Bulgakov was not present, Stanislavsky proposed a completely new manner of staging Act Three Scene One, the meeting of the anti-Molière plotters with the Cabal, that is, the Brotherhood of the Holy Writ. This was the purest fantasy on Bulgakov's theme, introducing divisions and conflicts between the characters where there was no real need for these.[120] When he had studied the record of the rehearsal, Bulgakov wrote two letters, similar in content, to Gorchakov and Stanislavsky. To the latter he said:

'I feel compelled to refuse categorically the changes made to my play *Molière*, since the changes in the Cabal scene noted in the record, like those noted earlier for other scenes, as I have become convinced, completely destroy my artistic concept and are aimed at writing a different play, which I cannot write because I disagree fundamentally with it.

'If *Molière* is unacceptable to the Art Theatre in its present form, although the Theatre accepted it and has rehearsed it in precisely this form for several years, I request that you take *Molière* off and return it to me.'[121]

Stanislavsky yielded, but he continued to move slowly with the rehearsals. Then they were again suspended. In early 1936 Nemirovich-Danchenko took charge of the directing; in the light of the internal situation in the Art Theatre, this was a significant change. It is clear that desperate efforts were being made to find a solution. By this time the play was fully ready. Bulgakov, incidentally, had little

---

[119] Quoted in *Neizdannyi Bulgakov*, p. 95.

[120] Ibid., p. 134.

[121] Ibid., p. 135; also in *Dnevnik. Pis'ma*, p. 368.

time for Nemirovich-Danchenko, although the director's surviving comments about the writer are filled with respect and recognition; perhaps this lack of mutual feeling was a consequence less of their artistic views than of Bulgakov's coolness towards the plainly stated conformism of the Art Theatre's second-in-command. Whatever the truth of the matter, this was of little importance with regard to the play. The whole affair was escaping the control of its creators and taking on a momentum of its own. Only at the last moment did the theatre, in self-defence, attempt a stalling action; Gorchakov in a press interview, like Nemirovich-Danchenko at a rehearsal, described *Cabal* as a 'historical melodrama'.[122] This has little in common with the textual reality, in which melodrama is a peripheral element, a reagent showing up the drama of the artist. This, however, is obviously an attempt to diminish the impact of the play and suggest a new system of meaning. But by now the play had a life of its own.

This proved to be a short life. The premiere took place on 15th February 1936, with a set designed by Williams and costumes by Ul'ianov; Molière was played by Stanitsyn, Louis XIV by Bolduman, Bouton by Ianshin, Madeleine Béjart by Koreneva and Armande by Stepanova. Judging by the reports, the play was sound and generally well acted, with sumptuous, striking décor. Perhaps the fact that it was the product of various people's efforts lent it a certain eclecticism, and the unconscionably long preparatory period had made the material slightly heavy and tired. Nevertheless, the audience welcomed it very warmly. Its long-term success seemed assured.[123]

In the meantime, on 9th March an editorial entitled 'Outward Glitter and False Content' appeared in *Pravda*, subjecting *Cabal* to harsh criticism. In the view of the anonymous author, the play relied on 'cheap effects and piquant situations in the spirit of the worst efforts of Dumas and Scribe', showing instead of the historical Molière 'a run-of-the-mill stage hack, who, to please the narrow-minded, leads a chaotic private life'; the theatre had 'focussed all its attention on the external aspect' of the play. This was one level of attack, at times recalling – as can be seen

---

[122] Nemirovich-Danchenko said, 'the play resembles the model of a splendid historical melodrama' (*Zapis' dlia teatra*, MAT Museum); see also Gorchakov's interview with *Literaturnaia gazeta*, 10.2.36, in which he says, 'We treated the the play in full, including its production, as a modern transcription of a once famous genre of historical melodrama.'

[123] Chudakova, 'Arkhiv...', p. 121.

– what had already been said about the play. There was, however, another level; it was asserted, for example, that 'the severity of Louis XIV is totally unexpected', and that the author was 'trying, while taking refuge behind a historical setting, to cast a reactionary eye on artistic creativity as "pure" art'. At least these comments dealt with things that really mattered, whereas the other accusations were merely a pretext, constituting criticism on trumped-up charges. This then is the last act of the cabal surrounding *Cabal*, very likely indicating that the *Pravda* reviewer well understood what the play was about. Otherwise it would be difficult to understand why such heavy artillery should be turned on a play which was recognized as feeble, or why so much emphasis was given to the Art Theatre's 'drawing the appropriate conclusions'.[124] It is true that the central party organ had just launched a series of denunciatory articles to inaugurate a campaign of annihilation against so-called 'formalism' in art,[125] but not even the broadest definition could place *Cabal* in this category. This case was accorded special treatment.

Other press organs followed the lead given by *Pravda*. The time had now come when the view of the party's main mouthpiece had the force of law. A theatre with the standing of the Art Theatre may still have had the right of appeal, but it clearly did not attempt to exercise it. After several hundred rehearsals and seven performances the play was taken off by the theatre management, as one which, to quote Gorchakov, 'did not meet the requirement of truthfully showing on stage the life and work of one of the greatest classics of the theatre.'[126] This verdict, from a book written in the Stalin period, bears that period's authentic stamp.

The end of *Cabal* produced a swift chain reaction. The limits of Bulgakov's immunity again turned out to extend no further than *Days*, as everybody immediately realized. One after another, various plans foundered. In May the Satire Theatre withdrew *Ivan Vasil'evich*, which had reached dress rehearsal.[127]

---

[124] 'Vneshnii blesk i fal'shivoe soderzhanie', *Pravda*, 9.3.36.

[125] See the following in *Pravda*: 'Sumbur vmesto muzyki', 28.1.36; 'Baletnaia fal'sh', 6.2.36; 'O khudozhnikakh-pachkunakh', 2.3.36.

[126] Gorchakov, p. 563.

[127] Shortly before Bulgakov's death the Travelling Theatre expressed interest in the play. Aleksandr Gladkov, to whom I am grateful for this information, approached Bulgakov on its behalf. The idea soon proved unrealistic.

The Vakhtangov Theatre dropped *The Last Days*; other theatres which had shown interest did the same.[128]

Thus a new phase of hope came to an end – according to the stage-directing of fate as Bulgakov had known it since 1929: everything fell through at once.

Bulgakov's reaction is also familiar: immediately, without wasting so much as one day, he set to work on new projects.

And thus began the last years of his life.

---

[128] The play was finally accepted by MAT in January 1940 and produced on 10th April 1943.

Chapter Nine

Essays in Almost Everything

    I. End of the dramatic works. A textbook of Russian history. A planned play about Stalin.
    II. *A Theatrical Novel* as revenge and psychological catharsis.
    III. Work at the Bolshoi Theatre; reviews and librettos. *Minin and Pozharsky*; more frustration.
    IV. Adapting *Don Quixote*.
    V. More redactions of the novel about the Devil. The definitive title appears. MAT commissions *Batum*. An attempt to modify it; final failure.
    VI. Illness, last works and plans. Brave last days. Death.

I

We may recall Bulgakov's sentence about the equal validity of prose and drama, recorded by Popov, in which he said, 'the two forms are bound together, like a pianist's left and right hands.'[1]

Ten years after his début as a playwright the word 'bound' had acquired a more mundane sense. Both hands were equally manacled. The 'move into the theatre', about which Boris Leont'ev had written,[2] had led into a narrow cul-de-sac, at least in Bulgakov's lifetime. One play and one adaptation marked the upper limit of opportunity. Beyond this, as he found to his cost again and again, stood a blind wall.

'I'm very tired and have been reflecting lately,' Bulgakov wrote to Veresaev on 4th April 1937, a year after *Cabal* had foundered. 'My last attempts to write for

---

[1] See Chapter Five.

[2] See Chapter Five.

the drama theatres have been the purest quixotry on my part. I shan't ever repeat it. I won't do anything more on the drama theatre front.'[3]

At about the same time, when asked about his creative plans for the twentieth anniversary of the October revolution, he replied, 'The removal of my various plays from the repertoire has been accompanied by newspaper articles which have made it irrefutably clear to me that writing more plays and offering them to the theatres is a complete waste of time. I have been forced to seek work of a different kind and have become an opera librettist.'[4]

Before this came to pass, immediately before *Cabal* was taken off, Bulgakov tried his hand at something else that was completely new to him. In response to a competition announced in the press he went to work energetically on a textbook of Russian history. His interest in this area had manifested itself long before. He soon dropped the project, but what he produced demonstrates that he was going about it in a professional manner, with much expert knowledge and the ability to expound it with transparent clarity. Clearly this interlude – in the tradition of Pushkin – was necessary for him. It would have been difficult, however, for the aspiring historian to avoid the conclusion that in this undertaking he would have even less room to manoeuvre. Perhaps there were also other factors, but, whatever the case, the plan went no further than fragments and notes.[5]

At the same time another plan was conceived – to write about Stalin. From his wife's diary we learn that on 6th February Bulgakov decided to write a play about Stalin's youth.[6] After some preliminary work, it was temporarily set aside. The idea itself, properly considered, has nothing astonishing about it, although when juxtaposed with *The Master and Margarita* – which was created at the same time – it looks strange. In both cases, however, the act of creation was an act of explanation – to the writer himself – of the mysterious nature of the world. He was interpreting life according to Gogol and Pushkin, but also – and above all –

---

[3] Quoted in M. Chudakova, 'Arkhiv M. A. Bulgakova. Materialy dlia tvorcheskoi biografii pisatelia', in *Zapiski Otdela rukopisei Gos. Bibl. SSSR im. Lenina*, Moscow, 1976, p. 122. Also in *Dnevnik. Pis'ma 1914–1940*, Moscow, 1997, p. 437.

[4] Quoted in Lesley Milne, 'K biografii M. A. Bulgakova', *Novyi zhurnal*, No. 111, 1973, p. 159.

[5] Materials, notes and fragments from the textbook are held in the Bulgakov archive in the Lenin Library.

[6] See Chudakova, 'Arkhiv...', p. 121.

according to Bulgakov. He was not the only one who must have been fascinated at that period by the mysterious figure of the ruler, whose soaring rise and towering position seemed explainable only in some special, possibly mystical terms. At almost exactly the same time Boris Pasternak confessed his own fascination in the well-known words of his poem 'The Artist':

> И этим гением поступка
> Так поглощен другой поэт
> Что тяжелеет, словно губка,
> Любою из его примет.
>
> Как в этой двухголосной фуге
> Он сам ни бесконечно мал,
> Он верит в знанье друг о друге
> Предельно крайних двух начал.[7]

Besides Pasternak's absolutely typical transports of rapture and admiration before the vision of something far from elevated, there was already Mandelstam's iconoclastic, sarcastic interpretation – an isolated one, it is true –, in which Stalin is 'the Kremlin mountain-dweller' with 'cockroach whiskers' and 'fingers as fat as worms'.[8] Bulgakov, we may surmise, held a place somewhere in between; we have no grounds to assume any iconoclastic intent, but what he would soon write would be free of rapture and very far from the banal panegyrics which were beginning to dominate literature. He himself owed his continued existence to Stalin's mercy; he knew from the evidence of history of examples of such mercy, the mechanism of its operation, and its limits; he knew the corrupting influence of

---

[7]   [And a poet is so entranced
By this genius of action
That he grows heavy, like a sponge,
When he absorbs any one of his distinguishing marks.

No matter how infinitesimally small he himself is
In this two-voiced fugue,
He believes that the two opposing principles
Know about each other's existence.]

First published in *Izvestiia*, 1.1.36, reprinted in B. Pasternak, *Sochineniia*, Ann Arbor, 1961, Vol. 3, pp. 240-241. [The English version of the second stanza is taken from Olga R. Hughes, *The Poetic World of Boris Pasternak*, Princeton University Press, Princeton, 1974, p. 103. *Trans.*]

[8] O. Mandel'shtam, 'My zhivem pod soboiu ne znaia strany'. First published in *Mosty*, No. 10 (1963), p. 159.

tyranny and the opportunities a tyrant had – if he valued such opportunities – to curb, when he chose, the bloodthirsty fervour of his paladins in order to appear better than they. Knowing all this, he may have wished to understand, within the limits open to him, how the situation in which he and his country found themselves had arisen. And it is likely that he wished to travel to the land of the despot's youth – the Caucasus – in search of the foundations of such an understanding.

For the moment, however, the journey had to be postponed. Some changes – the last changes – had occurred in the his professional circumstances. Some time earlier, Bulgakov had drawn closer to the musical milieu connected to the Bolshoi Theatre. In June the management proposed that he write the libretto for the opera *Minin and Pozharsky* for the composer Boris Asaf'ev. Bulgakov accepted the proposal. The next offer, made in September, was of full-time work. At the same time another conflict had erupted between Bulgakov and the Moscow Art Theatre about the writer's new version of *The Merry Wives of Windsor,* with which Gorchakov was dissatisfied. Bulgakov must have considered the litany of insults too long, for he tendered his resignation and signed on with the Bolshoi as a consultant in the repertoire department.[9] By his own previously cited account, he also became a librettist.

The Art Theatre connection was not yet terminated, but it was temporarily broken off. It is beyond doubt that this occurred at a time when there was ill feeling on Bulgakov's side. He been stung by the haste with which the theatre dropped *Cabal.* Being particularly alert to the loyalty of his friends, he was also hurt by an interview with Mikhail Ianshin on this occasion, in which Ianshin levelled some fundamental reproaches at him.[10] All this came to a head when an atmosphere of ever-deepening artistic paralysis was taking hold of the theatre and a vulgarized MAT style was being proclaimed as obligatory for other theatres as well. 'MAT is now in a state of the deepest crisis, even though it is well regarded, lauded and upheld as a model to be emulated,' remarked Aleksandr Afinogenov at this time.[11]

---

[9] On these matters and the surrounding circumstances see Chudakova, 'Arkhiv...', pp. 121-122.

[10] M. Ianshin, 'Pouchitel'naia istoriia', *Sovetskoe iskusstvo,* 17.3.36. The actor maintained subsequently that the sense of his statement was utterly distorted by the reporter (see Ianshin, 'Dni molodosti – *Dni Turbiykh*', in *Neizdannyi Bulgakov,* Ann Arbor, 1977, p. 53).

[11] Aleksandr Afinogenov, *Stat'i, dnevniki, pis'ma, vospominaniia,* Moscow, 1957, p. 137.

Many of the friendships Bulgakov had made at MAT withstood this trial, but his bitterness comes through clearly in one of his letters to Popov:

'Today is a holiday for me. Exactly ten years ago the premiere of *The Turbins* took place. I sit by my inkwell waiting for a delegation from Stanislavsky and Nemirovich-Danchenko to open the door and come in, bearing a congratulatory scroll and a precious gift. The scroll will list all my mutilated and mangled plays and all the joys that they, Stanislavsky and Nemirovich, have given me in the ten years I've spent at the Art Theatre. The precious gift, however, will be in the form of a large saucepan made of some precious metal (perhaps bronze) filled with the blood they've sucked out of me in these ten years.'[12]

II

It is not surprising that he needed his pen to master his bitterness.

The letter to Popov was written on 5th October, and at the end of November he began work on *A Theatrical Novel*, most probably returning to the idea, mentioned in his letter to the government, of a novel entitled *The Theatre*. We can at once recognize in the text the outlines of the sketch 'To a Secret Friend', but this time the autobiographical material is pushed a little further into the background, enclosed in the frame of convention, in a mould; no doubt the distance made life's difficulties more bearable.

The retreat into the background is effected in two ways. Firstly, by one of Bulgakov's ritual devices: the novel, which has the sub-title 'Diary of a Dead Man', is presented as the work of another. It is written by one Sergei Maksudov, who subsequently committed suicide. Bulgakov supposedly did no more than arrange publication. Secondly, by depicting Maksudov himself so that he hardly resembles Bulgakov. The writer makes him a complete literary outsider, a plain-minded man to whom the ways of the thespian fraternity are a mystery and theatrical life an unending series of surprises. This is the result of Bulgakov's playful treatment of the facts of his own life, a variation on an autobiographical theme which allows him to cool his emotions and sublimate his anger in an ambiguous denial of identity. It is also an opportunity to give a particularly striking view of the shape of the real world through the eyes of the ordinary man in a state of constant surprise.

---

[12] Quoted in Milne, 'K biografii...', p. 168.

This also has significant consequences in the area of style. His earlier autobiographical or semi-autobiographical jottings, were, as we know, somewhat untidy in form, clipped and staccato, hurried and jerky in their rhythm. Being literary meant being orderly; this is apparent when we compare *Notes on Shirt-Cuffs* with 'Diaboliad'. This time things are even clearer. *A Theatrical Novel* is presented within the convention of transparent psychological realism, with all its sensitivity to the sphere of meanings concealed and revealed, with equal penetration of the inner and outer worlds, with graphic descriptions and a measured balance in the structure of sentences. However, as befitted the effects of the naïve viewpoint, this realism, of a plainly Gogolian stamp, is as it were overdrawn and disturbingly clear, containing constant surprises; and the sharp outlines of the images are almost reluctantly eroded, creating the effect of a theatre of shadows – as when Maksudov walks for the first time through the corridors of the Independent Theatre. This type of realism is essentially the obverse of the fantastic, and the reader of *A Theatrical Novel* is present in both spheres at the same time. The unexpected guest who stands in the doorway to the accompaniment of *Faust* is actually the real editor, not an imagined Mephistopheles, yet his actions will suggest secret powers and a game according to unclear rules, and thus be traditionally diabolical. The behaviour of thespians will again produce a game, subject to secret rituals, on the background of which a real theatrical rehearsal will assume the features of a double game, a puzzle from the fringes of the absurd. The normal laws of space and time seem to cease to function in the enclosed space of the theatre. There is an element of parody in this, organically present in the material of the descriptions, as well as psychological truth, for this is exactly the way the theatre must have appeared to the novice entering it for the first time.

A Theatrical Novel repeats, in slightly altered form, the description of a publishing adventure familiar from 'To a Secret Friend'. This time the background – the literary milieu – receives more extensive treatment. After the disappearance of Rvatsky and Rudol'fi, Maksudov, by force of inertia, wanders for a time through literary salons, where he is treated by his colleagues with either contempt or envy. He is surrounded by figures who can mostly be easily identified in life, depicted with waspish and witty satirical verve.[13] This is also a world governed by its own

---

[13] For example Bondarevsky is Aleksei Tolstoi, Likospastov – Slezkin, Agapenov – Pil'niak, the elderly writer – Kataev.

strange rules, but stripped of any magic: it is ruled by false appearances, anticipatory cunning, arrogant self-advertisement and intrigue-mongering, while the driving force is the law of all-out competition, which demands that all remain in a state of conflict and queer the pitch for everybody else. With his rough-hewn naïveté, Maksudov thinks about literature more deeply, being more honest; thus he is condemned in advance to outsiderhood, which corresponds psychologically to the experience of the author. As usual in such cases, Bulgakov's characters and situations undergo cross-fertilization and modification, while states of mind and the content of experience appear to be authentic. In the end the dalliance with the literary fraternity turns out to have little importance, but it leads into a much more significant dalliance with the theatre, even into a theatrical romance – the double meaning of the Russian word 'roman' ('novel' and 'romance') will permit either interpretation. Here lies the novel's centre of gravity, outside the sphere described in 'To a Secret Friend'; and here it enters a higher orbit all its own.

It was clear from the beginning that the Independent Theatre was the Moscow Art Theatre, recreated with most careful precision and with less fictionalization than usual. A plausible list of easily identifiable prototypes could be drawn up.[14] Some situations which are typical of MAT are also highly plausible, for confirmation may be found in other accounts: among them are the complex relations between generations, the delicate and tense relationship between the two doyens of the theatre, the manoeuvrings, which the novice cannot understand, around the new play. Throughout all of this, however, *A Theatrical Novel* remains a work of literature, and thus can be treated as belonging to fiction – though fiction with a basis in fact. The fiction is also replete with Bulgakov's tendency towards extremes of confabulation, and with the emotion of psychological revenge taken in the most easily accessible form. This is why the images are highly coloured whenever and wherever this suits the author. What is significant is less the plausibility of the details than the deeper truth, which he captured with particular

---

[14] 'For the history of its creation, the list of prototypes of the characters is important, as are the materials for the factual commentary compiled by Elena Sergeevna and her elder son Evgenii Shilovsky (1922-1957) in the 1950s.' M. Chudakova, 'Arkhiv...', p. 123. The following are not in doubt: Aristarkh Platonovich – Nemirovich-Danchenko, Ivan Vasil'evich – Stanislavsky; Tulumbasov – Mikhal'sky; Strizh – Sudakov; Il'chin – Vershilov; Panin – Markov; Priachina – Koreneva, Patrikeev – Ianshin; Toropetskaia – Bokshanskaia.

clarity in the rehearsal scenes presided over by Ivan Vasil'evich (Stanislavsky), where the stage-production took second place to the caprices of the director's fevered imagination. I repeat: there was little that Bulgakov needed to add, and the MAT actors who were invited to a reading of *A Theatrical Novel* immediately saw for themselves that the parodic caricature was accurate.[15]

Maksudov does not believe in the system adhered to by the theatre and is planning a frontal attack on it when the novel breaks off in mid-sentence.[16] This in no way negates the fact that, as he confesses two sentences earlier, he is 'pining away for love of the Independent Theatre' and is 'pinned to it like a beetle to a cork'.[17] The fascination, the magic, the dream – as well as the torment, the anxiety, the disappointment – everything of consequence that Bulgakov experienced at MAT and in connection with MAT is present here in summary form. Most of the novel is wonderfully funny, but Maksudov's painful pleasure is also profoundly dramatic and draws him, with good reason, towards suicide. An earlier situation is repeated: a body appears, almost conventionally, as a literary device, but it nevertheless appears; moreover, the suicide preparations are made earlier and the reader witnesses them. There are therefore good grounds for supposing that the romance with the theatre, if taken to its conclusion, would have shown the same hopeless situation as the romance with literature. Desperation was overcome yet again, but Bulgakov's laughter comes through clenched teeth; the comical carnival is played out on the threshold of destruction. Fate willed that the lightly parodic ritual shown in the novel of bidding farewell to the theatre's dead fireman should be repeated soon at a similar ceremony on Bulgakov's death. And the fervent exclamation of farewell to Filia, alias Fedor Mikhal'sky, the brilliant reader of

---

[15] 'Bulgakov read chapters from this book [*A Theatrical Novel*] at his home to Moskvin, Kachalov, Litovtseva and Markov. Elena Sergeevna recalled that during his readings everybody laughed a lot, but Kachalov suddenly became sad and said, "We all laugh. But the worst of it is that this really is our theatre and all this is true..."' V. Lakshin, 'Eskizy k trem portretam', *Druzhba narodov*, No. 9, 1978, p. 218.

[16] Note the new ending, recreated from the manuscript, which suggests that Bulgakov generally queries the possibility of the comprehensive illusion of the stage. M. Bulgakov, *Romany*, Moscow, 1973, p. 420.

[17] Ibid.

human hearts, true friend and good spirit of the theatre, is very clearly the author's own, without any disguise:

'O glorious world of the office! Filia! Farewell! Soon I shall be no more. You too must remember me!'[18]

This is the same parting message as the one previously addressed to the Molière monument. An end which is already in sight and no longer distant looms ever larger in his consciousness. The Filia sequence, often cited by critics and commentators, with its bravura description of the virtuoso performance by the manager, is one of the outstanding passages of the novel. But it too has its own deeper meaning. Filia is an artist – not only in his own line of work, but *tout court*, without reservation or qualification – because he can see right through people 'into their very hearts', and discern 'their passions and their flaws, everything, good or bad, that is hidden inside them.' Moreover, unerring in his ability to distribute tickets, he is the spokesman of infallible justice, knowing 'who should come to the theatre and when; who had the right to a seat in the fourth row and who belonged in the crowded stalls.'[19] Here we see something that penetrates the essence of things and gives back to the world – if only on a small scale – part of the order that is proper to it; and this, as we shall shortly see, would become central to Bulgakov's literary endeavours. This is why he writes in all seriousness that 'Filipp Filippovich is in a class all his own.'[20] A true writer and a true administrator are both artists, equal in standing and worthy of each other.

The writing of the novel broke off at a point which we may suppose is roughly the middle, probably in the autumn of 1937.[21] Perhaps the writer sensed that he was entering a channel that was too narrow, marked out by experiences that were strictly personal, with an excess of in-jokes for the initiated. Perhaps his hurt feelings, once spilt onto paper, had cooled, and the act of writing had performed its therapeutic function. Or perhaps, in addition to these factors, his main project called for more attention and there was insufficient time for anything that distracted him from it. From Vladimir Lakshin's account, we know that Bulgakov planned 'to show in later chapters the return of Aristarkh Platonovich [the name given to

---

[18] Ibid., p. 353.

[19] Ibid., p. 348.

[20] Ibid., p. 348.

[21] M. Chudakova, 'Arkhiv...', p. 123.

Nemirovich-Danchenko in the novel – A.D.] from India, to add an uproarious scene in which he gives a talk in the theatre about his travels, to show the subsequent fate of Maksudov's play, critical absurdities about the play, and the hero's failed love affair.'[22] All of this remained to be done and, moreover, what was done was left unpolished. A definitive version of this work has yet to be established.[23]

To this day efforts have continued to soften or neutralize the impact of *A Theatrical Novel*. It is true that the Art Theatre tradition is no longer fully immune to criticism, but a substantial part of it enjoys protection, so a work which is in the nature of a pamphlet on this theme causes embarrassment. There were difficulties involved in the first publication, probably overcome only thanks to the adroit manipulation of Aleksandr Tvardovsky. In its essence the novel, while in a sense a form of revenge (and so the product of a psychological situation similar to that which led to *The Crimson Island*), is nowhere intemperate, and the feelings attributed by Bulgakov to Maksudov are closest to the Russian formula of the love-hate relationship, in which, however, the former clearly predominates. Knowing everything about the Art Theatre, the author – at least in the part that was written and which it is fair to judge – makes his hero experience a fascination with this theatre in spite of everything. This treatment makes all the clumsy attempts to give *A Theatrical Novel* a certificate of loyalty completely superfluous.

This excursion into autobiography, veiled by another name and a partial change of personality, and probably undertaken to a large extent as psychological catharsis, results in a description so graphic that every reader must feel a pang of regret when it breaks off in mid-sentence. The regret is heightened by a very human interest in prying into characters and situations *à clef*, and among Russian readers also by the author's unfettered treatment of mummified values – in a sense an attack on official idols. In Bulgakov's homeland such actions have special merit, and the relief which the writing clearly brought him communicates itself to the reader. But at the same time the emerging product elevated a formula for revenge to a higher plane, where the novel may simply have ceased to seem

---

[22] V. Lakshin, introduction to M. Bulgakov, *Izbrannaia proza*, Moscow, 1966, p. 40. The source of this information is Elena Bulgakova.

[23] See Chudakova, 'Arkhiv...', p. 123, on the problems related to establishing a definitive text.

necessary. While regretting that it is incomplete, we must acknowledge the author's sovereign right to see it in this light.

III

Bulgakov had declared his affinity with the established theatrical tradition as long ago as his *Nakanune* period. Now he found this tradition splendidly epitomized, based on high art, in his last refuge, the Bolshoi Theatre. The building itself, its fittings, its interior, its atmosphere, everything that had escaped the ravages of the liquidators formed a visible symbol of the endurance of certain principles and tastes, and this must have produced a comforting impression. Bulgakov liked attending evening performances to experience again and again the emotions he had described years earlier, when 'the triumph of Radames rolls in waves of sounding brass and the peals of the chorus' and 'in the intervals the Theatre gleams with gold and crimson and seems just as elegant as ever.'[24] In addition, in accordance with his principle of making himself useful when the opportunity arose, he reviewed librettos and attended rehearsals, evaluating professionally the activity on stage.[25] Here his innate musical sensibility must have served him very well. At the theatre he was greatly esteemed and his opinion counted for much. 'When he started nervously pacing the hall,' said Iakov Leont'ev at a soirée dedicated to the memory of Bulgakov, 'we knew he had noticed something, but was too modest to bring himself to mention it. Then we would go up to him, knowing that by asking leading questions we would be able to learn much from him.'[26]

Again Bulgakov was leading a strange sort of life, in which only a fragment of his personality was engaged. As in his *Gudok* days, everything that mattered took place at home. But his connection with the Bolshoi also led to certain

---

[24] M. Bulgakov, 'Sorok sorokov', *Nakanune*, 15.4.23. Also in M. A. Bulgakov, *Sobranie sochinenii*, Ann Arbor, 1982, Vol. 1, p. 300.

[25] Inter alia *The Decembrists* by Shaporin, *Arsena Shanshashvili* by Alibegov, *The Gentry are Coming* by Baranov and Beletsky, and many others. Bulgakov's appraisals, comments and suggestions are held in his archive in the Lenin Library.

[26] Iakov Leont'ev, speech at a soirée dedicated to the memory of Bulgakov. Quoted in 'Materialy o M. A. Bulgakove', *Mosty*, No. 11, 1965, p. 397.

profitable endeavours, probably undertaken principally to earn money. Over the years several libretti arose. These included *Rachel*, based on Maupassant's story 'Mademoiselle Fifi', for which the musical score was to be composed by Izaak Dunaevsky, and *Peter the Great*, showing the figure of the 'shipwright of Saardam' at key moments in his life. Material close to that of *Flight* gave rise to *The Black Sea*, in which a *chanteuse* rescues a Bolshevik conspirator, her husband kills an officer of Wrangel's counter-intelligence, and a Red Army commander who has some features of Frunze prepares the final storming of the White-held Crimea, where an atmosphere of drunken desperation reigns, with forebodings of imminent doom.[27] The music was to be composed by S. Pototsky, but this too came to nothing; the surviving text is limited to six scenes. The repertoire plans were changing, owing to various combinations of circumstances, so that some projects were postponed or simply abandoned. This time the writer probably cared little, as he was giving as little of himself as possible; the texts are mostly correctly presented and conventional, without reaching above the average standard of the genre.

The first of this cycle, the libretto for the aforementioned *Minin and Pozharsky*, based on a heroic episode in Russian seventeenth-century history, is the one which came closest to realization.[28] A period of pseudo-nationalism was just being inaugurated; selected elements of history were being demagogically pressed into the service of the Stalinist cause. The signal had been given by the demonstrative condemnation of Dem'ian Bedny's libretto for the opera *Bogatyri* [Knights] in December 1936. Bulgakov could not have discerned immediately the cynical and manipulative nature of these moves. As a confirmed and straightforward traditionalist, he must have been pleased by the affirmation of certain features of Russian-ness, particularly as this came after a long period of anti-nationalist nihilism. To this cause he could lend his pen with conviction.

But when he did so and wrote his libretto, it seemed as if fate itself wanted to protect him against the future charges of opportunism which would inevitably have followed if Bulgakov's contribution had found its way into the structure of

---

[27] The texts are held in the Bulgakov archive in the Lenin Library. The libretto of *Rachel* was published by A. C. Wright in *Novyi zhurnal*, No. 108, 1972, pp. 74-80.

[28] The libretto of *Minin i Pozharskii* was published by A. C. Wright in *Russian Literature Triquarterly*, No. 15, 1978, pp. 325-340.

Stalin's imperial edifice. At first the libretto appeared to be accurately aimed at current needs. It was discussed at meetings. Platon Kerzhentsev, the chairman of the newly convened Committee on Artistic Matters, reported to Boris Asaf'ev, who was expected to compose the music, that he had discussed the matter 'with comrades from the leadership at their initiative.'[29] Kerzhentsev then conveyed to the author the comments and requirements of 'the comrades', insisting that, among other things, he should write 'a full-scale political aria for Minin, along the lines of "Oh, grant me freedom" from *Prince Igor*. This should be Minin's solo aria, delivered, let's say, on the bank of the Volga, early in the morning, about the Volga, the oppressed people and the country laid waste by foreigners.'[30] In this edict, in which we may read everything that was to happen later to Russian culture, the spirit of the times is frightening. Bulgakov accepted the advice and completed the aria, adding heroic and patriotic elements to the libretto.[31] The result was a kind of historical melodrama with some emphasis on 'the people' and 'the nation' rather unhappily appended, along with a cloak-and-dagger espionage intrigue and a thoroughly comical ending. We witness an exchange of courtesies; the chorus sings, 'Glory to the saviours of the people!', to which the leaders graciously reply, 'Oh no, not to us! Glory to the people!',[32] recalling the ritual of mutual applause between the presidium and the hall on ceremonial occasions. There is probably nothing less like Bulgakov than this text. Perhaps, apart from anything else, the convention of the libretto itself imposed a pattern.

But in any case it was all to no avail. It turned out that the new image of the new era had to be drawn from traditional sources of the highest order. The Bolshoi had started work on Glinka's *Ivan Susanin*. Bulgakov's libretto was no longer needed and was relegated to the archive. According to Iakov Leont'ev, the writer, 'without being offended, and having no personal interest, joined all the others in working on *Ivan Susanin*; he offered comments and gave advice, using the vast body of knowledge he had accumulated for *Minin and Pozharsky*.'[33]

---

[29] Letter from P. Kerzhentsev to B. Asaf'ev, dated 20.12.37. IRLI, Fond 369.

[30] Ibid.

[31] This is evidenced by the two versions of the libretto, one of which, dated 20.8.36, is held in the Lenin Library, and the other, dated 1937, in IRLI, Fond 369.

[32] *Russian Literature Triquarterly*, No. 15, 1978, p. 340.

[33] Leont'ev, *Mosty*, No. 11, 1965, p. 397.

Was he really not offended? And what were his feelings, if even the attempt at opportunism had come to nought? It is not for us to judge. No doubt, true to himself, he wanted to find a useful role in something else, especially as he was surrounded by the friendly atmosphere of the Bolshoi. What else could he do?

IV

While repeating to himself, 'Whom shall I adapt tomorrow: Turgenev, Leskov, Brockhaus and Efron, Ostrovsky?' he could still adapt Cervantes for the stage. In MAT Bulgakov was apparently dubbed 'a knight of art', underscoring the constancy and incorruptibility of his artistic persona. As time went on his knightliness came to look somewhat errant, or aberrant, since, against the background of numerous conformist manoeuvrings, Bulgakov's fundamental fidelity to his calling looked anachronistic. This was particularly so when many people believed in the higher necessity for engagement, and common sense dictated that one learn a practical lesson from this. Bulgakov, as we know, did his best to come through with head held high. He discovered that the wall was all around him. He collided with it, crashed to the ground, got up, and tried again. He asserted that writing plays was 'pure quixotry', but went on writing them, so it is clear that in the list of kindred spirits he invoked from the past he found a place for the knight of La Mancha. In solidarity and understanding. Don Quixote would be his penultimate spokesman. There was much bitterness filtered and condensed in the choice that he made.

As usual, the writer conscientiously immersed himself in the literature of the subject and the text itself. He even studied Spanish for the purpose. From a plot which is elaborate and full of digressions he isolated a number of the hero's adventures. To these he added an ingenious and witty artifice in the style of the *Commedia dell'arte*, in which the members of Don Quixote's household and his neighbours are at once themselves and fictional figures created by them. He modelled his hidalgo in the spirit of the novel, but lent him a definite bias, highlighting his active kindness and his passion for assisting the humiliated and wronged. In his relations with Sancho Panza a spirit of solidarity occupies the foreground; two people who are utterly dissimilar understand and complement each other. Don Quixote becomes less an idle dreamer and eccentric creator of a non-existent world than a man who cannot be measured by sober, earth-bound criteria –

an active non-conformist. Cervantes's masterpiece, which reveals different facets of itself at different epochs, makes such an interpretation fully possible. To Bulgakov it was certainly the only possible one.

The change of emphasis in the ending, which departs from the model, is noteworthy. The Don Quixote of the original dies when overcome by sobriety, killed by normality. The Don Quixote of the adaptation dies when deprived of his freedom, which is the air he breathes, killed by the artlessness of the kind souls who would apply their own standards to him. Being true to his knightly word, the hidalgo is obliged to turn his back on his own essence, which means his self-destruction. The conclusion of the play, based on the hero's fervid soliloquies, is a moving cry of protest against enslavement and the frustrations of life. This may do something to blunt the message of the work, but the identification of author and character is so painfully apparent here that, in the name of simple tact, critical functions should probably be suspended. Such moments do sometimes occur in literature.

The adaptation was commissioned by the Vakhtangov Theatre; the contract was signed in December 1937; and work on the text lasted with long interruptions until September 1938. The set was designed by Williams, who was close to Bulgakov, and the title role was to be played by Ruben Simonov.[34] This time no major obstacles arose in the path of the play, but even so it was not staged until a year after the writer's death, first in Leningrad, and a month later in Moscow.

'I once called on Mikhail Afanas'evich when he was ill,' recalls I. Rapoport, of the Vakhtangov Theatre. 'He was lying screened from the light by large cupboards. When I entered he sat up and settled on the white pillow, in a white shirt, black cap and dark glasses. Everything about him seemed youthfully alert. I couldn't see his eyes but he was all ready to listen to me. I told him about the rehearsals, and I felt that Don Quixote of la Mancha must have been just as strangely majestic. He listened to his interlocutor and heard something else besides – something that appeared to be accessible to him alone. This image remained in my mind while we rehearsed the last scene of Don Quixote.'[35]

---

[34] See Chudakova, 'Arkhiv...', p. 134, and I. Rapoport, 'Moi liubimye roli sozdannye M. Bulgakovym', *Neizdannyi Bulgakov*, pp. 68-69.

[35] Rapoport, p. 69.

Thus did life and literature authenticate each other, and thus did fulfilment crown the kinship Bulgakov had found – together with death, which he had invoked and alluded to so often and so purposefully, which he had apportioned to others and therefore in a sense prescribed for himself.

It would not be long in coming.

V

This period was taken up with intense activity. The major novel was again pressing in upon work that was urgent, offered and undertaken for remuneration, and this novel would not leave him.

In July 1936, while taking a short break from one of his libretti, Bulgakov wrote the conclusion of the third redaction of the novel. In the latter half of 1936, five chapters were written of the fourth redaction – subsequently abandoned – , which harked back to an earlier compositional structure. In 1937 Bulgakov began the novel again and wrote roughly one third of it before once more dropping it. This was therefore the fifth redaction. The sixth began to take shape in the autumn of the same year and the writing went on until May 1938, to become the second complete redaction. It now bore its definitive title, *The Master and Margarita*. It was in this version that the concept of the Master's work finally defined itself as 'a novel within a novel', which, according to Chudakova's description, was in the nature of 'a kind of Ur-text which has existed from time immemorial but is brought forth from the gloom of oblivion into the light of the modern consciousness solely thanks to the genius of the artist.'[36] The conclusion and the nature of the destiny granted to the Master and his beloved, described in the end as 'peace', were subject to constant modifications. No sooner had Bulgakov completed the manuscript text than he began dictating the novel to Olga Bokshanskaia. In the course of this work he introduced new corrections, making this the seventh redaction, which was completed on 25th June 1938. A year later, on 14th May 1939, he completed the epilogue, and the novel was read to friends (such readings had been held earlier,

---

[36] Chudakova, 'Arkhiv...', p. 130. For a discussion of this stage of Bulgakov's literary career, see pp. 124-136.

starting in 1929). 'The impression made upon all of us was overwhelming,' Vilenkin recorded years later.[37]

The fact, unprecedented for Bulgakov, that he kept revisiting the work and revising it indicates its exceptional importance, as does the sheer number of versions. In many other of his works the central idea crystallized so clearly in his mind in the initial stages that there were no rough drafts at all. They were not necessary; the text was born in its final form! Yet this last novel was not even now seen as ready.

By the law of unlikely but psychologically understandable juxtapositions, alluded to earlier, another project took shape alongside it. MAT knew of the Stalin theme. At the end of 1938 representatives of the theatre opened negotiations, which clearly were not easy, with the author. These were resumed in the New Year, 1939.[38] This was the year of Stalin's sixtieth birthday, for which tributes on an appropriate scale were planned. Bulgakov's play was seen as a chance for the theatrical community to present a suitable gift. No doubt note was taken of the particular favour the leader had bestowed upon the author of *The Days of the Turbins*. Bulgakov's pen was a guarantee in advance that a certain level would be maintained and insipid panegyrics avoided. It may be assumed that, while wishing to improve its own position, the theatre was also hoping to help Bulgakov. It is easy to imagine the point being made that the play could bring about a change in the writer's fortunes and pave the way for other works.

In reply Bulgakov apparently made free with harsh words to the theatre. He resisted all attempts at persuasion for a long time, even though his wife evidently supported the project, sincerely wishing that her beloved husband should enjoy a normal position in literature. He must have had a clear idea of what he was being urged to do. He apparently said, 'This will end badly.' At last he gave in. Even if he was still reluctant, the act of making the decision was to him, a man of strong will and firm resolve, the crossing of a frontier beyond which energetic creative activity began. The first three scenes were written in January. He resumed work on it in May, and the partial results were read at MAT. The text was finally completed on 24th July and read in full at a meeting of the theatre's party

---

[37] V. Vilenkin, 'Nezabyvaemye vstrechi', *Neizdannyi Bulgakov*, p.57.

[38] For the fullest account of matters related to *Batum*, see Vilenkin, pp. 57-60; also Chudakova, 'Arkhiv...', pp. 135-137.

organization, where the decision was taken to prepare the premiere for the hero's birthday, 21st December.

The play was originally entitled 'The Pastor', but in the end received the title 'Batum'.[39] It opens with a prologue in which the young and insolent Djugashvili is expelled in disgrace from the seminary. The budding revolutionary, already equipped with leadership qualities, makes his way to Batum; there he organizes a strike, marches at the head of a street demonstration which is brutally suppressed, is arrested, imprisoned and condemned to exile. After escaping from his place of exile he appears in the epilogue in the apartment of an old party comrade who has previously given him refuge. Here it is discreetly suggested that the hero and his host's daughter are linked by something more than an ideological affinity.

The whole play is a desperate attempt to emerge with honour from a dishonourable situation. But again this meant having to overcome natural impulses. The effort needed to surmount resistance to alien material can be physically sensed. The whole shows precision in the design and professional composition; it has contrasting characters, strong emotional accents, humour and lyricism. The scenes showing the dull-witted governor and a grotesque audience that a government minister has with Tsar Nicholas II introduce elements of satire *bouffe*. Nothing is missing, and this is really not a bad play, but it is precisely the polished technical perfectionism that betrays the paralysis of the imagination. A skilled craftsman has forced himself to exceed his personal limits. The result is a carefully retouched, approximately historical picture, with only a thin layer of varnish. But it means no more than it shows and bears no deeper meaning. This alone is quite unlike Bulgakov. The fact is that, leaving aside some purely satirical or comic works, he had never placed a primitive individual at the focus of attention. He simply had no feeling for such people, and lacked the gift for total transformation, of feeling his way into personalities that were fundamentally alien to him. He therefore depicted Stalin as he had once depicted a Chinese coolie in 'A Chinese Story' (Bulgakov's only other departure from the rule stated above), entirely from the outside, on the basis of the effect of strangeness. He shows a fighter committed to his cause but bereft of any charismatic indications of future greatness. Insipid panegyrics were thus avoided. The play actually gives strong emphasis to the ordinariness of the

---

[39] The text may be found in *Neizdannyi Bulgakov*, pp. 137-210; also in Mikhail Bulgakov, *Sobranie sochinenii v piati tomakh*, Moscow, 1990, Vol 3.

hero, whose outward appearance, according to a description given by the police, 'produces no impression'.[40] Bulgakov's well-wishers would later try to interpret this as a conscious polemic against the burgeoning cult of the dictator. The choice of an episode from his youth was also explained by a wish – in the best tradition of Pushkin – to remind the ruler of the best part of his life story, to urge him to reflect and come to his senses. This is a permissible interpretation, but – if we are honest – an unproven one, which must be treated as 'wishful writing'.[41]

There were few writers in those terrible years who made no compromises. As long as these did not violate fundamental ethical norms they should be treated with understanding, even lenience today. We know how steadfastly Bulgakov guarded his pride. He understood Molière, of course, for whom morality was what was good for *Tartuffe*, but he licked nobody's boots. He may have bowed his head a little. There was nothing servile about *Batum*, but it departed quite dramatically from the figure thus far known as the creator of *A Cabal of Hypocrites* and *The Last Days*. It was a step in a direction which few would have wished to see the writer take, and if it had secured for him a turnabout in his destiny we would surely look upon it today with very mixed feelings. But the same destiny as ever took good care to ensure that Bulgakov's reputation remained unsullied.

At first the outlook seemed propitious and much nervous activity began to surround this particularly important play. It was rigorously vetted at various levels, but the conclusions were uniformly favourable. The author worked hard on the final version of the text. Accounts show that he was by turns fired with optimism and gripped by doubts. 'When I get tired,' he wrote in a letter to Vilenkin, 'I push aside my notebook and wonder what fate awaits the play. Just try to guess! A lot of work has gone into it.'[42] In the theatre there was satisfaction – no doubt sincere – at Bulgakov's return. The roles were allocated: the lead role went to Khmelev, who, according to Bokshanskaia, 'simpered and repeated that he would not be able to cope and that he would rather play the governor, but he was clearly pleased to be

---

40 *Neizdannyi Bulgakov*, p. 163; also in *Sobranie sochinenii*, Moscow, 1990, Vol 3, p. 532.

41 In English in the original [*Trans.*]. Certain scenes and components are now said to suggest connections with the Stalin period. This concerns, for example, the prison scenes and the relations between political prisoners and criminals. It seems unlikely, however, that with the knowledge Bulgakov then possessed he could have introduced such effects consciously.

42 *Neizdannyi Bulgakov*, p. 59. Also in *Dnevnik. Pis'ma*, p. 517.

persuaded.'[43] A field trip for a special working party under Bulgakov's leadership, leaving for Batum and Kutaisi on 14th August, would permit a detailed study of the setting. This was something no doubt demanded by MAT's attention to detail and the gravity of the situation. The world was about to burst into flames, but in the meantime everything proceeded normally. The working party, dubbed a 'brigade' in the spirit of the times, boarded its train, drank to the success of the mission and moved off at noon.

The blow could hardly have been staged more dramatically: at Serpukhov a cable from the theatre reached the train. It read, 'Journey not needed return Moscow.' MAT had received an order banning the play from the stage.

Accounts differ on this point. One attributes the decision to the hero himself, who managed successfully to present himself as the soul of modesty.[44] Another has it that a member of Stalin's inner circle, probably Zhdanov, blocked the play. This is not of fundamental importance, since it is not difficult to divine the true motives. By this time, as later, plays by out-and-out lickspittles and sycophants had an easy path to the stage, such as Shalva Dadiani's *From the Spark*. Bulgakov represented a brand of chivalry that stayed within the bounds of propriety, and there was no need for theatre of that kind. His offer of a conformist compromise had been rejected. This was his last and most crushing collision with the wall of impossibility. There was no longer any place for anything that was normal. He had no way out.

VI

On 14th September the limits of endurance were evidently exceeded. What followed was a watershed, this time a physical one. That evening Bulgakov

---

[43] Letter from O. Bokshanskaia to V. Vilenkin. IRLI, Fond 369.

[44] Stalin is said to have uttered the sentence, 'All children and young people are the same. There is no need to stage a play about the young Stalin.' Quoted in V. Petelin, 'M. A. Bulgakov i *Dni Turbinykh*', *Ogonek*, No. 11, 1969.

returned with his wife to Moscow by taxi as a sick man. He was suffering from acute pains in his eyes.[45]

Bulgakov's own diagnosis, enunciated in 1931, was, as we know: 'The cause of my ailment is the hounding I have suffered for many years, followed by silence'.[46] As a doctor turned writer, and thus an expert on the body and soul alike, he could hardly go wrong. Eight years later he might well have used exactly the same terms.

The illness had been gaining on him for some time and Bulgakov was able to detect its onset, although he concealed it from his circle of friends. His attitude to life did not permit self-pity. He complained only when things were very bad, and then only to those he could trust.

But it may have been no accident that the blow fell at this particular moment.

The diagnosis was made by some Leningrad doctors and then confirmed in Moscow: nephritis, the disease which had killed his father. Bulgakov apparently foretold to friends the exact course his illness would take, to the very end, which he knew to be inevitable.

A further deterioration of his eyesight ensued, necessitating visits to sanatoria. The last time he returned home, on 28th December, he wrote to Aleksandr Gdeshinsky, a childhood friend and witness at his first marriage, whom he had asked in earlier letters about details of life in Kiev:

'To be honest, and between ourselves, I have a nagging feeling that I have returned home to die. This bothers me for one reason only: it is tiresome, tedious and tasteless. As we know, there is only one decent form of death – by a firearm, but alas I have none.

'With all my heart I wish you health and the pleasure of contemplating the sun and listening to the sound of the sea and to music.'[47]

In this way he recovered his self-control, which helped him turn everything into a joke, right up to the end, and including the end. The courageous manner of his death was admired by all who visited him in his last months.

---

[45] For the fullest account of the last period of Bulgakov's life see Chudakova, 'Arkhiv...', pp. 137-142. See also the memoirs of S. Ermolinskii, 'O Mikhaile Bulgakove', *Teatr*, No. 9, 1966, with the proviso that any precise factual information is to be treated with caution.

[46] Quoted in Milne, 'K biografii...', p. 155.

[47] Quoted in Milne, 'K biografii...', p. 169; also in *Dnevnik. Pis'ma*, p. 536.

He was still able to go out. One day he turned up unexpectedly at a rehearsal at the Bolshoi. 'He was convinced that he was returning to life,' one of the theatre staff said later. 'He said with his modest smile, "You see? I've cheated medical science after all." Unfortunately, my dear Mikhail Afanas'evich, this situation again showed your exceptional honesty: you didn't cheat it.'[48]

He was consumed by his final frenetic mental activity. His wife took down numerous letters from his dictation, made notes from books and recorded his plans for future projects. He resumed work on the project which was to be his last, a play entitled *The Swallow's Nest* but also known as *Richard I*, first mentioned in May 1939. It seems this was to be about the strange link between the artist and the powerful ruler-patron, the decline of the ruler and the uncertainty of the existence which then revealed itself before the artist.[49] The revisiting was brief as he lacked the strength: 'I can't write anything; my head is pounding like a jackhammer ... I'm ill, I'm ill,' he recorded.[50] In a letter to Popov dated 24th January, very likely the last letter he ever wrote, we read, 'Are you alive, my dear Pavel? The frosts have utterly crippled me and I don't feel well. Phone me! Yours, M.'[51] A day later Bulgakov went out for what was, in all likelihood, the last time.

But work on *The Master and Margarita* continued. There were numerous corrections and additions, reaching as far as the scene at the funeral of Berlioz and making it possible to speak of a last unfinished version, the eighth.

A chosen handful of friends – Boris Erdman, Dmitriev and Williams – were frequent visitors. The Ermolinskys kept a close eye on the Bulgakovs and helped Elena Sergeevna, who maintained her brave self-control. Other friends also dropped in;[52] as long as Bulgakov had the strength, elaborate parties and revels

---

[48] B. Mordvinov, funeral speech. *Mosty*, No. 11, 1965, p. 394.

[49] See P. Popov's description: 'the end of an all-powerful man in Bulgakov's last, incomplete play *Richard I*' (*Zametki avtobiograficheskogo kharaktera*, Manuscript Department of the Lenin Library, Fond 218); note also 'the failure of *Richard* also meant the failure of the writer.' (Chudakova, 'Arkhiv...', p. 140). Unfortunately the details of this project, though recorded by Elena Bulgakova, have not yet been made available.

[50] Chudakova, 'Arkhiv...', p. 139.

[51] Ibid., p. 140. Also in *Dnevnik. Pis'ma*, p. 539.

[52] See the accounts cited earlier by I. Rapoport and R. Simonov in *Neizdannyi Bulgakov*, pp. 69, 71.

were held, at which everybody made determined efforts to present a jolly face. On several occasions Fadeev, now a very influential figure in the literary world, called on Bulgakov. There is every indication that Bulgakov's personality fascinated him and that he sincerely tried his best to help. This fearsome and complex figure, who retained his human impulses, had already been an accessory to many deaths, having sanctioned the arrest of writers. But this particular death stirred something in him. As in all those previous cases, however, it was too late.

The last days were an unrelieved period of great suffering. The patient lost his sight completely and lost weight. The slightest movement caused him pain. The last photographs were taken and the last sketches made of him. His wife promised him that she would publish *The Master and Margarita*. 'He listened carefully,' she wrote, 'then said twice, "Let people know".' According to the diary of a nurse who tended him, he also whispered the strange words 'donkey hot', which could be interpreted as 'Don Quixote'. In this way he seemed, with the strength he had left, to reaffirm his final incarnation, one which corresponded to the impressions of those who saw him on his death-bed. And in this way he took his leave of the world of his heroes, as it saw him off to the other world, with an apparently meaningless phrase, as if existence itself were giving a mocking grin.

Some say he uttered other words too, perhaps addressed to God.[53]

Olga Bokshanskaia wrote in a letter to her mother, 'He died on the tenth, at twenty to five in the afternoon. After the dreadful suffering he had endured in the last stages of his illness, the day of his death was quiet and calm. He was unconscious..., having fallen asleep early in the morning, and Liusia was compelled to lie down and take a sleeping tablet. As she told me: "I woke up at about two. The house was unusually quiet and from the next room I could hear Misha's calm, steady breathing. And suddenly I felt that everything was all right, that that terrible illness had never been, that Misha and I were living together normally, as we had before the illness, and he was asleep in the next room and I could hear his steady breathing. Of course this happy thought lasted no more than a second. He went on sleeping peacefully and breathing evenly." At about four she went into his room with a close friend who had just arrived [probably Boris Erdman, who lacked a permit to stay in Moscow – A.D.]. And again he was

---

[53] He is alleged to have said, 'Forgive me and receive me.' Quoted in 'Smekh pisatelia', *Russkaia mysl'*, No. 2739, 22.5.69, p. 7.

sleeping so soundly and breathing so deeply and evenly that Liusia said she thought a miracle had happened, that the crisis was passing, that he had beaten the illness and would begin to recover. (All the time she had expected this of him, given his extraordinary personality.) Thus he went on sleeping, until at about half past four a slight shiver ran over his face, he seemed to grind his teeth, and his even breathing resumed, but increasingly feebly as the life ebbed very gently from him.'[54]

---

[54] Quoted in Chudakova, 'Arkhiv...', pp. 141-142.

Chapter Ten

Victory

    I. The funeral. Hopes of publication. The role of Elena Bulgakova. The writer's return in the post-Stalin period. The discovery of *The Master and Margarita*.
    II. The Master and the Greater Devil.
    III. The leading role of the Lesser Devil. Human devilry and infernal life. Fiendish unfreedom.
    IV. The biblical motif. The secularization of the Gospels and the sanctification of life. Bulgakov as *anima naturaliter christiana*.
    V. The eponymous heroes and the Faust legend. Death in life and posthumous resurrection. A chance for compassion and creativity. Masters and disciples. Hope.
    VI. The novel's play of meanings. A fantastic time and a special place. Sun, moon, darkness and thunderstorms. Satan's ball. The narrator. The romantic tradition. Two styles. Lightness. Attempts at interpretation. A synthetic formula.
    VII. *The Master and Margarita* as the culmination of Bulgakov's oeuvre. The presence of earlier motifs. Realia. Overthrowing tyranny. Liberation and the final flight.

I

    No sooner had Bulgakov died than words were uttered about him which had never been officially spoken in his lifetime. On 15th March 1940 an obituary in *Literaturnaia gazeta* spoke of a writer 'of very great talent and splendid art', who had 'had a difficult and complex career and would enter the history of Soviet literature as an outstanding and original artist'. Bulgakov's great merits had been lauded equally loudly at the funeral service, which took place at the Union of Writers on the day after his death.[1] A guard of honour was placed beside his

---

[1] For the record of speeches given on this occasion see *Mosty*, No. 11, 1965, pp. 391-395. Information concerning the funeral and decisions on his legacy are given according to the separate collection of this material compiled by Elena Bulgakova and held in IRLI, Fond 369.

coffin. On 12th March, on the way to the crematorium, the funeral procession halted in front of the Art Theatre, then in front of the Bolshoi. The staff of both theatres came out to bid their farewells. This was exactly the ritual anticipated in *A Theatrical Novel*, and the solemnity of the proceedings indicated that official sanction must have been granted at a high level. The cremation took place at five in the afternoon.

A writer who for fourteen years had published nothing at all had no sooner died than a committee was set up to manage his literary heritage. This was announced on 14th March, demonstrating that a writer who in life had been subjected to spiritual torment and cast out of official literature had in death been accorded the rank of *Décédé* First Class. The hierarchy of posthumous honours was now so finely calibrated that chance could play no part in it.

The reason for the honour may reside in the fact that Bulgakov now appeared to pose no threat; and the strange aura of royal favour was visible to all. It shone much more brightly for a dead writer than for a living one. There was a certain logic in this, and nobody could have appreciated it better than Bulgakov.

But its glow was short-lived, and there was logic in this too.

The initial prognoses were good. The committee soon resolved to publish a collection of Bulgakov's works comprising *The Days of the Turbins, Flight, A Cabal of Hypocrites, The Last Days, Ivan Vasil'evich* and *Don Quixote*. The collection was to be accompanied by a literary biography written by Pavel Popov and an essay about Bulgakov by an author not as yet selected. A month later, in June 1940, the editorial board of the publisher Sovetsky pisatel' took the decision to publish. 'As unfortunately happens all too often, in times to come he will be better known than in the time he lived in,' wrote Fadeev to Elena Bulgakova immediately after the funeral, apologizing for his absence.[2] There can be little doubt that here too he was sincere, even if all his belated interest in Bulgakov and his works stemmed from an order he had received.

But not everything depended even on him. The publishers' plans were most likely disrupted by the war, which also put an end to the long stage life of *The Days of the Turbins* at MAT; after 987 performances, the costumes and props were completely destroyed in a German air-raid on Minsk in June 1941. During the war years Bulgakov's presence was evidenced only by *The Last Days*, performed on

---

[2] A. Fadeev, *Pis'ma*, Moscow, 1967, p. 159.

10th May 1943, and his adaptation of *Dead Souls*, which was played in various guises, including a concert version. This situation continued after the war. The spirit of late Stalinism would tolerate only so much, and no more. At this period there could be no place for more of Bulgakov.

This is all the more reason why we should bow our heads to the endurance and devotion of Elena Bulgakova. She proved to be one of those great Russian widows without whom Russian literature would have suffered irreparable spiritual losses, over and above the physical losses. Her long life was dominated by the memory of Bulgakov. She guarded the archive, helping all who were interested in the writer and defending his good name with all her strength.[3] Above all she prepared his texts for publication and was tireless in protecting them. The domestic archive contains two bound volumes of his works, dated 1954-1955, in every detail imitating a published edition, as a touching sign of hope.

Elena Sergeevna felt a particular responsibility for *The Master and Margarita*. Having made a promise to her dying husband, she tried to give effect to that promise, in her own words, 'six or seven times, each time in defiance of the prevailing circumstances and common sense.'[4]

Stalin had to die before the efforts of people of good will could bring the first modest results. In 1954, at the Second Congress of Soviet Writers, Veniamin Kaverin mentioned Bulgakov's name in public for the first time in many years, and in the Soviet Union such facts usually had special meaning or predictive force.[5] In the same year, *The Days of the Turbins* returned to the stage, this time at the Stanislavsky Theatre, thanks to the determined efforts of Mikhail Ianshin and under his direction. This was seen above all as a great victory for Elena Bulgakova: 'If Mikhail Afanas'evich were alive,' friends from Leningrad wrote to her, 'he would have led you out onto the stage and said to the audience, "Thank her! She's the one who has achieved the impossible. She has resurrected the Turbins!"'[6]

---

[3] For example, denying in a letter to the *Great Soviet Encyclopedia* the claim in the first edition that Bulgakov had lived abroad from 1921 to 1923. She appended a modest selection of favourable comments about him. (Letter dated 19.1.51; copies of it and other materials are held in IRLI, Fond 369.)

[4] V. Lakshin, 'Eskizy k trem portretam', *Druzhba narodov*, No. 9, 1978, p. 316.

[5] *II Vsesoiuznyi s"ezd sovetskikh pisatelei. Stenograficheskii otchet*, Moscow, 1956, p. 170.

[6] Bulgakov archive, IRLI, Fond 369.

We know nothing of the efforts which came to nothing, but we must bear these in mind too in evaluating the work of Bulgakov's widow and supporters then and later. Without an awareness of those unavailing but necessary efforts, no appraisal can even approach the reality of the matter. In any case, after the Moscow premiere the process of the restoration of Bulgakov gained momentum. A year later Leonid Varpakhovsky staged *The Days of the Turbins* in Tbilisi. In 1957 the premiere of *Flight* was held in Stalingrad. The '60s saw part of Bulgakov's dramatic oeuvre introduced to the stage in the Soviet Union and abroad. Productions to date have had mixed success, but in general, returning to the analogy of the two hands, prose was unmistakably Bulgakov's right hand, markedly stronger than his left. Nevertheless he maintains a presence today in various theatres.

Hopes of publication met with stiffer resistance. The first swallow in Bulgakov's homeland was a slim volume published in 1955 containing *The Days of the Turbins* and *The Last Days*. A larger collection of plays appeared in 1962, and a larger collection still came three years later, but without *The Crimson Island*, *Zoika's Apartment* and *Adam and Eve*. These and other omissions were made good by foreign editions. The revival of his prose works began only in 1962 with *The Life of Monsieur de Molière*. A year later came an incomplete version of *Notes of a Young Doctor*; in 1965 *Novy mir* published *A Theatrical Novel*; and the following year his *Selected Prose Works* appeared, in which *The White Guard* was printed in full for the first time in the USSR.

All of this, however, was merely the prelude to Bulgakov's second life, which began with the publication of *The Master and Margarita*. When this happened, in late 1966, the result was the establishment before our eyes of a new and dynamic scale of values.[7] Everything that Bulgakov had written before and beside his main work now had to be re-evaluated; the author was reborn at the end point of his life, compelling us to reappraise his previous self. Until now this main work had been present only in the consciousness of a small and restricted circle. It had lived a life which, though secret, was by no means safe from the threat of physical destruction; during the Terror, texts were destroyed just as zealously as people. Later, when the atmosphere had relaxed somewhat, occasional signals were given of its existence. As a result of its publication, the picture of literature in

---

[7] *Moskva*, No. 11, 1966, and No. 1, 1967.

the 1920s and '30s was altered, but that of literature in the present was altered even more. Removed from its chronological context, *The Master and Margarita* turned out to be a novel of our time and it is precisely the perspective of later experience provided by the ponderous movement of destiny that permits a full appreciation of it.

'You ask what will happen,' wrote Bulgakov to his wife while working on the seventh version. 'I don't know. You'll probably put it in a desk drawer or a cupboard with my dead plays and think about it now and again. But we can't foretell our future.

'I've given my verdict on this book and if I can manage to improve the conclusion a little I will think it worth proof-reading and putting in a dark drawer.'[8]

After the bitterness of successive events, these words contain a filtered and concentrated bitterness and a fear of voicing any hope.

But in truth 'we can't foretell our future.' Bulgakov's future materialized in this very text and is with us now.

II

The Master and the Greater Devil

Where does this book have its deepest origins?

Perhaps in an awareness of the presence of the devil, but a different devil from the one we spoke of at the beginning.

We have acknowledged that it is very convenient to have one's own devil. We have seen how often Bulgakov invokes him. *Diabolus minor* serves him very well, being ready at various times to open a door for Chichikov, assume the guise of a blizzard, leap to the top of a belfry, mix up Persikov's parcels or perform a dozen other functions peculiar to the demonic condition, or at least be named by every character who needs his name to fill a space in his life.

---

[8] Quoted in M. Chudakova, 'Arkhiv M. A. Bulgakova. Materialy dlia tvorcheskoi biografii pisatelia', in *Zapiski Otdela rukopisei Gos. Bibl. SSSR im. Lenina*, Moscow, 1976, p. 132; also in Mikhail Bulgakov, *Pis'ma. Zhizneopisanie v dokumentakh*, Moscow, 1989, p. 434 and *Dnevnik. Pis'ma 1914-1940*, Moscow, 1997, p. 474.

But there must have come a time when the author of *Diaboliad* became aware of the weakness of traditional diabolical powers in the face of the phantasmagoria of life itself and the chasms that yawn on even its safest roads; in the face of the semblance of sense accorded to nonsense; in the face of the delusion of conventions which are the more meaningless the more insistently they are imposed; in the face of false certainties, enduring phantoms and fleeting endeavours; in the face of rules that run counter to the deepest content of experience, but are acted on in the name of the highest imperatives.

Bulgakov had experienced all of this in turn, day after day. He was permitted to exist, but suspended in a vacuum. He had the measure of the tyranny, but enjoyed the protection of the tyrant and was even asked mockingly, 'Do we annoy you beyond all measure?' He was not listened to, but he could work, although his work turned into frustration for him; he was obliged to spoil what he did or look on while others spoiled it for him – and all to no good purpose. He read his plays to actors with superb skill, but in most cases could never hear them performing for him. He directed solemn celebrations and attended sessions of ideological instruction where he learned about the union of opposites, while about him people were disappearing; his neighbours and friends were arrested for poems and jokes; his one-time tormentors were annihilated even though they had never ceased to be obedient lackeys; he himself was questioned and informers were sent to watch him. He lived among people who pretended that everything was normal, when the reality was close to that described by Gogol: 'Without any metal chains they were all shackled by fear, which stripped them of everything: all their feelings, their intentions and their strength left them, leaving only fear.'[9] He must have known fear even when he read *The Master and Margarita* aloud to his closest friends, for now writing and listening were equally dangerous. He himself therefore restricted the circle to people who were truly close to him; he took careful precautions and looked upon more distant acquaintances with mistrust. He ceased to keep a diary. He found an outlet in acting, as in a second self, as if trying to elude yet again a fate which he had not successfully cheated by his first change of profession. He bluffed: 'It's a matter of complete indifference to me whether the cover of one of my books adorns a bookshop window. At heart I'm an actor, not a

---

[9] N. Gogol', 'Strakhy i uzhasy Rossii', *Sochineniia N. V. Gogolia*, St Petersburg, 1900, Vol. 7, p. 140.

writer.'[10] But when his spirits were low his voice changed: 'The eldest son chose not to become anything...'; 'Fate has me by the throat,' and 'I died every day...'[11]

Many matters have been soured by silence: eye-witnesses have died or maintained a discreet silence; his wife's diary was kept under seven seals and only fragments of it were published. The aim was to produce the impression today that life at that time was normal.

But it takes little imagination or knowledge of what was happening around him, of what was being said and written, who was arrested, repressed or eliminated, to picture the daily fabric of that life, even if the horror of it was concealed in pseudo-normality, or indeed precisely because of this. So it was then, even if it was possible to make light of some things.

'In the case of *Bliss*,' Bulgakov wrote to Popov from Leningrad on 10th July 1934, 'there has been an incident that quite oversteps the bounds of reality. A room in the Astoria Hotel. I'm reading aloud. The theatre manager, who is also a producer, expresses complete and obviously unfeigned delight. He intends to produce it, he promises money and says that he'll come and have a meal with me in forty minutes. Forty minutes later he appears, has dinner, says not a word about my play, then disappears as if the ground had swallowed him up, never to be seen again. I can only assume he has migrated into the fourth dimension. Wonders will never cease!'[12]

These were familiar wonders: already Rvatsky and Rudol'fi had disappeared, and some of the characters in *The Master and Margarita* would soon follow them. This was the pattern of normality in an abnormal way of life, in which people removed themselves or were removed, obligations ceased to oblige and the accepted sequence of cause and effect was suspended. Traditional diabolic prerogatives could reach only so far. In his *Mystery-Bouffe* Maiakovsky made fun of a hell which was fitted out with contemporary tortures. Since his time reality had made considerable strides along the scale of brutality. No longer was there any need to go to the devil, since devilry of the highest order was all around you and formed the experience of the citizens of the twentieth century.

---

[10] Quoted in Chudakova, 'Arkhiv...', p. 105.

[11] See Chapter Eight.

[12] Quoted in *Sovetskie pisateli. Avtobiografii*, Moscow, 1966, Vol. 3, p. 99; also in *Pis'ma*, p. 303 and *Dnevnik. Pis'ma*, p. 346.

'The Satan of the twentieth century,' wrote the Polish poet and essayist Mieczysław Jastrun, 'would need to be the personification of the hell of the concentration camps, of the confutation of all world-views and of the meaning of life; he would need to embody not only the negation of all values, but something much worse and more insidious: an inversion of the meanings of words, along with coercion to enforce public recognition of primary meanings. In other words the Satan of the Apocalypse and the Satan of complete duplicity bordering on the absurd.'[13]

A Satan of inverted meanings, of the negation of the sense of previous human experience; a Satan 'of complete duplicity', or of reality with a minus sign, but 'with coercion to enforce recognition of primary meanings'. Which is to say: one persuades oneself that all that is profoundly abnormal is absolutely normal. A Satan of our time, *diabolus major*, the spirit of utter evil, the prophet of self-destruction.

It was very likely he who skulked behind everything that surrounded Bulgakov and revealed himself to him. And if not fully understood, his presence there was sensed. The evidence for this is Bulgakov's main work.

Before adducing the proof of this, it is necessary to give an example which makes manifest the impersonal detachment of the greater devil. The incident occurred while Bulgakov lay gravely ill, one month before his death.

Three friends, all MAT actors, sent a letter to Stalin's personal secretary Poskrebyshev, informing him of Bulgakov's illness and stating that recovery was unlikely, while voicing the hope that some 'sudden, joyous event' might 'offer hope of a cure.' The letter, dated 8th February 1940, goes on:

'Bulgakov often used to say how indebted he was to Joseph Vissarionovich for his extreme kindness and support. He often recalled with sincere gratitude his telephone conversation with Joseph Vissarionovich ten years ago, which so inspired him then. We, Bulgakov's friends, seeing him now close to death, cannot neglect to inform you, Aleksandr Nikolaevich, of his plight, and hope that you will find it possible to convey this news to Joseph Vissarionovich.

---

[13] M. Jastrun, 'Historia Fausta', *Literatura*, No. 42, 1972.

(Signed) USSR People's Artistes Vasilii Kachalov, Alla Tarasova, Nikolai Khmelev'[14]

The present writer has been assured by a reliable source who was instrumental in creating this document that it was written in all good faith. Three eminent theatrical figures, recently decorated with new honours, apparently sincerely believed that if Stalin saw fit to repeat his gesture of ten years earlier, his voice could prove more powerful than medical science: by administering a jolt to the patient and restoring him to life. There is nothing ridiculous about this, for then and later many tales were told of such conversations and the effects they produced. Thus was history's greatest mass murderer, the perpetrator of the greatest crimes against humanity, abjectly implored to deploy the supernatural attributes he was thought to possess and work a miracle. In this calm insanity, dictated by an impulse of devoted hearts and providing clear evidence of the state of their minds, *diabolus major*, the master of inverted meanings, can be plainly seen.

This is the devil of silence, of the void, of the minus sign, of the word *nihil*. Stalin duly did what he could be expected to do: he did not telephone.

III

In his stead, *diabolus minor* appeared, by way of *The Master and Margarita*.

This was his benefit performance and his star turn. Hitherto he had been invoked frequently, but always in asides and hushed tones, always placed on the periphery and mentioned fleetingly as a rhetorical figure in the subjunctive mood ('it seemed as if Satan the practical joker had opened a door'; 'as if Satan had climbed the belfry in a cassock and was amusing himself by raising bedlam').[15] Thus, in accordance with his traditional nature, he became a sign of ambivalence and lack of clarity, a form of word-magic, or a pseudonym.

---

[14] Part of the letter appears in Milne, 'K biografii...', p. 160. A copy of the complete letter is in IRLI, Fond 369.

[15] M. A. Bulgakov, *Sobranie sochinenii*, Ann Arbor, 1982, Vol. 1, p. 263; M. Bulgakov, *Romany*, Moscow, 1966, p. 225.

Now he became the executor of an ultra-Bulgakovian design. Being freedom itself, the personification of free will, he is released with full autonomy, as the moving spirit, into the midst of un-free life – to bring reality to the cry of 'May the Devil take it!'

This is vengeance in the grand style, far grander than in 'The Fatal Eggs', *The Crimson Island* or *A Theatrical Novel*, and the Lesser Devil has in it his most important role yet.

He takes complete command of the plot. The action is fitted into three days, from Wednesday to Saturday evening, between the arrival in Moscow of Woland and his retinue and their departure. Their actions determine the course of events; a series of scandals disrupts the cohesion of Moscow life. This is the first level. The second level, which as we know did not take shape immediately under Bulgakov's pen and which is not evident at the beginning of the novel, is provided by the fate of the eponymous hero and heroine. Demonic power enables them to overcome earthly obstacles and opens before them a new dimension of existence. Lastly, it is Woland who initiates the projection of a reconstituted and secularized biblical myth, by the end offering the opportunity to conclude it by an act of liberating compassion. This is the third level. In a structural sense, the link between these three levels is the work of the Devil. Having organized the spectacle of the novel as if it were Satan's own ball, having assured himself that the results are as planned and having played the part of master of ceremonies, Woland flies away with his retinue. And when the design reaches its fulfilment and the fundamental principle 'the Devil take it!' is fully implemented, the work, logically titled by the author 'a novel about the Devil', itself reaches its conclusion.

But what sort of devil is it about?

First we need to enquire who the new arrivals in Moscow really are. It is easy to say that they are the possessors of some well-known names which appear in various texts.[16] Bulgakov knew the literature of his subject. He drew on it, however, without pedantry, inwardly agreeing with what the Devil says to Leverkühn in *Doktor Faustus*: 'Aber du hast ja all die skurrilen Necknämchen noch

---

[16] See for example A. Vulis's afterword to the first published edition of Part I of *The Master and Margarita*, Moskva, No. 11, 1966, pp. 127-130. Also V. Lakshin, 'Roman M. Bulgakova *Master i Margarita*', *Novyi mir*, No. 5, 1968, pp. 284-281; Chudakova (various works), and other sources.

von der Hohen Schulen her im Gedächtnis, von deinem ersten Studium her, als du noch nicht die Heilige Geschrift vor die Tür und unter die Bank gelegt hattest. Hast sie alle im Schnürchen und magst darunter wählen, – ich habe ja fast nur solche, fast nur Necknämchen, mit denen man mir, so zu reden, mit zwei Finger unter dem Kinn spielt.'[17]

And further on: 'Sei versichert, ich schenke meinem Äußeren gar keine Aufmerksamkeit, überlasse es sozusagen sich selbst. Das ist reiner Zufall, wie ich aussehe, oder vielmehr, es macht sich so, es stellt sich so je nach den Umständen her, ohne daß ich auch nur acht darauf gebe.'[18]

Bulgakov acts in similar fashion: he calls together a team and equips its members with conventional demonic attributes. The leader bears the mask of controlled suffering worn by Milton's rebel; Korov'ev is a cousin of Dostoevsky's and Mann's devils, the mocking demon, the personification and purveyor of irritating tawdriness; Abadonna is the spokesman of the forces of retribution; the dissolute, mermaid-like Hella seems to have been borrowed straight from Gogol's story 'Vii'; finally Behemoth, who concludes the long line of Bulgakov's cats, is a traditionally fiendish animal, while at the same time a domestic one, as if taken from folk wood-engravings, in which large cats with pointed whiskers once stood as symbols of Peter the Great. Bulgakov, however, for the moment displays no wish to meddle in matters of demonic guild demarcation. The matter is handled in a Manichean spirit: the world is an arena in which good and evil coexist, both sides observe a division of jurisdiction, and any tensions and conflicts which there might have been belong to the past. Thus traditional struggles, rebellions, divisions and excesses of censorious righteousness are bypassed as irrelevant to this particular

---

[17] Thomas Mann, *Gesammelte Werke*, Vol. 6, *Doktor Faustus*, Frankfurt am Main, 1960, p. 226. ['But you can still recall all the scurrile nicknames from the schoole, from your first studies, when you had not put the Good Boke out of the door and under the bench. You have them all at your fingers' ends, you may elect one – I have scant others, they are well-nigh all nicknames, with the which people, so to speke, chuck me under the chin.' Thomas Mann, *Doctor Faustus*, translated by H. T. Lowe-Porter, Harmondsworth, 1968, p. 219].

[18] Ibid., p. 229. ['Be sure, I reck nothing at all to my outward appearance. I leave it so to say to itself. It is sheer chance how I look, or rather, it comes out like that, or rather, it happeth like that according to the circumstances, without my taking heed.' Thomas Mann, *Doctor Faustus*, translated by H. T. Lowe-Porter, p. 221].

book. This is fully consistent with Bulgakov's predispositions, for he was a thinking writer without being a thinker and was not inclined towards philosophy. He was engaged not with the problem of existence *per se*, but with upsets in the fundamental humanistic consensus in the world about him. He therefore treated his devils as instruments, as conventional codes, as call-signs, as key words to evoke specific associations, as means to activate chains of cause and effect that conflict with those phenomena generally held to be 'normal'; he garnered them like flowers for a posy from different shelves, drawers and havens of tradition, since this method suited him best.[19]

These demons also speak for a highly Bulgakovian view of their contextual situation, but differ considerably from their Bulgakovian predecessors. The earlier demons did what demons traditionally do: they meddled, confounded and led into temptation, always reserving the right to explain themselves in rational terms, as the products of human fears and anxieties, of mental disturbance or a hyperactive imagination. The members of Woland's retinue have a graphic precision about them, that hyper-realism of unreality which Andrei Bely called 'the personification of fiction'; their characters are etched with clear contours, without fuzziness or ambiguity. The tasks set for this team are equally well defined and typify a working party on official infernal business, each member with his own particular area of operation. They are also far from seeking to destroy. It is true that Bulgakov refers to Faust, in which Goethe's Devil presents himself as a force with an internal contradiction – 'that power which wills forever evil, yet does forever good' – but the demons in *The Master and Margarita* are not trapped in any contradictions. They operate according to accepted rules and above all do not want evil, so are in no way subject to the Faustian formula.[20] They have specific organizational matters to attend to in Moscow. If they interfere in the realm of human reality it is *en passant* and with reluctance, not to destroy but rather to

---

[19] A different view, that the choice of demonic figures is motivated by very careful forethought, is upheld by Lesley Milne in her work *'The Master and Margarita'. A Comedy of Victory*, Birmingham Slavonic Monographs, No. 3, Birmingham, 1977.

[20] They more closely resemble Dostoevsky's Devil, who says, 'I'm probably the only person in the universe who loves truth and genuinely desires good...', '... and in the meantime I am genuinely kind-hearted and completely incapable of negation.' F. Dostoevskii, *Brat'ia Karamazovy, Sobranie sochinenii*, Moscow, 1957, Vol. 10, pp. 177, 169.

correct errors and make adjustments to systems that are out of kilter. From time to time, having an excess of supernatural powers, they casually play pranks, but this apart they ensure that all receive their due; they complete the ruination of things partly spoiled, trip the tottering, demolish what is rotten and urge the ill-inclined on to greater evil. 'Darum, zu deiner Beruhigung sei es gesagt, wird dir denn auch die Hölle nichts wesentlich Neues, – nur das mehr oder weniger Gewohnte [...] zu bieten haben,' Leverkühn is warned.[21] 'We have everything that you have,' Ivan Karamazov is told.[22] This closeness will turn out to have far-reaching consequences and will impart a different air to Bulgakov's demons: it will secularize and humanize them. It is true that they have the ability to don and doff their corporeal reality, to foretell the future, transmigrate and displace people and things in place and time. But these actions accord with traditions which have been described many times and need not be manifestations of infernal powers. They belong to the arsenal of black magic, wizardry and the investigation of hidden forces, to the realm of the occult, of spiritualist mediums and parapsychology. Woland himself, with his world-weary and cynical self-knowledge and condescending aloofness, has about him something of Faust, who having explored various mysterious areas, including the black arts, experiences the illusory nature and bitterness of cognition.

Devils such as these, hardly marked by devilry at all, conventional, fully earthly and deeply engaged in earthly matters, are clearly invoked to administer a shock to a system which is described very precisely in the novel. This is the material of everyday life, the material of custom and social psychology. It is formed from habit, reactions, responses and reflexes. It emerges in expressions from the period such as 'greetings, wrecker!', 'a typical little kulak', 'an enemy provocation', 'that man Kant should be packed off to the Solovetsky Islands for three years'; from good-naturedly acerbic reproaches between neighbours: 'You have to switch off the light when you come out of the lavatory, Pelageia Petrovna. Otherwise we'll have to see about getting you evicted';[23] and from the 'highly

---

[21] Mann, p. 247. ['Therefore, to your reassurance be it said, even hell will not afford you aught essentially new, only the more or less accustomed.' Thomas Mann, *Doctor Faustus*, translated by H. T. Lowe-Porter, p. 239].

[22] Dostoevskii, p. 171.

[23] *Romany*, p. 651.

disagreeable thoughts' which take possession of Likhodeev at the sight of the officially sealed door of his neighbour's room. It is an atmosphere of spy mania, denunciations, demagogy and violence, which in no way change their essential nature when turned into a joke, for this is one of Bulgakov's self-defensive stratagems which is already quite familiar. It is a structure built of ersatz materials: an apartment is not an apartment, nor a shop a shop, while a literary organization deals with anything but literature – but the need to pretend that abnormality is normality dictates that appearances be treated as truth. This gives rise to an unreality which is at once nightmarish and oppressively trivial: the fantastic denial of fantasy which occurs when a man who has been turned into a pig seeks a certificate stating that he has 'spent the aforementioned night at Satan's ball, having been enticed there in a vehicular capacity',[24] and when a cat which wishes to pay its fare on a tram is treated as a violator of the regulations.

It is the reality of pseudo-logical phrases such as 'sturgeon of secondary freshness', of lines of argument such as 'I took it, but I took what belonged to us – it was Soviet', and rhetorical questions: 'and Pushkin will pay the rent, will he?' This is the same reality in which a theatre manager has 'moved into the fourth dimension', and a cunning tyrant is implored to perform a miracle. Bulgakov felt this reality with his whole being, with all his experience of life and all his sensitivity. 'When you speak, Ivan Vasil'evich, I have the impression that you are delirious,' says the inventor to an administrator who is armed with official phraseology.[25] 'You're a phantom!' exclaims Eve, the wiser for her dreadful experience, to Adam, whose orthodoxy remains unwavering. 'You're a phantom. You're all the same. I sit here and suddenly it dawns on me that the forest, the bird-song and the rainbow are real, while you lot with all your cries of fury aren't real. [...] No, I'm not raving. You and your kind are all just a dream, just some kind of bizarre mystification.'[26]

---

[24] Ibid., p. 707.

[25] M. Bulgakov, *Ivan Vasil'evich*, Munich, 1964, p. 19.

[26] M. Bulgakov, *Adam i Eva, P'esy*, Paris, 1971, p. 59. See also Ermolinsky's precise formulation: 'Even real life can depart from reality and the commonplace and turn into a vision, replacing these with sheer invention in order to banish vulgar everyday comings and goings and rampant evil.' (Sergei Ermolinskii, 'O Mikhaile Bulgakove', *Teatr*, No. 9, 1966, p. 95.)

This was an early adumbration of the significant reversal of roles implemented in *The Master and Margarita*: a human devil sets an infernal life to rights.

The repair is effected by destruction: like cures like. The traditional Evil One in the guise of a gallant knight is a measure of the depth of Bulgakov's bitterness, but again the seriousness is overcome by lightness of touch, and while we laugh we may hardly notice the menace which he has turned into a joke. His vengeance is effected with sparkle and fireworks; speculators, con-artists, loud-mouths, dullards, embezzlers and informers receive summary justice. There are four significant outbreaks of fire. Fire, which, according to Azazello, 'puts an end to everything' and which provides a traditional act of purification, and thus a way of putting reality to rights, engulfs Berlioz's apartment, the Master's basement, the House of Literature and the shop for the privileged classes.[27] A mini-deluge is unleashed upon the home of the spokesman of falsehood, so another element is deployed in addition to the element which is traditionally Bulgakov's.

But where does this all lead?

The buildings will be rebuilt. The people will come to their senses. The demonic visitation will receive its pseudo-rational explanation *ex post facto*. Almost everything will remain as it was before. The system of inverted values will prove fairly elastic. The great act of retribution will appear impressive, but, when closely considered, it will also be superficial. The situation is pregnant with meaning, but its significance makes for even greater bitterness. It should not surprise us if the novel about the Devil is at one point consigned to the flames and if the fire expresses only the extremes of doubt and desperation. The Devil might do his damnedest yet fail to dominate the world he has been released into. He can cause only the merest flutter, without any serious tectonic disturbance. He may be the master of the plot, but not of life under the lifeless crust of oppression. This moribund form of life is diabolical in a different way – in a broader and deeper sense. It is typical that Satan's ball should be a grand and macabre spectacle but

---

[27] 'In Flat No. 50 the flames devour all that causes feelings of pain, impotence and horror in the reality of the satirist's time. We may further suppose that in Torgsin [...] material and social inequality burn, along with abhorrent privilege, while in the House of Literature it is falsehood, the servility of pseudo-art, and the sterile semblance of spiritual activity that are turned to ashes.' W. Woroszylski, 'Rękopisy nie płoną - obiecał diabeł', *Więź*, Nos. 7-8, p. 55.

one that is quite tolerable for normal human sensibilities, shaped by the romantic tradition of horror, the paintings of Bosch and Goya or modern horror films. This is a bravura variation on well-known themes, reminding us constantly that it is playing with conventions. What is intolerable is the writers' tedious party, a banal evening's dancing, with certain features placed in sharp focus to bring out for us in heightened form the misery of life, the painful triviality of existence, from which there is no escape: '... there stands a stunted linden tree and an iron railing, and beyond it the boulevard... And some ice is melting in a glass, while at the next table sits a man with ox-like, bloodshot eyes, and it's dreadul, dreadful... Oh gods – poison! Give me some poison!'[28]

The Lesser Devil's gala performance provides evidence of his powerlessness. The conclusion of the novel sets the seal on this. Here we learn that Woland's assistant Korov'ev is a knight, who 'once made an unfortunate joke [...] and subsequently had to keep joking rather more and rather longer than he had expected'.[29] No doubt the other members of the Devil's organizational team, parading in guises not of their choosing, have been in similar situations. We do not know whether the mission they are engaged in is also a form of penance for their sins (which, and against whom?), or a form of demonic shift-work, or a perverse fulfilment of a wish for 'earthly realism', like the reincarnation longed for by Dostoevsky's Devil, as 'a fat, sixteen-stone wife of a merchant'.[30] Bulgakov bypasses these elements of the demonic condition as well. He clearly needs to show one thing only: his *diabolus minor*, the traditional apogee of freedom, the epitome of free will, turns out not to be free. He is neither master of the situation, nor master of his own actions. From this standpoint, the stress placed on precisely this unfreedom in the last words of the third redaction, cited earlier, becomes understandable:

'So I have been ordered...'
'Can you really be given orders?'
'Oh yes. I have been ordered to escort you...'[31]

---

[28] *Romany*, p. 477.
[29] Ibid., p. 795.
[30] Dostoevskii, Vol. 10, p. 165.
[31] Chudakova, 'Arkhiv...', p. 111.

He, who in the earlier version can give orders to devils, in the final version merely *asks*. He cannot do otherwise, being the giver of freedom – through compassion. And the freedom is for everybody, including the Devil. He who does good is free.

IV

Bulgakov's devil-cum-magician has no sooner materialized at Patriarchs' Ponds than he begins to weave the novel's biblical thread. He could cite once again at the very beginning the question from *Doctor Faustus*: 'Ich hoffe doch, du wunderst dich nicht, daß dir Sankt Velten vom Religiösen spricht? Potz Stern! Wer anders, möcht ich wissen, soll dir wohl heute davon sprechen?'[32] Indeed, in a world of banal and trivialized verisimilitude which is in fact a wild indulgence of the fantasy, the evocation of the myth of Jesus is the work of the Devil. He, who in the current view is an impossibility, a kind of demonstration of Chekhov's words 'It cannot be, because it can never be',[33] is legitimately invoked to testify to the existence of one of whom it is exclaimed at one point in Bulgakov's writing, 'He never existed!'

It is true that the literature of the Soviet period often drew on biblical motifs, but with few exceptions (Esenin and sometimes Kliuev) this was purely in order to refute them, whether to express the supposed scale of the Bolshevik coup and sanctify it by means of borrowed accessories, or to proclaim the continuity and fulfilment of some messianic Russian mission. This was the fashion in the early days; later the Bible would be primarily something to be turned inside out and parodied by the ideologists of atheism.

Bulgakov's intentions are different. As work on the novel progressed, the biblical strand, which at first was only briefly sketched, gained in depth and objectivity. It is independent of the Moscow events, though connected to them by a deep-seated body of shared meanings, proceeding in the same time frame, seeming to renew itself constantly and create a system of higher references that operates

---

[32] Mann, p. 244. ['But I hope you do not marvel that "the Great Adversary" speaks to you of religion. Gog's nails! Who else, I should like to know, is to speak of it today?' Thomas Mann, *Doctor Faustus*, translated by H. T. Lowe-Porter, p. 236]

[33] A. Chekhov, 'Pis'mo k uchenomu sosedu', *Sobranie sochinenii*, Moscow 1960, p. 5.

continually. It is a way of extracting from humanity's collective experience a primary, in some way archetypal situation of denial and cowardice, confronted with loyalty to the ideals of truth and to one's calling. Here the author appeals most directly to the general consciousness and gives his earlier motifs their surest grounding. In Pilate's ritual phrase honouring the rule of Tiberius Caesar an echo can be heard of Bouton's jabbering sycophancy: 'Is our king the best and most magnificent monarch in the world? [...] Of course he is. I have always shouted and will continue to shout: "Long live the King!"'.[34] Every form of coercion generates insincere praise, establishing an unreal world of inverted meanings, and destroys freedom of thought, which by its nature presents a danger. The confrontation between Yeshua and Pilate will thus be a model and prototype for the relationship between Molière and Louis XIV and that between Pushkin and Nicholas I, forming in historical space a continuity of regularly renewed tension between the free intellect and domineering tyranny. Looking upon the dramas of these artists in the light of his own experience, Bulgakov now placed a broader construction upon them – as an adventure of the human spirit, to which he brought evangelical motifs.

Thus a secularized gospel arose, one which deliberately departed from strictly religious categories so as to establish common ground for people of all opinions and attitudes – this is one possible interpretation of Bulgakov's design. The lowering of the sacred is accompanied, however, by a simultaneous elevation of the profane, or of ordinary secular categories, to the Christian Heaven. At the intersection of the upward and downward movement, at about the half-way point, a new element takes shape and is tested by experience: individual value systems, rescued from inversion and denial, travel a roundabout route to meet Christian ethics, and the two turn out to be alike on the most important points. This is not a matter of belief in God, but of both believers and non-believers accepting the same precepts. Grigorii Pomerants has stated this very precisely: 'the modern religious mind [religioznost'] finds itself facing not so much the God of Abraham, Isaac and Jacob made flesh in Christ, as the mystery of life *apparently* before God, who demands a moral answer.'[35]

---

[34] M. Bulgakov, *Dramy i komedii*, Moscow, 1965, p. 274.

[35] G. Pomerants, '"Evklidovskii" i "neevklidovskii" razum v tvorchestve Dostoevskogo', *Kontinent*, No. 3, 1975, p. 147.

Bulgakov's ethical answer is given in the categories of guilt and punishment which are manifested thanks to moral memory – the conscience. The torments of memory, familiar earlier to Khludov and the narrator of 'The Red Crown', now return as punishment for evil-doing. Numerous criminals of all epochs and countries are punished in the novel, perhaps by nothing more than the perpetual repetition of their own situation, renewed again and again and monitored by the duty demons. By this means Bulgakov conveys to us his belief that evil-doing does not go unpunished.

But he also believes in the possibility of forgiveness. The Christian idea of a Christ who atones for the sins of humanity is set aside, in accordance with the position adopted. Bulgakov's Yeshua, stripped of any god-like attributes, dies only to live at peace with himself and his nature. We can guess, however, that for the author it is enough to know that this death has changed the world by setting in train a series of consequences that will last for centuries. One of these consequences is compassion.[36] It is experienced in the novel by Pilate and the child-murderer Frieda; in other words, by a mythical figure who initiates a chain of evil, and a small link in that chain, one sinner among many. Perhaps this means that compassion is always possible, and for all. Sergeant-Major Zhilin, seen in Turbin's dream in *The White Guard*, assures him that God receives everybody in Heaven,[37] while Woland studies the audience at the Variety Theatre and observes, 'They're just ordinary people [...] but sometimes compassion finds its way into their hearts.'[38] Thanks to the legacy of Yeshua-Christ, everybody has the capacity for compassion, while the omnipotence of the Devil does not reach that far. Margarita herself sets Frieda free, just as the Master himself frees Pilate; both have only to discover the powers that are theirs, and both break the determinist cycle of guilt and punishment by their freely chosen actions. In this way Bulgakov's favourite gesture of resistance and free choice, previously accorded to Malyshev, Khludov and Turbin, acquires a deeper, ethical meaning. The central figures of the

---

[36] The credit for first seeing the thematic problems of *The Master and Margarita* in terms of 'forgiveness, compassion and absolution', as for many other things, must go to Marietta Chudakova. See her 'Tvorcheskaia istoriia romana M. Bulgakova *Master i Margarita*', *Voprosy literatury*, No. 1, 1976, esp. p. 240 ff.

[37] *Romany*, pp. 71-72.

[38] Ibid., p. 541.

novel become free by setting others free; when the Master calls out to Pilate, 'You are free!', this applies also to the Master himself; everything that exists and is part of the human condition, including things that most clearly belong in the realm of myth, is subject to human choice.

Thus it emerges that in his writing Bulgakov is *anima naturaliter christiana*. It seems that religion played its part in his life too, though hidden from the eyes of strangers. Here he drew hope and here, via secret inspiration and the hidden pathways of inheritance, the spiritual legacy of his father revealed itself, for, as will be remembered, it was recorded that the figure of his father 'should be the point of departure for another planned work.'

The Devil tells this story – puncturing the conceit of the arrogant pseudo-rationalists – with the added aim of being able, by virtue of his universal presence in time, to testify that the myth had been realized in life in the way the Master describes. As we know, Bulgakov believed deeply in the power of true literature to penetrate to the very heart of things, in the intuitive faculty granted to an artist to grasp the essence of man and the world (after all, Filia, the 'artist of the office', also has some of this power). He would no doubt have endorsed the words Pushkin wrote not long before his death: 'A genius can discern the truth at first glance, and truth, as the Scriptures tell us, is stronger than the Tsar.'[39] Yeshua's wish was to live according to truth; here the Master becomes his disciple, and the certificate issued by the Devil applies also to Bulgakov himself. Marietta Chudakova points out perceptively, 'As he sees for himself how accurately the Master has guessed the truth of the Gospels in every detail, the reader is in some fashion compelled to believe that the creator of the Master, the author of that "other" novel which contains the first, has applied the same acuity of vision and faithful attention to detail to the study of the contemporary life which he shows.'[40]

The Devil's diminished powers are still more than sufficient for this.

V

They are also sufficient to help the Master and Margarita, although only to a limited extent.

---

[39] A. Pushkin, *Polnoe sobranie sochinenii*, Moscow, 1949, Vol. 16, p. 224.

[40] Chudakova, 'Arkhiv...', p. 130.

The two lovers make a belated entry into the novel, in all likelihood at the moment when the author begins to come to terms with the fact that this novel will not be merely his 'next' but his last, the one which will encapsulate everything that he holds to be most important, the one which will set him free, and make up for his foreshortened life. For this reason, availing himself of his prerogatives as author, he writes himself and the woman he loves into his main work. But, ever true to his principles, he alters the features of reality so that these will prove correct when checked against a different logic, the artistic and intellectual logic which applies only in the novel. He acts like a painter who paints himself into a crowd scene among many other figures, but the scene as a whole is in truth him, because it is his vision. In *The Master and Margarita* he expressed himself through all the characters, putting into their lives elements of his own side by side with the sum of his reflections on the relationship between man and the world.

The Master is therefore far from being an unambiguous figure. Propounding his truth, mocked, slandered, imprisoned and condemned to suffering, he stands at the end of a series of Bulgakov characters which opens with Yeshua, and, like Yeshua, he is resurrected to a new life. At the same time, when he burns his manuscript and shows disloyalty to his calling as a writer, he is also Pilate; and when he reconstructs the past through accurate guesswork he is also Woland. In this last connection a reference to the Faustian myth can be seen; Bulgakov actually makes repeated allusions to it, in many different ways. However, the tradition is subjected to characteristic bifurcation. The Devil, who does not have the role of tempter, has, as we know, the facial features and the wry grimace of self-knowledge of Faust in his later years; the Master, on the other hand, is the merest shadow of that Faust, ailing and hounded by a cabal of persecutors who, in the words of a Polish interpreter of Bulgakov, 'might deserve to be termed a collective Pilate'.[41] In the reverse of the situation in Goethe, it is Margarita, not the Master, who treats with the Devil as she struggles to save him, the Master. She is one of a number of Bulgakov's redeeming women, by now familiar. (Note that they are completely devoid of sensuality: eroticism generally was an area in which, in a literary sense, he was never at home, and, conscious of this, he very rarely ventured into it.) The Margarita motif is a form of enciphered love letter to a mistress, a tribute to her courage and devotion, revealing and

---

[41] Woroszylski, p. 51.

concealing the story of his own feelings. In hindsight it may also be read as a tribute to Russian womanhood, ready when necessary to sally into the seven circles of contemporary Hell. But here again tradition is bypassed, as it would demand that Margarita's symbolic surrender to the Devil should bring with it torments, perplexity, the spectre of damnation – anything that would leave its mark on the personality of the heroine. But it brings with it absolutely nothing of this, and Bulgakov expressly emphasizes this point.[42] Is Margarita so powerfully protected by love? No doubt she is, but this may be yet further proof of how innocuous the Lesser Devil really is. What does real damage is a life subject to a superior form of devilry, but there is no harm in plunging into traditional satanism.

Thus, in addition to the Bible, the Faust legend has also been dethroned. More than dethroned, because in the process it has collided with the hard carapace of reality and been shattered. If Christ was a tormented, itinerant philosopher, Faust turned out to be a tormented and lonely artist. Here we see in concentrated form Bulgakov's knowledge of the real burden of existence, of its clouded, untidy and essentially non-linear nature, which cannot be subsumed into any mythical categories. This is no doubt why he so spectacularly flouts tradition, challenges its component parts, makes a travesty of them: the Devil is better than humans; the sale of one's soul costs nothing; the beloved mistress is the saviour of the hero, and both, instead of living long and happily ever after, live short lives and die happy.

This last point is particularly significant. We can give no conclusive answer to the question of what is the key to Bulgakov's overall scheme. *The Master and Margarita* may be equally well understood as the Master's novel, surrounded by the free play of his compensatory imagination, the dream of a deluded artist – or one thought to be so; or as a similar vision of Bezdomny's, inspired by the consciousness he later acquires; leaving aside the possibility that, in a possibly naïve and unconsidered reading, it may be taken to be what it says it is – a story which might just happen. Bulgakov deliberately hides the key, leaving multiple possibilities open, and in this flickering play of meanings the freedom of the creative act, represented by this novel, finds fulfilment. The ambivalent feeling which the reader experiences and relishes, not knowing which world he is really in, is intentional. In fact he is in fiction and reality at the same time, subject to literature's right of invention; and so in a third dimension, in which, in the words

---

[42] See *Romany*, p. 747.

of the poet, 'everything is logical and nothing is impossible'. If this is so, the Master may be redeemed by love, rescued by the Devil and condemned to eternal rest in his romantic little house, which is the synthesis of his dreams and a happy refuge – but at the same time he must die. Bulgakov places particular emphasis on this duality – in a way which looks like an inconsistency but in fact is logic of a higher order: the two lovers, each separately, really do die, in the clinic and at home. Then we learn that they have vanished without trace, leading the police investigators to suspect kidnapping.[43] If the only escape from the stifling grip of life is with the help of Satan, this means there is no escape but death. But at the same time Azazello is right when he says, 'Do you really need to sit in a basement in your shirt and hospital underpants in order to feel that you're alive?'[44] There is such a thing as death in life and resurrection after death.

To the reader, the fact of the real death of the hero and heroine tears away the last veil. Previous half-real deaths and suicides for literary effect, followed by the discovery of Poliakov's and Maksudov's manuscripts, still had something of a game about them, although in *A Theatrical Novel* it had become a very real game, of which Tsvetaeva once said, 'Our real death can't be any more palpable than this.' The author by now had a foreboding of the end, then a certainty of that end, added to the certainty that nothing would change before he died; there is a personal and very moving touch in a small episode added at a late stage to *The Master and Margarita*, in which the barman Sokov, on learning that he is soon to die, begs Professor Kuzmin, 'Please stop my cancer'.[45] Nothing can ever be stopped, for the harsh words of *The White Guard* about suffering and death hold true. This is made manifest in Bulgakov's masterwork, in spite of the whole weight of tradition which, by the power of associations already set in motion, propels the action towards a previously sensed conclusion: the Master will thank the Devil for his help, then return to his basement and again resume his struggle against fate. But no. The cruel chaos of real twentieth-century existence stifles such traditional gestures at birth and makes a mockery of them. Bulgakov is absolutely true to the truth of the time which destroyed him. *Anna Karenina* contains a passage dealing with precisely this theme: 'It was cruel mockery by some evil force... It was

---

[43] Ibid., pp. 789, 791, 804, 805.

[44] Ibid., p. 787.

[45] Ibid., p. 629.

necessary to find deliverance from it, and deliverance was in the hands of everybody. It was necessary to break that dependence on evil, and there was only one way – death.'[46]

This truth has to be confronted. But a chance of liberation – through compassion – is also truth. Thanks to it an enslaved individual may be freed – free from others and free from himself. It is also a chance to work creatively. The writer at his work finds himself freer than the enslaved Devil. His work is his freedom. In this way the shattered Faustian myth, proclaiming opportunities for compassion and creativity, is gathered together piece by piece and reassembled, and only then, scarred and bespattered with earthly mud, does it regain its importance.

Against this background the Lesser Devil assumes even less significance than in the previous two areas: everyday Moscow life, and legend. He turns out to be an obliging intermediary, an efficient go-between. He could well repeat after Mann's Devil, 'Wir schaffen nichts Neues – das ist andrer Leute Sache. Wir entbinden nur und setzen frei.'[47] This is exactly right: his business is to unlock potential and help make people aware of opportunities. He does this with the aid of his dazzling manipulation of time, space, objects and people. But these modest sallies beyond the bounds of normality serve only to reaffirm a deeper abnormality. This is the Devil's sphere of action. However dazzling, however stunning the performance, behind it there will always stand the blind walls of impossibility which surround the domain of the Greater Devil. And man will always be alone within them.

But the devilish intrusion will not pass entirely without trace. Its traces will be imprinted jointly by the Devil and the Master (the alliance is significant) on the career of Bezdomny. There exists the punishment of consciousness, which Pilate and Frieda undergo – and the reward of consciousness, conferred upon the impetuous poet. At first, assuming a modish pseudonym, he blindly submits to the herd mentality of the period with its aggressive atheism. The shocks he receives compel him to give serious thought to the meaning of existence, seek his own identity and reject his pseudonym. The end result of this process has clear significance: the erstwhile nihilist and blustering boor appears in the epilogue as

---

[46] L. N. Tolstoi, *Anna Karenina*, Moscow, 1953, p. 857.

[47] Mann, p. 237. ['We make naught new – that is other people's matter. We only release, only set free.' Thomas Mann, *Doctor Faustus*, translated by H. T. Lowe-Porter, p. 230]

Professor Ivan Nikolaevich Ponyrev, 'a fellow of the Institute of History and Philosophy'. He is the one who is visited in his dreams by Pilate, who is 'pardoned on the eve of Sunday, the day of Resurrection', and the very last sentence of the novel, with its matchlessly fluent cadences that all readers remember invoking the name of the Fifth Procurator of Judea, concerns him. This concluding note clearly has very special significance to Bulgakov. He signals it earlier and repeats it three times, savouring it as he does so,[48] (the last sentence of 'The Fatal Eggs' was similarly structured); he uses it to link Bezdomny and the Master yet again, as if by a magic thread. Perhaps it was the author's intention to indicate that the memory of the myth which is made real by the Master endures, carried forward by his successors. It endures – and bears with it a warning. Moreover, in spite of the destruction of apparent meanings, in spite of inverted meanings, it binds human consciousness by an understanding of true meanings.

The title 'master' has its own special lustre in the novel.[49] Some elements of it also extend to the title 'disciple', which is bestowed upon Bezdomny in his valedictory scene. Disciplehood may be effected in a perverse way: the Master's weakness calls forth the courage of Margarita, and Yeshua has as his disciple not only Matthew the Levite, but also Pilate – just as previously Bitkov had become infected with Pushkin's art and become his 'disciple', and Efrosimov's one-time persecutor Markizov becomes his disciple. Bezdomny, on recovering from his blasphemous fanaticism, like Rusakov, and recovering his senses, like Markizov, will become a historian, like the Master – and perhaps he is the one who sets down the whole story.

The chain of historical acts of violence is interlinked with acts of resistance. It is not only the case that manuscripts, as Woland assures us, do not burn; nor do people perish. There are successors to repudiate the loneliness of their forebears. In the intricate dialectic of Bulgakovian meanings, which accumulate at many levels and cancel one another out, there is no definite conclusion, just as there is none in the fate of the main characters. This leaves one thing above all with which to look to the future – hope.

---

[48] *Romany*, p. 554, 799, 812.

[49] See Ibid., p. 553. Note also Lakshin's interesting observations in his 'Eskizy...', pp. 302-303.

VI

The play of meanings finds expression at every level and every dimension of *The Master and Margarita*.

Time in the novel is handled in such a way that the events of the Bible story should be perceived as contemporaneous with the Moscow events. The time is exclusively present time, constantly reactivating the past and turning what is and what was into elements of a shared conduit of thought. It might be termed fantastic time. On the one hand it is time without the attributes of being continuous and uninterruptible: 'It is a pleasure to stop the clock on a festive night such as this,'[50] says Woland; on the other, it is measured most precisely: the alternating Moscow and biblical episodes, with a single exception,[51] are exactly matched to one another. Space is similarly elastic. It is possible, as Chudakova suggests, that Bulgakov, as an attentive reader of *Imaginary Quantities in Geometry* by the eminent philosopher Pavel Florensky, was attempting a literary materialization of the possibilities so graphically presented in it of treating temporal and spatial categories in a new way; of 'overcoming space and turning bodies inside out.' Bulgakov underlined another sentence in this philosopher's work and added an exclamation mark: 'In this way, disrupting the flow of time, *The Divine Comedy* lies not outside our present science but before it.'[52]

The impression of a cogent connection between the two story-lines is reinforced by the repeatedly emphasized presence of two silent witnesses: the sun and the moon, with a meticulous division of functions. The physically palpable oppressive heat, familiar from the Constantinople scenes in *Flight*, in a sense compels us to recognize the obvious and accept exaggerated forms of everyday reality as the only reality; it accompanies the apparently irrefutable arguments of Berlioz and timid sobriety of Pilate. The moon shows up deeper meanings and the true state of affairs. (It is no accident that the Master glances at it while explaining

---

[50] *Romany*, p. 709.

[51] Note the end of Chapter 2, where the moment the cavalry ride past is precisely recorded: 'It was about ten in the morning' (*Romany*, p. 458), and the beginning of Chapter 16: 'The squadron of cavalry which had held up the Procurator at about midday...' (p. 588).

[52] Quoted in M. Chudakova, 'Usloviia sushchestvovaniia', *V mire knig*, No. 12, 1974, p. 80. Note also the sentence uttered by Timofeev in *Ivan Vasil'evich*, quoted in Chapter Eight, Part IV.

what has happened to him and saying, 'We must face the truth.')[53] It is also the object of constant attention at every point of its journey through the heavens. It accompanies the events in Yershalaim on the night Judas is murdered, highlighting the informer's sandal as a mute memento of the occasion. It is refracted in Berlioz's very last glance when he is decapitated by the tram. It lights the way for the Master when he is summoned by Woland. And lastly it provides the grand concert finale, being at once the path of Pilate's redemption, the violator of Ponyrev's peace of mind and the 'deluge of moonlight' of the concluding sentences; a powerful *fortissimo* and a cathartic cleansing.

So everything becomes clearer in the dark, when the play of appearances ends. Night is the time to draw the correct conclusions from the mixed and often deceptive signals of the day. This is a projection of personal situations by a man who in the daytime discharges the obligations imposed on him by circumstances, while doing his real work by night, fascinated by the presence of the moon. But this too is another way of making the novel's metaphorical structure express resistance to the dictatorship of appearances and the imposed obviousness of what merely seems. Hence yet again the significance of nightfall, as in 'The Red Crown' and *Flight*: 'an important and terrible time of day', when meanings are evaluated, contours eroded and the hour of truth approaches; this is the time when Pilate, like Gogol's Foma Grigor'evich, does not know if the cloak on his throne is only a cloak...

The storm cloud that bears down on Moscow straight from Yershalaim also has a special role to play and reinforces the impression that they are linked. This recalls the well known device of simultaneity used in Joyce's *Ulysses* when Dedalus and Bloom view the same cloud from different parts of town. The explosive discharge of the elements is both the background and the sign of human fates;[54] Yeshua and the Master die at the same time (just as Judas and Baron Maigel

---

[53] *Romany*, p. 522. Note also: 'E. S. Bulgakova said that Bulgakov was in the habit of standing by the window for a long time with his eyes fixed on the object of his observations: the moon had some special attraction for him!' Chudakova, 'Arkhiv...', p. 132.

[54] A storm also breaks in *A Theatrical Novel* at the moment when Maksudov enters the Independent Theatre, at a critical moment in his life. Note also another 'biographical' negative aspect of storms: according to Elena Bulgakova, 'Whenever Bulgakov had something banned or when some unexpected misfortune struck, there was always a storm [...] That's how it was with

perish simultaneously at the culminating point of the night); the menace of nature reflects the menace of human undertakings. The passing of the storm, on the other hand, brings a feeling of relief, of a crisis overcome, of ultimate liberation and hope; it shapes the bewitching atmosphere of parting with things worldly, the atmosphere which prevails as the author concludes the story of his hero and heroine, as well as his own life. Seeking to achieve maximum emphasis, Bulgakov speaks in the language of the elements he has invoked, and the purifying storm takes on the same depth of meaning as in Pasternak's late poem 'After the Thunderstorm' [Posle grozy]:

> Воспоминание о полувеке
> Пронесшейся грозой уходит вспять.
> Столетье вышло из его опеки.
> Пора дорогу будущему дать.[55]

Satan's ball contains a gamut of meanings and is a well-known feature of Russian literature. Pushkin had invited his readers to just such a ball in the draft of his planned epic poem about Faust, and in his 'Undertaker' he had offered an excursion into the macabre similar to Bulgakov's. In Vladimir Odoevsky's miniature 'The Ball', the ornate setting of a society ball takes on a disturbing aspect and turns into a *danse macabre*. These were popular devices and Bulgakov shows himself a consummate stylizer; seeming to blow the froth off the procession of whirling human and demonic dances described with such enthusiasm by the Russian Hoffmannists, he piles effects one upon another with the zest of a virtuoso, to create the ball to end all balls. It is not pure entertainment, however, since, as we have seen, it turns out to be much less demonic than literary – an informer is executed and an unbeliever brought low, and the setting brings out all the more clearly the hopeless and endless chain of penance for villains.

---

his last play [*Batum* – A.D.]. There were four meetings to discuss it, and four times, with comical precision, a thunderstorm broke out.' Quoted in Lakshin, 'Eskizy...', p. 220.

[55] Boris Pasternak, *Sobranie sochinenii v piati tomakh*, Moscow, 1989, Vol. 5, p. 125. ['The memory of fifty years// Recedes like a storm which has just swept through.// The century is no longer under the guardianship [of those years]//. It is time to give way to the future.' (English translation in Olga Raevsky Hughes, *The Poetic World of Boris Pasternak*, Princeton University Press, 1974, p. 157)]

As usual with Bulgakov, the light touch veils the anxiety and overcomes the greatest obstacles. As in *The White Guard*, the narrator-cum-impresario shows himself from time to time behind the text (in the earlier versions his role was intended to be greater) to place the clear stamp of his personality on the Moscow scenes, taking care to measure out the effects and shaping the background of successive scenes with evident pleasure. Sometimes he confines himself to a discreet indication of his presence; sometimes he is careful to ensure that the flow of his story should have all the features of an unhurried exchange with a reader whose presence he sees and feels. More often, however, he expresses sadness, perplexity and weariness; he emphatically repeats that things are terrible, echoes Pilate's request for poison, and begins the last chapter in a tone of melancholy resignation:

'Ye gods, how sad is the world at evening, how mysterious the mists over the swamps! He who has strayed in these mists, he who has suffered greatly before dying, he who has flown over this earth carrying an unbearable burden knows this. He who is weary knows it and he is ready without regret to leave the mists of this earth, its swamps and rivers; he is ready to give himself up to the arms of death with a light heart, knowing that death alone [can comfort him].'[56]

This is another living link with the romantic tradition. Gogol's 'Sorochintsy Fair' ends with a doleful confession of the loneliness of the author in very similar if not identical tones. But at the same time Bulgakov's novel bears the deep imprint of the trials of his own life and authenticates the death of the hero and heroine, clearly sensed through his certainty of his own approaching death; it expresses his awareness that the conclusion of the book would coincide with the conclusion of his life; this is the point at which literature and its conventions almost come to an end, and, in Pasternak's words, 'dyshit pochva i sud'ba' [the soil and destiny breathe deeply]. It is not surprising that this invocation took its place in the novel only a matter of weeks before Bulgakov's death,[57] and that in the unfinished sentence with heavy heart we hear the fading voice of a sick man, dictating his last corrections while he still has the strength. The narrator of *The White Guard* still resisted the course of events, even though he knew that this was futile; he uttered exclamations, warnings and advice, while wringing his hands. The narrator of *The*

---

[56] *Romany*, p. 794.

[57] See Chudakova, 'Arkhiv...', p. 140.

Master and Margarita, the wiser for his unhappy experience, understands that events are inevitable and irreversible, and therefore joins his voice to the Master's in pleading for eternal rest. But owing to the multi-levelled dialectic of meanings, the result is the opposite. In *The White Guard*, the narrator's anxieties concealed an acceptance of fate; in *The Master and Margarita* resignation is denied by the creative act itself, which opposes any fatalism and becomes the final victory of the previously defeated writer.

The romantic tradition is alive in the novel, and meetings with Gogol occur at points of great importance.[58] Conscious, however, of the fact that not all conventions were applicable to the turbulent and uncertain present, Bulgakov succeeds in mocking the superficial aspects of that tradition while exploiting the inner potential of romantic irony. This we see when the administrator of the Variety Theatre is subjected to a devilish attack amidst the crash of thunder and flashing lightning, in an atmosphere of mystery and menace, but with a public lavatory as its setting; and when Margarita takes her nocturnal ride to something resembling Golgotha, in a scene which stands as a separate study and a rehearsal of the most spectacular motifs of wizardry and black magic, a naked drunkard appears from a different dimension – a human dimension – and receives from the heroine a thoroughly modern 'extended, unprintable oath'.[59] The real link with the past is maintained in the most essential matters – the independence of spirit and the traditional understanding of the calling of the true writer. The costumes, on the other hand, are loosely fitted, for the novel as a whole sets out to reclaim freedom.

The romantic tradition also plays its part in the style of the narrative concerning the Moscow events. Here the dominant mode is a fluent eloquence with impeccably measured cadences, subject to the form of a free exchange, with its own variable but carefully marked rhythms. Bulgakov is a very deliberate stylist, sparing in the effects he applies; proof of this may be seen in his interpolation into 'normal' syntactic structures of inversions such as 'empty was the alley', 'and the glass was drained, and help it did', or in the bold accumulation of epithets, such as 'empty, black and dead'. There are moments when the Moscow scenes show almost too much eloquence in the descriptions and betray their origins in his early

---

[58] On the links between Bulgakov and Gogol, see Chudakova, 'Arkhiv...', p. 129, and at greater length her 'Bulgakov i Gogol'', *Russkaia rech'*, No. 2-3, 1979.

[59] *Romany*, p. 661.

feuilletons. But in reclaiming his freedom Bulgakov evidently wished to deny himself nothing that might boost his descriptive zest and recall the days of his youth. The mythical scenes, on the other hand, have about them a quality of succinct compression and a classical simplicity, free of ornamentation, in the descriptions. Here the author achieves almost absolute vision, in which his style becomes transparent and crystallizes the objects described. The seemingly sparing details selected combine to build up a vivid, sensual picture which gives the impression of complete authenticity. It is also faithful to the topography and layout of a city which Bulgakov had thoroughly studied from historical sources,[60] but which – above and beyond this – he was able to feel and transmute artistically into a structure which is truthful in the highest degree. The narrator makes no intrusions into these scenes; the description is fully objectivized; this is the very essence of literature as an act of evocation of the visible world, almost an additional proof of the fact that the artist's creative powers are absolute, like the powers of the Devil. There is also an abundance of highly expressive scenes in which, following Bulgakov's own established traditions, realism takes on the quality of fantasy – as in the almost surreal images of buildings in Yershalaim picked out of the darkness one by one by lightning flashes and seeming to soar skyward. All these are the very summit of a genre and unquestionably belong to the very best pages of their kind written in our time.

Thus a sense of the strangeness of life, which placed some strain on Bulgakov's vision in his early works, but which he soon began to overcome by precise and clear formulae, found expression in the language of his full maturity, in that inspired, limpid form which is sometimes found in his late works. This did not, however, impart any special high seriousness to those late works. On the contrary, in the Moscow scenes Bulgakov is extraordinarily light-hearted – at moments almost light-headed – considering the conditions in which he was writing, as if he really had started his book with a desire to bring to life the expression 'let it all go to the Devil!' His imaginative *brio* puts him beyond fear of anything. He has no qualms about the use of supernatural powers as a kind of master-key,

---

[60] A comparison of the descriptions in the novel with a reconstruction of Herod's palace shows a high degree of accuracy. On the sources Bulgakov used or might have used to establish his facts in the biblical chapters, see Chudakova, 'Arkhiv...', p. 72; Chudakova, 'Usloviia sushchestvovaniia', p. 79; I. Belza, 'Genealogiia *Master i Margarita*', *Kontekst*, 1978, p. 157 ff.

opening the way to many improbable twists in the plot – a use which does not fully accord with the rules of high art; no qualms either about his 'personified fictions', depicted in loving detail: cats with gilded whiskers and ladies' opera-glasses and pigs that glide through the air with briefcases tucked under one leg; nor about the realistic scenes, also clearly written with great relish, such as the scandal at Torgsin, the special shop for holders of hard currency and gold, in which a customer is hit on the head with a tray and his head produces a most precisely-described sound 'such as is heard when sheet iron is thrown down from a lorry', and the victim 'turned pale and fell back into a tub of salted Azov herring';[61] it is as if the author enjoys stressing that he sees and knows everything he is creating, including the brand of herring! He has no qualms about those acts of demonic spite which seem excessive and – occasionally – misdirected, such as the beating of Berlioz's uncle and the public strip-tease to which the Moscow ladies who hunger for basic worldly goods are subjected. ('That fool Bulgakov found something to laugh at,'[62] wrote Nadezhda Mandelstam indignantly). Nor about giving in to what may be described as *Lust zu fabulieren*, to the pleasure of wielding creative power, of prolonging the enjoyment of creating a world which obeys his pen, of commanding the moment to stay. This is most apparent in the farcical scenes involving Korov'ev and Behemoth. Like Shakespearian jesters, they seem to be called upon not only to discharge tension in intervals of jollity, but also to expose a jesting – though menacing – aspect of the world. They neutralize it by laughter; while pretending to adopt its rituals, they expose the hollowness of those rituals and demolish them from within. The parodically elevated tirades of both these scoundrels, their horseplay and banter may at times appear exaggeratedly grandiloquent. Perhaps the author's final revision would have eliminated some of these excesses, for it should not be forgotten that the novel, though complete in essentials, was not judged by Bulgakov to be finished – and we should make allowances for this. In what we have, in what was left in precisely this form, we can again feel the extra-literary warmth of the author's touch, a substitute for limited vital activity, an extension of the process of bidding farewell to life.

The richness, even extravagance of vision, has led some commentators to invoke the concept of the Menippean genre, popularized in the superb studies of

---

[61] *Romany*, p. 767.

[62] Nadezhda Mandel'shtam, *Vtoraia kniga*, Paris, 1972, p. 136.

Mikhail Bakhtin. And indeed, many elements of Bakhtin's definition of this genre perfectly match Bulgakov's novel. Yet the synthetic formula of the novel defies satisfactory classification in existing categories, while nevertheless inspiring such exegetic urges. These span a broad range, from Lesley Milne's very interesting attempt to place the novel in the medieval mystery tradition, to the admirable erudition and ingenuity of D. G. B. Piper, who treats the work as an elaborate political allegory of much breadth and detail, although it may seem reckless to suspect Bulgakov of such a thing.[63] There will doubtless be more such attempts; the possibilities are legion (for example: *The Master and Margarita* as a fable with deliberately inverted themes, in which everything is turned upside down). The fact is, however, that this novel, situated at the crossroads of many traditions,[64] makes such free play with them that it is in a category all its own; like *Don Quixote*, *Gulliver's Travels* and *Faust*, it inaugurates a new tradition.

VII

If this novel is considered in the light of the totality of Bulgakov's writing, it becomes clear that he was writing it all his life. There is hardly anything in what we have already seen that does not find some place in *The Master and Margarita*, and conversely, there is hardly anything in *The Master and Margarita* that did not arise earlier. This principle of two-way interpenetration in no way diminishes the fact that a new tradition has been inaugurated: the supreme secret power of transmutation is bestowed upon devils and artists alike. If, however, Bulgakov's oeuvre is seen as a pyramid, this book will be its apex, the point at which all lines converge. Or it may be seen as the keystone completing an arch and giving it a higher, harmonious meaning. In my attempt to reconstruct Bulgakov's career, I have frequently had occasion to draw attention to various things that recur at the

---

[63] Milne, *Comedy*...; D. G. B. Piper, 'An Approach to Bulgakov's *Master and Margarita*', *Forum for Modern Language Studies*, Vol. 7, No. 2, 1971, pp. 134-157.

[64] There is already a substantial body of literature dealing with the potential and obvious affinities of *The Master and Margarita*. In addition to the sources cited so far, there is, for example, E. Stenbock-Fermor's article, which carefully traces the Faustian motifs: '*The Master and Margarita*. and Goethe's *Faust*', *Slavic and East European Journal*, Vol. 13, No. 3, 1969, pp. 309-325. See also the select bibliography at the end of this volume.

end of it; Bulgakov's themes traverse the boundaries of successive works, bounce off one another, intertwine, divide, recur, change and disappear, only to reappear at last in this novel – we know how faithful the author is to the motifs he selects in literature, and to those that select him.

Almost all of them are here, beginning with Bulgakov's fundamental narrative fabric. There is the dense, closely-woven texture of Moscow custom and style of life from his early feuilletons; the ordinariness, and the strangeness that peers forth from the ordinariness; the meeting-cum-concert, the palatial restaurant, the living dead and the self-appointed mediums who publicly elicit lurid secrets. Bulgakov's own experience is here: the torments of the housing crisis, the intrigues of neighbours, the high-handed administrators, the obtuse Annushkas, the welcome refuge of one's own home – which we see combined with the cosiness of friends' homes – in the Master's basement. There are the musical accompaniments, the leitmotifs that mimic the events, the polyphony of domestic mayhem. The topography of much-loved corners of old Moscow: a little square with a pond, the streets and back alleys between Sadovoe Ring and Prechistenka; Griboedov House, in reality Herzen House, the Rumiantsev Museum, Sparrow Hills with its view of the forty times forty domes of Moscow's churches in the light of the setting sun. The people: the demagogic critics, the suspicious editors, the jealous writers, the informers great and small, the functionaries of the political police and civil police, uniformed and detective branches. The atmosphere: suspicion, spy-mania, fear, the certainty that if a stranger accosts you it is to arrest you, the reflexes of a world of eavesdropping and denunciation. Searches, arrests, interrogations; so many in the novel that they are hard to count. But there is also a woman's total devotion. The skulduggery of rogues, but also the torments of conscience, responsibility, the punishment of memory, atonement, compassion, kindness. The flight to a psychiatric hospital – the only available refuge, and the forced treatment applied in that refuge. The blasphemy of those who know not what they do – until they find out. The quest for peace, and the vengeful gesture of burning. The eyes uplifted to the stars, and death which is never out of sight, pushed into the background and made light of, but biding its time. The novel which results is partially distanced by a fiction of authorship and slotted into the context of a situation. We see airy frolics of the pen beside the firm tread of prose dealing with the things that matter most. And increasingly we see the impotence of shallow common sense when faced with the real mysteries of life, the fate of the artist confronted with despotism and depravity, the counting of costs which must be borne in exchange for the right to exist, and the avenging pen as the only chance. We see the religious sense, no doubt always present but deeply hidden and only revealed in glimpses, which did not inhibit mockery of certain elements of the religious tradition but which later was invoked in the inverted legend of Adam and Eve and the origins of mankind, and which now becomes the ethical mainstay of hope. And more broadly still: we see the world explained with the aid of Gogol, a natural sense of the mystery of life, when 'the Devil himself lights lamps to show everything in an unreal form', and the presence of that Devil is traced to produce the feeling that we are dealing with devilry of a special kind... And finally, at the very summit: the innately playful turn of mind, that impish gleam in the eye and the tilt of the head with the question, 'What if there's something in it?'

All of this is here, with characters and events drawn from real experience,[65] in a life-size surrogate world which Bulgakov has created for himself. It is a Noah's Ark which Bulgakov has entered with his whole technical inventory, with everything he has written and everything he has not managed to write, with what he only sketched and what has been taken from him. He withdrew into it one step at a time as he constructed it and fitted it out, learning from his previous failures – but this time his own wishes were sovereign. And as he withdrew he moved steadily forward and upward; in literature such apparently conflicting movements are possible. He could have said, with his heroine, that 'the novel contains life'.[66] His recompense for his spiritual half-life and the irrevocable process of dying, foretold at an early stage, made of the novel not merely literature but also a moving human document. The whole work is a gesture of liberation. It not only speaks of freedom, it reifies it. The writer who had earlier given his characters a chance to

---

[65] For example Baron Maigel, in reality Steiger (see A. Słonimski, *Moja podróż do Rosji*, Warsaw, 1932, pp. 54-55, 140. I am grateful to W. Dąbrowski for drawing my attention to this.) The principle of displacement and cross-fertilization is always applied, however. Bulgakov's personal experience is palpable in the critical campaign against 'Pilatism' (cf. the article 'Strike a Blow against Bulgakovism'); allusions can be heard in the surnames Lavrovich (Lelevich?), Latunsky (Litovsky?), Ariman and Berlioz (possibly a phonetic reference to Averbakh); other types of allusion – as usual broadly elaborated – also operate, for example, musical allusions.

[66] *Romany*, p. 558. [Drawicz slightly alters the sense of this line. In the Russian original the wording makes clear that Margarita says the novel contains *her* life {v romane ee zhizn'} *Trans.*]

free themselves by a gesture of resistance from the grip of inescapable circumstances now affirmed it himself. He authenticates the spiritual order he himself has established and becomes the last hero of his own life-long oeuvre.

It is not surprising that he delays again and again the moment of parting. The novel does not want to end; his hero and heroine gaze at 'the city spread out beyond the river with fragments of sun glittering from thousands of west-facing windows, and at the onion-domes of the Novodevichii Monastery.'[67] the Master gazes at them for a long time and only the devilish whistle breaks the elegiac tone and makes it possible for him to tear himself away from the city, which has been 'swallowed by the earth, leaving only mist where it had been',[68] but which then returns from a great distance as 'the city they had just left, with its onion-domed monasteries and fragmented sunlight reflected in its windows'.[69]

Freed by his novel and free in it, Bulgakov is himself in everything he accepts and rejects. Exercising compassion, he gives almost everybody a chance, with the exception of the two informers who are sentenced to death. He turns the greatest of all modern fears, fear of the political police, into a form of joke, viewing them almost through an inverted pair of binoculars. What is real and brutal – the seizure of valuables – is turned into a show, a dream, and disarmed. In this way the world Bulgakov lived in is rendered harmless. This time he passes over its rulers in silence – a fact that also has its significance. At times he does point his finger at tyrants; in the biblical section he again showed how the psychological terror imposed by the Roman despot could break people and make criminals of them. But in the Moscow part he restricts himself to little people and petty functionaries. Those above them are left alone. Only in the ball scene, where he picks the face of Maliuta Skuratov out of the crowd, does he give us to understand that he knows where he is and what he is up against. Possibly he meant to tackle in another place, in the play *Richard I*, the problem he could not avoid indefinitely: the conflict between the indulgent treatment of some and the brutal treatment of others. This novel was not intended to deal with this. Here tyranny is demolished from the inside, by the complete negation of the criteria, parameters and thought processes that it creates, by shaking these off and finding freedom from them. This is

---

[67] Ibid., p. 791.

[68] Ibid., p. 793.

[69] Ibid., p. 798.

sufficient; the settling of personal scores is superfluous. In a letter to Bill'-Belotserkovsky, cited earlier, Stalin three times says of Bulgakov's characters that they are 'honest' – in quotation marks. This was in full accord with the spirit of the time, when traditional norms had ceased to exist and served only as the butt of mockery. Bulgakov does no more than remove the quotation marks, along with others enclosing the words 'goodness', 'justice', 'compassion' and finally 'freedom'. This is what he sets against the 'overwhelming power of Bolshevism', which, however, overestimates itself.

Bulgakov well knew the grip of that power; he had felt it in his own life and that of his contemporaries. He knew that it could not be directly confronted; for people in his situation that time had not yet arrived. But with a light touch he could find a way round it. He could rise above it by applying at once everything he knew – devils, the Gospels, humour and style. None of this belonged to that oppressed world. It was no accident that in the dedication to his wife he wrote, 'you will fly with me on my last flight'. *The Master and Margarita* is full of flight; the attribute of weightlessness makes the main characters the equal of the devils and frees them from the grasp of that greater earthly devilry. But this apart, the whole novel has the wings of inspiration in its structure. What we might have taken for light-mindedness flows no doubt from a wish to break free once and for all from the gravitational pull of the 'overwhelming power'. Bulgakov was its prisoner. But here he was finding his freedom. This is where the novel's most important lines of meaning ultimately converge. A book about freedom, filled with freedom of movement and liberating its author – in a surprising but profoundly logical way – found its own freedom in addition to all this. Having escaped being crushed, it began its flight to our own time; its fate became its own sequel.

It is here that Bulgakov's victory lies: in saving the meaning of his own life by means of a book which would save itself according to rules established within it. It turns out that free art is more real than enslaved reality.

Lifting one's eyes to the stars in the closing lines of *The White Guard* thus takes on more meaning than when those lines were written. And the question, 'Why do we not turn our gaze towards them?' no longer applies.

The flight goes on.

The Master

The place Bulgakov came to occupy after his death – considering his work from the end to the beginning – is diametrically opposed to the one he held in his lifetime.

Fortunately literature knows no exact weights or measures and is subject to no table of ranks. We do not know which writer holds first place or which of two or three great writers is the greatest. We know only that this particular writer is counted among the most important of our century in the literature of his country. He has also turned out to be sufficiently universal to speak to and fascinate readers in many languages.

Among his contemporaries in his own country he cuts a fairly lonely figure, separated from most by his early and abiding attachment to tradition, and – more important – by what flows from this attachment: a traditional understanding of the writer's calling. He became an innovator, like any true artist, as a result of an inner need. He was not susceptible to fads or to blind faith in the idea that all that is new, unprecedented and unheard of dismisses and disqualifies all that has gone before.

He was an extremely gifted playwright, one of the few born artists in this field among his Russian contemporaries. But stage production is an institutional matter, requiring the right conditions. From the beginning, conditions were very difficult. He either wrote to the dictates of his internal censor, or he was censored and suppressed *post factum*. The results were uneven; next to some very good plays there are weaker ones with splendid passages, and others which are slighter, more conventional and frankly feeble. He did not create any great theatrical work. If he is foremost among the Russian playwrights of his time (for that at least can be stated almost for certain), that rank is his only by virtue of the absence of competition, if we are honest about it. His only rival, Nikolai Erdman, was unfortunately able to achieve creative fulfilment to an even lesser degree than Bulgakov.

He was a superb prose-writer, able to write almost anything, holding his own in every genre and every form that he tried his hand at. Both his novels are masterpieces. *The White Guard* is the more artistic as literature. *The Master and Margarita* reaches both deeper and higher, playing a special synthesizing role in the writer's own life as an artist, and this special quality also plays a role in the reader's reception of it. The unfinished *Theatrical Novel* is also splendid in its own way. Of the shorter works, his *Heart of a Dog* stands out prominently, crowning the works in which Bulgakov scrutinizes the society he lives in and voices his hopes, fears and warnings through his individual brand of creative imagination. But he was also at ease in the conventions of precise realism, as is demonstrated by his *Notes of a Young Doctor* and 'Psalm'.

Having served a patient apprenticeship in literature, he tried his hand in turn at anything that offered him the chance of being an honest writer. All opportunities turned out to be blocked. He wanted to be a witness to history, showing honestly how it was made. He wanted to be a witness to modernity – fully loyal, deeply convinced of many things, but incorruptible. He wanted to be a jolly writer of comedy, giving vent when necessary to a satirical temperament. He wanted to seek a chance for himself and others like him in art. He wanted to delve deep into history, examine the lives of great artists and consider their drama. He was even willing to make concessions of a far-reaching nature, while preserving his dignity; towards the end of his life he found himself in a morally exposed position owing to *Batum*, and could as a result appear harnessed with those who sang the praises of the cannibal. He was, as we know, a favourite without favours, trapped in an exceptionally difficult situation, allowed the favour of existing, living on his royalties and dying in his own bed. No doubt he felt morally obliged to repay this. But he did not know how to abase himself or lick boots, and his tyrannical patron would accept nothing less.

He tried with all his creative being to grasp any possible chance to subsist. None came. He could only hang by the thread of one play in one theatre, and one adaptation. There were two small books, from his early period, and then, for fourteen years to the end of his days, in the prime of his creative life, no publications at all.

Even if all the other shocking evidence were absent, the 'normal' fate of Bulgakov alone would tell us what had been done to Russian culture. Yet, thanks to its conclusion, this fate gives cause for optimism. Bulgakov was not the only one to be silenced as an artist. There have been many literary careers in the last sixty years which first soared to a height, then subsided into works of lesser significance, or were punctuated by long silences. This phenomenon is so common that no amount of manipulation by critics can conceal it. Few writers were granted the opportunity of a second birth and the recovery of their powers. Bulgakov was among those who were. He survived the great crisis of 1929. What he wrote thereafter bears many traces of that watershed. It is more than likely that his literary nerve centres were permanently affected. This can be seen if we compare his writings of the 1920s and '30s.

Right up to *The Master and Margarita*. Here he overcomes his own weakness and the power of his opponents – in grand style. He liberates himself and offers a chance of freedom to his future readers. The physical and spiritual system in which Bulgakov had to live is rendered null and void by this book; it ceases to exist. The book creates its own world, in which inverted concepts are returned to their normal position, in which there is no longer any compulsion to see evil as good, and Stalinist 'honesty' again becomes honesty without quotation marks. It is not as if the book were anti-Soviet; this classification does not apply to *The Master and Margarita*. It is simply a-Soviet. It has nothing in common with those things that go to make up the system in which it came into being. It nullifies that system – by what it says and by what it passes over in silence. It has its own specific weight of words unspoken and things not shown, which for Bulgakov simply do not exist, even as the target of mockery. 'You're a phantom, a ghost,' one of his heroines, Eve, had once called out to her inadequate Adam when she decided to leave him. 'You're all just a dream.' *Diabolus major* is the absence of goodness, or a void, in short nihil, the temptation of self-destruction, best neutralized not by struggling against it but by denial. Perhaps this was the meaning of the lines of obituary in verse written by Akhmatova after Bulgakov's death:

Ты так сурово жил и до конца донес
Великолепное презрение.[1]

---

[1] [You lived such an austere life and carried to the end your magnificent contempt.] Anna Akhmatova, 'Pamiati M. B-va', *Den' poezii*, Leningrad, 1966.

'Magnificent contempt' can nullify 'overwhelming force'. In his country today Bulgakov's novel plays on a substantially broader scale the role that his *Days of the Turbins* once partially filled: it sets people inwardly free and helps 'detotalitarianize' their minds. We may pause before calling it a 'great' book; this description seems to be reserved for works aimed at the very heart of existence and posing fundamental philosophical questions. Bulgakov was deeply concerned with the practice, rather than the theory of human existence. He chose the lightness of being, or rather became light, when he resolved to be free in everything, including the very act of writing. What he wrote was no ordinary book. However it is described, it is clear that it is now a book of major importance.

Thus the writer who was so often defeated achieved victory when he brought his work on a dream to its splendid fulfilment.

The scale of this fulfilment makes it an extraordinary phenomenon in Russian literature. While his early work brought him close to many writers, his later work distanced him no less from them. Aleksandr Grin went in for compensatory fantasy-writing, creating imagined worlds. Andrei Platonov showed the madness of the age in satirical masks. Evgenii Shvarts used traditional fairy-tale motifs to fashion decidedly didactic allegories. Il'f and Petrov practised social satire for as long as this was possible. Demons were invoked and biblical motifs exploited, if for completely different purposes. But nobody had drawn all this together in a single work and by doing so invalidated the system. There is only one book which may be compared for its effect with *The Master and Margarita*, and that is *Doctor Zhivago*. Pasternak's novel also gave back spiritual freedom to the individual, making the life of the individual independent of the conditioning factors and determinants which the heralds of the new age held to be decisive, and thus rejecting them, though in a less radical manner. With this one exception, Bulgakov remains peerless; he has only imitators. He clearly has much appeal for his successors, though so far this is mainly manifested in superficial ways.

Feeling a spiritual affinity with creative artists of various eras and countries, he made them his heroes and himself exploited this kinship. He placed himself, by a grand gesture, in several different areas of the European tradition at once, exposed himself to their influences, but drew from them moral guidance rather than stylistic models. He felt equally independent in the Russian tradition. Here he was closest to Gogol, the writer to whom he was most indebted; they were linked simply by their vision of the world. Pushkin was to him, as befits a Russian writer, the supreme measure of responsibility for the culture of his country. To Chekhov he was indebted – if only subconsciously – for much when he described the collapse of his former world and when he brought this description to the stage. He was deeply involved in Dostoevsky, partly taking on his demon, his symbolism and the torments of his conscience, and – while he apparently disliked him – he turned out to be, at a deeper level, the executor of his legacy. Dostoevsky was horrified by a vision of a world without God, a world in which human beings could feel absolutely free. Bulgakov, 'seeming to stand face to face with God vis-à-vis the riddle of existence', used his experience to show that absolute freedom meant slavery, and he found hope for true liberation in the principles of the Gospels. The dimensions of these statements by these two writers are difficult to compare; the depth and breadth of their vision differ, so the greatest caution is required in any comparison. There may, however, be a non-Euclidean geometry of Russian thought in which, different though they are, they draw closer.

With his view of the writer's calling, his artistic tastes and even his mode of being, Bulgakov often seems to have emerged from the nineteenth century. This does not in any sense mean that he is 'old-world' in the usual sense of the expression; on the contrary, his art benefited from the artistic revolution of the twentieth century. It does mean that he assumed the guise and role of a classic, even though the world which surrounded him lacked the preconditions for this. It became apparent, nonetheless, in the longer term that there was still a powerful social need for a classical presence of precisely this kind, which seemed to belong in another temporal dimension. Here we move a little closer to his phantasmagoria. Could his major work be, apart from everything else, a metaphor for his own fate? Could he himself be a kind of Woland, charged with a special mission and released into modern literature to show up evil and assist goodness – in other words, his own devil?

Whoever he was, what he had to offer was a kind of profoundly humane order. In this he believed – instinctively, profoundly and unshakeably. In the hope of ultimate order, the belief that 'life would always reassert its own', that 'if people... have truly human feelings, they will find a way out.'

Near the end of that major work Woland says to Margarita, 'Don't be alarmed; everything will be as it should. That's the basis the world is built on.' (Все будет правильно, на этом построен мир).[2]

Perhaps this is Bulgakov's most important sentence. Its ordinariness is illusory. If everything that the writer did came together in *The Master and Margarita*, then the meaning of the book is concentrated in that line.

A natural, humane order of things. Nothing more. Which is what Yeshua died for.

---

[2] *Romany*, p. 797.

The Devil

It is convenient to have a devil of one's own, good to be such a devil, and not advisable to think that he does not really exist, or that when he is set free at the end of *The Master and Margarita* we shall never meet him again.

This would be un-Bulgakovian. The book was not finally concluded. Which means that it goes on; it remains open-ended. Which means that something else ought to happen.

Let me reveal, in closing, that I looked for him. Following in Bulgakov's footsteps I waited for some sign, even the slightest. At Patriarch's Ponds, at dusk, over the water, in the deepest shade and in the already lit patches. In Prechistenka, in Denezhny, Plotnikovsky, Chisty and Bol'shaia Pirogovskaia Streets, and on Sparrow Hills at sunset. On Andreevsky Hill, under the old street lamps, in front of the little house, the House that squats on the slope.

To no avail. Sometimes I had the feeling that he was almost present, that he seemed to be giving signs of life. But I was never sure.

Of course, it was clear that the Greater Devil existed. Nobody could fail to notice that. He did what he could and was often successful. If Bulgakov had to exist at all, there should be as little of him as possible. He may continue his half-life, subject, like others of his ilk, to the refined manipulations of limited editions. These appear seldom and in small print-runs (any conformist hack receives print-runs many times larger), designed as a kind of vindication: we do publish him, after all. But he himself, the author of wicked portraits of NEP-era profiteers, is the object of profiteering: on the literary black market the price of a copy of his collected novels exceeds the average monthly wage. He, the creator of the scene in Torgsin, is for sale in today's Torgsins for dollars. For many years a collection of reminiscences about him has awaited publication.[1] Beneath the terrace of 'one of Moscow's finest buildings' lies Bulgakov's archive and the documents from it are cut and pasted lest they reveal too much of the truth, while admission to the Novodevichii Cemetery is now restricted to permit-holders. His first memorable play maintains a presence in his theatre, but in a feeble production, and the staging of his last novel, which has a great deal to say, has been attacked by the methods the author knew so well.

All this – but not only this – is harmoniously crowned by the following singular fact: one of the most serious studies of Bulgakov speaks of *The Heart of a Dog* without mentioning the title ('his third novella', 'the novella which Bulgakov was writing in early 1925' and so on);[2] if the work has not been published in its own country it does not exist, and if it does not exist it shall be nameless, but it is permissible to treat it as if it existed as long as it is not named – the black magic of totalitarianism.

Bulgakov's posthumous history is very telling. If he has managed to survive, he must be assimilated into the environment. When his writings again began to appear in print, many people who had a role in their publication and joyfully welcomed his presence judged, clearly in all sincerity, that the price was worth paying. Yet again a form of cabal arose; carefully measured half-truths were written, in a kind of exchange of knowing winks. This kind of thing continues. Perhaps the price really is worth paying in order to reach Russian readers and influence them. But the limits of compromise, the question of when something ceases to pay, and the value of uttering half-truths about this writer when one wishes to best serve his interests – these are matters each must resolve for himself.

This refers only to people of good will, of course. The spokesmen of ill will can have no such problems. Today the number of these jostling around Bulgakov is considerable. They seek to belittle him or place him on a false

---

[1] These lines date from c. 1979, when Bulgakov's *Romany* changed hands at prices greatly exceeding the nominal price of one rouble, fifty-three kopecks. The collection of reminiscences was eventually published in 1988: *Vospominaniia o Mikhaile Bulgakove*, edited by E. S. Bulgakova and S. A. Liandres, Moscow, 1988 – *Trans.*

[2] Drawicz is referring to M. Chudakova's 'Arkhiv M. A. Bulgakova. Materialy dlia tvorcheskoi biografii pisatelia', in *Zapiski Otdela rukopisei Gos. Bibl. SSSR im. Lenina*, Moscow, 1976, p. 44. For this information and that in the following note I am indebted to Lesley Milne. *Trans.*

pedestal. Two of them, operating independently, have gone further than all the rest: in their writings about him they make him an accomplice of the evil he opposed and a kind of alibi for the tyranny he detested.[3] His very existence should supposedly be credited to Stalin and should proclaim him patron saint of the neo-Stalinists, although he was a spiritual martyr to Stalinism.

If it is indeed true that *The Master and Margarita* is still continuing, these two tormentors of the late author will eventually appear at Satan's ball. Everything will be as it should.

The Greater Devil cannot be forgotten. But what about the Lesser Devil, Bulgakov's faithful servant?

He is nowhere to be found. Even at 10 Sadovaia, alias 302B Sadovaia, alias Number 13. I called there more than once at various times of day, mostly at dusk. I glanced into the courtyard and the stairwell.

There was nothing.

Until at last, one day, going back out of the gate into Sadovaia Street, I saw it. Nothing of any consequence, but...

The point is that Number 10 presses up tight against Number 14, so close that the walls meet. Anybody who is in Moscow and wishes to check this may do so. Wall against wall. Without the slightest gap or chink between them. Nothing.

So where is Number 12? It does not exist. But can this really be so?

Perhaps it does exist, but in some other way. And perhaps somebody lives in it after all.

I mentioned this to one of my Moscow friends. He shrugged. 'You're trying to make a mystery out of it,' he said. 'We know your tricks.' 'I'm not,' I replied. 'Take a look. The walls meet. Not so much as a chink.' 'Then it must be somewhere round the back,' he said. 'There's no room round the back,' I replied. 'In that case,' he said, 'it must be further back, in the yard, as a separate block.' 'But in Moscow the blocks have their own numbers in series, or letters of the alphabet, so...' 'Look, my friend,' he said, getting a little annoyed. 'Forget it. The house must be there somewhere. The Devil only knows...'

At this point he seemed to break off and choke on his words.

---

[3] One of these critics is apparently Viktor Petelin, the author of 'M. A. Bulgakov i *Dni Turbinykh*', *Ogonek*, No. 11, 1969, and *Pamiat' serdtsa neistrebima*, Moscow, 1970. The identity of the other is less certain. *Trans.*

I think I know what Bulgakov would have done at that moment. He would have inclined his head in his typical fashion, with an impish twinkle in his eye, and said, 'You don't say!'

So let this be the way we remember him.

1972-1973;
1978-1979

Glossary

Below are listed some events, personalities, acronyms and Russian terms which may not be fully explained in Drawicz's text. (*Trans.*)

Antosha Chekhonte (see Chekhonte, Antosha)

Bely, Andrei (pseudonym of Boris Bugaev, 1880-1934): prominent poet and novelist, representative of the Russian Symbolist school. Known also for his experimental novels, especially *Petersburg* (1916). Highly regarded as a literary critic, especially for his work on Gogol.

Bender, Ostap: picaresque hero of the novels *The Twelve Chairs* (1928) and *The Golden Calf* by Il'ia Il'f and Evgenii Petrov (1931). The name of this character became a byword in the Soviet Union for one bent on making money by whatever means.

Blok, Aleksandr (1880-1921): leading exponent of Russian Symbolism in poetry and drama. Drawicz's mention of Blok's vision of the October revolution as an act of historical justice (p. 106) refers primarily to his narrative poem 'The Twelve', in which a rag-tag band of revolutionaries marching through the streets is said to have 'Jesus Christ at its head'.

boyars: the landed nobility of Muscovite Russia. Their influence was greatly curtailed by Ivan IV (Ivan the Terrible) in the sixteenth century.

Chekhonte, Antosha: pen-name of Anton Chekhov (1860-1904) in the early years of his career (the early 1880s), when his output consisted mainly of short, humorous stories.

chinovnik: junior official of the Tsarist civil service, in the literary tradition established by Gogol and Dostoevsky, usually underpaid and downtrodden.

Enukidze, Avel' Sofronovich (1877-1937): Georgian Bolshevik and comrade of Stalin. Executed during the purge of 1937.

Erdman, Nikolai (1902-70): playwright, best known for *The Mandate* (1925) and *The Suicide* (1928), both banned in 1932. Exiled to Siberia in the 1930s. Bulgakov's intervention with Stalin may have speeded his return to literary life (see p. 228). Younger brother of Boris Erdman (mentioned on pp. 284-5).

Fadeev, Aleksandr (pseudonym of Bulyga, 1901-56): prominent novelist, member of RAPP (q.v.) and literary functionary. Author of *The Rout* (1927) and *The Young Guard* (1946), held to be models of Socialist Realism in literature. Secretary General of the Union of Soviet Writers in the later years of Stalin's rule. Committed suicide in May 1956.

Frunze, Mikhail Vasil'evich (1885-1925): commander-in-chief of Bolshevik forces on the southern front in late 1920. Later Chief of Staff. Met a mysterious death during a surgical operation in 1925, an event described by Boris Pil'niak in his 'Tale of the Unextinguished Moon' (1926).

Glavlit: *Glavnoe upravlenie literatury* (Central Administration of Literature). For many years the official title of the censor's office in Soviet times.

'Karamazov demon': on p. 136 Drawicz points to connections between the stage version of *The White Guard* and Dostoevsky's novels. In *The Brothers Karamazov*, the devil appears to Ivan Karamazov in a dream and a long conversation takes place.

Kaverin, Veniamin (pseudonym of Zil'ber, 1902-89): prose-writer, first published in the 1920s. Known for his popular novel *Two Captains* (1940) and later for his memoirs of literary life in the early Soviet period. In his later years an influential voice calling for increased intellectual freedom.

Khlestakov: the allusion on p. 146 is to the blustering hero of *The Government Inspector*, the play by Nikolai Gogol.

MAT: in Russian MKhAT *Moskovskii khudozhestvennyi akademicheskii teatr* (Moscow Art Theatre).

Mechik: a character in *The Rout*, a novel of the Civil War, by Aleksandr Fadeev (q.v.) (1927). Mechik is a student of middle-class background, who is attracted by the romantic appeal of the revolution. He proves unable to endure the hardships and finally deserts his comrades.

Meyerhold, Vsevolod Emil'evich (1874-1940): theatre director, famed for his inventive and imaginative staging of Maiakovsky's plays. Arrested 1939, executed 1940. On p. 85 Drawicz cites a playful mention by Bulgakov which refers to Meyerhold's 'Constructivist' directing, which took liberties with the playwright's text.

Na postu: (On Watch). Journal of RAPP (q.v.).

NEP: *Novaia ekonomicheskaia politika* (New Economic Policy), entailing a partial return to private trading in the years 1921-28, instituted by Lenin to foster stabilization in the aftermath of the Civil War.

NEPman: one who profited from the limited private enterprise of the NEP period (q.v.).

oprichniki: members of the Oprichnina (1564-72), a corps of special troops formed by Ivan IV in his struggle to overcome the power of the boyars (q.v.).

Perekop: in the lines quoted on p. 153, Simonov is referring to the decisive battle of November 1920, in which Frunze's Bolshevik army inflicted a crushing defeat upon Wrangel's White forces and enabled the Reds to capture the Crimea and end White resistance in the region.

Prechistenka: a street in central Moscow where many representatives of the intellectual and artistic elite lived in the 1920s. See p. 71 for more detail on the associations of the 'Prechistenka' spirit and the 'Prechistenka' figure (referred to on p. 93).

RAPP: *Rossiiskaia assotsiatsiia proletarskikh pisatelei* (Russian Association of Proletarian Writers). A group of writers who actively upheld ideological purity in literature in the 1920s and early 1930s. The journal of the Association was *Na postu* (q.v.). The leading figure was Leopold Averbakh.

Raskol'nikov, Rodion: hero of Dostoevsky's novel *Crime and Punishment*, who commits a brutal double murder and attempts to explain it in his own mind as the act of one who stands 'beyond good and evil' and cannot be judged by ordinary moral standards.

skaz: form of narrative in which the narrative voice is characterized by the speech-forms of the protagonist, usually those of the uneducated classes.

Smena vekh [Change of Landmarks]: a school of thought among *émigrés* in the immediate aftermath of the revolution and civil war, which held that the Bolsheviks had proved the only group capable of restoring any kind of authority in Russia. Since they had succeeded in maintaining a form of Russian statehood, incorporating much of the old Tsarist empire, and since NEP (q.v.) had replaced 'war communism', with its uncompromising socialist-run economy, opponents of communism could now lend their support to the new state.

'Shakhty' trial: (p. 83) in 1928 fifty-three engineers were put on trial for sabotage in the Donbass coal mines, following a series of explosions, fires and other mishaps in the pits. Further well-publicized trials of specialists followed.

Tvardovsky, Aleksandr Trifonovich: (1910-71) poet and editor of the leading Moscow literary journal *Novy mir* throughout the 1960s. This was the period when Bulgakov's *Theatrical Novel* appeared in this journal. Tvardovsky was personally responsible for a large number of daring publications, including that of Aleksandr Solzhenitsyn's *One Day in the Life of Ivan Denisovich* in 1962.

Vladivostok: in the lines quoted on p. 153, Simonov is referring to the final establishment of Bolshevik rule in the Far East of the country. This was not achieved until October 1922.

'wise monk': on p. 179 Drawicz has in mind the Dostoevskian figure of Zosima in *The Brother Karamazov*.

Wrangel, Baron Petr Nikolaevich: (1878-1928) general, senior figure in the White movement during the Civil War. Evacuated with his forces from the Crimea in 1920.

Select Bibliography

I. Main editions of Bulgakov's works

a) Collected works

Sobanie sochinenii v desiati tomakh, Ann Arbor, Michigan, 1982.

b) Other editions

D'iavoliada. Rasskazy, Moscow, 1925.
Traktat o zhilishche, Moscow-Leningrad, 1926.
Sbornik rasskazov, New York, 1952.
Dni Turbinykh. Poslednie dni, Moscow, 1955
P'esy, Moscow, 1962.
Dramy i komedii, Moscow, 1965.
Izbrannaia proza, Moscow, 1966.
'Master i Margarita', *Moskva*, No. 11, 1966, No. 1, 1967 (incomplete text).
Master i Margarita, Frankfurt/Main, 1968 (full text).
P'esy, Paris, 1971.
Romany, Moscow, 1973.
Ranniaia neizdannaia proza, Munich, 1976.
Ranniaia nesobrannaia proza, Munich, 1978.
Izbrannoe, Moscow, 1980.
Ranniaia neizvestnaia proza, Munich, 1981.
Zabytoe. Ranniaia proza, Munich, 1983.

II. Secondary Sources

Al'tshuler, A. [A. Smelianskii], *'Dni Turbinykh' i 'Beg' Bulgakova v istorii sovetskogo teatra 20-ykh godov*, Moscow, 1972.

Belozerskaia-Bulgakova, L., *O, med vospominanii*, Ann Arbor, Michigan, 1979.

Chudakova, M., 'Arkhiv M. A. Bulgakova. Materialy dlia tvorcheskoi biografii pisatelia', *Zapiski Otdela rukopisei Gosudarstvennoi Biblioteki SSSR im. Lenina*, No. 37, 1976, pp. 25-151.

Chudakova, M., 'K tvorcheskoi biografii M. Bulgakova 1916-1933', *Voprosy literatury*, No. 7, 1973.

Chudakova, M., 'Tvorcheskaia istoriia romana M. Bulgakova *Master i Margarita*', *Voprosy literatury*, No. 1, 1976.

Chudakova, M., *Zhizneopisanie Mikhaila Bulgakova*, Moscow, 1988.

Ermolinskii, S., 'Mikhail Bulgakov', in *Dramaticheskie sochineniia*, Moscow, 1982.

Ianovskaia, L., *Tvorcheskii put' Mikhaila Bulgakova*, Moscow, 1983.

Jovanović, M., *Utopija Mihaila Bulgakova*, Belgrade, 1975.

Karaś, J., *Proza Michała Bułhakowa. Z zagadnień poetyki*, Wrocław, Warsaw, Cracow, Gdańsk, Łódź, 1981, Moscow, 1988.

Lakshin, V., 'Eskizy k trem portretam', *Druzhba narodov*, No. 9, 1978.

Lakshin, V., 'Roman M. Bulgakova *Master i Margarita*', *Novyi mir*, No, 6, 1968.

Lakshin, V., 'Uroki Bulgakova', *Pamir*, No. 4, 1972.

Levshin, V., 'Sadovaia 302-bis', *Teatr*, No. 11, 1971.

'Materialy o M. A. Bulgakove', *Mosty*, No. 11, 1965

Miln [Milne], L., 'K biografii M. A. Bulgakova', *Novyi zhurnal*, No. 111, 1973, pp. 151-174.

Milne, L., *The Master and Margarita. A Comedy of Victory*, Birmingham, 1977.

Mindlin, E., 'Mikhail Bulgakov', in *Neobyknovennye sobesedniki*, Moscow, 1968.

Neizdannyi Bulgakov. Teksty i materialy, ed. by E. Proffer, Ann Arbor, Michigan, 1977.

Proffer, E., *Bulgakov. Life and Work*, Ann Arbor, Michigan, 1984.

Rudnitskii, K., 'Mikhail Bulgakov',*Voprosy teatra*, Moscow, 1966.

Sakhnovskii-Pankeev, V., 'Bulgakov', in *Ocherki istorii russkoi sovetskoi dramaturgii*, Moscow-Leningrad, 1963-1968.
Sovetskie pisateli. Avtobiografii, Vol. III, Moscow, 1966,
Stenbock-Fermor, E., 'Bulgakov's *The Master and Margarita* and Goethe's *Faust*', *Slavic and East European Journal*, No. 1, 1969.
Vinogradov, I., 'Zaveshchanie mastera', *Voprosy literatury*, No. 6, 1968.
Wolicki, K., 'Wycieńczony Faust i krwista rzeczywistość', *Twórczość*, No. 9, 1969.
Woroszylski, W., 'Rękopisy nie spłoną – obiecał diabeł', *Więź*, Nos. 7-8, 1971.
Wright, A. Colin, *Mikhail Bulgakov. Life and Interpretations*, Toronto, 1978.

Index of Names

Abramovich, S. 251
Afinogenov, Aleksandr 233, 266
Akhmatova, Anna 189, 191, 248, 250, 251, 327
Alibegov 273
Al'tshuler, Anatolii 15, 101, 102, 111, 152, 185, 326
Angarsky, Nikolai 73, 120
Antokol'sky, Pavel 133
Asaf'ev, Boris 266, 275
Aseev, Nikolai 56
Averbakh, Leopold 88, 89, 201, 321

Babel, Isaak 85, 89
Bachelis, I. 183, 185
Bagritsky, Eduard 56
Bakhtin, Mikhail 319
Balzac, Honoré de 31
Baranov, K. N. 273
Barkanov, M. 78
Bedny, Dem'ian (pseudonym of Pridvorov, Efim) 274
Béjart, Armande 197, 259
Béjart, Madeleine 259
Beletsky, Aleksandr 273
Belotserkovsky, Vladimir (see Bill'-Belotserkovsky, Vladimir)
Belozerskaia, Liubov' (see Bulgakova, Liubov')
Bely, Andrei (pseudonym of Bugaev, Boris) 40, 42, 120, 191, 222, 224
Belza, Igor' 317

Benediktov, Vladimir 250
Berkovsky, Naum 152
Beskin, Emmanuil 153
Bestuzhev-Marlinsky, Aleksandr 2
Bezymensky, Aleksandr 158
Bill'-Belotserkovsky, Vladimir 157, 171, 183, 323
Blium, Vladimir 90, 150, 151, 153, 156, 170
Blok, Aleksandr 124
Bogoliubov, V. 158, 167
Boguslavsky, A. 90
Bokshanskaia, Olga 221, 269, 278, 281, 282, 284
Bolduman, Mikhail 239
Borsh, G. 87
Bosch, Hieronymus 302
Briusov, Valerii 84
Broide, M. 155
Bulgakov, Afanasii I. 7, 8, 11
Bulgakov, Ivan A. 7, 20, 21
Bulgakov, Konstantin 11, 18, 23, 26, 27
Bulgakov, Nikolai A. 7, 20, 21, 165, 189, 190
Bulgakova, Elena A. 72
Bulgakova, Elena S. 7, 46, 72, 76, 93, 107, 134, 192, 202, 224, 225, 242, 246, 247, 248, 269, 270, 272, 284, 285, 287, 288, 289, 290, 291, 293, 313, 323, 331, 326

Bulgakova, Liubov' 37, 67, 69, 70,
   73, 148, 149, 163, 176, 189,
   212, 237
Bulgakova, Nadezhda A. 7, 14, 23,
   27, 29, 32, 39, 56, 70, 131
Bulgakova, Tatiana N. 11, 12, 13,
   29, 32, 33, 38, 39, 69, 70
Bulgakova, Varvara A. 7, 99
Bulgakova, Varvara M. 7, 8, 11, 20,
   32, 34, 37, 98, 99
Bulgakova, Vera A. 7, 20
Bunin, Ivan 26, 111

Cardanus, Hieronymus 3
Cervantes, Saavedra Miguel de 276,
   319
Chaikovsky (see Tchaikovsky)
Chebotareva, V. 24, 39, 47, 77, 120
Chekhov, Anton P. 52, 115, 123,
   147, 150, 152, 153, 190,
   223, 302, 329
Chekin, I. 158
Chudakova, Marietta 20, 23, 30, 32,
   42, 46, 47, 56, 72, 73, 75,
   76, 91, 93, 98, 99, 107, 120,
   126, 132, 162, 168, 170,
   173, 175, 180, 188, 189,
   192, 193, 194, 196, 197,
   199, 200, 204, 206, 214,
   220, 221, 223, 226, 232,
   233, 237, 238, 239, 242,
   245, 246, 247, 289, 264,
   266, 269, 272, 277, 278,
   279, 283, 284, 286, 291,
   293, 296, 302, 305, 306,
   312, 313, 317, 332, 326
Chushkin, Nikolai 228
Colan, Militsa 179

Dadiani, Shalva 282
Dąbrowski, Witold 121, 321
d'Anthès, Georges 2, 251, 254
Denikin, Anton I. 27
de Visé 235
Dickens, Charles 162, 230
Diev, Vladimir A. 90
Dmitriev, Vladimir 205, 220, 284
Dobronravov, Boris 146
Doroshevich, Vlas 41
Dostoevsky, Fedor 2, 40, 81, 111,
   127, 136, 178, 179, 190,
   252, 298, 299, 302, 329
Dragomiretskaia, N. 116
Dumas, Alexandre, *père* 197, 259
Dunaevsky, Isaak O. 274

Enukidze, A. 215, 232
Erdman, Boris 284, 285
Erdman, Nikolai 3, 164, 166, 228,
   325
Ehrenburg, Il'ia 84, 102, 103, 190,
   191
Ermolinsky, Sergei 75, 246, 283,
   284, 300, 326
Ershov, V. L. 173
Esenin, Sergei 54, 163, 303

Fadeev, Aleksandr 125, 285, 288

Fainzil'berg, Il'ia (see Il'f, Il'ia)
Faiko, Aleksandr 164, 166
Fedin, Konstantin 54, 114, 116, 125, 252, 253
Fedorchenko, S. 72
Fitzpatrick, Sheila 181
Florensky, Pavel 312
Fogelevich, L. 157
France, Anatole 190
Freidkina, Liubov' 253
Freud, Sigmund 55
Frunze, Mikhail V. 274

Gałczyński, Konstanty Ildefons 45
Gdeshinsky, Aleksandr 283
Gladkov, Aleksandr 260
Gladkov, Fedor 115
Gladyrevsky, Nikolai 32, 73
Glagolev, Aleksei 11, 108
Glinka, Mikhail A. 275
Globa, Andrei P. 253
Goethe, Johann Wolfgang von 251, 298, 307, 319
Gogol, Nikolai 2, 3, 5, 10, 40, 44, 48, 62, 66, 70, 78, 81, 84, 86, 90, 91, 111, 119, 175, 179, 180, 191, 194, 196, 204, 205, 215, 217, 221, 222, 223, 224, 229, 234, 244, 245, 246, 247, 262, 289, 292, 313, 315, 316, 321, 325
Goncharova, Natalia 250
Gorbachev, Grigorii 154

Gorchakov, Nikolai 140, 207, 226, 255, 256, 257, 258, 259, 260, 266
Gorky, Maksim 26, 36, 89, 93, 114, 124, 180, 200, 230, 237, 240
Gounod, Charles 112
Goya, Francisco 302
Griboedov, Aleksandr 70
Grin, Aleksandr 328
Grossman, Leonid 248

Hoffmann, E. T. A. 3
Hugo, Victor 116

Iakulov, Georgii 163
Iakut, V. 254, 255
Ianovskaia, L. 131, 227, 248, 326
Ianshin, Mikhail 146, 151, 173, 188, 257, 259, 266, 269, 289
Iaron, Grigorii 130
Il'f, Il'ia (Fainzil'berg, Il'ia) 51, 52, 92, 162, 190, 328
Isakov, Sergei 166
Iusupov, F. 64
Ivanov, Vsevolod 3, 54, 81, 115, 133, 137, 141, 159

Jastrun, M. 294
Joyce, J. 313

Kachalov, V. 173, 270, 295
Kagansky, Zakhar 120, 192
Kaluzhsky, E. 134, 215

Karum, Leonid 99
Kataev, Evgenii (see Petrov E.)
Kataev, Valentin 51, 54, 84, 133, 164, 190, 268
Kaverin, Veniamin 289
Kerzhentsev, Platon 275
Khmelev, Nikolai 146, 157, 173, 281, 295
Khodasevich, Vladislav 212
Kirov, Sergei 233
Kirshon, Vladimir 233
Kisel'gof, Tatiana (see Bulgakova, Tatiana)
Kluev, Nikolai A. 303
Knipper-Chekhova, Olga 133
Konchakovskaia, Inna 7
Kor, I. 183
Koreneva, L. 259, 269
Korostin 245
Korotkov, N. 87
Kozintsev, Grigorii 246
Kozlovsky 166
Kuprin, Aleksandr 26

Lakshin, Vladimir 236, 270, 271, 272, 289, 296, 311, 326
Lappa, Tatiana N. (see Bulgakova, Tatiana)
Lavrenev, Boris 115, 125
Lelevich, G. (pseudonym of Kalmanson, L.) 88, 89, 321
Lenin, Vladimir 54
Leonidov, Leonid 215, 221, 254

Leonov, Leonid 56, 89, 141, 190
Leont'ev, Boris 132, 263
Leont'ev, Iakov 273, 277
Lermontov, Mikhail 251
Leskov, Nikolai 40, 139, 229, 276
Levin, V. 19, 60
Levshin, Vasilii 37, 70, 112, 163, 326
Lezhnev, Isai 120, 121, 192
Liamin, Nikolai 72
Liandres, S. 121, 134, 149, 165, 202, 331
Likhachev, Dmitrii 162
Lilina, M. 221
Listovnichii, Vasilii 7
Litovsky, Osaf 150, 151, 153, 166, 183, 184, 232, 321
Litovtseva, Nina 270
Livanov, Boris N. 207
Louis XIV 198, 199, 200, 202, 236, 259, 260
Luk'ianova, L. 170
Lunacharsky, Anatolii 135, 137, 138, 141, 150, 151, 153, 155, 156, 158, 159, 167, 185
Lunts, Lev 80
Lur'e, Ia. 134
Luther, Martin 75, 112
Luzhsky, Vasilii 135

Maiakovsky, Vladimir V. 56, 137, 151, 169, 202, 239, 240, 241, 293
Malyshkin, Aleksandr G. 115, 116

Mandelstam, Nadezhda 29, 265, 318
Mandelstam, Osip 54
Mann, Thomas 1, 109, 297, 299,
 303, 310
Mansurova, Tsetsiliia 166
Mariengof, Anatolii 163
Markov, Pavel 131, 133, 134, 138,
 145, 173, 182, 207, 208,
 226, 270
Maupassant, Guy de 274
Medvedev, Roi 120
Meyerhold, Vsevolod 44, 85, 130,
 141, 153, 222, 227, 228, 246
Mikhal'sky, Fedor 215, 269, 270
Milne, Lesley 135, 136, 145, 149,
 159, 201, 205, 206, 207,
 209, 215, 216, 220, 221,
 225, 227, 228, 229, 230,
 231, 232, 237, 247, 255,
 264, 267, 282, 295, 298,
 319, 332, 326
Milton, John 297
Mindlin, Emilii 54, 326
Minsky, K. 166
Mlechin, V. 222, 224
Molière (Jean-Baptiste de Poquelin)
 3, 167, 195, 196, 197, 198,
 199, 200, 202, 203, 219,
 229, 230, 234, 235, 248,
 250, 254, 255, 256, 257,
 258, 259 281
Mordvinov, B. 284
Moskvin, Ivan 133, 221, 270

Nemirovich-Danchenko, Vladimir I.
 181, 220, 221, 226, 227,
 253, 255, 258, 259, 267,
 269, 271
Nicholas I 202, 206, 250, 251, 253,
 304
Nicholas II 280
Novitsky, Pavel 170, 183, 222
Nusinov, I. 145, 171, 184, 201

Odoevsky, Vladimir 2, 162, 314
Olesha, Iurii 51, 52, 72, 145
Orlinsky, A. 150, 151, 152, 156,
 166
Orlov, Mikhail 194
Osinsky, N. 123, 139
Ostrovsky, Aleksandr 229, 276

Pasternak, Boris 101, 124, 265,
 314, 315, 328
Paustovsky, Konstantin 9, 10, 103,
 125, 206, 254
Pel'she, R. 183
Petelin, V. 152, 282, 333
Peter I 113
Petliura, Semion 16, 17, 18, 19, 22,
 100, 103, 108, 110, 113,
 136, 138, 139, 142, 143,
 151, 152
Petrov, E. (Kataev, Evgenii) 51,
 52, 162, 190, 328
Pikel', R. 183, 185, 201
Pil'niak, Boris A. 115, 120, 125,
 185, 268

Pil'sky, Petr 122
Piper, D. G. B. 319
Piscator, Erwin 229
Platonov, Andrei 86, 125, 328
Pokrovskaia, Varvara (see
　　Bulgakova, Varvara)
Pokrovsky, Mikhail 73
Pokrovsky, Nikolai 73, 92
Poliakova, E. 140, 157
Polonsky, Viacheslav 180
Pomerants, Grigorii 304
Popov, Aleksei 165, 227
Popov, Pavel 7, 33, 65, 71, 93, 98,
　　99, 106, 107, 112, 116, 117,
　　131, 176, 191, 196, 205,
　　215, 216, 219, 223, 225,
　　229, 230, 237, 239, 242,
　　244, 247, 255, 256, 263,
　　267, 284, 293
Popova, Anna
Poskrebyshev, Aleksandr 294
Pototsky, Sergei 274,
Pravdukhin, Valerii 154, 158
Pridorogin, A. 37
Proffer, Ellendea, 13, 134, 326
Prudkin, Mark 146
Pushkin, Aleksandr 2, 28, 70, 85,
　　111, 179, 196, 202, 206,
　　242, 247, 248, 249, 250,
　　251, 252, 253, 254, 255,
　　265, 281, 288, 304, 306,
　　314, 328
Pyr'ev, Ivan 244, 245

Raaben. I. S. 76, 97
Raevsky, I. M. 207
Rapoport, Iosif M. 277, 284
Raskol'nikov, Fedor 159, 181
Rasputin, Grigorii 39, 64
Rastrelli, Bartolomeo 5
Remizov, Aleksei 2, 40, 120
Reshetar, J. S. jr 104
Reznik, Osip 221
Rodov, Semion 88
Rolland, Romain 89
Romashov, Boris 164, 166
Rudnitsky, Konstantin 146, 163,
　　165, 220, 221, 222, 224,
　　226, 227, 229, 244, 257, 326
Rydel, Christine 213
Rykov, Aleksandr 180
Ryndin, Vadim 170

Sakhnovsky, Vasilii 147, 204, 205,
　　221, 227, 255
Sakhnovsky-Pankeev, Vladimir 204
Saltykov-Shchedrin, Mikhail 91
Scribe, Eugène 259
Seifullina, L. 141
Sel'vinsky, Il'ia 221
Selikhanovich, Aleksandr 99
Selivanovsky, Aleksei 183
Senkovsky, Osip (Sękowski, Julian)
　　2
Serafimovich, A. 116
Serman, Il'ia 134
Shakespeare, William 229
Shaporin, Iurii 273

Shatova, Zoia 163
Shchedrin (see Saltykov-Shchedrin, Mikhail)
Sheremet'eva, E. 209, 214
Sheshukov, Stepan 182
Shilovskaia, Elena (see Bulgakova, Elena S.)
Shilovsky, Evgenii 225, 269
Shklovsky, Viktor 80, 87
Shtein, Aleksandr 211
Shtok, Isidor 141
Shvarts, Evgenii L. 328
Simonov, Konstantin 153, 154, 183, 211
Simonov, Ruben 165, 166, 277, 284
Simov, V. A. 220, 221
Skoropadsky, Pavlo 15, 16, 19, 100, 117, 135, 142
Slashchev-Krymsky, Iakov 177, 178
Slezkin, Iurii 24, 25, 28, 39, 41, 54, 72, 100, 126, 268
Słonimski, Antoni 321
Slonimsky, Mikhail L. 3, 89
Smirnova, Vera 254
Sokolova, Vera 146, 151, 173
Sologub, Fedor 2
Stalin, Joseph V. 87, 156, 157, 158, 171, 184, 199, 201, 206, 208, 215, 228, 230, 258, 260, 264, 265, 266, 267, 275, 279, 280, 281, 282, 292, 294, 295, 298, 323, 326
Stanislavsky, Konstantin 138, 140, 141, 159, 203, 204, 208, 215, 216, 220, 221, 222, 226, 255, 256, 257, 258, 269
Stanitsyn, Viktor 230, 259
Steiger 321
Stenbock-Fermor, E. 319
Stepanova, Angelina O. 259
Sudakov, Il'ia 134, 135, 138, 139, 143, 180, 181, 232, 255, 269
Sukhovo-Kobylin, Aleksandr 2
Svetin, L. 19
Svetlov, Mikhail 56
Svidersky, Aleksei 180, 181

Tairov, Aleksandr 170, 227
Tarasova, Alla 295
Tarkhanov, Mikhail 221
Tarnovsky, Evgenii 73
Tchaikovsky, Piotr I. 150
Tikhonov-Serebrov, Aleksandr 236, 237
Tiurin, Iu. P. 245
Tolstoi, Aleksei N. 69, 84, 125, 177, 178, 191, 268
Tolstoi, Lev N. 71, 111, 124, 127, 179, 214, 229, 309, 310
Topleninov, Sergei 72
Trauberg, Leonid 246
Trenev, Konstantin 125, 137, 152
Tsetlin, Mikhail 122
Tsvetaeva, Marina 309
Tur brothers 78
Turbina, Anfisa 8
Turgenev, Ivan 229, 276
Tvardovsky, Aleksandr 272

Tynianov, Iurii 80, 248

Ul'ianov, Nikolai 147, 259
Ushakova, Natalia 72, 189

Vakhtangov, Evgenii B. 166
Vaks, B. 190
Vardin, Illarion V. 87
Varpakhovsky, Leonid 290
Vasil'evsky, Il'ia (Ne-Bukva) 69
Vel'tman, Aleksandr 2
Venkstern, Natalia 72, 215, 230
Verbitsky, Vsevolod 207
Veresaev, Vikentii 73, 89, 124, 176, 206, 225, 230, 231, 237, 242, 247, 248, 249, 252, 254, 263
Verne, Jules 62, 66, 168
Vershilov, Boris 133, 135, 269
Vesely, Artem 115, 116
Vilenkin, Vitalii 230, 255, 257, 279, 281, 282
Vinogradov, Igor' 327
Vishnevsky, Vsevolod 169, 220, 228, 247
Voloshin, Maksimilian 53, 54, 118, 120, 127, 176, 191
Voronsky, Aleksandr 89
Vorovsky, Vatslav 59
Voskresensky, Ivan P. 8
Vulis, A. 296

Wędziagolski, Karol 100, 101

Wells, Herbert George 86, 93, 213, 239
Williams, P. 259, 277, 284
Woroszylski, Wiktor 301, 307
Wright, A. Colin 72, 274, 327

Zagorsky, M. 181
Zaiaitsky, Sergei 72
Zakhava, Boris 166
Zamiatin, Evgenii 40, 41, 42, 58, 80, 81, 86, 168, 185, 191, 240, 241
Zavadsky, Iurii 234
Zemskaia, E. A. 20, 32, 76, 131
Zemskaia, Nadezhda (see Bulgakova, Nadezhda)
Zemsky, Andrei 32, 34, 37
Zemsky, Boris 32, 34
Zhdanov, Andrei 282
Zhukovsky, Vasilii A. 173
Zorkaia, N. 146, 149, 151
Zoshchenko, Mikhail M. 2, 3, 36, 52, 89
Zubilo (see Olesha, Iurii)

STUDIES IN SLAVIC LANGUAGES AND LITERATURE

1. Peter I. Barta and Ulrich Goebel, **The Contexts of Aleksander Sergeevich Pushkin**
2. Mark J. Elson, **A Diachronic Interpretation of Macedonian Verbal Morphology**
3. Colin Partridge, **Yuri Trifonov's Moscow Cycle: A Critical Study**
4. Gareth Williams, **The Influence of Tolstoy on Readers of His Works**
5. A.D.P. Briggs, **A Comparative Study of Pushkin's** *The Bronze Horseman*, **Nekrasov's** *Red-Nosed Frost*, **and Blok's** *The Twelve*: **The Wild World**
6. Edward E. Ericson, Jr., **The Apocalyptic Vision of Mikhail Bulgakov's** *The Master and Margarita*
7. Peter E. Barta (ed.), in collaboration with Ulrich Goebel, **The European Foundations of Russian Modernism**
8. János Pilinszky, **Metropolitan Icons: Selected Poems of János Pilinszky in Hungarian and in English**, Emery George (ed. & trans.)
9. N.V. Gogol, **РЕВИЗОР/The Government Inspector: A Comedy in Five Acts**, M. Beresford (ed.) with English Introduction and Notes
10. Wendy Rosslyn, **Anna Bunina (1774-1829) and the Origins of Women's Poetry in Russia**
11. Nina A. Efimov, Christine D. Tomei, Richard L. Chapple (eds.), **Critical Essays on the Prose and Poetry of Modern Slavic Women**
12. Lauren G. Leighton (compiler), **A Bibliography of Alexander Pushkin in English: Studies and Translations**
13. Juras T. Ryfa, **The Problem of Genre and the Quest for Justice in Chekhov's** *The Island of Sakhalin*
14. Yuri Druzhnikov, **Contemporary Russian Myths: A Skeptical View of the Literary Past**
15. Robert Whittaker, **Russia's Last Romantic, Apollon Grigor'ev (1822-1864)**
16. Roger Cockrell, **Bolshevik Ideology and Literature, 1917-1927**
17. Marina Kanevskaya, **N.K. Mikhailovsky's Criticism of Dostoevsky: The Cruel Critic**
18. Andrzej Drawicz, **The Master and the Devil–A Study of Mikhail Bulgakov**, Kevin Windle (trans.)

DISCARDED